Collective Bargaining

Consulting Editor • ALBERT A. BLUM • Michigan State University

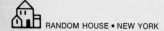 RANDOM HOUSE • NEW YORK

Collective Bargaining

Howard D. Marshall
Vassar College

Natalie J. Marshall
State University College at New Paltz, New York

ISBN: 0–394–31422–0

Library of Congress Catalog Card Number: 70–141963

Manufactured in the United States of America. Composed by H. Wolff, Inc., New York, N.Y.
Printed and bound by The Kingsport Press, Kingsport, Tenn.

Design by J. M. Wall

First Edition

9 8 7 6 5 4 3 2 1

Cover photograph by George W. Gardner.
Cover design by Hermann Strohbach.

PREFACE

All too often, the student of industrial relations and collective bargaining, whether he is a newcomer or an old-timer to the subject, will conclude that the field is one easily mastered, or that on the basis of his knowledge and experience he knows all that there is to know.

As will quickly become evident to anyone reading this book, the authors' conviction is that the subject material is more difficult to master than it first appears to be. This is due less to inherent complexity in the material itself than to the almost infinite variety of ways in which the process of collective bargaining can be played. Not only does it vary from industry to industry but from plant to plant within an industry, and the practitioner with years of experience in one plant or industry will find a quite different set of rules at another location. We have tried to capture and emphasize some of these differentials but the reader should be cautioned to watch for generalizations and to question whether the given definitions would apply in each specific instance.

Even more striking are the differences in industrial relations systems as one moves from one country to another. Due to this wide variety, in treating each of the issues and questions related to collective bargaining we have centered our main focus on aspects relevant to the United States; however, we have closed each chapter with a brief summary noting some of the major characteristics of the chapter's particular aspect of collective bargaining in each of eight other countries. Our bases for selection of countries were simple ones—first, to give the student some idea of the richness and degree of the variety, and second, to focus upon countries about which our own knowledge was most complete.

It is customary for the authors of a book to acknowledge the assistance they have received from others, and we would indeed be remiss did we not do so. In addition to our many colleagues whose advice we sought regarding the structure of various chapters or bits of analysis, we owe a deep debt of thanks to the many students in our classes who have participated in constructing, revising, and reworking the manuscript. A special word of acknowledgment is owed to Professor Albert A. Blum, who served as consulting editor for the book and who provided innumerable helpful corrections and suggestions. While we borrowed freely from the ideas of our readers, pride of authorship sometimes—perhaps too frequently—led us to reject their suggestions; remaining faults and errors must therefore rest on our shoulders.

Finally, we should like to thank our typists for long hours of typing and retyping, and Vassar College for financial aid in helping to defray some of the costs involved.

CONTENTS

1

The Institutional and Historical Background

1
The Many Faces of Collective Bargaining

There is no standard pattern of collective bargaining.

—Richard Lester

☐ LIKE so many other terms in the social sciences, the meaning of collective bargaining at first glance appears to be deceptively simple. As one pursues the subject more intensively, however, one soon discovers that there is much beneath the surface that is never made apparent by reading a newspaper account of negotiations between a company's union and its management.

The term *collective bargaining* is in itself misleadingly concise. Few individuals, even those who have never been exposed to the study of industrial relations, could fail to note the significance of the word *collective* as distinguished from *individual* bargaining. Under collective bargaining workers band together to present their demands with a single voice, a voice that is far more powerful than that of a worker speaking on his own behalf. The word *bargaining* suggests a spirit of give and take—not in the sense in which management sometimes describes it, as a process by which they give and the union takes—but one in which both parties have to make concessions in order to win other demands.

So far so good. But this simplified distinction between individual and collective bargaining fails to take note of a number of the important changes that occur when bargaining on a col-

lective basis begins. First of all, while the term collective bargaining is on the surface self-descriptive, it is misleading in the sense that the workers, as a group, don't really bargain with the employer. Instead, they elect representatives who speak on the group's behalf and negotiate a contract for the group. As the scope of the bargaining unit broadens, to an industrywide, regional, or national basis, the individual worker becomes more and more divorced from the bargaining process.

Furthermore, although the term seems self-descriptive, it has not been easy to define precisely what collective bargaining is or to analyze its functional purpose. A quick review of a number of labor textbooks will provide a series of definitions. Collective bargaining has been defined as "a method of making decisions" (in its refined form, this definition specifies that the decision making takes place between two institutions), or "a method of resolving disputes by compromise," or "a method of adjusting to change," or "a struggle between parties with the outcome dependent on the relative strength to withstand a strike." Although all of these definitions have elements in common, they emphasize quite different aspects of the bargaining process.

One of the most careful attempts to analyze the nature of collective bargaining has been set forth by Neil Chamberlain.[1] Chamberlain has suggested that collective bargaining can be analyzed as functioning in three different fashions, depending upon its setting. He suggested that it might be viewed as (1) an exchange relationship between the two parties, that is, it furnished the means for selling labor; (2) a constitutional system in industry where the union shares sovereignty over the workers with management; and (3) a method by which the union can join management in making joint decisions on issues of concern to both parties.

Joseph Shister has argued that the differentials established by Chamberlain are not operationally meaningful. He has suggested instead that collective bargaining can best be analyzed by listing its principal characteristics. In any such list Shister would include the fact that collective bargaining involves group relationships, that it is both continuous and evolutionary, that it interacts with the socioeconomic climate, that it is private but at points involves government action, and that it varies from setting to setting.[2]

It is not our intention here to add still another definition to the already swollen list. We do wish to emphasize, however, that the relationship between the two parties—labor and management—may be entirely different in one plant or bargaining unit from what it is in another. Furthermore, these relationships change over time. In the remainder of this chapter we will discuss some of the reasons for this diversity.

We can begin by noting that today it is not even easy to itemize all of the topics likely to be on the agenda in a collective bargaining session. This has not always been the case. Prior to the 1930s, the items entering the typical contract were relatively few and thus simple to enumerate. A union would seek recognition, an increase in wages, and the settlement of certain key grievances. With the passage of time, however, the scope of bargaining, particularly in this country, has expanded enormously. Today it is difficult to think of a single item of possible interest to both parties that is not subject to negotiation somewhere. Since the succeeding chapters deal with the contents of collective bargaining contracts in some detail, no enumeration is necessary here. An examination of the Table of Contents, however, reveals that not only has the range of protections afforded workers been broadened but protection of the institutional rights of the union and management has come to play an increasingly important part at negotiation sessions. Meanwhile, the settlement of grievances has become a day-to-day affair that does not wait until the negotiation of a new contract.

The Union Organization

Historically, collective bargaining in all countries has been inextricably linked with unions and real collective bargaining does not begin until unions have become sufficiently established to undertake the task.

The existence of the union as an intermediary speaking on behalf of the workers introduces a third voice into the bargaining process. For the union as an institution has goals and a life of its own. A union's leaders must concern themselves not only with how any settlement will affect the fortunes of the union's members but also with the future of the union itself. It is possible, for example, that a demand for higher wages, if met, may decrease the number of jobs in a plant, while at the same time increasing the number of workers willing to join the union. A union under the guidance of its leaders develops a life of its own, and the preservation of that life becomes more important than the betterment of the life of even a substantial minority of the union's membership. What the union seeks to maximize may be quite different from what individual workers, if left to their own devices, would have attempted to achieve. It is obvious, however, that the union must make and win demands satisfactory to the majority of the membership or find its membership rolls rapidly melting away.

A failure to understand this dichotomy is at the root of frequent wonderment at the willingness of workers to undertake a strike when their demands and the employer's offer are only two or three cents apart. Preservation of the union's power and its future ability to bargain may be the real issue rather than the minor wage discrepancy.

One thing, then, is clear even at this stage of our discussion. Collective bargaining is with rare exceptions a major *raison d'etre* for the existence of labor unions. Unions exist neither as educational institutions nor as purveyors of charity, although to a limited extent, unions have played both roles. Nor have political objectives been the primary preoccupation of unions. Unions in the United States have never been as completely free of political entanglements as is sometimes believed, and unions in other countries have been far more completely involved in political affairs than have unions in this country. Nevertheless, even among the most politically conscious unions, including those dominated by Marxist leaders, involvement in collective bargaining plays a major if not dominant part. A union is organized to improve if not maximize the interests of its membership. While a union's vision of this goal may become blurred at times as it finds itself distracted by various bureaucratic considerations, if the loss of vision is too great, the union cannot survive. Workers join unions for the protection and benefits membership will bring. The bulk of a union's membership is, except in periods of crisis, at best apathetic. If the union does not succeed in winning for workers some of their demands (with the promise of more to come), apathy is likely to be converted into hostility and abandonment.

To say that unions all have the common objective of entering into collective bargaining, however, conceals the wide variety of goals and objectives different unions may have and the different ways they go about obtaining them. Given this diffusion of objectives, how do a union's leaders decide which objectives are the most important and therefore to be accorded priority in their bargaining with the employer?

There are two general considerations of paramount importance, each of which can be subdivided into a number of elements. The first is the character of the union itself—the degree of democracy present in its organization, its relation to the national or international union, and the degree of danger faced by the union's membership from raids by a rival union. The second broad category consists of external factors—the general state of business conditions with particular reference to the industry in which the union is directly involved and the character of contract settlements elsewhere.

Seen from the eyes of an outsider, virtually all unions give the appearance of being highly democratic. Most unions have constitutions that read as models of democratic principles. In such constitutions rank-and-file members are given every right to express their views and to remove their leaders from office whenever it seems appropriate. For a substantial majority of unions, particularly at the local level, this picture of internal democracy is accurate. The length of tenure in office of local union leaders is very short, averaging about two years. The more democratic the union is, the greater the role played by the rank and file in shaping the union's demands.

A truly democratic union, however, often creates serious problems for its leaders. Obviously the leaders face an increased danger of losing their positions since other members are free to criticize them and to run for office against them. Furthermore, the democratic union is likely to force the union leader into making demands upon the employer that the leader knows are unwise or impossible to attain even if the rank and file were willing to support a long and costly strike. Similarly, a democratic union is likely to be more unruly, less willing to fulfill its contractual commitments, and frequently guilty of unauthorized strikes.

Not all unions, of course, are so highly democratic in their operations. A lack of democracy may arise either by default, through the failure of the members to act upon their rights, or through a process of centralization in the bargaining process. Both phenomena are not uncommon and tend to have quite different impacts on the position of the union's leaders.

A number of studies of local unions in action have revealed that union democracy is plagued by the same difficulties that beset most democratic organizations—the apathy of the average individual who belongs.[3] Typically, except at moments of crisis, union members do not take a keen interest in their union's activities. An average union meeting will often find only 10 percent or less of the union's members in attendance.

A failure to attend the union's meetings is not always a sign of disinterest, however. Furthermore, members often have an opportunity to discuss issues at the workbench or during lunch and coffee break. They are thus able to communicate their views to their leaders in the shop. Quite frequently, the absence of a good turnout at the union meeting will work to the leader's disadvantage just as much as an excess of rank-and-file participation. Often a small but determined minority is able to seize control of a meeting and force unrealistic demands upon the local's leaders or even overthrow them. It is an astute leader indeed who manages to find compromises at the same time suitable to the majority of the workers, acceptable to management, and not too distasteful to a dissenting minority.

When collective bargaining takes place on the national level, however, the position of the union leader becomes more secure because the difficulty of overthrowing him increases. It is more difficult for a would-be rival to a national officer to become sufficiently well known to the larger membership. Even a national officer, however, may remain secure only as long as his demands upon management reflect the views of his constituents, and the most powerful labor union leaders like John L. Lewis and James Hoffa have held their power less because of their ability to centralize the reins of power than because of the great benefits they have been able to win for their followers. Nevertheless, national leaders do tend to have considerably wider discretion in formulating their demands on employers and often retain their offices even when their unions achieve only relatively minor gains.

Sometimes a local officer in trouble with some of the members of his union can extricate himself by "passing the buck" to the national office. Demands that he considers inappropriate or impossible to win can be forwarded to the national office for rejection without the local officer jeopardizing his own position.

Less significant today, since the AFL-CIO has established its "no raiding" pact among its unions, but of considerable importance historically, has been the threat posed by other unions who may seek to capture a union's membership for their own rolls. Whether organizing hitherto unorganized workers or those already members of another union, there is a tendency for those leading the drive to make elaborate promises—some of which may be impossible to fulfill. Where workers are attracted by these promises and threaten to bolt their present union membership, the current leaders may be driven to make similarly exaggerated promises that will be equally difficult to meet. Once again, the union leader is put in a difficult position. To avoid continuous threats of this nature he may seek some form of union security clause from the employer. Although raiding is considerably reduced today, major unions outside the AFL-CIO such as the Teamsters still pose an ever-present threat to unions within the federation's jurisdiction.

It is apparent from what we have just said that the process of collective bargaining is as much a political as it is an economic process. Any union leader who wishes to remain in office must be attuned to which way the political tides within his union are running.

In addition to factors within the union that influence the character of its collective bargaining practices are the settlements obtained by rival unions. Union members are keenly sensitive to the relative position of other workers vis-à-vis their own as well as to their union's performance in comparison to others. Because contract settlements nowadays receive prominent attention both in the newspapers and on radio and television, the union member has little difficulty keeping abreast with current developments even if he is not an avid reader of the union newspapers.

It should be quickly added that developments elsewhere may raise hopes that cannot be fulfilled because of variations in economic conditions from one industry to another and from one plant to another. Union leaders also have to shape their demands to the exigencies of the market situation. Even in a period of general prosperity, when the climate for wage increases and other demands is most auspicious, there may be industries and firms in a weak financial position that are unable to match the concessions granted by other firms. Although union members often reject employer claims to financial debility as familiar cries of "wolf," the astute union leader needs to be able to judge when the employer's protests are well founded and where the closing of the plant or a drastic curtailment of employment is likely should the union persist in its demands.

Much of the analysis thus far can be applied to both industrial and craft unions. Historically, there has been a sharp difference between these two types. Industrial unions have attempted to organize all workers in a plant, both skilled and unskilled, while craft unions have admitted only those workers trained to a particular craft or skill. More recently, however, the base of the craft unions has broadened considerably, and many now have memberships nearly as diverse as industrial unions. Other differences between the two types, although important, can also be overemphasized. Craft unions are sometimes harder pressed to cope with technological change, which makes the skill of their members obsolete, but to a large extent this depends on the state of the market faced by either type of union encountering such change. It is also true that craft unions have relied more upon market restrictions made possible by their members' skills and have sometimes acted outside the areas usually prescribed for collective bargaining, but bargaining has grown increasingly important for crafts through the years and often their objectives at the bargaining table are identical to those of the industrial union. More and more craft unions, for example, seek pensions and similar benefits from the employer rather than supplying them to the membership from the union's treasury. One important administrative distinction between the two that frequently exists is worth noting at this point. Many of the negotiations on behalf of craft workers employed by small employers in a local market are carried on by a union business agent. The business agent is a paid professional who normally handles the affairs of the union members on a full-time basis. Business agents take their guidance not only from requests of the rank and file and other union officers but also frequently consult with fellow union business agents.[4]

Management

The same rich variety in goals and attitudes toward collective bargaining characterizes the management of different firms as it does the leaders of various unions. In one respect, however, the attitude of most management toward collective bargaining is usually quite different from that of union leaders.

If anything, most management tends to see collective bargaining not as the reason for its existence but as a threat to its survival. This is not true for all members of management, of course; some, such as personnel directors and the industrial relations experts, owe their jobs to collective bargaining. Nevertheless, the relationship of management to, and its attitude toward, collective bargaining is quite different from that of union leaders. As we shall soon see, although unions have not always been wedded to collective bargaining, in recent years it has been management rather than the unions who have dragged their feet on the way to the bargaining table. Until the passage of the Wagner Act in 1935 and its subsequent seal of constitutionality

by the Supreme Court, many American managements never came to the bargaining table at all. With the passage of time, however, management has grown increasingly concerned with the quality of labor relations. A 1957 study of some 714 firms showed that there was, on the average one person in personnel for every 125 employees. In contrast, unions had one full-time official for every 300 union members.[5]

The reluctance of management to engage in collective bargaining is not difficult to understand. They see themselves as having much to lose and very little to gain from recognizing and bargaining with a union. A loss of autonomy, a need to increase costs by paying higher wages and by cutting the workday were (and to some extent still are) likely to be deemed too great a loss for the compensating gain in improved plant morale.

In other respects, the variety of management positions with regard to collective bargaining is just as broad as it is for unions. Management structures range all the way from one-man leadership to giant corporations with many layers of management. The attitudes of management toward collective bargaining do not vary consistently with the size of the firm involved, however. The single manager, operating a small plant, may be more sympathetic to unions because he himself may have risen from the ranks of labor and thus be more aware of the problems facing workers than the executive of a large corporation would be. Equally often, however, the owner-manager of the small plant may feel his whole position threatened by the union and therefore be more antagonistic toward the union than his fellow executive in a large corporation.

In evaluating the attitudes of management toward collective bargaining, however, we will concentrate on the large companies. These are the firms that provide the bulk of the nation's employment opportunities and they are the ones most frequently organized and involved in collective bargaining. It should be noted, however, that there are long-standing bargaining arrangements between the members of craft unions and their employers, and, in such fields as construction and clothing, many of these employers are very small. As the next chapter points out, these parties have had a long bargaining history. Although their relative importance has declined today, they should not be dismissed too readily.

Ever since 1932 when Adolf A. Berle and Gardiner Means wrote their classic study *The Modern Corporation and Private Property,* students of the corporation have been aware that the frequent divorce of ownership and management creates problems in studying decision-making in the large company.

Of the various goals and objectives toward which a management may strive, the aim of maximizing profits has been the one most frequently emphasized by economic theorists in the past. By seeking to maximize profits, the manager ensures that his plant will be run in the most efficient manner possible, thereby guaranteeing the utilization of the best combination of factors of production.

Largely because of the existing (and increasing) lack of congruity between ownership and management, a number of the more recent theorists have questioned whether the typical chief executive (or he and his fellow officers) actually does seek to maximize profits.[6] It is easy to conceive of a variety of other motives that may prompt executive decision-making. Considerations of power, prestige, a sense of social responsibility, the desire for a good public image, fear of government intervention, and a desire to maximize output or to maintain a certain percentage of the market may all be involved in varying proportions. It is quite possible that each of these goals, if seriously pursued, will come in conflict with the profit maximizing principle.

Pursuit of these other goals, however, does not mean that concern over profits cannot remain an important and even dominant part of management's thinking. A company may have a fixed target of a certain rate of profit on sales or on capital investment and be satisfied provided that target is achieved. Management may seek a level of profits designed to keep the stockholders happy without incurring the risk of losses that might lead the stockholders to seek new management.

Not all observers of the corporate scene are agreed that the old theory of profit maximization is as far wrong as some of its critics imply. Note that a failure to maximize profits implies some degree of discretion in the hands of management. It has already been noted that the absence of direct control over the business by its owners because of the divorce of ownership and management grants management a certain latitude. In addition, management requires a certain freedom from the exigencies of market competition of the character envisioned by Adam Smith. If the firm is in a fiercely competitive market, it may be compelled to try to maximize profits lest it wind up with sizable if not maximum losses.

In response to critics of the profit maximization principle, some management experts have denied that the separation of ownership and management is as general as has been depicted. They argue that there is still a high concentration of stock ownership, assuring the owners a considerable degree of control over their companies. It is also questioned whether management, in firms where ownership is so widely diversified as to make owner control impossible, acts in any significantly different fashion than they would if they were the sole owners.[7] The growth of stock option plans and similar devices has also meant that many managers have a far more extensive investment in the company than was true a quarter of a century or more ago.

Although a completely satisfactory answer to the controversy is difficult to provide, the importance of profit maximization in shaping the attitude of corporate managements toward collective bargaining is readily apparent. A management that is determined to maximize profits is likely to take a quite different approach toward the demands of a union than is one that has a less rigid goal in mind.

Like a union, a corporate management has both internal and external forces acting on it as it faces any business decision. Essential to a good profits record is a high level of productivity within the plant and an atmosphere of peace uninterrupted by slowdowns, frequent strikes, and so on. High levels of productivity are also dependent on the ability of the company to attract top-quality workers and the ability to avoid losing them to rival plants. The greater the skill requirements and the longer the period of training necessary, the more important is a low rate of turnover among the plant's labor force.

Corporate executives may disagree among themselves, however, particularly when there is a union involved, as to the best means of preserving labor peace and achieving peak productivity. Some officers may see union-management cooperation as the best course and encourage the union to take an active role in production decisions. Others will see the union as a threat to harmonious plant relations and a menace to production standards,

and they may urge that the union be opposed at every step. Industrial relations in various plants may thus be a reflection of which group is in control.

Even within a given company, moreover, disagreement among management officials may exist to an extent sufficient to make the company's policies vacillating and uncertain. Sometimes a union leader is able to recognize which members of the management team are likely to support a particular union demand and he will seek to win support from those individuals.

Part of the rift within management's ranks may be based on the conflict between a desire for recognition from the public as a "good employer" and a desire to avoid any loss of managerial autonomy. While it is nice to have the reputation of being a good company with which to work, too many concessions and too much wooing of workers may lead (at least in the view of many managers) to a loss of management's right to manage. Not only may individual management personnel at the same level in different departments view a given question with quite different perspectives, but the viewpoint may change as one ascends or descends the managerial ladder. Nor is it easy to predict in advance whether a foreman, for example, will want to take a firmer or more conciliatory line toward a union demand than upper-echelon management.

The contrasting role played between different levels of management is neatly exemplified in two plants with whom we have had personal contact. Both plants employ about 2,500 workers; one is in the printing industry and the other makes auto parts. In one case, all bargaining over new contracts is conducted by the company's vice-president in charge of labor relations in consultation with the local industrial relations officer. It is quite clear, however, that the vice-president has the say in all final decisions. In the other plant, bargaining is left much more in the hands of the local company officials. The general nature of the settlement expected as well as the acceptance of any new proposal made by the union (such as a new fringe benefit not available in the company's other plants) must be cleared by the top management. In many other ways, however, the local management is remarkably free to work out its own settlement with the various unions in the plant.

It is evident from the preceding examples that the personnel director or the officer or officers charged with the responsibility of bargaining with the union has some of the same diversity of opinion on his team as the union leader has on his. It should be noted, however, that the company official faces a loss of position or prestige because of a rejection of his settlement by the stockholders more rarely than the union leader does from a rejection by the members of his union. Furthermore, the not infrequent rejection of a settlement by the rank-and-file union members is viewed by management officials as further evidence of the basic irresponsibility of unions. Even in a company where sharp internal divisions exist between different members of the management team, everyone will almost always support the final decision. The more democratic is the operation of the institution in question, the greater is the opportunity to voice dissension. To a certain extent, the lack of democracy in labor unions can be blamed on the management that prefers to deal with a realistic union leader who will insist that his union abide by the signed contract.

The advice and counsel received from individuals outside the corporation may also play a role in shaping the attitude management decides to assume at the bargaining table. The advice of banking officials close to the company, suppliers, and customers may all play a role. Just as settlements recently achieved at other plants may shape the character of the union's demands, so may these settlements be important in determining management's response. Once settlement has been achieved elsewhere, it becomes difficult for the company to make a good case for refusing to grant a similar settlement. Not only is the resolve of the union's membership strengthened, but public opinion is likely to be less sympathetic to an employer who is unwilling to grant terms already won elsewhere.

It goes without saying, of course, that there may be very good reasons why a particular company cannot match the terms offered by other employers. Its internal cost structure may make such concessions impossible. Any firm, then, cannot simply blindly play "follow the leader," but must weigh the nature of its labor costs as a proportion of total costs and its competitive position in the market. Several times in past years, after the UAW had won sizable wage increases from the big three auto manufacturers, American Motors avoided comparable increases and in one case even secured a wage reduction based on its weak market position.

Effect of Environment

The various environmental factors that impinge on collective bargaining and contribute to its richness of variety warrant somewhat more detail. Collective bargaining is such a familiar part of our contemporary scene that we complacently assume that we know everything there is to know about the subject. As Alfred Marshall once said about economics, however, the more one studies the subject, the more one finds to learn.

There are over 73,000 local unions operating in the United States, each possessing different leaders, bargaining with different employers under a variety of economic conditions; over 150,000 labor contracts have resulted from these negotiations. Clark Kerr has suggested a number of ways in which the environmental settings of collective bargaining may differ.[8] Included on his list are the size of the plant, the amount of investment per worker, the nature of the company's product market and cost structure, and the relationship of the plant to the community, including the plant's relative size and whether it considers itself a permanent member of the community or is prone to moving about the country. The atmosphere of the community itself and whether or not it is a "union" town may also have some bearing.[9] The age of the union and the collective bargaining process may also be significant; as the years pass, bargaining may become more peaceful, as both parties temper their approach toward their opponent. Some unions or industries may, on the other hand, develop a tradition for "tough" bargaining that may continue and grow in intensity decades after the union has become well established.

While all of these factors may have a significant impact upon the shape of collective bargaining in a particular situation, it is difficult to judge how any individual variant will affect the bargaining scene. A large plant is likely to have more formal relations with a union, with the terms of the contract spelled out in greater detail. However, in some big plants the relationship between management and the union is very congenial. Similarly, a picture of the small plant is sometimes drawn where everyone, workers and management alike, are all members of one big happy family. The absence of a union is frequently justified by the lack of a need for one. While this may constitute an accurately drawn picture for many plants, it is surely not always the case.

In some cases, these environmental factors may operate in opposing directions with one factor outweighing one or more others, thus tending to produce varying relationships. Nor should one become too doctrinaire; collective bargaining, above all, involves relationships between human beings. Strong personalities do not simply mirror the economic and political environments in which they exist, important though those may be; such leaders put their own personal stamp on the character of the bargaining process.

With all of these varying and often conflicting forces at work, it is not surprising to find that the range in the character of industrial relations is enormous.[10] In some plants, collective bargaining may constitute little more than an armed truce with open warfare between the two parties breaking out regularly. Management seeks to limit the influence of the union at every step while the union tries to take over operation of the plant. Management in these circumstances is likely to see the contract as a defensive armor against the union's encroachment, while the union views the same contract as an offensive weapon providing an opening wedge into the plant's operations.

At the other extreme is union-management cooperation, where management seeks the union's advice and help in making decisions. Examples of union-management cooperation are not difficult to find but constitute a distinct minority of collective bargaining situations and usually prevail in small companies that have faced a serious financial crisis sometime in their past.

The majority of collective bargaining situations fall in between these two extremes. Unlike the armed truce, in which the two parties are barely civil to each other, in the majority of cases, both parties find considerable room for tolerating each other's viewpoints. Warfare (strikes and lockouts) may still occur periodically, but both sides make a greater effort to understand the other's position and to examine the facts. As conditions or leaders change, the relationship may grow closer or deteriorate—and these general trends may remain unchanged for considerable periods of time. Rarely, however, do they move to the two extreme positions sketched above.

Although collective bargaining displays great diversity within a given country and although the collective bargaining process in part reflects the mores and culture of the country in which it takes place, many of the basic issues remain unchanged. For example, the insecurity and dissatisfaction created by the inequities of early capitalism fostered union growth in many countries around the world, just as it did in the United States and England. A more generally applicable statement, however, would be that unions developed because of the stresses and strains concomitant with the process of industrialization. Although some craft unions antedate industrialization and the factory system, unions everywhere developed as a significant force only as the pace of industrialization quickened.

Unions are, however, not simply a reaction to big business and the modern industrial giants. John K. Galbraith's suggestion that unions in the United States emerged as a "countervailing power" to big business is the result of a misreading of labor history in the United States. But the anxieties, uncertainties, and insecurities that came with what Karl Polanyi has called "the great transformation" meant that workers were cast like straws in the wind, helpless to protect themselves before the gusts of change.

Although in many countries the stresses of industrialization have taken similar forms, the defenses constructed by unions against the forces of change have differed markedly from country to country. More than the unions in any other country in the world, American unions have sought to better the position of their members by concentrating their efforts on collective bargaining. Unions in other countries have been far more prone to rely on political pressure to achieve desired objectives. Unions elsewhere have also been more given to espousing socialistic objectives; for a number of them, collective bargaining with private employers is but a temporary (hopefully) stage until a system of public ownership has been achieved. Most American unions, by way of contrast, are as loyal to a private enterprise system as the management with whom they negotiate.

Consequently, foreign labor unions have been far more involved in political affairs than have their American counterparts. Many foreign unions have organized political parties of their own or aligned themselves with a party sympathetic to their interests. As a result, foreign labor unions place far greater reliance on the actions of their governments to provide them with certain of the same protections that American unions have sought through collective bargaining. Despite the anguished cries of conservatives who have charged for the past thirty years that the United States is a welfare state well on its way to socialism, the fact is that, judged by the standards of other industrialized nations, the United States has been very slow to adopt welfare measures. Whether this is a cause for praise or blame has been a subject for fierce debate. Without engaging in further acrimony, we can simply point out that this slow pace (which in part resulted from the failure of American unions to push for such protection) has forced American unions to furnish such protection for their members from their own funds or seek protection from the individual employer through collective bargaining. This fact explains much of the postwar drive by American unions for fringe benefits.

The exclusive reliance of American unions on collective bargaining has precluded any great interest in consumer cooperatives. Beginning in England with the Rochdale Plan, the idea of workers banding together as consumers to protect their purchasing power has had wide success in England and in many countries on the continent, particularly in the Scandinavian countries. In some of these countries consumer cooperatives account for 20 percent or more of the total retail trade. By contrast, consumer cooperatives have never gained more than 1 percent of the retail trade in the United States. There are many reasons for this failure, but the disinterest of unions and workers in general has been a major contributing factor.

It is true that there was scattered interest on the part of some early union leaders, such as William Sylvis, in the organization of producer cooperatives, but the idea never caught on with the vast majority of the union members and was never developed far beyond the dream stage.

One can also find fleeting instances when American unions also toyed with the idea of true consumer cooperatives. In 1845 the Boston Mechanics attempted to organize a cooperative but it was short lived. Interest in consumer cooperatives was rekindled after the depression of 1873, but the failure of the cooperatives to extend credit and their payment of low wages to their employees, violating the philosophy of unionism, helped spell their early demise.

American Business Unionism

Much of our preceding characterization of the American labor movement as it differs from foreign ones can be summarized by saying that American unionism from its conception was strongly oriented toward the principle of *business unionism.* Samuel Gompers, the first president of the AFL, is often cited as one of the founders of business unionism, and the famous labor historian Selig Perlman has argued that business unionism was a product of the 1880s and 1890s when the union leaders became disenchanted with dreams of broad social and revolutionary reform.[11] While there may have been a change in tone at that time (as indicated by the collapse of the Knights of Labor), we are inclined to agree with Philip Taft who argues that the seeds of American business unionism were planted and grew from the time when unions first became organized in this country.[12]

What is *business unionism* and how does it differ functionally from the unionism of other countries? A business union is one that concentrates on the bread-and-butter issues of workers' lives, focusing its efforts on raising the wages and bettering the working conditions of its members through collective bargaining rather than such other means as political action. To do this, it seeks to control the supply of labor by various devices such as apprenticeship rules and skill requirements. To ensure its control, the union usually maps out strict jurisdictional boundaries and attempts to control all jobs that fall within them. Business unionism thus tends to seek improvement in the situation of its own members, even at the expense of other workers.

Clearly the distinction is to some extent a matter of degree. Unions that would not meet the general specifications to be called business unions may also seek to better the position of their memberships through collective bargaining. Nor are the leaders of business unions as completely lacking in idealism as the definition sometimes seems to imply. Nevertheless, the degree of distinction is sufficiently important to bring a marked difference in the approach towards collective bargaining as shown by business unions and by those unions more concerned with general social and economic reform.

Another major factor in setting the tone of collective bargaining in one country in contrast to others or even for different regions within a country is the attitude of the national and local governments and their officials. As will become readily apparent as this book proceeds, collective bargaining has been at times seriously hampered by government action, while at other times the power of government has nurtured unions and kept them alive. At times, unions have been legally ruled as conspiracies subject to civil and criminal action. At other times, the right of unions to be recognized and the obligation of employers to bargain with them has been specified by legislative enactments. Students of the subject will be able to identify such periods in American labor history and the same pattern has taken place in many other countries as well.

Even while establishing the legal right of unions to bargain, however, a government may limit the range of subjects about which a union is free to negotiate. The Taft-Hartley Act in the United States is a good illustration. Under that act such subjects as the closed shop are barred from the bargaining table even though both parties may wish to discuss them. Similar limitations can be found in other countries.

The subject matter of collective bargaining thus varies not only from plant to plant and industry to industry but from country to country. Even more striking than the differences between bargaining in the United States and in the Western European countries is that between developed and still-developing nations. The developing countries' unions are even more prone to be involved in politics and dependent upon a political party or the government for support than those in Western Europe. Collective bargaining in these countries is likely to be less fully developed not only because the unions themselves are less mature, but because the government is likely to impose heavy restrictions on strikes and the general nature of the demands made by the unions lest they hamper economic growth. While the major emphasis of this book will be on collective bargaining as it is practiced in this country today, where it is appropriate and possible, comparisons will be made with the way collective bargaining operates in other countries to give the reader some idea of the richness of variety involved.

In addition to variations in culture, modes, geographical environment, and the structure of the government the character of collective bargaining in any country is also a function of time. The existence of collective bargaining is so commonplace today that it is difficult to remember that only a little over a century ago the phrase had not yet been coined. The coining of the term is usually attributed to Beatrice or Sydney Webb. The Webbs were distinguished British economists and Fabian socialists of the late nineteenth and early twentieth century and authors of many books, including *Industrial Democracy.* At the time they used the term, the practice was a rarity everywhere. Judged by United States standards, collective bargaining is still in a primitive state in many countries.

NOTES

1. Neil Chamberlain, *Collective Bargaining* (New York: McGraw-Hill, 1951), Chap. 6.

2. Joseph Shister, "Collective Bargaining," in Neil Chamberlain, Frank Pierson, and Theresa Wolfson (eds.), *A Decade of Industrial Research* (New York: Harper & Row, 1958).

3. See, for example, Leonard Sayles and George Strauss, *The Local Union* (New York: Harcourt Brace Jovanovich, 1967); Theodore Purcell, *The Worker Speaks His Mind on Company and Union* (Cambridge, Mass.: Harvard University Press, 1953).

4. Hjalmar Rosen and R. A. Hudson Rosen, "Decision Making in a Business Agent Group," Industrial Relations Research Association, *Proceedings,* 1955, pp. 287–297.

5. Dale Yoder and Roberta J. Nelson, "Salaries and Staffing Ratios in Industrial Relations, 1957," *Personnel* (July 1957), pp. 16–22.

6. R. A. Gordon, "Short Period Price Determination in Theory and Practice," *American Economic Review,* 38 (June 1948), 265–288; F. E. Hoogstraat, "Attacks on the Value of the Profit Motive in Theories of Business Behavior," in J. W. McGuire (ed.), *Interdisciplinary Studies in Business Behavior* (Cincinnati: Southwestern Printing, 1962); and William J. Baumol, "On the Theory of Oligopoly," *Economics,* 25 (August 1958), 187–198.

7. Earl F. Cheit, "The New Place of Business," in Earl Frank Cheit (ed.), *The Business Establishment* (New York: Wiley, 1964) pp. 152–192.

8. Clark Kerr, "The Collective Bargaining Environment," in Clinton S. Golden and Virginia D. Parker (eds.), *Causes of Industrial Peace Under Collective Bargaining* (New York: Harper & Row, 1955), pp. 10–22.

9. Milton Derber, W. Ellison Chalmers, and Ross Stagner, "Environmental Variables and Union-Management Accommodation," *Industrial and Labor Relations Review* (April 1958), pp. 413–428.

10. This point is further developed in Benjamin M. Selekman, "Varieties of Labor Relations," *Harvard Business Review,* 27 (March 1949), 175–199.

11. Selig Perlman, *A Theory of the Labor Movement* (New York: Macmillan, 1928).

12. Philip Taft, "On the Origins of Business Unionism," *Industrial and Labor Relations Review* (October 1963), pp. 20–38.

2
The History of Collective Bargaining—Here and Elsewhere

The overshadowing problem of the American Labor Movement has always been the problem of staying organized. No other labor movement has ever had to contend with the fragility so characteristic of American labor organizations.

—Selig Perlman

☐ RECENT critics have argued that American labor historians pay too much attention to the history of organized labor and too little to the history of the unorganized.[1] Whether or not such criticism is justified for labor history in general, it quite obviously is irrelevant when applied to the history of collective bargaining. In order to have collective bargaining it is necessary to have unions which, if not permanent, are at least organized on a long-term basis and unions that are anxious and willing to engage in bargaining. For more than half a century after the first stirrings of a labor movement, neither of these prerequisites existed in the United States.

Labor Unions

It is true that the labor union antedates the corporation in United States history. The seeds of early unionism can be discerned in groups formed shortly after the American Revolution and one can find cases of real collective bargaining in the 1790s. Both, however, were exceptions and oddities of their time rather than the general rule.

Early efforts to form unions were frustrated by the unwillingness of employers to recognize their existence, let alone engage in collective bargaining with them. The union movement as a potent force in the American economy is a phenomenon of recent vintage.

Perhaps the first point to be emphasized in selecting the key points that have shaped collective bargaining in this country and helped to distinguish it from bargaining as it has developed elsewhere in the world is that although labor unions have a long and an honorable history in the United States, their strength has never been as great as in many other industrialized countries. As late as 1897 total union membership in this country accounted for less than 4 percent of the labor force; at its pre-1930s peak in 1920 it had risen to 19 percent, but by 1933 it was back down to 7 percent. Even in 1970, unions in the United States accounted for only about 28 percent of the nonagricultural labor force and about 23 percent of the total labor force.

Although the current figures represent a slight retreat from the previous high mark set during the years immediately after World War II, they are in vivid contrast to the levels of union membership forty years ago. Thus, while forty-one of the national unions existing today were established prior to 1890, unionism on a national scale did not really begin until after the Civil War. There had been scattered attempts to organize national unions and even a national labor movement (as evidenced in the work of the National Trades Union in 1834), but such efforts were doomed to failure. Most of the early United States unions were short-lived local organizations that were confined to a single city.

17

A national union, which may be organized along either industrial or craft lines, consists of locals organized in the same general field or area. Although the national union is in effect the parent body, the degree of autonomy accorded to the locals in collective bargaining varies from national to national. There are some 180 national unions in the United States, and most of these are affiliated with the AFL-CIO. Local unions may pay part of their dues to the national on a per capita basis. The nationals may in turn pay a per capita tax to the AFL-CIO (if they are members). An international union, which has local affiliates outside the United States, resembles the national union. Its foreign membership is usually confined to Mexico or Canada.

Although collective bargaining also dates back far into our history, it did not develop fully until after World War II. The great upsurge in union membership during the 1930s did not immediately produce collective bargaining because of the tenacious resistance of employers to all forms of it. During World War II, collective bargaining necessarily functioned under wartime conditions that made the government an inevitable party to every important dispute. Furthermore, cost-plus contracts often made management less cost conscious than is customarily the case. Thus, it is important to bear in mind that as a significant phenomenon collective bargaining in this country has a record of less than two decades.

What accounts for the early weakness and ephemeral character of American unions? Labor historians have supplied us with a wealth of explanations—enough to hamstring the labor movements of several countries! In addition to the employer and governmental opposition that slowed union development elsewhere, there were a number of characteristics unique to the American economy that made the path toward unionization a particularly rocky one to tread.

One of the most obvious features distinguishing the United States from most other countries was the flood of immigrants who came to this country throughout the nineteenth and early twentieth centuries; between 1891 and 1920 over 18,000,000 immigrants landed on our shores. Although the immigrant ranks included a number of men who later served as leaders of the American labor movement, they also represented a huge supply of workers willing to work at very low wages. Employers were thus able to ward off the demands of unions for better wages by hiring labor "fresh off the boat."

The famous labor historian John R. Commons has stressed the important role the unions played in the "Americanization" of these immigrants.[2] Ironically, however, the same flood of immigrants was responsible for the emphasis placed by American unions on securing contracts assuring the *closed shop* (where all workers have to be members of the union prior to being employed). The greater insistence on the *closed shop* has been a characteristic historically distinguishing American unions from those in other lands. Early associations of workers, for example, often put great social pressure on other workers to join the union. Typical of their practices was a refusal to stay at boarding houses that also lodged "scabs." As a result of this insistent pressure for the closed shop, employers frequently formed their own associations in order to be better able to combat it.

The immigrant was brought to this country by the fact that America has been traditionally the "land of opportunity"—a high-wage country. This has also made the case for unions less pressing and urgent in the minds of many workers, particularly those having recently arrived.

The existence of the open western frontier as a "safety valve" throughout much of the nineteenth century should also be emphasized. Although economic historians have debated the question of who settled the West and how much influence the frontier had on workers back in the East, it seems safe to say that its existence tended to relieve some of the stresses of low wages and city life by providing workers with the possibility, when things became too rough, of quitting and moving West. This possibility, however illusionary it may have proved to be in reality, helped to reduce the interest of workers in organizing unions to fight for better working conditions.

The existence of the frontier accounted in part for another facet of our economic environment that is of sufficient importance to merit separate attention—the degree of social and economic mobility that gave the Horatio Alger story a chance to be repeated over and over in real life. While the opportunity for such mobility has sometimes been overstated, it did exist, and workers' dreams of one day being their own boss or the boss of others had a chance to come true. Who would want to help organize a union when someday he might be an employer himself?

Unlike workers in other countries, American workers, whether unionized or not, never completely lost faith in the capitalist system and the belief in private property. The sacredness of private property proved to be a major stumbling block in the path of union organization in the United States. All efforts at unionization were seen by the general public as a threat to private property and the courts repeatedly held unions to be a conspiracy against property rights. Between 1806 and 1842 there were seventeen conspiracy trials involving unions; in each case the union was found guilty.

When, for example, the Typographical Society of New York petitioned the New York State legislature in 1818 for a charter, the appeal was granted but with the proviso that the society make no effort to alter the wage levels in that occupation. Any effort to compel an employer to pay higher wages was a threat to his property rights and therefore illegal.

The surprising thing is not that conservative judges could render such decisions but that the bulk of the population would support them in these decisions. The fact that there was not more general protest may be the result of a wide acceptance of the doctrine of property rights.

Such court decisions, however, were not readily accepted by individual union workers and by the many groups of workers seeking to organize, despite their support of capitalism. American unionism, like unionism in other countries, was a response to the employer-employee relationship and a society where a small group of men controlled the working lives of large groups of other men. It would be a bad misreading of our labor history to conclude that workers were never seriously dissatisfied with their working conditions. The use of guns, clubs, and dynamite repeatedly demonstrated the willingness of workers to damage property and shed blood in behalf of their cause. Selig Perlman and others, however, have suggested that such violence when it occurred was less a matter of class antagonism than a reflection of the early frontier spirit of this country.[3] It should be added that much of the early violence was also a product of the stubborn refusal of employers to recognize unions. When the fight is for survival, the battle is likely to be more intense.

What has differentiated our unions, then, from those in many other countries has been a general acceptance of capitalism and a willingness to work within its framework rather than seeking its overthrow. Sometimes, as in the case of Samuel Gompers and other early labor leaders, this attitude represented a pragmatic decision, based less on any great admiration for capitalism than on a feeling that efforts to overthrow it were futile. Often, however, the labor leader has been as firm a believer in private property as the employer whom he faces across the bargaining table. Only the communist-led TUUL (Trade Union Unity League, 1929–1935), the IWW (Industrial Workers of the World, 1905–1920), the Knights of Labor, and a handful of smaller unions have worked toward a substantial or complete recasting of our society.

As noted in the previous chapter, the result has been that throughout the history of unionism in this country unions have far more consistently turned to the bargaining table for their gains than have unions elsewhere. Our unions have never displayed a keen interest in the game of national politics and have tended to be wary of government action lest it work more to their disadvantage than to their benefit. Again, however, we must be careful not to leave the impression that American unions made no efforts to secure legislative protection. Earlier efforts by American unions to reinforce by appropriate legislation their collective bargaining demands for such things as shorter hours were largely unsuccessful and by the early decades of the twentieth century, union leaders even opposed social security legislation lest it undermine the attractiveness of union membership! American unions tended to confine their interest in politics to the immediate local scene and their political activities accordingly manifested themselves at the state and community level.

Part of the responsibility for the short life span of early unions and the ineffectiveness of their demands rested with the membership of the unions themselves. Although it is true that American unions, including those interested in radical reform, have generally placed great emphasis on collective bargaining, this has not always been the case. Largely because employers refused to recognize unions for bargaining or for any other purpose, workers formed the habit of pressing for unilateral demands rather than undertaking collective bargaining.

The first recorded attempt at true collective bargaining in the United States took place in 1799 involving the Philadelphia Cordwainers. An earlier attempt of the Cordwainers to organize had collapsed within a year, and this second attempt, which was embellished with feeble efforts at collective bargaining, had also failed by 1806. The Grand National Consolidated Trades Union collapsed in 1834. There were other isolated but significant instances of collective bargaining throughout the first half of the nineteenth century. Most of these involved skilled workers and an interesting characteristic of the demands of these early unions was the effort to obtain the same wage for good and bad workers in order to meet the problem of "runaway apprentices" who, having partially learned the trade, would seek work in a nonunion shop at a wage rate below that being paid the union members. The tendency to "jump" jobs in this way threatened the wage standard set by the union. Similar attempts to make the less-skilled worker unattractive have been continued by skilled workers right down to the present day. Craft unions found much of their success resulted from their ability to "control the job," which involved strict controls over the right of the employer to hire and fire including stringent limitations on the use of apprentices. Such attempts were responsible for putting the early American labor movement at odds with many of the rank-and-file semiskilled and unskilled workers.

During the pre–Civil War days of American unions, when a group of workers decided that the time for a wage increase had come, they would meet and draw up a proposal including the sought-for increase as well as whatever other adjustments they deemed proper. This new "contract" was then submitted by a committee to the employer on a take-it-or-leave-it basis. Either the employer accepted the new terms as presented or the committee had the right to call a strike. The strike continued until either the employer capitulated or the workers were compelled to surrender. Often these early "strikes" involved a mass decision on the part of the workers to seek employment at other plants. If the employer was unable to recruit substitutes possessing similar skills, he might be forced to close down. The resolution of the issue thus became a question of the relative economic endurance of the two parties.

An interesting variant of these take-it-or-leave-it tactics of early unions was their frequent practice of inviting an employer to attend one of the union meetings at which the basis for the new demands would be discussed by the union's membership and the employer was expected to respond.

Although the balance of economic power was undoubtedly tipped in favor of the employers, workers were able to gain temporary successes in this fashion with a fair degree of regularity, especially when they pressed their demands during periods of prosperity when business was booming and the demand for labor high. In prosperous times the weaker employers often conceded rather quickly thereby making it impossible for employers to maintain a united front and putting great pressure on the more powerful employers to make settlements also. Victories over the weak employers also stiffened the resolve of the workers to continue the battle against the others.

However, the best word to describe these early gains won by workers is "temporary." Since most employers continued to refuse to recognize or negotiate with a union, they were bound by no signed contract requiring that they continue to pay the increased wages for a specified period of time. The result was that employers frequently seized upon the first opportunity that presented itself to cut wages back to their previous level. A downturn in business conditions was particularly conducive to such wage cuts. The ranks of union membership fell sharply after the depressions of 1812, 1837, 1854, 1857, 1873, 1921, and 1930, and a decline in wages followed each time.

The primary responsibility for the failure to enter into true collective bargaining at an earlier date must be placed on the shoulders of employers. However, because they had been repeatedly rebuffed by employers and because their efforts at unilateral demands had shown some degree of success, unions were not always willing to undertake collective bargaining even when the chance arose. Friends of labor like Horace Greeley upon occasion scolded unions for this display of unwillingness.

From the beginning unions in the United States generally pressed for what was then called *compulsory arbitration.* The term arbitration in early American labor history had a considerably broader meaning than it has today. The term collective bargaining had not yet been invented, and such words as arbitration and conciliation were sometimes used in its place. When they pressed for compulsory arbitration, however, most early unions were really seeking compulsory recognition by employers, that is, they were really demanding that employers be compelled to meet with them and settle issues peacefully, thus avoiding the necessity to resort to strikes.

Arbitration in those early days was thus an extremely loose term used to cover everything from collective bargaining to some form of mediation or conciliation. It was not until the early 1900s that arbitration came to have the distinctive meaning it bears today— this despite the fact that as early as 1829 the Cabinet Makers of Philadelphia had referred to arbitration in their constitution.

It might be noted parenthetically that neither mediation nor conciliation gained much early support from the federal or state governments. Although the two terms are used almost interchangeably today, they formerly had quite distinct meanings. Mediation, much more than conciliation, implied that government officials actively participated and offered suggestions. Neither service was available on a formal basis until comparatively recently, however. New York and Massachusetts were the first to establish permanent bureaus (1866), and while by 1913 thirty-two states had established such facilities, they were rarely used. Federal facilities were not provided until 1913, when the U.S. Department of Labor was established. Thus for over a century, collective bargaining remained solely a matter between union and employer with the government's role limited to interventions, usually on the side of the employer, when public interest seemed to demand it.

After the Civil War, a variety of forces, both on the employer and the union side, fostered the adoption of collective bargaining. Earlier, employers had been inclined to insist upon their right to bargain with each worker on an individual basis. As unions increased in strength, however, an increasing number of employers (the proportion of this was still small) adopted the policy of organizing company unions as a defense against outside organizers. Although negotiations between a company union and an employer could seldom if ever be termed bargaining in the true sense of the word, they did accustom employers to dealing with workers as a collective group. As a result, the old insistence of employers that each worker should have the opportunity to speak for himself lost much of its force.

At the same time, unions began to acquire a greater degree of permanency so that they remained to enforce contracts and negotiate future agreements. The spread of collective bargaining was also fostered by the growth of the national unions, which supervised bargaining and discouraged locals from engaging in unilateral action. By the late 1850s national unions were beginning to develop in response to the emergence of national markets; between 1854 and 1860 six craft unions, including the Printers (this union still exists today) became organized on a national basis. The trend toward national unions continued during the Civil War, but some years passed before most of the nationals acquired any bargaining power and control over their locals.

The origin of the implementation of collective bargaining in the United States in large part was the responsibility of Samuel Gompers. Gompers and other AFL leaders found lessons for the building of a successful labor movement in the experiences of the first major labor organization in the United States—the Knights of Labor.

The Organizations

This brings us to another distinctive facet of American labor history—the number and diversity of bodies engaging in collective bargaining. Collective bargaining has never been as centralized in this country as it has been in Europe, and there has been greater room for variety and experimentation. In many respects, as we will see in later chapters, this diversity has enriched and broadened the character of collective bargaining in this country. At the same time, the existence of what are often called dual unions has weakened the bargaining strength of American unions and led to internecine warfare at the expense of a united front against the employers. The AFL, which has often levelled the charge of "dual union" against its would-be rivals, itself began as a dual union to the Knights of Labor.[4]

The Knights of Labor

Founded in 1869 by Uriah Stephens as a secret society of workers and brought to full bloom after Terence Powderly became the Grand Master Workman in 1879, the Knights of Labor marked a new development in American labor history. Until that time, American unions had been confined almost exclusively to skilled workers, but Stephens and Powderly both concluded that craft unions inevitably produced divisions that weakened the labor union movement. After the early secrecy feature of the Knights had been removed, the doors to membership were flung open to all save a few unregenerate groups such as gam-blers, bartenders, lawyers and bankers, as the Knights sought the enrollment of all workers including farmers into "one big union."

The history of the labor movement and collective bargaining in this country might have been quite different if the ideals of the Knights of Labor had prevailed. Interested in social reform, they were adverse to violence and dubious about the efficacy of the strike as a weapon for labor. Ironically, both the early success of the Knights (whose membership grew from 9,000 in 1879 to about 750,000 in 1886) and their subsequent rapid collapse (membership had been reduced to 100,000 by 1890) can be attributed in part to their involvement in strikes. For the Knights, collective bargaining was a centralized process with much of the responsibility for final decisions resting in the hands of the top officers.

It was this centralization of decision making that left no room for the local and national officers and thus was responsible for the final collapse of the Knights. By the end of the Civil War, collective bargaining in general had ceased to be a solely local affair. Much bargaining was still done by the single local, but a number of national unions had been formed and within the cities attempts had been made to form city central bodies consisting of workers who were in the same field (such as construction) but belonged to different unions. Collective bargaining after the Civil War also ceased to follow the earlier pattern of unilateral demands by unions. By the end of the Civil War a clear distinction had also been made between items that were properly a part of day-to-day bargaining and those that were subject to renegotiation at contract time.

The Knights of Labor's concept of "one big union" came in conflict with the aims of already established national unions, which were structured on occupational lines. The organization of the Knights called for local assemblies at the lower levels, which were composed of skilled and unskilled workers alike. While the Knights favored mixed locals, their organization had many "craft" locals as well. The local Assemblies owed their allegiance and took their lead in collective bargaining from the district assemblies and the National Assembly above them.

Since the organizational structure of the Knights of Labor left little room for the national craft unions, local unions that joined the Knights found themselves torn by two appeals for loyalty. Both the leaders of the Knights and the national union officers demanded a voice in all bargaining decisions made by the locals. Since some national unions dated back to the 1850s, they had a strong historical claim on workers' loyalty. The seeds of conflict were planted from the moment the Knights were organized, and the battle increased in intensity as time went by.

At first there had been some clashes between the Knights and independent unions of skilled workers, but such clashes had been minimized by the fact that the Knights had undertaken the organization of skilled workers hitherto unorganized. By the mid-1880s, however, the independent unions complained increasingly of raids on their membership by the Knights. Things came to a head when the Knights took into its fold a cigar workers' union and settled with the cigar manufacturers after a strike called by both the Knights' newly admitted member and Local 144 of the Cigarmakers' International. In what was perhaps the crowning blow, the Knights supplied the manufacturers with their own union label identifying the work as being performed by union

labor. The International, on the other hand, tried to impress smokers that only its own label provided proper identification of union labor.

Among those left furious by the Knights' tactics was Samuel Gompers —then a member of Local 144 and soon to be the leader of the new AFL.

In 1886, when the Knights' membership rolls were at their peak, a meeting was held between the leaders of the national unions and the leaders of the Knights. As a concession to the national leaders the Knights offered to accept no local for membership without the consent of the national union concerned. The leaders of the national unions rejected this offer. At its 1886 convention, the Knights' leaders ordered all members of the cigarmaker's union to resign from their national, and in December of that year the leaders of the national unions held a separate convention. Here was founded the first permanent national labor federation in America— the American Federation of Labor.

American Federation of Labor

The Knights of Labor merit only brief mention in any history of collective bargaining because bargaining was not their prime objective. In contrast, the American Federation of Labor was and still remains the epitome of "business unionism"—dedicated to the task of improving the condition of its membership through the collective bargaining process.

Unlike the Knights of Labor, the growth of the AFL at first proceeded very slowly. After its founding in 1886 nearly fifteen years passed before the AFL reached the size achieved by the Knights of Labor at its peak strength. To a large degree the very characteristics that made the AFL's growth so slow, and thus were targets for criticism, were also responsible for the sureness of its footing and its ability to weather attack.

The AFL leadership avoided entanglements with the lower classes of workers. Organizational efforts were confined to the highly skilled and there was no sense of solidarity among workers like that which developed in many European labor unions. The AFL leadership held the organization aloof from the battles of other workers. The Homestead strike (1892) at the Carnegie Steel plant, which resulted in a pitched battle between union members and Pinkerton detectives, and the Pullman Strike of 1894 were both important battles lost by labor, but they were battles in which the AFL leadership played no important role.

The success of the AFL was based in part upon lessons learned from the Knights of Labor and it spelled the eventual end of the Knights. In the first place, whereas the Knights of Labor had been organized from the top down with responsibility for all major decisions, including bargaining, held at the top, the AFL was a federation in which virtually all power was retained by the national unions. Collective bargaining was the responsibility of the national unions and the locals under them. Each set its own policies without interference from the parent federation. Jurisdictional lines[5] were sharply drawn, with each national union having exclusive control within its hegemony. Because the philosophy of the AFL was basically conservative and because the leaders followed the good "business unionism" tradition and were scrupulous in abiding by the terms of their contracts, gradually, even without the threat of legal coercion, a sizable number of employers began to sign bargaining agreements.

Despite numerous setbacks, the AFL continued to expand. For the first time, unions succeeded in surviving

business depressions. They remained intact, ready to renew their demands when business conditions improved. The newly found ability of the craft members of the AFL to survive a depression encouraged the formation of other craft unions. Between 1897 and 1904 the number of national unions belonging to the AFL more than doubled, rising from 58 to 120.

Much of the early success of the AFL can be attributed to its policy of exclusive jurisdiction and its willingness to declare unions outside its domain "dual unions." Unions that belonged to the AFL enjoyed both the protection of exclusive jurisdiction and the right to make their own decisions. While this policy had obvious advantages and in some respects strengthened the bargaining position of AFL unions, it also meant that in later years the AFL was plagued by the emergence of rival dual unions and by jurisdictional rows within its own structure. One of the early powers reserved to the parent body was the settling of intra-AFL jurisdictional disputes. However, this power was lost seventeen years after the federation was formed when in 1903 a national convention reversed an order by the AFL's central board to revoke the charter of the Brewery Workers. The convention went even further, denying the board power to revoke other charters without permission of two-thirds of the delegates at the next national convention. Jurisdictional disputes grew more and more serious as changing technology, new industries, and new products made old jurisdictional demarcations less and less distinct.

The attitudes of the AFL toward collective bargaining largely reflected those of its leadership. Samuel Gompers was a firm believer in militant "business unionism" in which the labor movement confined most of its efforts to negotiations at the bargaining table. Although he never championed apparently hopeless causes, he was willing to fight to the death for those principles important to the interest of the AFL. Under the leadership of William Green, Gompers' successor, the AFL veered from militancy to respectability. Typical was Green's approach to the problem of organizing textile mills in the South. Repeated efforts to organize these mills had been defeated often by the use of brute force. Green's solution was sweet reasonableness. We must convince the employers, he argued, that ". . . it would be more profitable to deal with organized labor."

This approach was part of a new AFL campaign directed at all industries in the 1920s. Recognizing the importance of technological change then taking place, the AFL put great emphasis on cooperation between union and management as a way of increasing output and thereby making the union more attractive to the employer. Since the unions still wanted what employers regarded as an undue proportion of the resulting output, however, few employers were impressed, and little additional headway was made in organizing, particularly in the southern textile plants.

The unions were not the only ones to use a conciliatory approach. Employers in the 1920s also adopted numerous programs to woo the favor of their workers as they initiated various welfare programs such as pension plans. They also organized company unions. Such unions were not an innovation of the 1920s, however. Irving Bernstein has noted that some existed before the turn of the century,[6] although they did not come into widespread use until after World War I.[7]

Unions, of course, saw company unions for what they were—an attempt to weaken the labor movement—and dubbed all such activities paternalism. Although employers made a pretense of collective bargaining through company unions, the truth was that no real collective bargaining could exist under such conditions. Not only were the company unions unable to strike, but their leaders were often carefully screened by the company. Even when the company union's officers were anxious to do a good job, they were handicapped by their lack of information about wage scales and working conditions in comparable plants elsewhere. Rarely did company unions offer an opportunity for workers to settle their grievances. The labor historian Irving Bernstein reports, for example, that not a single grievance over dismissals was filed at Procter and Gamble during the first decade after its company union was formed.[8]

Later Rivals to the AFL

We have noted that one of the major sources of the AFL's strength and ability to survive employer opposition and periods of economic depression was its concentration on organizing only the skilled. While this policy protected the AFL from undue exposure to attack as employers could not easily substitute nonunion labor, it also limited the federation's ability to expand and meant that the bulk of America's laboring class went without union protection. A number of rival unions were formed to meet this need; most of them were radical in outlook and concentrated on organizing the unskilled and the semiskilled. Most notable among these were the Industrial Workers of the World (IWW), often referred to as the "Wobblies," and the Trade Union Unity League (TUUL).

Because the IWW and the TUUL were primarily political in character, they, like the Knights of Labor, do not figure prominently in a history of collective bargaining. Despite their political objectives, however, they did participate in collective bargaining, and the leaders of the Trade Union Unity League developed a technique that they brought to the Congress of Industrial Organizations when they later became organizers for that central union body. The TUUL organizers had discovered how to ferret out the grievances among workers in an unorganized plant and to exploit these with maximum efficiency in recruiting new members. John L. Lewis and the other CIO leaders were happy to make use of this technique in their own organizing campaigns.

It was, of course, the final schism marked by the breaking away of the CIO from the AFL that constituted the most serious threat to the supremacy of the AFL and that in the end greatly promoted the expansion of the American labor movement. Until the 1930s, the AFL leaders had continued to regard the great mass of unskilled and semiskilled workers as largely unorganizable. In earlier years the AFL officials had not made even a half-hearted attempt to organize the mass production industries. The *American Federationist* (the official organ of the AFL) had for years accepted advertisements from these nonunion plants, a practice that was bitterly attacked by Lewis. Favored by a change in the political climate and the blessing of public opinion, the CIO leaders succeeded in extending collective bargaining into sectors of the economy where it had never before existed.

Labor entered the 1930s in a weakened condition. Unlike earlier periods of prosperity, the 1920s had not witnessed growth in the labor movement. Buffeted by the campaign of welfare capitalism, the employers' drive for an "open shop" (closed to unions), and declining job opportunities in coal mining and the railroads, unions actually experienced a contraction in membership. In 1929 union membership stood at only 3.4 million—down 1.7 million from its peak after World War I. As a result of the depression the numbers showed a further decline to under 3 million in the early thirties.

Like many business leaders and the Hoover administration, the leaders of the AFL tended to minimize the seriousness of the business downturn. A number of AFL unions became involved in petty squabbles over the sovereignty of the local versus the national union in collective bargaining. Only the changed climate of labor legislation plus the threat of CIO competition finally prompted AFL leaders to undertake a great new organizing program of their own.

The success story of the CIO is too well known and too lengthy to merit retelling in a history of collective bargaining. We should note, however, that the CIO's rise involved a change in tactics by both labor and management. Management, which had tried to woo workers with various forms of welfare capitalism, such as pensions and company unions, during the decade of the 1920s again emphasized their earlier tactics of intimidation and coercion. These tactics persisted even after the Wagner Act's constitutionality had been upheld by the Supreme Court.[9] To counter this renewed opposition, the CIO leaders played on workers' grievances and employed the sitdown strike, in which workers seized plants and stayed in them until the union's demands were met. The sitdown strike was helpful in organizing the hitherto unorganized automobile and rubber industries.

Not unexpectedly the sitdown strikes raised all the old fears over the threat posed by unions to private property plus evoking fresh ones. The Hearst newspapers ran vigorous editorials denouncing them and Frank

Murphy, then governor of Michigan, was under heavy pressure in 1937 to use the state militia to eject the strikers from the General Motors plants. Murphy resisted these pressures and GM finally recognized and settled. Coupled with its victory at U.S. Steel (little steel continued to hold out) this achievement gave the CIO much to celebrate.

A major change was the eventual willingness of both parties to submit themselves to binding contracts on a wide range of topics. Prior to the 1930s, there had been a gradual move away from the unilateral demand by unions; some true bargaining by both parties had already taken place. The resulting contracts, however, tended to be skeletonlike in form and generally left the terms of working conditions to be settled by informal agreement.[10] These early agreements, which were characteristic of virtually all pre-1930 American labor contracts save those on the railroads, closely resembled the current form of labor contracts in Western Europe. Like contracts in Great Britain today, many of these earlier U.S. contracts contained no definite expiration date. The growth of the one-year contract on a widespread basis was a product of the 1930s and was prompted largely by uncertainty on both sides as to "what they were letting themselves in for."

The form of the contracts began to change in a number of other ways also. Earlier contracts had tended to be simple and had concentrated mainly on standardizing working conditions. For many reasons, not the least of which was hostile management's suspicions, contracts now became more legalistic as the management of large firms sought to deal at arm's length. Prior to the 1930s, except in the case of the railroads, neither party was likely to seek legal advice in drawing

a contract. Virtually none of the large firm's management had had any real experience in industrial relations or with collective bargaining and most tended to insist upon the inclusion of management-rights clauses as a price for settlement. The day of the lawyer in industrial relations had come.

The dominance of the binding written agreement has been most frequently attributed to the action of the National Labor Relations Board established under the Wagner Act. The timing of its adoption and the less frequent use of such agreements abroad suggest that there is much to be said on behalf of this view. Edward Peters, however, has suggested that the willingness of the CIO to push in the direction of signed agreements combined with the advantages to employers of being assured of "undisturbed working conditions and labor costs for a specified period of time" must also not be overlooked.[11]

On the whole, however, it would be improper to overemphasize the sharpness of the differences in the motives of the parties involved in collective bargaining in the 1930s and those practiced in early years. It is true that in addition to the differences we have just mentioned one can single out still others. The CIO placed far less emphasis, for example, on union security clauses than had unions of an earlier day. Instead what the CIO sought was exclusive bargaining rights. The fundamental objectives of the union movement in its drive for collective bargaining remained the same, however—better wages and job security for the members. It should be noted that wages were not as big an issue in the 1930s as they were to become later (and to some extent had been earlier). The tendency to downplay the wage issue reflected the economic conditions of the times. In the 1930s, however, the list of objectives was expanded to include many more than before.

Negroes in American Unions

One of the groups accorded greater attention by the CIO than they had previously received from any major labor organization were the Negroes. Antagonism between Negroes and union leaders had been fostered earlier by the use of Negroes as strikebreakers. First as slaves and later as free men, Negroes served as strikebreakers in coal mining, steel manufacturing, the railroads, auto manufacturing, and meat packing. Some Negro leaders (Booker T. Washington, for example) were suspicious of unions and looked to employers to protect the rights of the Negro.[12]

Negro hostility to the union was by no means unwarranted. Early unions either excluded Negroes entirely or segregated them into auxiliary locals often run by white leaders. At its inception, the AFL was dedicated to organizing all workers irrespective of their race or color, and Gompers declared his unwillingness to admit into the AFL any national union that discriminated. This commitment broke down with the admission of the Machinists in 1895, however, and a new policy was formulated. The plan now called for the AFL to work on unions within its ranks to get them to remove any discriminatory policies they might practice. Given the precarious health of the early labor movement the move is understandable, but it is also easy to understand why this new policy did not inspire among Negroes any great confidence about the interest of unions in improving the Negro's position.

In a number of the craft unions and particularly in the railroad unions, Negroes faced a stone wall of opposition partly because many of these unions had strong roots in the South, partly because of their fraternal character, and partly because many of them began as insurance companies and Negroes were regarded as a poor insurance risk. Even down to the present day, craft unions have often prevented Negroes from entering apprenticeship programs and thus closed them off from an important channel for advancement.

Negroes continued to be suspicious of unions into the 1930s and this skepticism was extended to the CIO during its early days. The CIO, however, was quick to encourage the enrollment of Negroes and its policies forced the AFL to adopt a more liberal attitude.

Although the CIO's leadership generally professed a much more liberal line toward the question of Negro rights than did the AFL, it would be a mistake to think that the CIO became the black man's champion. The attitude varied widely from union to union. Furthermore, although the CIO was more willing to endorse in principle the concept of equal rights for all men and to recruit black workers to its ranks, in practice it did little in its collective bargaining to assure that the Negro's rights were protected. Even the lofty statement of principles was to weaken with the passage of time by the failure of the member unions to observe it. The improved position of the Negro during the late 1930s and the 1940s can be attributed far more to the tight labor market than to any actions or speeches of the CIO. As a result the civil rights plank in the AFL-CIO merger had a hollow ring for most Negroes.

The reluctance of many local CIO unions to aid Negroes was and still is expressed in many ways. Sometimes a union has adopted a passive attitude, accepting discriminatory practices that were initiated by the employer or arose from local custom. Sometimes unions have taken more active roles—excluding Negroes or establishing separate seniority lists. Not too surprisingly, free admission of the Negro has been most strongly opposed in the South or where an integrated union would mean that Negroes would constitute a majority.

Nevertheless, the CIO was instrumental in enrolling large numbers of Negroes in the ranks of organized labor for the first time and extending to them at least part of the protections to be derived from collective bargaining. (See Chapter 3 for relevant legislation.)

Collective Bargaining Since 1930

Prior to 1940 little hint was to be found of the dramatic changes to come in the following two decades. Grievance procedures were still in a comparatively rudimentary stage; only about half of the contracts filed with BLS in 1940 contained provisions for the arbitration of grievances. Fringe benefits were still virtually unknown as a subject for collective bargaining.

Two marked changes did occur in the collective bargaining in the 1930s. One is so obvious that it needs no elaboration—for the first time free collective bargaining became the usual way of settling industrial disputes rather than governmental intervention or the company union. The second is the changed attitude of unions vis-à-vis government intervention. As the next chapter demonstrates, virtually all of the government intervention up to this point had been on the side of the employer and unions were understandably dubious about this method of settling labor disputes. Be-

cause they had long been accustomed to stand on their own and to win their protection at the bargaining table, unions began the 1930s with a general skepticism of all social welfare legislation. We indicated earlier that union leaders, like many others, at first tended to underestimate the magnitude of the prevailing recession. Their initial response to the mounting unemployment was the traditional recipe devised for depressions—maintenance and even the improvement of wages and a shortening of hours and work sharing. It soon became apparent, however, that the problem of unemployment plus many of the other social and economic ills that were plaguing the economy were of a magnitude impossible to handle by collective bargaining. As a result the whole attitude of the labor movement changed in favor of government participation. Whereas in the early thirties the AFL had opposed social security and similar legislation on the grounds that it undermined the function of unions, such legislation in the later thirties and thereafter was welcomed by labor with open arms. In addition, the unions increasingly turned to the NLRB and the courts to protect their rights.

Developments Since World War II

Many of the more recent changes in the labor movement and in collective bargaining will be detailed in later chapters. However, we will make brief note here of three major changes that have occurred since the end of World War II.

The first has been in the transformation of the climate of government attitudes toward industrial relations that culminated in the passage of the Taft-Hartley Act in 1947 and the Landrum-Griffin Act in 1959. After long years in the role of underdog, labor unions had by the postwar years acquired new power. Throughout World War II, unions had cooperated in the war effort and except in rare instances had foregone strikes; this increase in power had thus gone largely unnoticed by the general public.

Like the end of World War I, the end of World War II triggered a rash of labor disputes. The impact on public opinion was also similar; demands that something be done to check the power of unions were again voiced, leading to the passage of the Taft-Hartley Act. Evidence of union coercion and misappropriation of funds led twelve years later to the passage of the Landrum-Griffin Act. These pieces of legislation will receive more detailed treatment in the next chapter.

The second major change was a slowing of the pace of union growth. The extent to which this slowdown has been the result of unfavorable postwar legislation has been hotly debated. Union leaders naturally assign much of the blame to this legislation. However, other factors have certainly played a significant if not a major role. One such factor is the difficulty of organizing those not already in the ranks of unions—white-collar workers, agricultural workers, and the employees of small plants. In addition, many critics of the labor movement have attributed the decline in union membership to a loss of organizing zeal on the part of many unions that preferred to consolidate their forces rather than expand into new areas. While union membership has dropped both in absolute terms and as a percentage of the labor force, earlier-voiced fears that the movement would return to its 1920s' status have not been realized.

Perhaps partly because of these fears, an idea long in the minds of some union leaders began to be more and more seriously discussed; this was the third major change—a merger between the two rivals—the AFL and the CIO. A number of obstacles that had at first appeared to be insurmountable began to melt away. The issue of craft versus industrial unionism, which had at the beginning so sharply separated the two unions, grew less important. In the competition for new members, many of the AFL craft unions had become so altered that it was difficult to tell them from an industrial union. At the same time, the view of many AFL leaders that the CIO was "just a bunch of radicals" lost some of its force when the CIO expelled a number of Communist-dominated unions. Finally, with the passage of time and the retirement and death of old-time leaders, some of the early animosities had died down. Problems of leadership were resolved as AFL President George Meany, an active worker for unity, was named president of the AFL-CIO, while Walter Reuther, the CIO president, became one of the vice-presidents of the merged group.

It is still too early to be certain whether the new organization will prove a successful force in affording the union movement far greater power in its dealing with management or whether it will be the mere "rope of sand" predicted by John L. Lewis at the time of its formation. During recent years there have been new tensions in the AFL-CIO as a result of the renewed sense of craft consciousness within a number of the member unions. Considering the more than twenty years of rivalry between the two groups, the merger has achieved remarkable harmony with relatively little in the way of jurisdictional disputes. Nevertheless, the ambitious goals announced earlier have not been achieved. Total union membership has remained relatively constant (if anything, there has been some decline). In addition to the railroad brotherhoods, an increasing number of unions have for one reason or another moved outside the AFL-CIO. Most notable among these have been the International Longshoremen's Association and the Teamsters, both of which were expelled on the basis of corruption. The Teamsters have continued to remain outside the fold and have constituted a threat to the security of the AFL-CIO's power and membership.

Meanwhile the UAW under the leadership of Walter Reuther, after expressing increasing disenchantment with the goals and leadership of the AFL-CIO, disaffiliated in 1968.

The expressed dissatisfaction of the UAW with the AFL-CIO is in part a reflection of an increasing disenchantment by a number of scholars and students of labor who are dissatisfied with the growing impersonalization of collective bargaining, its divorce from the rank and file, and the increasing reliance on professional experts. In response to these changes and to altered circumstances that suggested greater possibilities for success, the AFL-CIO in recent years has taken a fresh look at the fields of white-collar workers and public employees and found favorable conditions for instituting collective bargaining.

White-collar unionism has been slow to develop in the United States. Even today, although there are slightly over 2 million white-collar union members, they represent only about 11 percent of the potential. European white-collar unions have had much more success, with union members accounting for 30 to 40 percent of the potentially organizable white-collar workers in many countries and 60 percent in Sweden.

Part of this disparity can be attributed to differences in historical background. The United States has had few foremen unions, while such groups are often strongly organized elsewhere. In addition, many white-collar workers employed in technical jobs in Europe have been drawn from blue-collar positions in which they had already become familiar with unions. In this country white-collar workers more often tend to be drawn from schools and colleges.

White-collar workers in this country, until recently, have often seen little reason to join a union. Frequently they have been well treated by management and have come to identify with it. Just as the AFL tended to ignore the needs of many unskilled workers, so did it (and the CIO) dismiss the white-collar worker as either largely unorganizable or unworthy of attention. The union movement largely failed to concern itself with the special interests and problems faced by white-collar workers even when such workers sought to organize and enter into collective bargaining agreements.

More recently there has been some change in the attitude of both sides. Several groups of white-collar workers (such as teachers) have begun to reconsider their previous feeling that unions were beneath their dignity, while others have turned to unions for protection from automation or the increasingly impersonal character of large organizations. Meanwhile unions, facing the facts that employment opportunities were actually declining in some blue-collar occupations and that white-collar workers had become a majority, have undertaken sophisticated campaigns to lure white-collar workers to their ranks. Radio and television programs, college-educated organizers, and the establishment of white-collar enrollments are up by union have all been tried. Thus far the statistics do not suggest that they have had any resounding success; total white-collar enrollments are up by several hundred thousand, but the percentage of white-collar workers unionized has remained virtually unchanged.

Meanwhile the unionization of public service employees and their participation in collective bargaining has been much more dramatic than white-collar unionization in this country. Public employees in Europe were unionized and engaged in bargaining about thirty years before their American counterparts. At every level of government, local, state, or federal, both unionization and bargaining developed much more slowly in this country. The right of federal employees to join unions was ensured by President John F. Kennedy's Executive Order 10,988 in January of 1962. Prior to that time only the postal employees had been well organized and actively involved in collective bargaining; elsewhere in the federal government instances of collective bargaining had been scattered and largely limited to shipyards, arsenals, and the TVA. Under the Kennedy executive order, workers were given the right to choose their exclusive bargaining agent. However, under a supplement to the order in 1963 they were forbidden to strike.

Associations of local and state government employees are not a completely new phenomenon in this country either—witness Calvin Coolidge's famous stern stand against Boston's striking policemen back in 1919. For a number of years following this famous episode, however, many of these associations such as the Patrolmen's Benevolent Association and the National Education Association accomplished little in the way of collective bargaining. Beginning late in the 1950s both these and similar groups of municipal and state employees such as the firemen, sanitation men, and construction workers began to form militant unions that not only demanded recognition and collective bargaining rights but engaged in numerous strikes. Although a sizable number of states still either bar or omit any reference to union activity by public employees, about half of the states have laws according bargaining rights to one or more of these associations. All of the states, however, have consistently barred strikes by public employees. (See Chapter 3.)

The pace of unionization and collective bargaining has been more rapid at the municipal than at the state level. Eighty percent of American cities having a population of 10,000 or more have one or more public employee unions.[13]

The Development of Labor Unions Abroad

By being ethnocentric and beginning first with a history of the American labor movement, we may have left the impression that the American movement preceded the development of unions in other countries. Any such generalization would be erroneous, however. It is Great Britain that is usually called "the mother of the labor union movement" and our brief historic sketches of labor movements abroad appropriately begin with that country.

Great Britain

Whether British trade unions trace their ancestry back to the early guilds or whether they were an independent response to working conditions as predicated by the Webbs is still debated by English labor historians. It is certain, however, that rudimentary labor organizations had made their appearance in England by the middle of the 17th century. Despite their early beginnings, British unions labored under serious handicaps in the form of governmental and employer opposition till the latter decades of the nineteenth century, and even then they still had to contend with unfavorable court decisions. Early efforts to organize the skilled and unskilled alike were abandoned for a number of years as the difficulties of organization compelled the unions to rely on organizing the highly skilled alone.

The first indication that the atmosphere was becoming more favorable for unions came in 1824 when the Combination Laws of 1799 and 1800 were repealed and the association of workers for the protection of their interests and for collective bargaining became legal. Although this marked a real change in the attitude of Parliament—during the last decades of the eighteenth century, Parliament had enacted forty separate pieces of legislation designed to curb unions—the path for union organization remained a rocky one. It was not until the Molestation of Workers Act of 1855 that the right of workers to picket in support of their demands for improvements in wages and hours was assured. Fuller legislative protection of unions did not come until the 1870s, and even after that time unions were still subject to the threat of court action. As late as 1903 and 1909, in the Taff Vale and Osborne decisions, the courts held unions liable for damages incurred by their officers during a strike and unions were forbidden to make contributions to political parties; both decisions, however, brought speedy remedial legislation by Parliament.

Around the middle of the nineteenth century, unions undertook to organize into national organizations. Aided by Robert Owen's early leadership, the Grand National Consolidated Trade Union won much support and grew rapidly during the first years of its existence. Lack of experience by its leaders, the disassociation of Owen from the union movement, and the hostility of public officials and employers caused it to collapse. It was not until 1868 that another convention of union leaders led to the formation of the Trades Union Congress—still the most powerful national union organization in Great Britain.

During this first phase of British unionism, English unions became interested in the cooperative movement and an extensive organization of consumer cooperatives took place continuing to the present time. When the early efforts to organize a national union failed, union officers turned to political activity and identified themselves with the Chartist movement for parliamentary reform.

In the middle of the nineteenth century the second phase of British unionism began with almost exclusive emphasis on organizing the highly skilled. Members paid high dues not only to receive the benefits of collective bargaining but for economic protection from accidents, unemployment, sickness, and old age.

Toward the end of the nineteenth century British trade unionism came increasingly under the influence of socialist and Marxist leaders. Although not all of the conservative leaders were displaced, the tone of the labor movement has remained distinctly different from that in the United States, with British labor leaders far less satisfied with the system of capitalism and far more inclined to seek its alteration by methods outside the framework of collective bargaining. The fact that British workers did not get the vote until toward the end of the nineteenth century did little to endear the economic system to them. These new leaders reinstituted a program of organizing the unskilled and the success of the Dock Strike of 1899 signaled the achievement of this goal, winning a permanent place for un-skilled workers in the labor movement. The collapse of the General Strike in 1926, however, took some of the militancy out of the British labor movement.

British unions have made remark-able gains in membership during the past century even though they never obtained the degree of protection awarded to American unions in the 1930s. Between 1892 and 1964 union membership jumped from 1.5 million to the present figure of about 10 million. This represents about 40 percent of the labor force.

Although there are over 600 unions in Great Britain, nine large ones account for better than 50 percent of the total membership. British unions have been somewhat more successful than their American counterparts in enrolling white-collar workers. Nevertheless, union strength has declined somewhat since the end of World War II when measured as a proportion of the total labor force. Despite this decline, it remains true that bargaining plays a far more important role in Britain than in either Italy or France.

The National Labor Party, established in 1906, has become a major force in British politics and several times has won control of the House of Commons.

Developments on the Continent

Because of considerations of space we will treat labor in other European countries even more sketchily than labor in Britain. Instead of attempting a complete historical sketch for each country, we will outline the major aspects that differentiate the development of unions on the Continent from those of Great Britain and the United States.

France

Among the many points of dissimilarity in the historical development of British and French unions, three differences are particularly significant:

1. French labor unions developed at a considerably later date and never became as significant a force. Although labor unions were anticipated by the mutual aid societies and the "resistance societies" of early French history, a real labor movement did not begin until the 1840s. This was partly due to the antiunion policy of successive French governments; it was not until 1864 that the legal ban on strikes was repealed and not until 1881 that the freedom to organize unions was recognized. Another thirty-five years were to pass before collective bargaining was granted similar legal recognition. The difficult legal position of unions reinforced an already fierce opposition by French employers to anything that threatened to endanger their ability to run their plants as they chose.

2. Added to the difficulties outlined in the previous paragraph have been the intense internecine battles between the unions themselves. A running battle has transpired between socialist and anarchist left-wing leaders and Catholic unions. The struggle was climaxed by the splintering of the Communist-dominated Confédération générale du Travail (CGT). Many workers who left the CGT remained unaffiliated with any union; between 1947 and 1951 total union membership was cut in half. Today, French unions can claim only about 2.5 million members divided among three major federations; the CGT, the Catholic Confédération française des Travailleurs Chrétiens (CFTC), and the socialist Force Ouvrière (FO).

3. The political diversity of French unions has meant that a sizable segment of the labor movement regards collective bargaining as, at best, a poor substitute for a complete overthrow of the economic system. Because of the weakness of French unions and their unwillingness to sponsor a strong effort to expand collective bargaining coupled with the resistance of employers to bargaining collective bargaining has remained much less fully developed than it has in Britain or the United States, even though legal protection for bargaining is now assured in France. In more recent years, however, ideology has come to play a less dominant role in the thinking of French union leaders and a wider use of collective bargaining has resulted.

West Germany

Although the subsequent chapters of this book will deal only with unions in West Germany after World War II, we will devote a few sentences to the earlier history of German labor unions in order to provide the reader with some comparison with union development in other countries.

Like English unions, the unions of Germany can trace their ancestry back to organizations of labor formed during the Middle Ages. Government opposition, however, was an even more persistent feature of German labor history. In 1713 all unions were declared illegal. Efforts throughout much of the first half of the nineteenth century by Socialist Workers Associations and others met with little success. In 1860, the printers and tobacco workers were first among a number of groups to organize successful unions, but efforts in 1868 to form a General Congress of German Workers ended in failure a short time later. Continued legislative enactments during the years between 1878 and 1890 that were designed to put down all socialist activity drove most unions underground. During World War I, the Kaiser encouraged unions as a means of raising workers' morale and for the first time German unions received official governmental recognition.

Under the Weimar Republic, unions continued to enjoy official sanction, but the government sought to force acceptance of a system of compulsory arbitration. The republic was unable to solve the problem of unemployment in the late twenties and thirties and the German people turned to Hitler; under the Nazi regime all pretense of a free labor movement was abandoned.

After the war, the Allied occupation forces reestablished conditions necessary for a labor union movement and unions have blossomed in postwar West Germany. West Germany's labor relations have been characterized by a remarkably quiet and peaceful climate at the bargaining table, but unions and management battle fiercely in the halls of the legislature. Like many European unions, the West German unions tend to bargain on an industrywide basis and have relatively little influence in the shop. The Metal Trades Union with 1.8 million members is the largest and most influential union and has acted as a pattern setter for the others.

The largest federation of unions is the Deutsche Gewerkshaftsbund (DGB) consisting of sixteen industrial unions with a total membership of about 6.5 million members. There is a smaller federation of another 1.2 million. Although German unions are strongly organized in order to undertake large-scale bargaining, their power and degree of organization are more than matched by that of the employers associations. Rarely does an individual employer ever bargain on his own.

The major problems of German

unions have paralleled those of unions in France and Great Britain—wage drift, in which many employers are paying wages in excess of those set by the union, plus the power of the West German government to extend union contracts so that they apply to non-union contracts as well. The result in both instances has been to reduce the appeal of union membership somewhat. Nevertheless, unions have done well in postwar West Germany; total membership is just under 8 million and accounts for approximately 40 percent of the nation's labor force.

Sweden

Like unions in many European countries, Swedish labor unions had their antecedents in the medieval guilds. Unions as we know them today, however, did not develop in Sweden until late in the nineteenth century when their formation was accompanied by a number of bitter strikes. These first unions were composed almost exclusively of skilled workers. In 1890, the organization of the General Factory Workers' union heralded the beginning of an effort to organize the unskilled. Thereafter local unions were increasingly organized into national bodies. In 1898 unions established a national federation called Landsorganisation (LO). A general strike in 1909 was a spectacular failure and resulted in cutting union membership by more than half. It was not until 1938 that a successful trend toward centralization began—a trend that was further developed during World War II. Today Sweden's unions are very successful; in a nation with a total population of about 8 million and a labor force of 3.8 million, there are nearly 2 million union members. Better than 90 percent of the industrial workers are unionized. The LO is the single most important union, and it has predomi-

nantly blue-collar members but includes many white-collar workers as well. The TCO (Central Organization of Salaried Employees) is the principal white-collar worker's union while the SACO (Swedish Confederation of Professional Associations) serves to organize professional workers.

At about the same time that Swedish unions were beginning to organize on a national basis, employers began to form associations of their own, with the SAF (Swedish Employers Confederation) number one in importance. Thus, as in West Germany, employers are as well organized as the workers. Not surprisingly, during and since World War II much bargaining has been on an industrywide basis. Although the majority of contracts are still negotiated on a local basis, over half of the workers are covered by industrywide agreements. Partly as a result, strikes have become a rare occurrence. With 13 percent of the agreements covering over 60 percent of all the workers, the government has inevitably intervened in the bargaining process often in order to ensure peaceful settlements. Most contracts expire between January 30 and March 30; most provide for a three-month notice so that most collective bargaining transpires within the six-month period from September 30 to March 30. If neither side indicates dissatisfaction with a current contract within a specified time (usually three months), the contract is automatically extended.

Israel

Although a scattered handful of Israeli unions date back to the beginning of this century, the labor union movement in Israel really began in 1920 with the formation of the Histadrut (General Confederation of Labor). It is safe to say that in no other country has a labor movement played such a dominant part in national life as the Histadrut has in Israel.

The Israeli labor movement developed for reasons quite different from those of any of the countries thus far reviewed. Until recently, there was no employer class in Israel against which workers could revolt; indeed there was no working class either, only people who wished to become workers. As a result, the Histadrut has been far more than just another labor union. It has served as an educational and training organization in the development of Israeli business and is itself an employer and operator of companies. It was instrumental in the organization of the *kibbutz* (communal farm) and helped to organize producer cooperatives in industry. The Histadrut has served as a recruiter of labor abroad and aided in the training and placement of the immigrants coming to Israel. Inevitably the Histadrut has been involved in the politics of Israel; it has experienced intense political factionalism within its ranks and it supplies the membership for the three labor-oriented political parties of Israel.

Labor unions in Israel predate the state itself and thus have never had to fight for the right to exist. Legislation guaranteeing the rights of labor has existed ever since Israel attained statehood. There has been a tendency in recent years, however, to transfer some of the Histadrut's early activities directly to the state. In 1959, for example, the labor exchanges were nationalized and removed from the auspices of the Histadrut.

Israeli unions are organized from the top down with much of the power and responsibility residing with the Histadrut. There are national and local unions that engage in collective bargaining, but neither is permitted to have an independent wage policy and must adhere to the standards of the Histadrut. Workers join the His-

tadrut directly and are then assigned to a national union in keeping with their occupation. There are over thirty national unions and each union elects its own officers. Union members elect representatives to the Histadrut convention held every four years.

The Histadrut has more than a million members—more members than the entire Israeli labor force. This is explained by the right of wives to belong to the Histadrut and to vote. Of the 854,000 in the labor force, over 790,000 of them belong to the Histadrut. (There is another minor labor organization, the National Labor Federation.) In its capacity as employer, the Histadrut provides jobs for slightly over 22 percent of the total labor force.

Bargaining on the employer side is also centralized, taking place under the auspices of employers associations set up in most industries. Typically, 70–80 percent of the employers in an industry belong to an association and membership is particularly heavy among small employers. Contracts may be for a specified or an unspecified period of time or may be broken down by item, with some provisions having a specified time limit and others none.

From the beginning, the government has tended to leave the issue of collective bargaining to the two parties most concerned. However, many items such as fringe benefits that have entered into collective bargaining in the United States are already provided for by national law in Israel.

India

Although the first recorded labor dispute in India dates back to 1817, true labor unions in that country are a product of the twentieth century. Until World War I, India's labor force can best be characterized as unhappy but undemonstrative. India's failure to support a union movement earlier can be attributed less to the attitude of the government or employers (the latter did not hold out a welcoming hand to unions, however) than to the lack of industrialization and the tendency of industrial workers to migrate back to their villages after a brief sojourn in the urban areas.

Interestingly, white-collar workers were among the first groups organized, with textile workers providing another source of membership. Once successfully launched in the years during and after World War I, India's unions immediately became involved in a series of factional disputes that have lasted until the present. The All-India Trade Union Congress was split when "moderates" pulled out to disassociate themselves from the communists, who had employed terror tactics and called for a general strike in the 1920s that proved to be an inglorious failure. The moderates then formed the Indian Trade Union Federation (ITUF) while the communists formed the Trade Union Congress. The splintering has continued until today; India has five major union confederations with economic and political philosophies ranging from communism at one extreme to anticommunism at the other. The government-sponsored anticommunist Indian National Trade Union Congress was formed in May 1947. Two of the major organizations, the Hind Nazdoor Sabba (HNS) and the United Trade Union Congress (UTUC) are both left-wing socialist oriented organizations and have been not only anticommunist, but also antigovernment.

The Indian government's attitude toward organized labor has been a mixed one from the beginning. In 1926 the passage of the Indian Trade Unions Act provided for the formation and protection of unions. Three years later, however, a second piece of legislation forbade wildcat strikes. In 1945 the Indian Parliament enacted the Trade Union Law that restated the right of all workers except policemen, firemen, and employees of penal institutions to organize and engage in collective bargaining. Both this and the Labor Relations Adjustment Act of 1946, which empowers the government to end strikes and lockouts and to impose compulsory arbitration when deemed necessary, were designed to help unions in their disputes with management, but many unions have to this day continued to view the actions of the government with suspicion. The socialist unions have been suspicious of the government's role in supporting the ITUF and wish to see unions keep clear from entangling alliances with employers, political parties, or the government.

Indian unions have had some growth in strength since World War II because of the encouragement given by the government and because of the miserable working conditions generally prevailing. Two postwar ministers of labor, Giri and Desai, have both opposed compulsory arbitration and supported collective bargaining. The desperate situation of many of India's workers is shown by the fact that in 1946 real earnings for industrial workers were 32 percent below the already low standard prevailing in 1940. Although recent statistics are sketchy, figures in the cotton textile industry and some of the other industrialized sectors indicate a slight rise in real earnings during the last half of the 1960s.

Although unions have been permitted to organize and bargain with governmental blessing, exclusive jurisdiction is not guaranteed and several unions may be functioning in the same plant—a situation that often exasperates union officials and management alike. The union is likely to sustain the most damage in this situation, since diversification serves to weaken a labor movement that is already far from strong. Local federations have been attempted in an effort to secure cooperation among the various unions, but these efforts have not been particularly successful. Movement in the direction of regional and national federations has also been made; the record of achievement has been clearer in this case.

The Indian labor movement is still relatively weak. Concentrations of union strength are found in the railroads, iron and steel, cotton textiles, and chemical products. India has over 11,000 registered unions, claiming membership in excess of 3.5 million. There is probably a considerable amount of inflation in those figures, however, and the Indian government estimate of about 2 million members is probably closer to the mark. As a percentage of the total labor force, this amounts to only slightly over 2 percent. Since four-fifths of the population is in agriculture, unions account for close to 50 percent of the industrial labor force. Craft unions are little known and most union members can be classified as unskilled except for white-collar workers who still make up a sizable proportion of the union membership.

Collective bargaining has made little progress in India. Contracts, where they exist, run for three to six years and usually provide for automatic increments. Unions have tended to resist tying wages to productivity increases because they fear displacement by automation and because the government limits the amount of wage increases possible. Because of the resistance to unions by employers, shop stewards have not had a chance to develop. Although free collective bargaining is encouraged by the government, the government also sanctions compulsory arbitration. Many of the items subject to bargaining are set by governmental standing orders, although these orders only set minimums and can be exceeded by the union if it has sufficient bargaining power.[14]

Japan

The Japanese labor movement has had a relatively brief history and has only developed as a significant force since the end of World War II. The first recorded Japanese labor union was an organization of rickshaw men who banded together to strike in protest against the introduction of horse-drawn trams in 1883. Most of the early unions took the form of mutual aid societies that emphasized political action designed to secure legislative improvement of working conditions. Strikes did occur, however, and in 1900 the government passed a law denying workers the right to strike. This law plus the depression that Japan was undergoing when it was passed spelled the demise of most of the existing unions at the time.

In 1912 there was another attempt to organize a worker's mutual aid society, called the Yuai Kai. As in the case of the earlier attempts, much of the impetus for organization came from the intellectuals—a group that historically has played a far smaller role in the American labor movement.

World War I stimulated the labor movement in Japan as it did in other countries. Despite the prohibition on strikes, a number of strikes took place, and wage increases were won. Workers now began to organize by themselves without the aid of the intellectuals, but union efforts were largely confined to the highly skilled workers, particularly those in engineering and transportation. Few factory workers joined in the movement. The effectiveness of the movement was further weakened by the development of numerous ideological disputes among the union leaders. The final death blows came when the Japanese government launched the nation on its Chinese adventure. Some unions were dissolved, some were pressured to disband, and those that remained became rightist organizations supporting the government's war policy.

After World War II, Japanese unions reappeared and grew rapidly under the nurture of Allied occupation forces. Three federations developed, split on ideological lines—one right wing, one left wing, and one centralist. In 1950, a new trade union federation, the Central Council of Trade Unions (Sohyo) was organized to unite the three federations and provide for coordinated action. Although it was established to promote what we would call "business unionism," it has become the scene for recurring ideological disputes and the Japanese labor movement remains very politically conscious. Most of the national leaders tend to be anticapitalist in their economic philosophy.

The only major limitation on Japanese labor unions today is a prohibition of membership in unions by supervisory or managerial employees and a limitation somewhat akin to our Taft-Hartley on Japanese unions' right to strike. Since 1952, strikes, lockouts, and slowdowns are prohibited for a ten-day period, during which a central labor commission attempts to mediate. Strikes that would seriously damage the public interest can be suspended for another thirty days by the prime minister in order to obtain further time for mediation. Thereafter unions can strike, but employers are free to punish strikers by firing, suspensions, and pay reductions if they can enforce such actions.

Today there are over 30,000 labor unions in Japan, but many of them are limited to a single plant. They resemble our industrial unions but are independent units, each making its own bargaining arrangements with management. There are national bodies, which are loose federations of these locals, but they have little power or control over the locals. The most important of these nationals is the Sohyo, which is primarily composed of leftist unions and is associated with the Socialist party.

Total union membership in Japan is now in excess of 8 million, which makes it the fourth largest labor movement in the world. About one-third of Japan's labor force is organized, but organization has been concentrated chiefly in the larger plants. The small plants have been virtually untouched by unionization and workers in those plants receive markedly lower wages and labor under decidedly inferior working conditions. This dichotomy between conditions in the large and small plants is sometimes referred to as Japan's "dual economy."

Mexico

Mexico is not a typical representative of union development in Latin America. Collective bargaining in Mexico resembles collective bargaining in the United States much more closely than it does that in the rest of Central and South America. Typically, Mexican unions are freer to bargain than are unions elsewhere in Latin America. This is only a recent development, however, and Mexican unions have obtained funds of their own and freedom from government intervention more recently still.

Although traces of a labor movement can be found prior to the turn of the twentieth century, it was not until 1906 that the Mexican unionization gained real momentum. In that year the Gran Círculo de Obreros Libres (Grand Order of Free Workers) was formed. The union consisted of textile workers in six cities and was basically socialistic in orientation.

At the same time miners were also demanding better working conditions. Like so many of the Latin American countries even today, Mexican labor unions had difficulty improving working conditions in the mines because the government feared that such changes might prompt foreign owners to withdraw their capital. When the Gran Círculo ordered a strike, Porfirio Díaz, the head of the Mexican government, commanded a resumption of work and enforced his order by the use of stern measures that resulted in considerable bloodshed.

The subsequent revolution against Díaz in 1910 intensified the spirit and value of union organization. In the years preceding World War I, union organizations came increasingly under leftist leadership and experienced a steady growth in popularity. Alarmed by this resurgence, the government ordered one organization, the Casa de Obrero Mundial (the House of World Labor), to disband and jailed some of its leaders. Despite such government restrictions, the labor movement continued to grow and the Casa along with two other national federations (Federation of Syndicalists and the Mexican Regional Confederation of Labor) in 1916 called a general strike.

The strike was repressed violently by the then-dictator, Venustiano Carranza. But in 1917 the liberal leader Alvaro Obregón forced through a constitutional provision (article 123 of the Mexican constitution) that guarantees not only the right of unions to organize, but also their right to strike and to bargain collectively.

Mexican labor unions have always been politically conscious, and in 1918 the Mexican Labor Party was founded. There is no labor party of significance today, but labor participates actively

in the PRI (Institutional Revolutionary Party). Until World War II, virtually all of these unions were extremely leftist in philosophy and some were openly Marxist in orientation. The most important Mexican union, however—the Confederation of Mexican Workers (CTM)—has gradually become more conservative in outlook after beginning as a Marxist organization. Communist influence has been reduced somewhat by the active participation of both the AFL and the CIO in guiding Mexican labor leaders, particularly since World War II. The strength of these ties has reflected variations in the cordiality of diplomatic relations between Mexico and the United States. During the middle and late 1960s the two countries' labor movements had a new problem with which to cope—the increasing migration of American industry across the border to escape the high wage rates in the United States. Although many items that are a subject of collective bargaining in the United States are determined by legal enactment in Mexico, the Mexican unions do participate in collective bargaining and have a much freer hand than any other nation in Latin America.

There are approximately 5,000 unions in Mexico, with most of them belonging to one of the three national federations—the Confederation of Mexican Workers, the Mexican Workers' Regional Confederation, and the Confederation of Workers and Agricultural Workers. There are in addition four important confederations of labor and twenty-five important national unions. Far and away the most important of the confederations is the Confederation of Mexican Workers (CTM). It has a total membership of over 1.5 million with twenty-six affiliated national unions. The CTM has been active both on the national scene and in attempts to organize throughout Latin America. The CTM also has a women's division with a claimed membership of over 300,000, but like the Israeli Histadrut membership, this includes the wives of workers. Total union membership is approximately 2.5 million and accounts for about 40 percent of the nonagricultural labor force; most union members are found in the industrialized sector around Mexico City. According to the 1960 Mexican census the total population of Mexico was 35 million, with a total labor force of 8.27 million. Any worker is free to join a union except for employers and a few government employees (airline pilots were forbidden to be union members until recently) and some peculiar exceptions like bank clerks. The most significant unit in the Mexican labor movement is the local union.

One of the peculiarities of Mexican collective bargaining is the vast detail included in all contracts. The result is that contracts tend to be excessively long, elaborate, and legalistic.

Summary and Conclusions

Although it remains true that the labor movement of any country in large part reflects the history of economic development of that country, it is also apparent from the above historical sketches that unions around the world have labored under the same handicaps from their beginning—the determined opposition of employers supported by the various branches of the government. Another common characteristic of early union movements in most of the countries in our survey was their vulnerability to downturns in business conditions.

Unlike most of the other countries surveyed, America never had a feudal period in its history. The result has been that American workers have been far less class-conscious and much more inclined to concentrate on bettering their economic position through collective bargaining. The general strikes, consistently a failure wherever attempted, that have been characteristic of unions elsewhere have not been a feature of United States labor history.

Although the current attitudes of the governments of the various countries toward unions and collective bargaining differ, the general trend has been in the direction of providing greater protection and security for both. As we will see in the chapters that follow, collective bargaining today also differs from country to country and reflects in part the past history and in part the differing needs and circumstances of workers in different countries, working under varying economic circumstances.

NOTES

1. See, for example, Herman Kohn, "Some Problems in the Writing of Labor History," Industrial Relations Research Association, *Proceedings of the 18th Annual Meeting* (1965), pp. 324–332.
2. John R. Commons, *History of Labor in the United States,* (New York: Macmillan, 1936) Vol. I, pp. 9–10.
3. Selig Perlman, *A History of Trade Unionism in the United States* (New York: Macmillan, 1922), p. 305.
4. A dual union is one organized in a trade or skill where there is already a union in existence. Thus in an earlier day the AFL deemed it had the right to condemn as dual unions all unions that arose in competition to one of its nationals.
5. International unions often lay claim to a particular area of employment. When two or more unions claim exclusive control over the same area a jurisdictional dispute arises. Such disputes have long been a part of the American labor scene and have been particularly prevalent in the construction industry. Unions under the old AFL were accorded specified jurisdictional

boundaries that other unions within the AFL were expected to honor. Non-AFL Unions that impinged on these boundaries were declared "dual." The present AFL-CIO has a "no-raiding" agreement to preserve jurisdictional boundaries within its membership.

6. Irving Bernstein, "Union Growth and Structural Cycles," in Walter Galenson and Seymour M. Lipset (eds.), Labor and Trade Unionism: An Interdisciplinary Reader (New York: Wiley, 1960), p. 87.

7. U.S. Department of Labor, Characteristics of Company Unions, 1935, Bulletin No. 634 (Washington, D.C.: U.S. Government Printing Office, 1938).

8. Irving Bernstein, The Lean Years (Baltimore: Penguin, 1966), p. 173.

9. The LaFollette committee's 1936–1937 hearings in the Senate took testimony that employers spent nearly $10 million and employed more than 3,800 labor spies during the 1930s. These figures were based on only incomplete evidence and were probably considerably higher for the entire economy. However, they have been credited with influencing the Supreme Court in its decision upholding the constitutionality of the Wagner Act.

10. Doris E. Pullman and L. Reed Tripp, "Collective Bargaining Developments," in Milton Derber and Edwin Young (eds.), Labor and the New Deal (Madison: University of Wisconsin Press, 1957), pp. 333–335.

11. Edward Peters, "Recent Literature in American Labor History," Industrial Relations Research Association, Proceedings (1965), p. 339. After 1941, of course, a written contract was declared mandatory by the Supreme Court in the Heinz Company case, 311 US 54.

12. Much of the material of this section is drawn from Ray Marshall, The Negro and Organized Labor (New York: Wiley, 1965).

13. Much of the data on public employee collective bargaining in this section is based on Kurt L. Hanslowe, The Emerging Law of Labor Relations In Public Employment (Ithaca, N.Y. New York State School of Industrial and Labor Relations, 1967).

14. Much of this discussion is based on Labor Law and Practice in India, Bureau of Labor Statistics Report No. 303 (Washington, D.C.: U.S. Government Printing Office, 1966).

3

Collective Bargaining and Governmental Policies

Collective bargaining in the past 25 years could be roughly described as a legislative triangle bounded on one side by the Wagner Act, on the second by Taft-Hartley, and the third by Landrum-Griffin.

—John Herling

☐ IN our sketch of the historical development of unions in the United States and elsewhere, we noted that the success of unions was often directly dependent on the manner in which the government protected their interests. When the various branches of government were favorably disposed toward unions, unions grew in number and size; when the government was unfriendly, unions and collective bargaining faltered. Although not all scholars are agreed as to the importance of government in aiding union growth, and calling it a simple cause-and-effect relationship would be inaccurate, the evidence does suggest that unions develop more easily when government is favorably disposed rather than antagonistic toward them. In this chapter we will treat in more detail the changing attitude of governments toward unions and collective bargaining. After a brief historical sketch of some of the major court decisions in the United States prior to the 1930s, we will outline the major legislation since that time and finally take a brief look at the record in other countries.

The 1930s in this country represent a major watershed in governmental attitudes toward collective bargaining.

Although some efforts had been made to protect labor in earlier decades, these efforts were largely ineffectual and were frequently overturned by court decisions. It was not until the 1930s that the courts relinquished their dominant role in making labor policy to the legislative and executive branches. It is perhaps questionable that even the courts had a "policy" toward unions in the early years. Inevitably, the first branch of government with which labor became involved was the courts since neither the federal nor state legislatures chose to make their position (assuming they had one) clear by enacting appropriate legislation. It was to the courts that employers turned when they saw their profits and businesses threatened by demands from their workmen.

Before proceeding further with our analysis of the role the courts played in shaping the early development of collective bargaining, however, we should pause briefly to identify the various policies any branch of government may take toward unions and collective bargaining has rested on a tremes are policies of repression and policies of encouragement. In this country, a policy designed to restrict collective bargaining has rested on a faith in the power of the market to establish the fairest prices and the best distribution of income. A belief in individualism and a desire to protect the right of the individual to improve his position as much as possible have also been used as grounds for restrictive policies. Individual rights were held to be superior to group rights and the power of group action (including, of course, union action) was likely to be viewed with suspicion. It is noteworthy that through the years unions have encountered the most hostile environment when operating in areas where there was a high percentage of rural inhabitants. Even today right-to-work laws and similar legislation occur most frequently in the less highly industrialized states.

Alternatively the repression of collective bargaining may derive from a desire on the part of the government to be in complete control of the nation's economic and political affairs. There is no room for collective bargaining under any variant of mercantilism and a country's free labor movement has always been an early target of any dictator. Nazi Germany serves as a prime example.

When a government chooses to encourage collective bargaining, it may do so for purely political reasons. In a highly industrialized nation with the free ballot, workers account for a sizable minority if not the majority of the votes. It thus behooves politicians to respond to these voters' demands. In addition to these purely practical political considerations, government officials may hold a real belief in collective bargaining as a way of greater freedom and what Beatrice and Sydney Webb termed "industrial democracy." In addition, members of the executive or legislative branch of government may favor unions for straight economic reasons—as a means of raising purchasing power and/or stabilizing the economy.

Between the two policy extremes of open support and avowed opposition to collective bargaining, governments may institute policies designed to correct problems arising when the two parties to bargaining are left to their own devices. Government officials, for example, may support collective bargaining but feel that it can only be successful if the power of the two parties is reasonably equal. It was in part fear of the power of unions that prompted our courts to follow English common law practice and to declare unions conspiracies while issuing injunctions with a generous hand. Simi-

larly, much of the legislation of the 1930s as well as the Taft-Hartley and Landrum-Griffin Acts represents not only changing sentiment toward the cause of labor, but also a reevaluation of the relative power of unions vis-à-vis management.

While it is obviously impossible to have real collective bargaining if one party is much stronger than the other, if the government is unduly preoccupied with this problem and attempts to see that the two sides are exactly equal, its efforts are likely to be self-defeating. First of all, the objective of exact equality is virtually impossible to attain and even if achieved is likely to be quickly altered as economic conditions change as a result of new competition, shifts in market demands, and the vagaries of the business cycle. Furthermore, the government is likely to continue to protect the underdog long after that canine has developed teeth and fighting capabilities of his own.

The best example of the last point is embodied by the early court decisions protecting business concerns against the group pressures of worker organizations. Judges tended to perceive the situation as an uneven battle between the single employer and a group of workers. Even after the growth of the corporations, the fact that the corporation for legal purposes was a legal person tended to perpetuate in the court's mind the image of the business enterprise as a one-man affair. Nor were judges familiar with or understanding about the potential danger of monopsony, where a single buyer faces numerous sellers.

Another basis for governmental opposition to collective bargaining may be the problems it creates for the economy. Thus, even those in general sympathy with bargaining may support government policies that limit it in order to protect the general public and the economy. The two most serious problems cited as arising from collective bargaining are the threat of inflation and the danger that failure to reach a settlement will result in a strike that will produce great inconvenience and loss of income to the public. Both problems will be treated fully in later chapters.

Because, prior to the 1930s, there was no statutory law (except in the case of the railroads) dealing with the question of collective bargaining, the issue was placed squarely in the laps of the courts. In rendering a decision, the courts relied on Anglo-Saxon common law. Contrary to a frequent misconception, common law is not unwritten. While the authors of statutory law are the various legislatures, however, common law is written by the courts themselves. Common law develops as a result of court decisions interpreting and clarifying situations that are either not covered by statutory law or where the existing law is unclear. Although common law rests heavily on precedents set by earlier court decisions, it can change and new decisions may rewrite the "law" just as much as legislative enactment.

The first major recorded case involving the question of workers' right to band together and demand a voice in the setting of wages involved the Philadelphia bootmakers (the old term is "cordwainers") in 1806. The shoemakers, dissatisfied with their wages, joined together and demanded that the master journeymen pay them more money. Anxious to capture a broader market and fearful of the effect the cost would have on sales, the master journeymen sought relief in the courts. The case was a celebrated one even from the beginning. Leading Whigs and Democrats served as lawyers for each side as the issue of state versus individual rights was argued in the courts.

The judge's charge to the jury, however, left no room for doubt and the jury found the union of workers to be an illegal conspiracy. The decision aroused the ire of many workers and even provoked adverse newspaper editorials, but the pattern had been set for a series of conspiracy cases in the years ahead; during the following thirty-six years there were seventeen more such cases. Not all of these ended with the union found guilty of criminal conspiracy as the Philadelphia cordwainers had been, but the results were much the same. Even when the union's right to existence was not challenged, the methods it used to implement its demands were held to be illegal.

It was not until 1842 that a second famous case, *Commonwealth v. Hunt,* restored some protection to unions. In reviewing a previous decision that had been adverse to the union, Chief Justice Shaw of the Massachusetts Supreme Court declared that ". . . a conspiracy must be a combination of two or more persons, by some concerted action, to accomplish some criminal or unlawful purpose, or to accomplish some purpose not in itself criminal or unlawful by criminal or unlawful means." In the course of the decision, Chief Justice Shaw not only upheld the right of unions to exist but also their right to strike, providing the strike was peaceful; he also approved of the closed shop as a legitimate goal for a union to seek. Although not many other courts immediately adopted Justice Shaw's interpretation and unions thus continued to be harassed in the courts, after 1842 no court declared unions to be conspiracies in and of themselves.

After the Civil War employers began to change their method of attack against unions. Beginning in the 1880s the use of the labor injunction developed and its use expanded after its effectiveness was amply demonstrated in quelling the Pullman strike of 1894. Whereas hitherto unions had been subject to prosecution on charges of criminal conspiracy, they now became the targets of civil suits. To achieve their goal of halting strikes, employers would file suit in courts of equity. These courts handle problems that defy settlement by a simple exchange of money for damages suffered. A plaintiff may argue that the actions of the defendant, if permitted, may result in losses impossible to calculate or assess. Employers thus found courts of equity a favorable vehicle for their attempts to protect their property from what they alleged to be menacing attacks from the unions.

An employer would request that the court issue an injunction prohibiting the union from taking strike action on the grounds that the strike would do irreparable damage to his property and his anticipated profits from that property. Since many strikes even during this fairly recent period of our history were marked with violence and destruction of property, the frequent issuance of injunctions on this ground is not too surprising. If the use of the injunction had stopped there, the cause of unions would have been less severely hampered.

The courts, however, were willing to entertain the argument that all work stoppages were a threat to the employer's business since they hurt his sales even though no physical damage to his property took place. Then too, many of the injunctions were "blanket" orders prohibiting almost any conceivable action that might be taken by a union's members and its supporters. In one case, for example, supporters of the union on strike in other parts of the country were even enjoined from sending telegrams of encouragement to the striking workers!

Perhaps most serious, however, was the willingness of judges to issue restraining orders despite the absence of evidence that damage to property was threatened. To obtain this restraining order the employer would appeal to the court for an injunction by filling out a bill of equity that described the property, alleged the union's intent to do irreparable damage, and pleaded for relief. The judge commonly responded by issuing a temporary restraining order, which forbade all action until the employer had time to prove his case. The next step would be the issuance of a temporary injunction. Preparatory to the issuance of this injunction, a hearing would be held during which the burden of proof was on the union to demonstrate why the temporary injunction should not be issued. Later a permanent injunction could be issued if the need arose. Usually, however, by the time the temporary injunction expired support for the strike had long since evaporated, and it was difficult if not impossible for the union to regroup its forces.

Another variation on the use of the injunction was its combination with the yellow dog contract, in which the worker agreed as a part of the terms of his employment not to join a union and agreed in advance that such action would constitute sufficient grounds for his dismissal. On the basis of these contracts, employers were able to secure court orders directing unions to desist in their efforts to enroll workers on the grounds that success in getting the workers to join would involve a breach of contract.

The injunction was a potent weapon in the hands of employers and it was frequently used. Up until 1931, over 1,000 labor injunctions had been issued and less than 50 of these at the behest of labor unions. Nearly half of the injunctions were *ex parte* injunctions issued at the request of the employer with little or no evidence to support the request. In addition, the union was given no opportunity to present its views prior to the issuance of the injunctions.

Antitrust Laws

The first piece of federal legislation designed to cope with the mushrooming corporation was the Sherman Antitrust Act of 1890. Although the prime target of the act was business monopolies, labor historians still debate today whether Congress intended it to apply to labor unions as well. In any case, for the first eighteen years after the passage of the act, only a half dozen minor cases came before the Supreme Court for review, although some diverse decisions concerning the new law's applicability to unions were made by lower courts.

The first major case, *Loewe v. Lawlor* (more popularly known as the Danbury Hatters case) came to the Supreme Court in 1908. The Hatters' Union had struck Loewe in an attempt to organize the firm. When the strike failed the union instituted a primary boycott against Loewe and a secondary boycott against the merchants who continued to handle his merchandise, urging the public not to patronize these stores. A primary or, as it is sometimes called, a product boycott is directed against the employer with whom the union is having a dispute. A secondary boycott involves placing economic pressure on other employers in order to induce them to persuade the first employer to make concessions.

Finding the boycott to be hurting his sales, Loewe, aided by financial support from some other employers,

brought a suit against the union for treble damages amounting to $240,000. (Treble damages was one of the remedies provided under the Sherman Act.) In the first hearing of the case, the Supreme Court in 1908 upheld the decision that the secondary boycott was an illegal act under the Sherman Act because it interfered with interstate commerce. In a second decision on the case in 1915, the Court upheld the lower court's decision that a conspiracy in violation of the Sherman Act had existed and that the workers' personal possessions including their homes were subject to seizure to make repayment. Payment of over $230,000 was finally made to Loewe, largely from funds raised by the AFL.

The danger of antitrust violation combined with the use of the injunction was emphasized in 1911 when, in the Buck Stove and Range Company case, the Supreme Court upheld the injunction forbidding the AFL from continuing its boycott of Buck company stoves. Four years earlier a strike had been called when the company, despite a contract with the Metal Polishers' union, lengthened the working day from nine to ten hours. The strike had failed and to help the workers the AFL had included the company in its "we don't patronize" list published in the *American Federationist*. The president of the company was a bitter foe of unions and was supported in his case by financial aid from other employers.

A lower court issued an injunction directing the officers of the AFL to cease publishing and distributing copies of the union journal containing the boycott list with the name of the Buck company. When the officers ignored the injunction, they were given jail sentences of up to one year.

The Supreme Court upheld the sentences and although the officials escaped jail because the time limit of the statute of limitations had expired, the illegality of the use of the boycott was no longer open to question. Even worse was the worrisome fear that strikes might be judged to be illegal on the same grounds. After all, a strike could just as easily interfere with interstate commerce as a boycott. The unions had ample cause to suspect that strikes might be the next target of court decisions.

Two points need to be made. The first is that of the two decisions, the Danbury Hatters case was the more sweeping in scope since it not only cast doubt on the legality of all union action but also made the individual union members responsible for the collective action of the union of which they were members. Second, the severity of the court decisions in these two cases was probably in large part a response to the extent and surprising effectiveness with which boycotts had been employed by unions after 1884 in supporting their demands at the bargaining table. Upon one occasion a brewery was even induced to refuse to furnish beer to a saloon that was serving strikebreakers.[1]

It is little wonder, given the hostile court decisions, that three years later labor greeted with great joy a second piece of antitrust legislation, the Clayton Act of 1914, that at first reading appeared to exempt unions from antitrust prosecution. Samuel Gompers and other labor leaders hailed the new legislation as "labor's Magna Carta." Such elation, however, was premature. The language of the Clayton Act was blurry and did not explicitly exempt the unions from all antitrust activity. Of the twenty sections of the Clayton Act, only two applied to labor. Section 6 read in part:

> . . . The labor of a human being is not a commodity or article of commerce. Nothing contained in the anti-trust laws should be construed to forbid the existence and operation of labor . . . organizations.

Section 20 read in part:

> . . . no restraining order or injunction shall be granted in any court of the United States . . . in any case between an employer and employees, or between employees, or between persons employed and persons seeking employment, involving or growing out of a dispute concerning terms or conditions of employment, unless necessary to prevent irreparable injury to property, or to a property right of the party making the application, for which injury there is no adequate remedy at law.

A brief résumé of two major cases that were tried after the Clayton Act was passed will indicate the way in which the courts interpreted this second piece of antitrust legislation as it applied to unions.[2]

The first case, which involved the Coronado Coal Company of Arkansas, began in 1914, the year the Clayton Act was passed. The company decided to terminate its contract with the United Mine Workers and reopen as a nonunion company. When the locals at one of the mines went on strike in an effort to force the company to reverse its decision, violence erupted and the mine was destroyed. In addition, several lives were lost in pitched battles between the strikers and the mine guards and the strikebreakers imported by the company. Once again the triple damages clause of the Sherman Act was brought into play as the company sued the union for nearly $750,000.

In June 1922, following lengthy litigation in the lower courts, the case was decided in favor of the union. The Supreme Court ruled that the company's case should be dismissed on the grounds that it did not come within the jurisdiction of the Sherman Act since the company had not proved that the union had sought to interfere with interstate shipments of coal.

But this was not the final disposition of the case. The case had a second hearing when a disgruntled union official testified for the company to the effect that the union really had attempted to prevent the company from distributing its coal throughout the country. In the face of this new evidence, the Court reversed its previous stand and found the union guilty. Save for an out-of-court settlement, the company presumably would have been awarded triple damages. What had begun as a victory for the union, apparently removing unions from the threat of antitrust violation for strike activity, was converted into a stunning defeat although the Clayton Act had been on the books for over eight years.

A few years earlier, *Duplex Printing Press Co. v. Deering* (1921) demonstrated that unions were still subject to the injunction. The Duplex Printing Press Company was operating with a ten-hour day (the norm was nine) in a nonunion shop. The New York City International Association of Machinists attempted to aid their union brothers in Michigan who were on strike against the company by refusing to install the company's presses.

Although the lower courts refused to issue an injunction on the grounds that the Clayton Act protected the union from such action, the Supreme Court, acting on an appeal, directed that an injunction against the union be issued and declared that the boycotting activities against the company's printing presses by the Machinists Union were illegal under the terms of the Clayton and Sherman Acts.

The decision was a split one but the majority concurred with Justice Pitney who rendered the verdict that the Clayton Act did not provide protection to unions from injunctions in such cases. Pitney argued that although labor was not a commodity (the language used in the Clayton Act), it was still possible to hold the actions of labor organizations to be in restraint of trade. Nothing else in Section 6 of the Clayton Act, said Pitney, could be construed to exempt unions from antitrust prosecution and this was not sufficient.

Section 20 of the Clayton Act had provided grounds for the lower courts' refusal to issue an injunction because such a court order would violate the terms of the act that forbade injunctions interfering with employer-employee disputes. The Supreme Court, however, accepted a narrower definition of the word employee and since none of the strikers were employees of the Duplex Company, their dispute with it *was* subject to injunction.

In this decision the Supreme Court in effect denied that a union had any legitimate interest in conditions in nonunion plants: a position with which unionists obviously took issue.

Other cases could be cited to demonstrate that the Clayton Act failed to provide unions with immunity from the Department of Justice antitrust division for a long period of time. During the 1930s, however, the environment for collective bargaining gradually improved and unions were granted wider and wider discretion.[3] An effort by Thurman Arnold, head of the antitrust division in the late 1930s, to apply the antitrust laws to unions with greater force met with little success.

It was not until 1941, however, that the Supreme Court clearly reversed itself and in *United States v. Hutcheson* declared that neither picketing nor a boycott involved in a jurisdictional dispute was enjoinable under the immunities accorded unions under the Clayton Act and the Norris-LaGuardia Act.

For a number of years unions breathed easier. Under the new interpretation unions were apparently safe from antitrust prosecution unless their objective was to affect the price of the product directly or collusion with the employer was involved.

The story is still not ended, however. In 1965 the Supreme Court awakened old fears by a decision involving the United Mine Workers (*United Mine Workers of America v. Pennington et al.* 85.5 Ct. 1585). The Court ruled that a union was subject to triple damages under the antitrust laws if it conspired with one group of employers to set wages designed to drive other companies out of business. Of the six judges who upheld this verdict three said that industrywide bargaining could produce a wage scale too high for some firms in the industry and that this fact in itself would be sufficient evidence of illegal action by the union. The other three judges suggested that additional evidence of an unspecified nature would be required to justify a verdict of guilty.

Whether the ramifications of this decision will be as far reaching as was at first feared still remains to be tested. Certainly friends of unions have seen real cause for concern. Already nearly $40 million dollars of damage suits are pending in the lower courts and the then Senator A. Willis Robertson, long a proponent of stiffer antitrust laws for unions, announced after the decision that the Court had done his job for him.

The question of whether the antitrust laws should be made more fully applicable to unions or whether unions should be left entirely exempt is still hotly debated. Those who argue for stricter application reason that labor monopolies are just as injurious to the economy as business monopolies and that fairness demands that both parties be treated equally by the law. There is also a widespread fear that unions are growing too powerful and can exercise undesirable effects on the economy unless their power is checked.

Certainly it would be difficult to maintain that unions are in no sense a monopoly force. From the beginning they have been dedicated to taking labor out of competition. Opponents of the application of the antitrust laws to unions argue, however, that union monopoly is different from business monopoly in the sense that unions are not profit-making institutions and thus should not be judged by the standards applied to business.

These critics also doubt the propriety of applying the same remedy to labor as to business monopoly. No one, they argue, even in this day of the talking product doing its own television commercial, has ever suggested that a product might veto the price placed upon it by its producer. Clearly unions do face this possibility; unions must obtain the consent of the members whose services they sell. In this variant and others, the age-old plea that labor is not a commodity and thus should not be treated as such is still heard. Supporters of unions add as a clinching argument the fact that the antitrust laws have done little to diminish the bargaining strength of employers and therefore to use them to weaken unions would be to accord management a major advantage.

Nevertheless, even the supporters of unions are forced to admit that there are occasions where the power of unions is excessive. The real problem of applying antitrust laws to unions, however, lies in deciding which of a union's monopolistic activities are essential for the improvement of workers' positions and which must be judged illegitimate because they too seriously impede the competitive system. There is also the possibility that both conditions may be true in a particular case, which obviously raises still more difficult questions.

It is quite clear from the preceding brief review of early policy toward collective bargaining that the environment as we know it today represents a marked change from the earlier period. Although the most dramatic changes came in the 1930s, it would be a mistake to conclude from our preceding description that the government made no effort to protect unions engaging in collective bargaining prior to that time.

State legislatures and Congress were both subject to greater political pressure than the courts and these bodies were by no means insensitive to the outcries of American workers in the early years. Labor's Bill of Grievances, submitted to Congress in 1906, was in part responsible for the passing of the Clayton Act. Even earlier, Congress had included in the Erdman Act, which dealt with the regulation of the railroads, a section forbidding the railroads from discriminating against those workers who were members of a union. Congress' disinclination to extend this protection to other workers was probably strengthened by the Supreme Court's declaration that the provision in the Erdman Act was unconstitutional.

State legislatures also did not completely ignore the interests of unions. By 1910 over twenty states, including most of the major industrial ones, had passed some labor legislation favorable to unions. One of the first pieces of legislation passed by many of these states was a law making it illegal for an employer to fire a worker because of membership in a union. As in the case of congressional actions, however, the Supreme Court rendered decisions that made the laws ineffective. All such laws were invalidated by the Court on the grounds that they constituted a violation of the due process clauses of the Fifth and Fourteenth Amendments.

Later, attempts by a number of states to prohibit such practices by employers as blacklisting (where the name of a worker known to be sympathetic to unions or otherwise objectionable is placed on a list circulated among employers) and the use of company stores (often workers were paid in scrip that was accepted only at company stores and these stores charged higher prices than elsewhere) also perished at the hands of the Supreme Court. The Court also overruled state laws that attempted to check the use of injunctions by courts of equity.

While it is true that the 1930s constitute a benchmark in labor legislation and mark the bestowing of congressional approval on collective bargaining, the really dramatic change lay in the fact that most of the labor legislation received the seal of approval of the courts.

We have already noted that an injunction in the Hutcheson case was refused by the Supreme Court partly on the basis of the existence of the Norris-LaGuardia Act. It is now time to examine in some detail this legislation, which was passed in 1932 on the eve of the New Deal and in one stroke removed most of the sting from both labor injunctions and the yellow dog contract.

Earlier in this chapter we stressed how great a handicap the injunction had been to labor unions. Employers could seek temporary injunctions restraining the union from striking until the employer had had the opportunity to show reason why the strike was likely to cause destruction of private property. Often the ability of the company to prove the existence of such a danger became irrelevant. By imposing a waiting period of thirty days or longer before the union was free to go on strike, the workers' will to strike was often broken. A union must strike when the iron resolve of its members is hot. Doubts about the success of the strike and the possible loss of his job begin to plague the worker when he has had a period of time to think things over.

Under the Norris-LaGuardia Act, courts can still issue injunctions in labor disputes, but only after sworn testimony subject to cross-examination has convinced the court that unlawful acts will otherwise be committed (or have already been committed) that would inflict substantial and irreparable damage to the employers' prosperity. Furthermore, the employer must provide evidence that he has no other recourse and that the law enforcement officers charged with the responsibility of protecting his property are either unwilling or unable to do so. Even if such evidence is furnished, the court must be convinced that the providing of the injunction will not do greater injury to the union than a failure to issue would do to the employer. Finally, the injunction could not be used to enforce a "yellow dog" contract in a federal court.

Other parts of the Norris-LaGuardia Act dealing with primary or product and secondary boycotts were less explicit and have been subject to prolonged court interpretation. The constitutionality of the act, however, has never been challenged successfully and it still remains as a pioneer piece of American legislation protecting the rights of unions. Twenty-five states have adopted similar anti-injunction laws.

The Norris-LaGuardia Act also aided the unions by clarifying the issue of what Congress deemed to be a legal labor dispute. Previously the courts had interpreted Section 20 of the Clayton Act to protect workers only in disputes involving a company and the workers employed directly by that company. The Norris-LaGuardia Act broadened this definition to include any dispute whether or not the workers were employees of the company in question.

Although the Norris-LaGuardia Act removed two of the major roadblocks to union organizing efforts and set forth congressional support for the right of workers to join unions of their own choosing and to select the leaders who were to represent them in collective bargaining, the act did nothing to ensure that employers would recognize unions or agree to bargain with them once they had been recognized.

The next step in this direction came with the National Industrial Recovery Act of 1933. Section 7A of that act provided that the industrywide codes of fair competition established elsewhere in the act should encourage the development of collective bargaining by providing that workers ". . . shall have the right to organize and bargain collectively through representatives of their own choosing." The section further stipulated that all of this was to be done without interference from employers.

Although bargaining rights were now clearly recognized under the law, no machinery for the enforcement of those rights was established. Both the original National Labor Board chaired by Senator Robert Wagner and the National Labor Relations Board that succeeded it lacked any statutory authority and employers defied the board's recommendations with impunity. The NIRA (National Industrial Recovery Act) placed great emphasis on the voluntary character of collective bargaining and when employers refused to cooperate, unions found the brick wall as impenetrable as ever. In 1935, Section 7A became inoperative when the Supreme Court declared the entire act unconstitutional.

National Labor Relations Act

Students of the New Deal era generally agree that one of the most revolutionary pieces of legislation passed during the Roosevelt administration was less the product of the President than of Congress and particularly of Senator Robert Wagner. It is for this reason that the 1935 National Labor Relations Act is most often known simply as the Wagner Act.

Although Congress had no direct authorization under the Constitution to legislate concerning collective bargaining, many members of Congress were anxious to enact a law that would more nearly equalize the bargaining strength of labor and management. Congress passed the Wagner Act on the basis of the commerce clause in the Constitution that gives Congress the right to regulate interstate commerce, although there were many initial misgivings that the Supreme Court would find this legislation to be unconstitutional too. In its general tone and spirit the Wagner Act resembled the Norris-LaGuardia Act and Section 7A of the National Industrial Recovery Act, but now all of the loopholes were closed.[4] The new law firmly established the right of workers to form independent unions of their own choosing. The act required that employers recognize a union that represented a majority of the members of an appropriate bargaining unit and that he bargain with that union. No longer could an employer hamstring a union by refusing to recognize the union's existence unless it had the economic power to compel its recognition.

The requirement to bargain did not mean that an employer had to accept a union's demands or sign a contract not to his liking (although the bargaining power of the union might compel him to do so, there was no legal obligation). However, it did mean that an employer had to meet with the union's leaders, listen to their demands, and make a reasonable counterproposal of his own. Later decisions of the National Labor Relations Board (NLRB) were to insist that the employer meet with the union's representatives in person; bargaining by mail was not sufficient.

Section 8 of the new act forbade employers to discriminate against any worker because of union activity. Furthermore, the employer was forbidden to support financially a union of his own in order to prevent an outside, independent union from organizing his plant. Another old enemy of organized labor—the company union—was now illegal. Independent company unions of the workers' own choosing could still exist, but any evidence of an employer's connection with that union was legally fatal.

The philosophy of the Wagner Act largely centered on the importance of *collective* bargaining as a means of promoting industrial peace and the need to protect the right of *groups* of workers. It stressed the importance of majority rule, although the rights of the minority were not completely ignored.

From the first day of its passage, many observers had serious doubts about the success the law would have when it was tested in the highest court of the land. Already numerous pieces of New Deal legislation, including the National Industrial Recovery Act had been found unconstitutional. In the months immediately after passage of the Wagner Act, many employers openly flouted its provisions, confident that their actions would be upheld by a subsequent court decision. Thus employers ignored NLRB orders and openly welcomed the necessity of the board to go to the courts to get its orders enforced in the expectation that their failure to comply would be ultimately upheld by the judiciary. Even today, incidentally, 30 percent of all NLRB rulings are still appealed to the federal courts,[5] even though these appeals may involve considerable delay. Although a considerable amount of pressure had been exerted on the Supreme Court to make the Court more liberal (including Roosevelt's proposal for its reorganization), it still came as a distinct shock to employers when in 1937, in the *National Labor Relations Board v. the Jones and Laughlin Steel Corporation,* the Supreme Court upheld the Wagner Act's constitutionality.

Although many employers learned to live with the Wagner Act during the twelve years before it was amended by the Taft-Hartley Act, there was always a certain amount of management unrest and dissatisfaction both with the act itself and the way in which it was administered. From the beginning, management complained that the act and the National Labor Relations Board it established were biased in favor of labor.

Given the friendly attitude of government toward management in the past, any change in the opposite direction was likely to be viewed with hostility by businessmen. Furthermore, many employers have never abandoned their basic suspicion of unions and collective bargaining. Complaints by unions to the NLRB about unfair employer practices remained as numerous at the end in the last year before the Wagner Act was amended as they had been in earlier years; there were 2,000 such cases pending when the Taft-Hartley Act was passed. Anyone who thinks that the issue of union-

ism is completely settled for most employers should try asking one how he feels about the unionization of his white-collar employees.

During the course of the twelve years before the Wagner Act was amended, over 40,000 workers were reinstated in their jobs and awarded over $12 million in back pay. While many of the most heated attacks against the NLRB came during the early years of its life, it is also true that the board continued into the 1940s to irritate employers by favoring the cause of labor whenever the situation left room for doubt.

Although many charges were leveled against the NLRB, we will concentrate on only three. One frequently expressed complaint was that the board was so zealous in protecting the union's rights that it trampled on the employer's rights in the process. An employer who attempted to express his views about the union and to explain his reasons for opposition to it was often charged with the illegal act of interfering with the organizing rights of the union. While the board had earlier taken the position that the employer should maintain a neutral position lest his obvious position of power unduly influence employees, it had taken verbal and written statements made by the employer in the context of other actions. In the important *Virginia Electric Band Power Company* case (*20 NLRB 911, 1940*), the NLRB found the company guilty of interference when it issued statements to its workers suggesting that they join an independent union that subsequently signed a closed shop contract. Workers refusing to join the independent union were dismissed. The Supreme Court at first held that there was nothing objectionable in the statement made by the company and called upon the board to determine whether there was accompanying coercion. Such a finding by the board was subsequently upheld, but the Court did suggest that the employer had a right to express his views although he was not free to coerce by words any more than by deeds. The assumption of neutrality as a proper stance for the employer— a view that the board had sometimes seemed to support—was repudiated by the Court. Critics were not appeased by the modification in the board's earlier position and the passage of the Taft-Hartley Act restated the position that an employer could honestly state his views.

Similarly, the employer had to be extremely careful lest he be charged with trying to influence unduly the union's leaders and members. Even the provision of a Coke machine in a room where the union held its meeting was seen as a subtle plot.[6]

While the NLRB at times may have been unduly protective of labor's rights, its attitude must be viewed in the context of past employer practices, the problems involved in getting a union organized, and the great effect that every word and gesture of an employer will have on workers trying to muster sufficient courage to form a union.

If one were to ask what impact the NLRB has had on collective bargaining, the first and most obvious answer would be that it did a great deal to make it possible. It seems doubtful, for example, whether even the upsurge of the CIO would have lasted without the support of the Wagner Act and the National Labor Relations Board.

The NLRB also influenced collective bargaining by virtue of its broad interpretation of the Wagner Act in regard to what subjects should be deemed bargainable. The language of

the act itself on this point is tantalizingly vague and general. The relevant passage reads as follows:

> . . . the performance of the mutual obligation of the employer and the representation of the employees to meet at reasonable times and confer in good faith with respect to wages, hours, and other terms and conditions of employment, or the negotiation of an agreement, or any question arising thereunder . . .

Employers charged that the board, by interpreting this clause in the broadest possible way, gave unions an open invitation to make all kinds of impossible demands and to invade areas traditionally reserved for management decision making.

Both of these charges are subject to important qualification, however. The very process of collective bargaining inevitably involves some loss of the employer's traditional freedom to act without being accountable to his workers for his actions. Furthermore, the mere fact that a particular subject is deemed proper for collective bargaining does not mean that the employer has to accept the union's demands or even a compromise. A refusal to accede to the union's demands has never been construed as a failure to bargain in good faith as long as the employer was willing to hear the union's demands and state his counterposition.

Employers even gain some advantages from the multiplicity of topics. It gives them space within which to maneuver—offering some things and rejecting others. Certainly it is by no means clear that the total gains achieved by the union in dollar-and-cents terms are any greater than if the scope of bargaining had been somewhat narrower.

A third criticism raised by some employers against the board was its choice of bargaining units. These employers claimed that the board discriminated in favor of industrial unions. Craft unions joined the employers in this criticism. Those employers who were critical of this alleged tendency (not all were and some actually preferred to deal with industrial unions) often found (or hoped to find) the craft unions easier groups with which to deal. The CIO industrial unions were often considered to be more aggressive and less easily divided and fragmented. Employers remembered the difficulty that the steel workers had had earlier in this century in bargaining successfully when they were split into a series of craft unions. The craft unions also quite naturally were sensitive to any possible slighting of their cause because of the intense rivalry existing between the AFL and the CIO at the time. Skilled workers were sometimes unhappy because they were included with semiskilled and unskilled workers and outvoted by the latter two groups. Much of the narrowing of wage differentials previously based on differences in skill can be attributed to the use of broad plant or employer units.

Whether the board's decisions as to the appropriate bargaining unit had any significant impact upon the winning or losing of union elections is difficult to determine. Certainly employers charged that the bargaining unit was set by the board to assure the maximum chances for the union winning an election. Again the board appears to have been motivated by the principle of providing protection to the greatest number of workers possible. While it is quite possible that some workers found themselves working in union plants against their wishes, dissatisfaction was probably more likely to result when workers found themselves represented by a union not particularly suited to their needs.

Taft-Hartley

During the years preceding the Taft-Hartley Act, a number of states passed legislation designed to curb the power of unions. Union organizers had to register with the state and standards were set for the payment of dues, the conduct of elections, and the tenure of union officers. All such legislation, however, was passed in the rural nonindustrial states. Little or no controls were imposed in those states where unions were already strong.

Nevertheless, a large segment of the general public felt that unions had acquired too much power under the Wagner Act, imperiling the collective bargaining process. This general feeling of uneasiness over labor's newly won power, capped by an exasperation over the rash of postwar strikes, led to the passage of the Taft-Hartley Act, more properly known as the Labor-Management Relations Act of 1947. The avowed intentions of the sponsors of the bill were to balance the alleged one-sidedness of the Wagner Act and to restore some of management's power in order to make the bargaining strength of the two sides more nearly equal.

The Taft-Hartley Act is a long (twenty-eight pages compared to the Wagner Act's nine) and complicated piece of legislation dealing with many diverse aspects of union activities. We will concentrate here only on those sections most relevant to collective bargaining.

One provision designed to accomplish both of the objectives espoused by the bill's sponsors was the employer free speech clause. As interpreted by the expanded NLRB also provided for in the act, this provision gives the employer the right to state his opposition to the union and its demands and to require that employees attend his speeches provided they are made on company time.[7] Unions have complained that the new freedom has been abused and employers have used their right of free speech to threaten dire events such as the closing of the plant if the union's demands are supported by the workers. One textile organizer recently told us that it had been virtually impossible to organize some plants since the free speech clause went into effect because of hints made by the employer of steps he would be forced to take if the union was admitted and the reinforcement of these hints by more direct warnings by his foremen to the workers. Thus while the free speech clause does not extend the right of the employer either to threaten retaliation or promise benefits, the wider latitude enables him to make use of these ploys covertly (or have subordinates do so).

Even granting these abuses, the free speech clause still seems a valuable change. Freedom of speech is such a precious part of our heritage that it is better to err on the side of giving too much freedom even though that freedom is abused than to attempt to curtail it.

Another part of Taft-Hartley designed to reduce the bargaining power of unions was the removal of certain topics from the area of collective bargaining. The closed shop was forbidden and states were given the power to legislate against the union shop. It is illegal under Taft-Hartley for the union to attempt to seek through collective bargaining anything specifically prohibited by law. At the same time, however, an employer cannot compel a union to bargain over its internal affairs. Nor can either an employer or a union require the other to bargain away any right granted to him by the Taft-Hartley Act.

It had been charged that without this protection unions might coerce employers into doing things not required or even specifically exempted under the law. The protection has been sought rarely, however, and there were other provisions of greater significance.

To parallel the list of unfair employer practices specified under the Wagner Act, Taft-Hartley announced a list of unfair union practices. For a list of these see the Appendix to this chapter.

None of these restrictions have proved very significant in practice. The board has dealt with relatively few cases involving union coercion of either employers or employees. The antifeatherbedding clause became almost completely inoperative thanks to court rulings that declared that as long as workers were willing to perform work (even though there was no work to be performed) the union could insist they be paid. The requirement of stand-by orchestras that never played a note was thereby declared legal and proper.

The "requirement to bargain" clause includes little more than the stipulation that a sixty-day notice of a desire to negotiate a new contract must be posted and that the union must refrain from a strike (employers similarly cannot lock out their employees) during that period. The need for the clause has always seemed in some doubt in any case. Although John L. Lewis was once quoted as saying to the mine owners that *they* had to bargain but he did not, the fact remains that the union is organized primarily for the precise reason of engaging in bargaining. Normally it needs no law to compel it to fulfill its function. There have been some cases where unions have stated their terms on a "take it or leave it" basis (the Teamsters have sometimes done so), but this is not the usual situation. Nor have there been many cases involving unduly high initiation fees. The basic problem here, of course, is the widely different traditions in the various trades; initiation fees that might seem excessive in one field may be perfectly acceptable in another.

More frequently unions have been charged with violations of the sections forbidding the use of mass picketing and the use of violence during strikes. A union cannot picket an employer to force him to bargain with it, if the employer has properly recognized another union under the terms of the NLRB. Nor can a union which has lost an election continue mass picketing of a plant and thereby prevent the delivery or shipment of goods. The union may, however, engage in "informational" picketing designed to inform the public that the plant is nonunion and thereby discourage customers from patronizing the company.

The most complex and certainly the most controversial section of the act dealing with unfair union practices has been the part concerning the secondary boycott. It will be remembered that the secondary boycott was the basis for numerous earlier court findings against unions.

Under Taft-Hartley, it is illegal for a union to picket an employer who is doing business with a company with which the union has a dispute. Early fears that the Taft-Hartley Act would also require workers to handle products farmed out by a struck plant to another plant were dispelled in the so-called "ally doctrine" involved in subsequent rulings of the NLRB such as *Local i291, 142 NLRB 37.* In this case the board ruled that the union

was not guilty of violating the prohibition against secondary boycotts when the second company was in some fashion related to the first plant (for example, if the two companies were under common ownership or management, or where work at a struck plant was being farmed out elsewhere).

Limiting the right of unions to engage freely in secondary boycott activity is generally justified by reference to the need to protect the employer from strikes arising from situations in which his own employees are not involved. Since his own workers are not questioning the terms of their own contract, the employer reasons, the union has no basis for disrupting his production or sales.

Not unexpectedly, union leaders reject the validity of this reasoning. They point out that workers may indeed be dissatisfied with their work when it involves working with goods upon which their comrades have refused to work. Union members argue that this provision requires them involuntarily to act as scabs. Because unions had long employed various forms of secondary pressure, it was not surprising that they sought a loophole in the law.

One major loophole was the so-called "hot cargo" clause. Initiated by the Teamsters, the clause was designed to circumvent the law by getting employers to agree voluntarily in their contracts with the union not to accept goods that were "hot" in the sense that they came from an employer currently engaged in a labor dispute. What the workers themselves could not collectively refuse to do, the employer could *voluntarily* reject. For some time the legality of this maneuver remained in question; the NLRB in some cases rejected such clauses and took no action in others. The usual NLRB position was that such clauses were legal and could be enforced in court but not through strike action. When the issue eventually came before the Supreme Court, it ruled that hot cargo clauses were legal, but that the union could not act to compel the employer to enforce such an agreement. The issue was finally settled by the Landrum-Griffin Act, which, with two specific exceptions, declared illegal all such clauses whether of a voluntary or involuntary nature. Note that an employer can still unilaterally refuse to buy the products of the struck company or can choose to patronize the output of a nonunion firm instead. Since unions believe that the latter is likely to be the more frequent occurrence, they argue that this freedom of employer action is discriminatory in light of the limitations imposed on union actions.

Another section of the Taft-Hartley Act that caused some early alarm among unions is Title III, Section 301, which exposes unions to law suits for breach of contract. Although union treasuries can be seized for the purpose of payment, the assets of individual members are exempt. This section has not proved of great significance.

Only thirteen states have their own labor relations laws patterned after the Wagner or Taft-Hartley Acts; nine of these are known as little Taft-Hartleys.

Landrum-Griffin

The Landrum-Griffin Act was largely an outgrowth of hearings of the McClellan Committee in the Senate detailing the extent of union corruption. The law seeks to check union malpractices by requiring scrutiny of unions' financial activities and by attempting to assure a greater degree of democratic procedure within local and national unions. The details of this part

of the law are not directly relevant to the topic of collective bargaining, although one of the law's goals was to improve the quality of collective bargaining by assuring the membership a greater voice in the union's internal affairs.

The attempt by Landrum-Griffin to expand the influence of individual union members has had one quite unexpected outcome: there has been a marked increase in the rate at which settlements achieved by the unions' leaders have been rejected by the rank and file. This has been somewhat disappointing to those persons who believed that the problems of industrial relations could be solved if only the workers were free to control their greedy, predatory leaders.

In general, the provisions of the Landrum-Griffin Act, designed to give the individual worker greater protection against coercive tactics and malpractice by his union, have been frustrated in two ways. First, the courts have been unwilling to interfere in what they regard as the internal or family troubles of the union. Second, there is a problem stemming from a basic flaw in the legislation itself—a failure to provide workers with any funds with which to challenge their unions. When the outcome is uncertain and the court costs have to be borne by the worker, the temptation to make even justifiable complaints is greatly reduced. While in some cases appeals may be undertaken by the Secretary of Labor, few appeals have actually been entered under his auspices and little additional protection has been afforded.

Title VII of the Landrum-Griffin Act covers a variety of miscellaneous items. As mentioned above, the act is more specific than Taft-Hartley in dealing with secondary boycotts and bans hot cargo clauses except in the cases of the clothing and construction industries. Other aspects of this section dealing with the question of secondary boycotts have yet to be clarified by court interpretation.

Although this section has been widely regarded as evidence of a general antiunion bias on the part of Congress, one important change was included that worked to the advantage of strikers. Under the Taft-Hartley Act, a worker who was on strike for reasons other than an unfair labor practice by the employer could be replaced and in the event of a vote on an employer's offer, his replacement rather than the striker was the person eligible to vote. Under the Landrum-Griffin Act, a worker on strike for economic reasons retains his voting rights for a period of twelve months.

Racial Discrimination

Considerations of space preclude a lengthy examination of federal and state legal actions that, beginning in the 1930s, were designed to end discrimination. We will thus confine our comments to the aspects of this legislation that are most directly relevant to unions and collective bargaining.

Although fair employment practices commissions have been constituted by every President since Franklin Roosevelt, racial discrimination in unions and collective bargaining has continued. Such commissions have been more effective in exerting pressure on employers (for example, by threatening the withdrawal of apartment contracts) than they have in changing the policies of labor unions and the contents of collective bargaining contracts.

Until recently, the NLRB has been reluctant to apply its jurisdictional powers to control acts of discrimination by unions. Prior to 1964 the NLRB had threatened several times to decertify a union for failing in its duty to provide fair representation, but in the Hughes Tool decision in that year it took decertification action and went one step further.[8] The board held that not only was failure to provide fair representation grounds for decertification but it also was an unfair labor practice, which meant the board could seek a cease-and-desist order from the courts in such cases.

Actually the courts, including the Supreme Court, had been somewhat ahead of the board in this area. But court action is a slow and costly process when undertaken by the individual and if the board continues to follow the Hughes Tool precedent it could do much to expedite enforcement of antidiscriminatory legislation as applied to unions.

The Civil Rights Act of 1964 supplies an additional source of protection to racial minorities. Title VII, Section 202 in part reads as follows:

(c) It shall be an unlawful employment practice for a labor organization—

(1) to exclude or to expel from its membership, or otherwise to discriminate against any individual because of his race, color, religion, sex, or national origin;

(2) to limit, segregate, or classify its membership in any way which would deprive or tend to deprive any individual of employment opportunities, or would limit, such employment opportunities or otherwise adversely affect his status as an employee or as an applicant for employment, because of such individual's race, color, religion, sex, or national origin;

The importance of this legislation is dependent upon the ultimate disposal by the Supreme Court of the Hughes Tool case.

Assuming that the board is upheld in its ruling, the 1964 Civil Rights Act is likely to have reduced importance in the area of industrial relations. Should the board's decision be overturned, however, the 1964 Act may provide important protection.

About half of the states and a number of the major cities have fair employment practice acts of their own. In some cases (in New York and New Jersey, for example) such statutes have influenced unions to remove formal restrictive clauses from their constitutions.

Public Employees

In a country in which the courts and many government officials were slow to abandon their suspicions of labor unions, it is not surprising to find strong opposition to the formation of unions or to petitions for collective bargaining by public employees. As late as the turn of the century, legislators and several Presidents deplored the combined efforts of government employees to petition Congress for improvements in working conditions. Presidents Theodore Roosevelt and William Howard Taft both issued orders banning such group activity. Not until the passage of the Lloyd-LaFollette Act in 1912 did the right of government employees to band together for such a purpose become legal. Although the act was at first interpreted to apply only to postal employees, its scope was gradually broadened to include the right of all federal employees to join unions. The right to strike, however, was clearly withheld. Indeed, the law did little to clarify the right of such unions, once organized, to engage in collective bargaining.

The situation remained unchanged until President John F. Kennedy, on the basis of a report submitted to him the previous fall, issued Executive Orders 10,987 and 10,988 in January 1962. The first executive order established a system whereby an employee could appeal against arbitrary action by a superior. The second order gave federal employees the right to form unions and to engage in collective bargaining. The right of employees to refuse to join a union was also guaranteed. In May of the following year, President Kennedy issued a supplement to Executive Order 10,988 that denied any right of federal employees to strike. Although considerable progress has been made (about a third of the 2.5 million government employees are organized), there are still numerous complaints. Early complaints about the Kennedy Executive Orders concerned the absence of any machinery for resolving impasses between employees and the concerned department and the wide-ranging managerial prerogatives left in the hands of a department, which limited the scope of the issues open to collective bargaining discussions considerably.

Following an investigation of these charges, President Lyndon Johnson on October 29, 1969 issued Executive Order 11491. Although this new order did not meet all the objections of the critics, the scope of collective bargaining for federal employees was considerably broadened. There is now more room for grievance procedure including arbitration with an opportunity for review of agency decisions by the Federal Labor Relations Council.

State legislation authorizing collective bargaining by state and local public employees is as recent a phenomenon as the federal orders and has mushroomed in the past five or six years. According to a survey of state labor commissioners made by the authors, in mid-1967 twenty states had some legislation allowing at least one category of public employees the right to organize and negotiate with the public employer. Of these twenty, thirteen gave broad coverage while the remainder confined themselves to one or more employee categories. Teachers have received perhaps the greatest amount of newspaper coverage, but other public employees, ranging from policemen, firemen, and nurses to ferry boat operators (Alaska), have been accorded increased bargaining rights through such state legislation.

In addition to the twenty states with existing laws, ten states reported attempts within state legislatures to have such legislation passed. Such legislation occurs with the greatest frequency in the Northeast, the Upper Midwest, and the Far West. In the South only two states—Florida and Alabama—have passed such legislation and in both states it is limited to specific groups of employees. As any reader of the newspapers is aware, however, the absence of legislation has not precluded the formation of unions by public employees seeking collective bargaining rights.

None of the states has resolved the problem of how to handle a strike by public employees. Legislation such as New York's Taylor Law has largely failed on this score. New York's Taylor Law, so named after its primary drafter, distinguished professor of industrial relations George Taylor, was thought to be a model labor law when it was passed in 1967. The Taylor Law substitutes fines on a striking union for the penalties on the individual striker (fines, loss of his job) provided by its predecessor, the 1947 Condon Wadlin Act. However, strikes by New York State employees continue to occur. Less troublesome but still unresolved is the problem of how to handle union demands for a union shop.

Summary and Conclusions

Although government's efforts to establish the environment for collective bargaining have changed markedly in the past two decades, the change has not been as complete as the unions at first feared and does not represent a reversion to the antiunion attitude of an earlier day. Today one seldom hears the Taft-Hartley Act described as a piece of "slave labor" legislation. This should not lead us to overlook the fact, however, that Taft-Hartley has made it more difficult to organize workers outside the union movement. While Taft-Hartley has left large unions relatively unaffected, it has been damaging to new and weak unions.

Even most supporters of the new legislation have been compelled to admit that comprehensive national legislation often proves to be unsuitable when applied to local conditions in a particular shop. The diversity of collective bargaining makes it difficult to formulate laws that will be applicable and suitable for all situations. The ban on the closed shop was opposed as strongly by some employers as it was by the unions. Traditional work rules made attempts to prohibit featherbedding almost impossible to enforce.

The Landrum-Griffin Act represents the first attempt by the federal government to interfere in the internal affairs of unions. While union members and union leaders may resent this intrusion into their private affairs, there is little evidence that they have had difficulty in complying with the terms of the act or that those terms have severely restricted their power. In fact, the law may have made it more difficult for employers to secure settlements because of the increased frequency with which the rank and file votes down settlements arrived at by the union's leaders. Without question, the section dealing with secondary boycotts has been a serious handicap for some unions, but the full extent of this problem can only be determined in the light of future court decisions.

The Role of the Government in Collective Bargaining Abroad

With the possible exception of France, the United States regulates industrial relations more strictly than the other countries (England, West Germany, Ireland, Sweden, Japan, Mexico) in our survey. Like the United States, most of the other countries have had a history of early opposition to the labor movement that has gradually relaxed with time. In the area of collective bargaining the distinction is less marked since the philosophy of the Wagner Act was to set the stage for collective bargaining and then let the two parties resolve their differences by themselves.

Great Britain

Both British courts and British legislatures regarded labor unions as outright conspiracies during their early years. In the early days of the nineteenth century, employers set up unilaterally boards of inquiry and arbitration to reduce the complaints of workers over wages. Employers tended to ignore unions as much as possible—a policy that received little opposition from the government. The Trade Unions Act of 1871 (amended in 1876) and the Conspiracy and Protection of Property Act of 1875 went a long way toward removing the label of conspiracy from British unions. But it was not until the Trade Disputes Act of 1906 that the last vestiges of legal

obstruction were removed from collective bargaining. In 1916 provision was made for a system of voluntary arbitration of industrial disputes by the establishment of an Industrial Court. During World War II, arbitration was made compulsory in order to avoid interferences with war production. In 1950, at the insistence of the unions, the prohibition against strikes and lockouts was lifted and only limited provisions for compulsory arbitration were retained. Since that time there has been increasing emphasis on the voluntary character of arbitration and today unions are again free to strike.

Unlike unions in the United States, British unions have no protection under the law. Employers are neither required to recognize unions nor to enter into collective bargaining unless the union can compel them to do so. Strikers have no protection under the law and may be discharged although in practice they rarely are. In fact, the British government's general "hands off" policy has worked more to the benefit of unions than to their detriment and recently there has been considerable agitation by British industrialists for a more forceful role by the government. Since labor contracts are unenforceable in British courts of law, employers often find themselves unable to secure the fulfillment of terms agreed to by the union's leaders in exchange for improvements in wages and working conditions by the company.

Both major British political parties have been discussing reforms in the present system, possibly including some movement in the direction of the United States model, with its exclusive bargaining rights, formal grievance procedures, and legally enforceable contracts. The Labor Party has understandably been less anxious to move in this direction and has been encouraged in its reluctance by British unions. Even Labor members of Parliament, however, have viewed with some sympathy such corrections as the proposal for a twenty-eight-day cooling-off period before a strike can be called, which is designed to curb one of the worst irritants to management, the "quickie" strike.

The British government sets no limits on the subjects considered appropriate for bargaining, nor does it attempt to control the size of the bargaining units. Both questions are left to labor and management to decide.

France

The French government has had a long history of intervention in labor affairs. It was not until 1881 that the freedom to organize was accorded to French unions, and twenty-eight years passed before the legal basis for collective bargaining was assured. The time lag is explained not only by the slowness of the French legislature to act, but also by the relative disinterest of many French unions in such legislation because of their preoccupation with political affairs. The 1919 legislation was actually passed in the hope that it might divert French unions into the more peaceful pastime of collective bargaining! In the years that followed the French parliament passed a series of statutes giving the minister of labor power to supervise collective agreements and to extend their terms to workers who were not covered by the agreement itself but who worked in similar plants located within the geographical confines of the agreement. Shortly after World War II, the power of the minister of labor was somewhat reduced although he still retains power to extend agreements to workers who are not covered if he sees fit. Agreements no longer require gov-

ernment approval, but the law requires equal wages for equal work regardless of sex and sets certain standards for the determination of a minimum wage.

Since the war, the French government has also attempted to set up work councils within the plants, but efforts in this direction have been notably unsuccessful.

Finally, it is important to note that, like Great Britain and several other European countries, the French government is inevitably more deeply involved than the U.S. government as a party in labor relations because a substantial proportion of the French economy is nationalized.

West Germany

Ending a long-standing German tradition of governmental opposition to labor unions and collective bargaining, the government established by the Allies after World War II has given unions a free hand. Great freedom is permitted both with respect to the choice of bargaining unit and the subject matter of collective bargaining. Extensive legal provisions for various fringe benefits, however, have reduced the importance of these items in bargaining contracts. Like its French counterpart, the German ministry of labor can extend the terms of a collective bargaining agreement to firms and employees not originally covered by the agreement. As in France, 50 percent of the employees of the industry or area must have been covered by the original agreement before the government can act.

This power to extend wage agreements apparently has affected collective bargaining in several interesting ways. Not only has it somewhat reduced the interest of workers in collective bargaining, but it has tended to encourage industrial over craft unions. It is easier to extend a contract when all of the workers are in one union rather than belonging to several craft unions.

Furthermore, although unions are theoretically free to bargain upon whatever subject they please, German labor contracts actually tend to be rather brief and broad enough to be applied to all employers whether they are parties to the agreement or not. The result is that some observers have seen German unions as little more than "quasi-legislative agencies" drawing up contracts that ". . . become more minimum wage and hour laws than union contracts."[9]

Since 1926 Germany has had a series of labor courts that settle not only disputes arising under the terms of an existing contract but the issues arising during the negotiation of a new contract as well.

Sweden

Swedish labor union leaders have continued through the years to encourage the government to follow a "hands off" policy in labor affairs. Unlike Norway, Sweden has managed to resist all proposals for compulsory arbitration. (By United States standards of definition, Denmark has no real system of compulsory arbitration either.) Nevertheless, as in any country where a large segment of the economy is nationalized, a substantial amount of government intervention is inevitable. The fact that the Labor Party is the party in power has helped to make such intervention more palatable to the unions if not to management. The need to keep the trade union movement free from the government has been a matter of real concern to union and government officials alike.

Unlike Great Britain, Swedish laws provide for the legal enforcement of labor contracts and the government takes a far more active role in the settlement of strikes (see Chapter 24). Disputes between labor and management over the terms of contracts are resolved in labor courts. These labor courts, first established in 1928, consist of seven members—two representatives from each side plus three disinterested persons, two of whom must have had previous judicial experience.

Although Swedish unions protested vehemently and undertook a series of strikes to reinforce their protests when labor courts were first introduced into Sweden in 1928, these courts have now become an accepted means of settling disputes arising under existing contracts.

Israel

The relationship between the government and the union movement in Israel is complicated by the fact that the Histadrut, the central union body, also played a major role in the formation of the Israeli government. It is not surprising therefore that the government has always been favorably disposed toward labor. Israel has numerous laws that set working standards with respect to hours and so on and protect the right of unions to organize and bargain. There is a system of mediation but arbitration takes place only if both parties have agreed in advance to accept a decision; thereafter if one party refuses to abide by it the decision can be made binding. On the whole, the two parties are left to their own devices in formulating a contract. Such contracts may be registered with the ministry of labor, although this is not required. When deadlocks occur, the Ministry may intervene and attempt conciliation.

India

In India, as in many developing nations, both employers and unions have been reluctant to engage in free collective bargaining, preferring to have the government make settlements for them. Neither side has wished to experience strikes, and neither has dared to risk the possibility that such strikes might arise from free bargaining. Employers worry that inexperienced workers might try to force impossible demands on them, while unions fear that employers will be too strong for them if government protection is removed. As a result of these attitudes, efforts by the Indian government to end compulsory arbitration of disputes have been opposed by both parties.[10]

Unions in India are given less protection under the law than they are in some developing nations. Although unions and collective bargaining are not deemed restraints of trade, employers, as in England, do not have to recognize or bargain with unions unless pressure from the union compels them to do so. In 1936 the checkoff (see Chapter 11) became illegal under a new law forbidding employers to deduct anything from workers' paychecks.

The Industrial Employment (Standing Orders) Act of 1946 provides a minimum standard of working conditions beyond which unions are free to go if they have sufficient bargaining power. Indian law also requires the establishment of work councils in all plants employing 100 men or more, but this effort has been even less effective than in France.

One problem of Indian labor legislation is the lack of enforcement. Much of the national legislation is enabling legislation. These laws grant the power of enforcement to the individual states, which all too often fail to take action.

Japan

As in Germany, the current labor union movement in Japan stems from the actions of the Allies, who instituted it after World War II in the hope of averting a resurgence of the military. Every encouragement has been extended to collective bargaining and only government employees are restricted in their right to organize and bargain. Strikes by government employees are strictly forbidden and some observers attribute the aggressive left-wing politics of these workers to that fact. However, since U.S. government employees have labored under a similar handicap without becoming radical, other factors must also be at work in the case of the Japanese government workers.

Mexico

Mexico has also gone through the familiar pattern of oscillating government attitudes towards labor unions, with the government evincing everything from deep hostility to strong support. For many years PRI, a party that often elects representatives of labor and is sympathetic to labor's interests, has been an important political force in Mexico.

In 1931 a federal labor law repealed all state laws controlling labor but left the enforcement of the new law in the hands of the states. Mexican labor laws run the gamut from minimum wages and rules pertaining to the employment of women to regulations concerning collective bargaining. There are associations of both employers and unions and both must be registered to be legally constituted. Mexico has a system of tripartite labor courts. These provide arbitration services but only after conciliation has failed.

Like the West German chancellor

the president of Mexico has the power to extend the terms of an agreement to all the workers in a specific branch of an industry or to a specific region; two-thirds of the employers and workers must already be parties to the agreement before he can so act.

Chapter Summary and Conclusions

It is difficult to predict what the impact of government on industrial relations is likely to be. A friendly climate does not automatically assure a strong union movement and successful collective bargaining. Nor does government interference unless extreme necessarily spell the doom of either unions or bargaining. Nevertheless, it seems quite apparent that the chance for a healthy system of collective bargaining is best when the government supports it.

How specific legislative acts will shape the character of collective bargaining is equally difficult to predict. When the law is too remote from traditional custom and practice both management and labor may tend to ignore it and follow the old ways for prolonged periods. In other cases, for example Germany's policy of extending the terms of contracts to non-covered firms, the entire flavor of the collective bargaining process may be changed by a single act.

APPENDIX

The major provisions of the four most important laws governing labor relations in the United States are outlined below.

I. Federal Anti-Injunction Act (Norris-La-Guardia Act), 1932
   A. Protected unionization and other activities by stating that they were not to be enjoined in federal courts. This has been held by the Supreme Court to supersede the Taft-Hartley

and to prevent injunctions against strikes in breach of contract (*Sinclair Refining Co. v. Atkinson*).
   B. Defined a labor dispute to include any controversy over the terms and conditions of employment "regardless of whether or not the disputants stand in the proximate relation of employer and employee" thus protecting secondary as well as primary boycotts.
   C. Established five-day limitation on temporary restraining orders.
   D. Established the requirement that a company seeking a restraining order must post bond for payment of damages if the union should be wrongfully harmed.
   E. Provided that before an injunction could be granted the employer must have sought a damage suit first or must be able to show why it could not be successful, and the firm must have fulfilled its own obligations by not violating an agreement and having tried bargaining, and the police must have stated that they are not able to provide protection.

II. National Labor Relations Act (Wagner Act), 1935
   A. Guaranteed the right of workers to organize and bargain collectively.
   B. Designated five unfair labor practices by the employer.
      1. interference with the right of workers to organize and bargain collectively
      2. domination of the union (company union) and statement of preference for one union or another by the employer in a jurisdictional dispute
      3. discriminatory hiring or firing because of union activity
      4. discharging or discriminating against workers for testifying before the National Labor Relations Board (NLRB)
      5. employer not bargaining in good faith with the accredited representatives of his workers
   C. Established the National Labor Relations Board with power to determine

the appropriate bargaining unit, call elections, prepare the ballot, conduct the voting, and certify a union as representative of a group of workers. Also power to hear complaints of unfair labor practices brought by companies and unions and to issue "cease and desist" orders to halt them.

III. Labor-Management Relations Act (Taft-Hartley Act), 1947
   A. Outlawed the *closed shop* and gave states the right to outlaw *union shops*
   B. Restored the injunction
   C. Guaranteed the right of workers to refrain from joining and participating in a union unless a union shop agreement exists
   D. Listed certain unfair labor practices on the part of the union:
      1. Unions cannot interfere with the rights of individual workers. Unions are forbidden to use coercive techniques against either the employer or workers in the choice of representatives for bargaining. The union cannot discriminate against any worker, whether he is or is not a union member, but must represent the interests of the worker in the unit.
      2. The union cannot refuse to bargain in good faith—this section was designed to parallel the requirement placed upon employers by the Wagner Act. Neither the employer nor the union is required "to agree to a proposal or mak(e) . . . a concession."
      3. The union cannot undertake certain types of unfair strikes and boycotts.
         a. no secondary boycotts—employer was free to do business with whomever he wished.
         b. no strikes or boycotts to force an employer to recognize an uncertified union or to compel the employer himself to join the union or an employers organization.
         c. no jurisdictional strikes.
         d. no featherbedding practices

(see p. 306 for definition and discussion).
      4. The union cannot picket to organize workers or to force recognition for twelve months after an employer has recognized another certified union.
      5. The union cannot impose unduly high initiation fees as a price of union membership
   E. A free speech amendment assured employers the right to state their views on unions—the NLRB had relaxed its position even before Taft-Hartley and employers do not need to furnish either equal time or facilities to the union for reply. As long as no threats of retaliation or promises of reward are involved, an employer is free to point out that he may be forced to close down if the union demands are successful.
   F. Foremen and guards must have separate unions.
   G. Required principal union officers to file affidavits that they were not members of or affiliated with the Communist Party; unless they do, the union loses the NLRB's services.
   H. Required unions to file certain financial statements if they wish certification from the NLRB.
   I. Increased the size of the NLRB and created the position of Counsel General with power to bring charges in his own right in cases of unfair labor practices and illegal strikes and secondary boycotts.
   J. Authorized the instigation of suits by and against unions for violation of contract.
   K. Forbade payments by employers to unions except in cases such as the check-off where safeguards have been made.
   L. Forbade political contributions by labor organizations.
   M. Forbade strikes by government employees.
   N. Made employees who were on economic strike and not entitled to reinstatement ineligible to vote in representation elections. This was subsequently amended by the Landrum-Griffin Act.

IV. Labor-Management Reporting and Disclosure Act (Landrum-Griffin Act), 1959
A. Enfranchised "economic striker" during first twelve months of strike.
B. Provided "bill of rights" for union members.
   1. right to participate in nominations and elections
   2. right to attend and participate in union meetings
   3. vote by secret ballot on an increase in dues, initiation fees, or other assessments
   4. right to see a copy of the contract under which an employee is to work
C. Set minimum democratic election procedures.
   1. national union elections to be held not less than every five years and local elections not less than every three years
   2. elections to be by secret ballot
   3. union not to interfere with right of any member to run for office, union funds may not be used for the campaign of any one candidate
D. Required comprehensive and detailed reports from union of such provisions as election procedures, membership requirements, dues and fees, and annual financial reports
E. Required supervision of "trusteeships" or suspensions of the autonomy of a local union by the parent body. Such "trusteeships" can be undertaken by the national only to correct corruption and assure carrying through of collective bargaining agreements or other legitimate union activities. They must file a report when the "trusteeship" is imposed and every six months thereafter. Meanwhile the votes of such a local delegate may not be counted at the national conventions until "trusteeship" has been removed.

NOTES

1. Joseph G. Rayback, *A History of American Labor* (New York: Free Press, 1966), p. 161.

2. Dallas Jones has argued that President Wilson must share part of the blame for the loose wording of the Clayton Act, which left it open to court interpretation. See Dallas L. Jones, "The Enigma of the Clayton Act," *Industrial and Labor Relations Review,* 10 (January 1957), 201–221.

3. See pp. 53–54 for the role of the Norris-LaGuardia Act in this connection.

4. Still earlier legislation had provided bargaining rights for a selected group of railroad employees under the terms of the Railway Labor Act of 1926. Although this act has often been cited as a model piece of legislation, some students have disagreed. See Herbert R. Northrup, "The Railway Labor Act and Railway Labor Disputes," *American Economic Review* (June 1946), pp. 324–343. Northrup asserts that labor peace in the railway industry has been bought by giving unions in the industry much of what they sought, rather than being the result of the law.

5. Robert Evans, Jr., *Public Policy Toward Labor* (New York: Harper & Row, 1965), p. 19. Evans points out that a complaint that the Counsel General part of the board (under the Taft-Hartley Board separated into prosecutor and judge) finds to have merit may be settled in two months or less if an informal agreement is achieved. A year's delay is likely if the case goes to the full board and added (often lengthy) time is involved if the case is appealed to the courts.

6. Harold W. Metz, *Labor Policy of the Federal Government* (Washington, D.C.: Brookings, 1945).

7. Robert Evans has pointed out that the NLRB and the courts have taken different views over the years as to whether an employer must grant the union equal time and the use of company facilities to answer the employer's position statement. In *NLRB v. Avondale Mills* (1958), the Supreme Court ruled that the employer must provide facilities when their lack elsewhere markedly damages the union's chance to present its answer to the company. Evans suggests that the NLRB (without complete support by the courts) appears to be trying to broaden this interpretation to include cases where the union was not granted the use of company property for a meeting even

though other facilities were available. Evans, *op. cit.*, p. 133.

Evans further points out that board decisions of the 1960s make it improper for an employer to "predict" (1) that if the union wins the election it will make impossible demands that the employer will be unable to meet and (2) that the result will be either a long strike or a forced closing of the shop. *Ibid.*, p. 134.

8. *Hughes Tool Decision*, NLRB *Tenth Annual Report,* 1945, p. 18. 147 NLRB n. 166.

9. Clark Kerr, "Collective Bargaining in Postwar Germany," in Adolf Sturmthal (ed.), *Contemporary Collective Bargaining in Seven Countries* (Ithaca, N.Y.: Cornell University Press, 1957), p. 200.

10. William Friedland, *Unions and Industrial Relations in Underdeveloped Countries,* Bulletin No. 47 (Ithaca, N.Y.: Cornell University Press, 1963), pp. 50–51.

2
Contract Time

4
The Bargaining Unit

There is a strong and understandable pressure on bargaining units to expand until they are coextensive with product markets.
—Neil Chamberlain

□ THE structure of collective bargaining is necessarily directly related to the way bargaining units for labor are defined as well as to the organization of industry. "A bargaining unit is an area of worker representation for purposes of collective bargaining."[1] What group of workers shall be considered a unit for bargaining purposes? Possible answers include all the workers in a shop or plant, all the workers in a particular industry in a city or region, or perhaps even all workers in a specific industry in the nation. The definition of a unit influences all aspects of the bargaining, including the content of the discussions as well as the participants in the discussion. The trend toward larger bargaining units and centralized decision making was noted as early as 1912.[2] To what extent is the scale of the bargaining unit determined by the size of the unit of management across the table? Or is there perhaps an inverse correlation?

At least in part the choice of the bargaining unit is determined by the organization of the industry. With the growth of the large corporation, the bargaining unit underwent commensurate growth. Technological innovation works both ways with regard to the choice of a unit. Larger industrial complexes lend themselves to larger bargaining units, but technological advances that ultimately reduce the number of men working in close proximity will weaken the community of feeling needed for collective bargaining. There is still considerable debate concerning which side first pressed for larger bargaining units—management or the unions. Frank Pierson believed it was management, stating "To a considerable degree, industry-wide bargaining is a defense measure utilized by employers to offset the advantages enjoyed by powerful unions."[3]

The ultimate form a bargaining unit takes, however, depends on a multitude of other relevant factors. Harold W. Davey adds six to the list: the wishes of the employees; the bargaining history of the plant; the membership requirements of the union involved; the presence of "community of interest" among employees; similarity of wages, hours, conditions of work; and the extent of self-organization among employees.[4] Obviously, both labor and management will press for a bargaining unit set at the scale or level that they believe will give them an advantage. Unions that have regulations requiring locals to have the approval of the national before settling a contract are more likely to turn to broader based bargaining units.

Consistent with the generally held belief that strength lies in numbers, unions seem to feel that they can best fight the large corporation with large blocs of workers. The union also believes that large-scale operations will cut off potential competition from other unions.

Frequently the distribution of bargaining units roughly parallels the distribution of business firms in size and number of employees covered. The parallel distribution indicates that bargaining is mostly on a firm-by-firm basis.[5] In 1956 the *Monthly Labor Review* noted that of the 1,737 known contracts covering 1,000 or more workers, multiemployer bargaining groups negotiated 557 agreements covering almost 4 million workers. Multiemployer arrangements occurred more frequently in industries characterized by small establishments, such as apparel manufacturing, printing, trucking, retail trade, hotels and restaurants, and service industries. While the majority of nonmanufacturing contracts were found to be multiemployer, this was not true of manufacturing contracts.[6]

One of the most difficult problems faced by the National Labor Relations Board has been the determination of the unit appropriate for collective bargaining. The board was given this responsibility by Section 9(b) of the Wagner Act (the section empowered the board to "decide . . . the unit appropriate for the purposes of collective bargaining . . . [whether] employer unit, craft unit, plant unit, or subdivision thereof . . .") but it was given little guidance. The disputes that arose were not only the expected ones involving the desires of small groups of employees. The latter disputes were about free choice as between the larger and the smaller groups. The board members differed as well: was their responsibility to decide in favor of whichever unit would be most effective or to follow the wishes of the employees (majority or majority and minority)? As John Dunlop has remarked, "From the importance of the bargaining unit to unions and managements, it follows that determination of the bargaining unit is the most significant responsibility exercised by the National Labor Relations Board for the future of collective bargaining."[7]

When the Wagner Act was passed in July 1935, the AFL dominated the labor scene, and at that time it could have been expected to solve any problems relating to bargaining units that might arise. But within months the issue of industrial unionism split the AFL's executive board and soon afterward the CIO came into existence. In an attempt to deal with numerous cases, each unique in some respect, the NLRB tried to set up certain standards. The factors that the board felt might determine the community of interest within a group of employees included: the duties, skill, wages, hours, and working conditions of the employees; the extent and type of self-organization; the history of collective bargaining in the plant under consideration and other plants in the industry; the desires of the employees; the eligibility of employees for membership in the union; and the relationship between the proposed unit and the administration and organization of the employer's business.[8] The most critical decisions were faced in cases in which an industrial union seeking a plantwide "P and M" (production and maintenance) unit came into conflict with one or more craft unions requesting separate units for workers in each of the crafts involved.

The issue first came to a head in the Globe decision (Globe Machine & Stamping Co., 3 NLRB 294) of 1937. In this instance rival unions claimed craft and industrial units and, while there had been a history of separate craft negotiations, more recently a plantwide agreement (industrial) had existed. The NLRB decided that either unit was feasible and that the employees themselves should decide. In an election to decide representation the craft groups would vote separately from the whole, and they could be included in the industrial unit or have separate craft units. As it turned out, the industrial unit was chosen but the craft workers had been protected. The "Globe election" continued to be used extensively by the NLRB to decide similar disputes.

The NLRB modified this solution in

1939 in the American Can case (13 NLRB 1252), which was decided after the composition of the NLRB had changed. The board held that a history of bargaining on an industrial basis prevented a later determination in favor of a smaller unit against the will of the majority of the employees. The AFL attacked this second policy as biased but there has been no proof of that charge.[9] From 1944 to 1947 the policy was again modified and more so-called Globe elections were held.

The NLRB ruled on the question of multiplant units in a relatively small number of cases. The board tried to recognize a unit as broad as the employees desired (or as was in accord with their community of interest) if it was justified by the form of organization of the business. "Before a multi-employer unit could be found appropriate under the Act . . . the Board required clear evidence that the association was authorized to act and was acting for the employers in collective bargaining, as well as that bargaining in such a broad unit was feasible."[10] If the union questioned the inclusion of any part of the unit the employees of that part could show their desires by vote. Although a union would have trouble justifying any attempt to revert to a smaller unit after years of bargaining in a larger one, an employer could easily accomplish the same end by simply withdrawing from the employers association.

Under the Taft-Hartley Act, the NLRB's decisions on unit issues were presumably intended to ensure workers freedom to engage in or to refrain from concerted activities. Supervisors were not to be called employees so were excluded from a unit question. With regard to the controversial question concerning craft versus industrial units, Section 9(b)(2) of the Taft-Hartley Act provided that the NLRB should not "decide that any craft unit is inappropriate . . . on the ground that a different unit has been established by a prior Board determination, unless a majority of the employees in the proposed craft unit vote against separate representation." The board did not interpret this to mean that craft unit elections were mandatory but rather that a prior determination by the board or past bargaining history "may not be the sole ground upon which the Board may decide election."[11] Nonetheless, one of the results of the passage of the Taft-Hartley Act was an increase in attempts to carve out various groups from old established bargaining units and the provision was interpreted as favoring craft unions.

Taft-Hartley added further qualifications to the original legislation (Wagner Act) on the choice of bargaining unit. The NLRB's discretion was limited on the question of giving recognition to bargaining units with partial or incomplete self-organization. Furthermore, the act placed an indirect obstacle in the way of industry-wide collective bargaining because if a union compelled an employer to join an employers association the act stated it was guilty of an unfair labor practice.

The National Labor Relations Board's position on choice of bargaining unit has continued to change over the past twenty years. In 1948 the board denied establishment of any separately represented craft units in plants in three industries: basic steel, basic aluminum, and lumbering. A 1954 decision permitted craft severance if the employees (other than those in the three industries mentioned) involved were members of a true craft or departmental unit and if the union seeking the change was one that traditionally had concerned itself with the special problems of the workers involved.

In 1966 the majority of the board said that henceforth it would consider a variety of factors in determining whether or not a group of workers should be separated on a craft basis. The decisions would be made on a craft-by-craft basis, thereby freeing craft workers in the previously mentioned industries from automatic exclusion. Factors to be taken under consideration in any NLRB decision include the history of bargaining at the plant and the degree of stability of relations, the degree of independence of the craft workers, their participation in the more general union, conditions in the industry as a whole, and the background of the union seeking to carve out a craft bargaining unit. The impact of this decision may be twofold. Although it may increase chances for separate representation of craft workers in the three industries previously excluded, it may make separate bargaining less automatic for craft workers in other industries.

The board has followed several policies concerning the method by which previously excluded workers may be included in a bargaining unit. One policy, for example, involves prior consultation of the additional workers followed by a vote of the whole body of workers (Petersen and Lytle, 60 NLRB 1070 [1945]; 16 LRRM 27 [reiterated in 1954]). Another policy provides for only one vote (Waterous Co., 92 NLRB 76 [1950]; 27 LRRM 1050 [reiterated in 1961]).

The board's determination of a bargaining unit could have repercussions on the content of labor's demands as well as on the type of union recognized. The industrial unions have worked for general wage increases on a cents-per-hour basis while the craft unions have distinguished between levels of workers when presenting their demands. The demands emphasized by a multiplant or multiemployer unit would be determined by the satisfaction of the greatest number of workers.[12] The AFL-CIO merger has had the effect of reducing disputes over bargaining units among rival unions. Less time and effort are spent in trying to induce a unit to change its allegiance. This in turn should lessen the task of the NLRB in choosing the proper unit for representation elections.

White-collar unions in some instances are treated differently from blue-collar unions by the NLRB. According to the Taft-Hartley Act no supervisors or foremen can be included in the unit. The act also specifies that professionals (the act includes a detailed definition of a professional) cannot be part of a unit determined by the NLRB unless the majority of these workers voted for inclusion. In other respects white-collar workers may form units or be included in units as other workers are. In practice, while plant clerical workers may join production workers in a unit, office clerical workers never join production workers. In practice also, technical workers have formed separate units, but they could combine with another group of workers if there was community of interest.[13]

The trend in American collective bargaining is distinctly toward greater centralization, whether this is achieved through greater use of industrywide bargaining or through increased reliance on pattern bargaining. These two forms will be discussed in detail later. First, however, we will explore the general advantages and disadvantages of increased centralization, with reference to the point of view of labor, of management, and of the general public.

Some writers have been rather

cynical about the advantages that a broad bargaining unit offers to the union. George Brooks, for example, has suggested that the only advantage that a large unit has from the union's point of view is that it insulates the leaders from the members.[14] Other observers are far more optimistic and note that in any case "local" labor markets are very broad these days, that management cannot compete by exploiting labor, that some decisions ought to have application throughout a specific industry (wage levels, job descriptions etc.), and that the larger bargaining unit enables participants to see industrywide problems like a declining market situation more clearly. Union advocates of increasing centralization stress that this trend would tend to bring wages out of competition and would increase the maturity and responsibility of the union leadership. The importance of standardization of wages will depend upon the fraction of costs that are wages. If wages are a small part of costs, employers will not fight wage increases. Standardization of apprenticeship and training requirements might promote more efficient use of the labor force. Another benefit that unions see as a result of increased centralization is the fact that a rival union will have a much more difficult time gaining recognition with a large bargaining unit in operation. Furthermore, the recognized union will presumably have an easier time withstanding pressures from nonunion personnel. Labor has also argued that centralized bargaining is the only feasible way to handle the larger employer. Certainly the union is in a better financial position to hire trained advisors for a single large-scale bargaining situation than it is to send trained people to several places for smaller sessions. Participants in a larger bargaining unit can also share the costs of any insurance schemes with resulting economies for the individual worker. Harold Davey notes that the principal pressures favoring the growth of multiemployer bargaining derive from management and union needs for greater institutional security.[15]

The major disadvantage from labor's point of view has been expressed by Neil Chamberlain:

> The basis for the danger is that centralized authority can extend its aegis over matters which are quite within the competence of local representatives: the industry pattern can be applied with excessive rigidity and in unnecessary detail to local settlements; the multiemployer bargain can determine matters which could well be left to individual employers and the union committee.[16]

As George Brooks points out, there is a definite and direct correlation between the size of the bargaining unit and the amount of local initiative and activity.[17] Anyone concerned with the internal democracy of the union cannot help but see the disadvantages of placing power and decision-making authority in the hands of a few, often hired technicians at the expense of the elected officers. The ability to "whipsaw" employers, or play one off against another, is forfeited if the union presses for industrywide bargaining rather than pattern bargaining. Although management often views the centralized bargaining unit as bringing greater peace, or at least less friction, unions have found that they sometimes have to pay the price in increased internal union conflict. Perhaps this outcome is to be expected when the power and prestige of the local union officials are cut. Furthermore, to the extent that personal knowledge of the other party at the bargaining table facilitates the discussion, a larger, more impersonal bargaining unit penalizes both sides.

Management gains obvious advantages from centralization. They know that once they arrive at a contract at least one of their costs is fixed and that, at least in the case of industrywide or pattern bargaining, they will not have to face the possibility of other firms competitively cutting wages. Perhaps management can plan for the future with more confidence because they possess a firmer picture of what to expect. A surprising number of employers supported industrywide collective bargaining at the hearings that preceded the passage of the Taft-Hartley Act.

The major potential disadvantage of large-scale bargaining from management's perspective is the increased strength it bestows on the union and its national officers, both with respect to bargaining and with respect to political activity. In addition, there is potential danger to the small businesses and those just beginning unless separate bargains are allowed on local issues (a frequent occurrence). Perhaps such firms would not be able to afford the terms agreed to by their larger neighbors. The individual firms might well be powerless to achieve policies suited to their own needs. A joint bargain tends to ignore special conditions in each plant, and a marginal firm may also be unable to meet any increase in costs even if the terms of a joint agreement force it to do so. Perhaps in the interests of efficiency such a firm should close its doors, but it would be difficult to tell its management (or its workers!) that. If increased centralization means involving the government in an attempt to control or regulate the bargaining process, both labor and management would be opposed.

The concept of previous agreement on wages or any other cost might be termed antagonistic to the free enterprise system and competition. The resulting condition has been likened by many to monopoly.

The third party with an interest in the collective bargaining process is, of course, the public. The major advantage from their point of view is undoubtedly the increased stability that comes from centralization. In addition, there may well be an increase in productivity after the marginal firms have been forced to close their doors. Proponents of increased centralization suggest that by ending wage competition the manufacturers will devote more attention to competition elsewhere, which will benefit the consumer.[18] Lack of competition in wages does not necessarily take prices out of competition.

If centralized bargaining increases labor peace, the general public is obviously benefited. On the other hand, centralized bargaining increases the possibility of major disruptions in the economy if a contract agreement is not reached, especially in the case of industrywide collective bargaining. Charges have also been made that such bargaining would become political rather than economic in nature. Of course, bargaining at any level has always contained characteristics of a political maneuver. Another matter of public concern might be that rigidities in wages could ensue from centralized bargaining, rigidities that could from time to time result in cost structures that are too high and thus lead to a stifling of individual creativity on the part of management. The introduction of new products or cheaper ways of producing the old might thus be curtailed. Finally, the public might worry about the implications of the obvious growth of monopolies on both sides of the bargaining table.

Is this trend inevitable? Are there natural limits to the size of the bargaining unit? The answers to these questions are, of course, not definitive but some judgments can be attempted. Several forces that contribute to the creation of larger units seem likely to continue. The first of these is the employers association. R. F. Hoxie observed as early as 1920 that "the employer association movement was in the beginning primarily defensive."[19] Nevertheless, these associations are likely to continue to exist, thus encouraging continued centralization of bargaining. Max Wortman, who studied the influences of the employer bargaining association on manufacturing firms in 1962, noted that manufacturing firms that were members of associations had less frequent work stoppages and lower grievance rates than those that were not. The differences were statistically significant. Severity of work stoppages and turnover rates were also less but not statistically significant.[20]

Management bargaining associations have taken different forms. Associations have been formed on a trade basis (some of these developed from trade associations formed for exchange of general information on the problems of the trade), on an industry basis, and on general bases. Labor economists have divided these employer bargaining associations according to their intended functions. The belligerent and the negotiatory associations are undoubtedly self-explanatory. The consultative form is as weak, or, if one prefers, as loose, as the title implies. Primarily found on the West Coast, the administrative association is the strongest form found in the United States today. Its strength lies in the fact that members must give their power of attorney to the association, a requirement that often causes management to shy away from joining.

The major problems of management bargaining associations are twofold. The first is lack of solidarity within the associations. Conflicts within an employers association may be as great or greater than within a union. The second problem arises when the association must make an offer to the union: How can several manufacturers with quite different cost structures agree to the same wage structure? These two potential sources of disagreement have been played upon by numerous unions; for example, the Teamsters, which we will discuss in detail later.

If in the case of a multiemployer bargain one employer is struck, the courts have held that it is acceptable for the others to institute a lockout.[21] Recent newspaper strikes in New York City provide examples of this activity.

The trend toward fewer and larger national unions also leads to increased centralization. In a 1957 study, Mark Kahn noted that the changing distribution of job territory (the functions within the job) among the national unions reflects the continuing search by every union for the kind of structure that would maximize what Selig Perlman and others have called "job control."[22] Perlman predicted that the bulk of organized labor would eventually fall within the jurisdiction of a small number of national unions, whose number would continue to decrease as time went on. Kahn defended this thesis by citing the following changes in the economy: the displacement of narrow-based unions by those with broader forms, the greater craft autonomy within industrial unions, the multiindustrial expansion of unions, the favorable consequences of size as such, and the very process of adjustment (meaning the settlement of jurisdictional conflicts and the like).

In 1966 eight unions dealing with General Electric demanded that the company meet with all eight at one time. The possible implications of this interesting development will be discussed later, but at this point we should note that such action may presage the formation of a different type of bargaining unit, one composed of several unions.

What will be the impact of a new form of general unionism on the bargaining structure within the American economy? If the Teamsters continue to gain in membership and if they succeed in their attempts to organize a variety of occupations will there be an increase in centralized bargaining? Will the Teamsters try to unify their bargaining?

Increased automation in industry will also affect the form bargaining takes. If increased technological innovation makes the assembly-line worker obsolete, what form will bargaining take? Unions have debated whether they can maintain interest and a sense of sharing a common purpose and problems (among workers) when a single worker operates one department, with the nearest other worker several hundred yards away. One is tempted to observe that if the initial problem of maintaining union membership is solved that form of bargaining is likely to be more centralized. The evidence presented in the 1956 *Monthly Labor Review*[23] suggests that multiemployer bargaining occurred more frequently in industries characterized by small establishments. If the number of workers employed by a large (in terms of capital investment) manufacturing concern is considerably cut over time, it is likely that those who remain will want to broaden their ranks and therefore their strength by bargaining jointly with employees of other firms. They would, of course, have to weigh the potential success of their combined force against the possibility that the managements involved might also choose to associate themselves for bargaining purposes.

Growing heterogeneity would cer-

tainly limit the size of the bargaining unit. When the interests of the employees involved become too diverse and when the problems of various management structures are too unrelated, pressure for centralization of bargaining will be likely to come to a halt. Many unions, aside from the Teamsters, are already dispersed across industry lines and many industries, aside from General Electric, have several unions to deal with.

Centralization takes a variety of forms. We will start with what might be termed the most extreme, industry-wide collective bargaining.

Bargaining is on an industry-wide basis when negotiations over one or more issues are conducted by two negotiating bodies, one of which on the workers' side represents, either by formal or informal authorization, a majority of all employees within the industry, or a majority of all employees in a particular category of work, and the other of which on the employers' side represents, either by formal or informal authorization, a majority of all firms and plants within the industry.[24]

There can be deviations from this generalized description or definition. Sometimes a minority of firms in an industry are not covered. The organization for bargaining may be formal, as in the case of an employers association, or informal, as a group of employers; the union involved may be a craft union or an industrial union. The word industry is usually applied to producers of a similar product. Thus it is possible that the industry does not coincide with the union's jurisdiction and problems may arise if there are attempts on the part of the union to broaden the definition of the industry. As noted previously, the Taft-Hartley Act provided that a union could not strike to force the employer to join a particular association. Industrywide collective bargaining then may mean bargaining with a relatively narrow, homogenous group of firms. Three industries are customarily discussed as being those in which industrywide bargaining is most fully developed: railroads, men's clothing, and coal. Coal mining will be discussed in detail later to show the actual operation of such a bargaining form.

Other multiplant bargaining systems include the companywide system and regional and local area bargaining. In the first situation, basic issues are settled on a companywide basis, but there is an effort on the part of management to adhere to local wage levels. Nonetheless this bargaining form does tend to resemble an industrywide bargaining situation. The regional and local area bargaining units probably predominate in the multiemployer bargaining. Many of these units came into being when craft unions insisted on the same treatment for their workers regardless of where they were employed. Single craft bargaining for a whole industry remains relatively rare. Within any of these situations exceptions to wage structures may exist, allowed by the union because of extenuating circumstances, but these are not publicized because the unions want to make employers whom they are about to deal with think that there are no exceptions.

Among the industries bargaining on a regional basis are the following: canning and preserving, dyeing and finishing, fishing, hosiery manufacturing, leather tanning, longshoring, lumbering, shipping, metal mining, nonferrous metal manufacturing, paper and pulp manufacturing, shipbuilding, shoe manufacturing, trucking (intercity), woolen and worsted textile manufacturing. Note the broadness of the product market in each case. Multiemployer bargaining units are more prevalent in big cities and are found more frequently on the West Coast than in other sections of the country.

In pattern bargaining, the other dominant form that centralization of bargaining takes, the union reaches a settlement or "key bargain" with one employer, hoping to gain the same terms from other employers. The term pattern actually refers to basic changes in wages and fringe benefits negotiated during the key bargain. The key bargain may be settled with the leader in the industry or with any of the large firms. Often the effects are little different from the situation of association bargaining, except that no employers association is involved. Oligopolistic industries have tended to favor pattern bargaining, but recently in single-unit (one employer–one union) bargaining the use of patterns has become more apparent. Often the patterns are not confined to a single industry, since one union may copy another.

The steel and automobile industries are often listed as major examples of industries in which pattern bargaining predominates, but the two situations are different. In steel the situation is that of price leadership.

The almost unvarying practice in the past had been for U.S. Steel to take the leadership in negotiations and settlements. Bargaining committees of other companies ordinarily marked time with their union counterparts until the settlement on a basic contract with U.S. Steel had been achieved. It should be emphasized, however, that the situation has not been quite as stereotyped as the foregoing generalization might suggest. There have been frequent variations from the U.S. Steel settlement on both wages and non-wage items to meet special situations, and there were occasions when a company other than U.S. Steel led in the settlements.[25]

In the automobile industry, on the other hand, each firm remains independent and innovating and the United Automobile Workers bargain on a company basis, choosing one company or another to set the pattern for the industry. The auto industry will be discussed in detail later as an example of pattern bargaining.

Although wage leadership predates the key bargain, the advent of unionization has strengthened the similarity of wage changes in an industry.[26] Arthur Ross refers to pattern bargaining as coercive comparison and speaks of the orbits within which it operates. How effective price leadership will be also depends on the situation in the community, since management will want to pay on a scale appropriate for the community in which they are located. The nature of the product market is also of great importance. If the product is highly competitive, union attempts to achieve a pattern of wage increases that will be passed on to the consuming public are much more likely to fail. It also is possible to have "fractional" pattern bargaining, in which the result is a satellite bargain that resembles the key bargain in many respects but differs in some way because it has been adapted to fit peculiar local conditions.

Another variation of pattern bargaining is the form contract as used by the Teamsters. The union draws up what it feels is a workable contract. This contract is then presented to each of the many employers with whom the union must deal in the hope that each will agree to the terms. This variation will be discussed in case-study form later in this chapter.

We will now discuss selected bargaining forms in detail. Our first example is that of industrywide bargaining. When this phrase is used, many

economists and historians immediately think of the bituminous coal industry. Although this industry does not present a perfect example of industrywide bargaining and although certain problems peculiar to the bituminous coal industry further cloud the picture, we will use it as our first case study.

The first attempt at industrywide bargaining in the bituminous coal industry dates back to 1885, when the National Federation of Miners and Laborers of the United States (the United Mine Workers of America was formed in 1890) adopted a constitution that contained in its preamble the following statement:

> Local, district and state organizations have done much toward ameliorating the condition of our craft in the past, but today neither district nor state unions can regulate the markets to which their coal is shipped. . . . In a federation of all lodges and branches of miners' unions lies our only hope. Single-handed we can do nothing, but federated there is no power of wrong that we may not openly defy. . . .[27]

For one year, 1886, a widespread agreement was in force, including miners and operators from Illinois, Indiana, Ohio, and West Virginia. During the following two years dissension among operators led to the gradual withdrawal of the participants in this agreement. In 1898 a broader agreement, called the Central Competitive Field Compact, was reached, covering operators and miners of Illinois, Indiana, Ohio, and Pittsburgh. This compact, which, with changing provisions, remained in force until 1927, covered length of workday, wages, and tonnage rates. Wages within the states covered by the compact were higher than in the southern area that included Kentucky, Tennessee, and West Virginia, but production increased more rapidly in the southern mining fields. As Waldo E. Fisher has pointed out, "The rapid increase in production in the southern fields, however, must also be explained in terms of the competitive advantage held by the southern operators as the result of more favorable terms and conditions of employment."[28]

The nature of this special industry deserves comment. In the 1970s we are well aware that coal is a declining industry as a result of the competition of other fuels. Furthermore, increased mechanization has cut the demand for labor in the mines. Early in this century, however, the industry could also be characterized as highly competitive, particularly between different geographic regions, and highly unstable (shifting demand and supply).

The goals of the United Mine Workers (UMW) have long been stated as: (1) the steady improvement of the economic well-being of the miners, (2) the stabilization of wage rates during downward cyclical fluctuations, and (3) the stabilization of competitive relationships among firms and producing areas in the bituminous coal industry.[29] The union early in its history accepted the introduction of mechanized production as a way of improving the status of the worker, deciding to seek to share the benefits of increased productivity that resulted.

In the last days of the Central Competitive Field Compact in the mid-twenties interregional competition increased as demand for coal declined, and John L. Lewis led the miners to demand "no backward step" in wages. To the UMW the source of the industry's problem is excess capacity and Lewis was perfectly willing to see a cut in the numbers of both mines and miners. Between 1927 and 1933 there was a return to smaller bargaining units than previously. However, after

the passage of the National Industrial Relations Act in 1933 the UMW entered into active organizing and soon completed this task. Although conflicts between mine operators continued, conflict between union and nonunion miners ceased.

The late thirties and the war years were more successful for the UMW than the late twenties. One indication of this success was the 1941 inclusion in each contract of a "most favored nation" type clause stating that should the union win a higher settlement from one employer it would immediately become effective everywhere. The fact that the operators could make such a guarantee, however, implies greater operator cohesion than really exists. The lack of cohesion or discipline between the operators is one reason for the bargaining strength of the union. In reality, important conflicts of interest in areas of differing profit margins and circumstances of production remain between the firms in the northern Appalachian fields and those in the southern area.[30] Lack of cohesion among the operators has prevented the establishment of lasting unity during periods of bargaining with the union. During World War II, there was a single bargaining unit of operators from the Appalachian fields but the southern operators withdrew from this shortly after the end of the war. During the last years of his presidency Lewis dealt successfully with operators at informal luncheon meetings. The miners joined the operators in the formation of the National Coal Policy Conference, an alliance to protect the industry.

Much of the union's strength is also derived from the broad discretionary powers of the presidency. Morton Baratz notes that all officers of the international union apparently owe their status to the president. Furthermore, 70 percent of the presidents of district unions are in a similar situation, since they are "provisional appointees."[31]

This close approximation to industrywide bargaining can be effectively compared to pattern bargaining. One of the most popular examples of pattern bargaining in the United States today is provided by the UAW and the automotive industry. Most of the material for this section is taken from Robert M. Macdonald's in-depth study of the industry (1963), although some reference is made to an earlier study (1958) by Harold M. Levinson. Levinson pointed out that pattern bargaining could result either in identical benefits provided in the key bargain, or in "an equivalent, or near equivalent, total 'package' of benefits, regardless of their specific form."[32] Because of the increasing complexity of contracts and the growing number and variety of fringe benefits, Levinson favors the second definition.

As Macdonald notes, although bargaining in the auto industry is done on a companywide basis it is pattern bargaining. "Through strong, centralized direction of negotiations, the international union has been able to pursue a tightly coordinated strategy that takes full advantage of the intense sales rivalry between firms."[33] The union technique of "whipsawing" the employers shows off to advantage in this case.

Management in the big three automobile companies (General Motors, Ford, and Chrysler) has not accepted these union techniques without a fight. For a time their actions resembled the first stages of industrywide collective bargaining. In 1958 the big three tried joint acceptance of common goals and pursuance of a common strategy. During this period of "parallel" bargaining these companies made comparable, and in some respects identical, proposals and concessions. Although this strategy was apparently successful in 1958, in 1961 the union countered it by inducing American Motors to set a substantially higher settlement pattern in return for improvements in its competitive position through concessions in the work rules area.[34]

Macdonald uses General Motors as an example of how an automobile company bargains with the UAW. Although 90 percent of General Motors' unionized workers are members of the UAW, they belong to 131 bargaining units in sixty-six cities in eighteen states.[35] The union has a national General Motors Council, which coordinates local demands and formulates policies in dealing with a common employer. Two delegates are sent from each bargaining unit. Additional representatives are also sent, according to the size of the unit. This council meets annually, with special meetings called as needed. Subcouncils are organized along functional lines; each sends a member to the negotiating committee. Macdonald notes that the international apparently handles major economic issues while the subcouncil representatives concentrate on modification of the working agreement.[36] Before any agreement can be submitted to local memberships for ratification it must be approved by a majority of the negotiating committee and of the national council.

Management policies at General Motors are formulated through two committees of the Board, the operations policy committee and the administrative committee. The administration of the policies and the negotiations are carried out by the labor relations committee under the vice-president in charge of personnel administration. Local committees on both sides negotiate local agreements.

Until the mid-1950s, locals of the minor automotive firms were comparatively independent, but as a result of the intense competition of that decade, the international, by bargaining for them, came to the rescue of the local officers who had to explain to members why increased demands were not going to be met.

Macdonald notes that the minor auto companies have given the UAW higher settlements in the past than have the big three. The commonly accepted explanation is that the minor firms are in a weaker bargaining position; they cannot afford to risk a work stoppage. Although he did not deny the relative vulnerability of these firms, Macdonald feels that the variations in efficiency with which the respective managements dealt with the labor relations function were at least partially responsible.[37]

Levinson's study, which covered the 1946–1955 period, was focused on the UAW also, but it omitted the major three auto producers and included some eighty-seven smaller firms (both inside and outside of the auto industry) in the Detroit area that had contracts with the UAW. Levinson found that pattern enforcement was much stronger in the larger units, particularly those closely tied into the auto industry. His study, however, concentrated upon deviations below the pattern, deviations caused by economic factors. Levinson contended that union negotiators did not consider the elasticity of demand for labor in the firm to be relevant to the settlement, although he admitted that there were deviations for economic reasons, and that internal political considerations appeared to play an insignificant role. Levinson summarized the union's approach in this way:

. . . given the key bargain as a standard, its primary objective is to en-

force that standard in order, in effect, to "take labor out of competition." However, the union does adjust its demands to the needs of the particular situation, either through a below-pattern settlement or increases in productivity, if these adjustments can be made without presenting any serious threat to this primary objective.[38]

Under the leadership of James Hoffa, the Teamsters attempted to establish a master contract that would apply to all areas of the country, a tactic that greatly resembles pattern bargaining. The unified approach that the Teamsters have assumed is not a reaction to existing management associations, although management is attempting to form associations in reaction to the union's threat. Multi-employer bargaining has been most noticeable in those industries characterized by small shops, each with only a few employees. Certainly the trucking industry fits that description.

The union's efforts in this direction coincide with the ascendence of Hoffa to the presidency upon the imprisonment of Dave Beck. Hoffa had reached prominence through the Central States Drivers Councils (CSDC), strengthening these area organizations as he grew in power. Although the Teamsters' attempts at unification have strengthened the employers associations, Hoffa's most successful bargaining technique appears to have been based on a divide-and-conquer strategy. His strike threats were selective, and never included all employers in an area. In most cases, although association bargaining existed, individual truckers have been found who were willing to sign before the association had agreed (even when these truckers were represented by the association), with the result that the truckers respect the union and Hoffa and direct their ill-will at their fellow truckers.[39] At one point in the 1960–1961 negotiations of the CSDC Hoffa taped the proceedings and played these tapes back out of context to union meetings.[40]

The other major geographic areas that bargain approximately as a unit are in New England and in the Western states. Differences occur, however. In New England, the trucking firms argued that because their hauls were shorter and because they encountered heavier traffic, their wage structures should remain different from those prevailing in the Midwest. The situation differed in the West because of the existence of a few unusually large and influential truckers and a history of reliance on an outside arbitrator (an idea that strongly appealed to management). The West also has had a shorter experience with anything resembling a master contract. Contracts were renegotiated in 1961 and then again in 1964, 1967, and 1970. In the latter year union members in various areas opposed a uniform contract, opposition which led to wildcat strikes.

The direction in which Hoffa was moving was obvious from the wording of the 1961 contracts, most of which contained some form of this clause taken from the CSDC contract: "The parties in this Agreement accept the principle of a National Over-the-Road Agreement and are willing to enter into negotiations for purpose of negotiating such National Agreement."[41]

Arthur A. Sloane has accurately summarized the current situation in the trucking industry. "Moreover, even the master contract might be more accurately described as a 'half contract:' geographic and other supplements to the basic contract still provide for differing working conditions and economic terms across the country, and only when these are appended can there be said to be a 'whole' contract in each case."[42] Of course, the contract signed by each automobile manufacturer with the UAW is also less than a whole contract until adjustments are made for conditions and problems in each plant.

In July 1966, the national convention of the International Brotherhood of Teamsters, Chauffeurs, Warehousemen and Helpers of America, reported on in the August issue of the *Teamster* magazine, amended the union's constitution to allow for industrywide and areawide collective bargaining:

Section 4 (a): If a majority of the affiliated Local Unions vote for area, multi-area or national, company-wide or industry-wide negotiations for an area, national, company-wide or industry-wide contract, all involved affiliated Local Unions shall be bound by such vote, must participate in such area, multi-area or national, company-wide or industry-wide bargaining and shall be bound by the contract approved as provided below. Upon completion of negotiation by a conference, trade division, or by any committee appointed by the General President, subject to the approval of the General Executive Board, to engage in negotiation of an industry, area, multi-area or national or company-wide contract, such contract shall be submitted to the membership covered by said contract proposal for their approval or rejection.

. . . Local Unions which are parties to such contracts may not withdraw from such bargaining unit except upon six (6) months' notice and for good cause shown to the satisfaction of the appropriate Conference, Trade Division or Committee, and approved by the General Executive Board of the International Union. If any company-wide, or industry-wide contract proposal will deprive its involved members of better existing conditions of general application to all such involved members of the local union it may appeal to the General Executive Board which shall have the final authority to determine whether such alleged better general conditions shall be continued or shall yield to the over-all gains of the proposed contract. Unless mutually agreed to, no Local Union shall suffer any economic loss.

The nationwide disunity in employer ranks that has appeared in the trucking industry can be attributed to two major factors. The first is the economic factor (some of the following points can be applied to other industries as well). Higher costs affect each trucker differently because each has a different cost structure. Therefore, a wage bill that is acceptable to one employer may be totally unacceptable to another. In addition, the trucking industry is particularly characterized by individualism on the management side. Trucking falls under the aegis of the Interstate Commerce Commission when state lines are crossed and individual firms feel the regulatory effects of the government differently.[43]

The second factor that contributed to employer disunity was, of course, Hoffa's divide-and-conquer technique. He supported group bargaining, getting mutually suspicious groups to unite. But the strike threats were against a few targets, which were not announced but rumored (and apparently chosen) in advance. Always Hoffa appealed to the self-interest of the employer.[44]

Whether the Teamsters' technique is too much the creation of one man to be carried over to another industry, or even to be applied to the trucking industry without Hoffa, only time can tell. However, all indications are that the master contract, half a contract though it may be, will be more and more widely applied. Teamster Acting President Frank Fitzsimmons achieved a personal victory with the ratification of a national contract by more than 70 percent of the membership in the spring of 1970 despite dissenting voices from Teamsters in Chicago and the steelhaulers.

The divide-and-conquer action used by Hoffa against management parallels the tactics often used by a single large employer who deals with a number of unions. In their efforts to counteract this technique unions are frequently led by the Industrial Union Department of the AFL-CIO.

In 1966 the negotiating sessions at General Electric and Westinghouse were considered headline material when eight unions united to state the wishes of 160,000 union members employed by the two firms. That they had the support of the AFL-CIO is evident in this statement from the AFL-CIO *The American Federationist.* "In pledging labor's full resources to the joint bargaining effort, the convention resolution warned that if these firms are permitted to maintain substandard conditions or flout the legal obligation to bargain in good faith, 'they will exert a drag upon the whole field of collective bargaining.' "[45] The "full resources" mentioned included $8 million or more to finance negotiations with General Electric. The two companies vowed not to sit down with the union group, but the leader of the group stated that it was only necessary for the involved unions to maintain the "same demands everywhere and stick to them."[46] The General Electric–Westinghouse negotiations represented the technique of *coordinated bargaining,* in which two or more unions negotiate for individual unit contracts containing similar terms.

The NLRB has upheld the right of advisors from other unions to be present in negotiating sessions[47] and the group of unions has tried this to assure that similarity of demands is achieved. Sharing of information by unions is, of course, not new. In August 1966, the NLRB petitioned for a federal injunction against General Electric on grounds of reasonable cause "to believe that G.E. is violating the Taft-Hartley Act in refusing to bargain with an IUE committee which includes coalition representatives." In June 1969 the U.S. Circuit Court of Appeals held that no employer might refuse to negotiate a contract merely because a union's bargaining team included representatives of other unions.

In *coalition bargaining,* the bargaining unit is actually changed (subject to NLRB acceptance). Although this form of bargaining is obviously more difficult to establish and maintain than coordinated bargaining, it has proved successful in some cases. In 1964, for example, American Home Products was successfully "taken on" by a five-union group led by the Oil, Chemical and Atomic Workers Union, while the UAW and the International Association of Machinists achieved similar results vis-à-vis Revere Copper and Brass in 1965. Occasionally, union discord ends an attempt to form a bargaining coalition. Such a failure appeared in negotiations with Wilson and Company, sporting goods manufacturers.

The technique of union coalitions raises interesting questions for the future. Will it eventually lead to union mergers or will controls be imposed by the National Labor Relations Board? Will public opinion be adversely aroused? The 1969–1970 union negotiations with General Electric produced a greater understanding between the United Electrical, Radio and Machine Workers and the International Union of Electrical, Radio and Machine Workers, which had long been competitors for the allegiance of electrical workers. Furthermore, the feuding labor leaders George Meany and Walter Reuther were able to agree on their support for this concerted union effort.

To test the impact of multiemployer bargains is not a simple matter. The available evidence suggests, however, that pattern bargaining has not produced uniform change in wages and fringe benefits in either oligopolistic or competitive industries, but that there has been some tendency in this direction. How is this tendency to be measured? Richard Lester and Edward A. Robie cite statistics to prove that wages have not risen more under this type of contract than they have under single-employer contracts. They refer to these wage decisions as more "sensible and far-sighted," but they do note that wages tend to be more stable and rigid than normal.[48]

Certainly the number of strikes is relevant. Is the trend to more or fewer strikes under multiemployer arrangements? What other factors might influence the number of strikes? Does a management bargaining association preclude the free entry of new firms to this particular enterprise? What has the impact of this bargaining situation been on the structure of the firm that is involved? On the structure of the union? How much voice has the individual worker surrendered? Are these last few questions answerable or subject to quantification?

Lester and Robie's 1946 study (which included data from the 1920s and 1930s) concerned seven industries in which national or regional bargaining had played a role: Pressed and blown glass, pottery, stoves, full-fashioned hosiery, silk and rayon dyeing and finishing, flat glass, and West Coast pulp and paper. They observed that wage patterns deriving from multiemployer agreements had not apparently placed any additional restraint on technological improvement and new invention. However, the age of the study calls the validity of this conclusion into question in the 1970s.

Another point to be considered when weighing the impact of nationwide bargaining is the possible increase in monopolistic or collusive practices. Here again, Lester and Robie note no significant impact, observing that "Local interests and the interests of smaller firms have generally been well represented in wage negotiations under national or regional bargaining in the seven industries."[49] They concluded that concentration of wage changes in "one industry-wide determination avoids the labor unrest and series of strikes that often accompany competition between firms in the timing of wage changes or competition between rival unions in exacting concessions from employers."

This 1946 study also points out that wage differentials may continue to exist despite the existence of industry-wide bargaining. We should also note that industry- or marketwide stabilization of wages and working conditions may occur without unionization. The steel industry provides a good illustration of the development of uniform wage rate increases at an early date (1904) in widely dispersed labor markets. A recent case study of collective bargaining is relevant to the question of the bargaining unit.

In his study of wages and fringe benefits in six West Coast industries (published in 1966) Harold Levinson considers economic, political, and "pure power" elements as determinants of bargaining outcomes. The union is in a better position if the market structure of the industry is such that the entrance of firms is difficult, assuming the union has established control of those in existence. Levinson does not put as much stress on the political aspect but concerns himself with "pure power." The union

or management capable of exercising militant power is most likely to be successful in wage settlements. Thus Levinson seems to place less emphasis on the scope of the bargaining unit.[50]

The most universal criticism of multiemployer bargaining centers on loss of worker sovereignty in the union. Centralization of decision-making is feared as is the labor monopoly that presumably ensues. George W. Brooks has stated:

I believe that the single most important characteristic of collective bargaining structure is the location of decision-making authority. . . . In its simplest terms I would favor plant-centered unionism. I would like to see the maximum amount of collective bargaining—both negotiations and grievances—handled and decided by local management and local union leadership on a face-to-face basis. With numerous qualifications for particular localities, it seems to me that this is the goal most worth pursuing, and that it is much more concrete and realizable goal than "democracy" or "participation."[51]

One possible line of action for critics who seek to end broader bargaining is a redefinition of the antitrust laws. Archibald Cox and Douglas Brown, like many others, believe that unions can only be covered by the antitrust laws when they are tampering with the product market.[52] The Supreme Court had seemed to follow this interpretation in the Apex Hosiery and Leader decision (1940), but more recently it appears to have changed its views (see Chapter 3). Legislation is occasionally proposed (so far unsuccessfully) in Congress to limit bargaining to a single employer and a local union.

Brooks' suggestion is to inject the competitive spirit into industrial relations, by breaking up industrywide bargaining units except when they are necessary to promote a stable market for the product.[53] In particular, he feels that the details of a contract could be settled locally. Some of the blame for the growth of the larger units is assigned to the NLRB, which agreed to them in the interest of stability. In this regard Brooks stated that the important relevant powers of the NLRB were: (1) rule of exclusive representation, (2) principle of majority rule, (3) the rule that the electoral unit for purposes of the NLRB election and the bargaining unit for purposes of negotiations are the same.[54]

The future of multiemployer bargaining in the United States depends upon the structure of unions and management, the attitude of the public, and the attitude of the government. The latter is evident in the conclusions reached by a congressional investigation committee in the mid-1960s: "[It] is our conclusion that in the area of multiemployer association collective bargaining the balancing of power between unions and employers has been quite successfully achieved. Those who fear the results of "big unions" and "big employers" will gain very little support for their positions from the history and results of multiemployer association collective bargaining."[55] In the eyes of this committee at least there is no point in the government's trying to curb multiemployer bargaining.

Again, as automation reduces the number of workers per shop pressure for larger bargaining units may increase, since the union may begin to feel that the single shop is too weak a base.

The Bargaining Unit Elsewhere

Although American unions have adjusted to the widening markets and to the increased size of businesses by forming regional and industrywide bargaining units the focal point of much union activity is still the local. Many industrial relations experts feel that the key to understanding collective bargaining still lies in the individual shop. By contrast, a far larger proportion of foreign unions engage in multiunit and even nationwide bargaining. Often they are virtually absent from the shop, despite a few efforts to gain access in recent years.

The other feature of bargaining units in the United States that distinguishes them from those elsewhere is their enjoyment of exclusive bargaining rights. Not only are unions in this country afforded certain guarantees of recognition and assurance that an employer will have to deal with them if they win a majority of the votes, but they are also guaranteed exclusive jurisdiction within the perimeter of the bargaining unit as defined by the NLRB. Unless a union is displaced from power by a majority vote of the unit's workers, no other union has the right to represent workers in that unit. Granted under the terms of the Wagner Act, such protection is unique.

Great Britain

Collective bargaining is less centralized in Great Britain than it is in other countries of Western Europe, but by American standards is still highly centralized. Key settlements, particularly in the railroads and in engineering, set the standards for elsewhere in the economy. The existing institutional arrangements make a high degree of centralization almost inevitable. Employers are highly organized into employers associations (the employers' equivalent of the Trades Union Congress is the British Employer Confederation [BEC]). Furthermore, strong informal pressure deters them from making settlements outside the one negotiated by the association (see Chapter 16). Similarly, British unions are best equipped to handle bargaining on a broad scale. Of the 635 national unions, nine account for over 50 percent of the total union membership in Great Britain. Furthermore, several different unions may be represented within a single plant or even department. To complicate things still further, a worker's membership in a particular union is usually determined by his place of residence rather than his place of work. Thus, the local to which he belongs may not even be in the plant in which he is employed.

In recent years there has been some trend toward plant bargaining conducted by the shop stewards (union representatives in the shop). Stewards (over 175,000 in number) handle such items as piece rates, bonuses, and individual grievances. The importance of these items should not be minimized —often more than one-third of a worker's earnings is accounted for under piece rates and bonuses. Ironically many items are settled orally between the foremen and the steward, and no formal written agreement between union and management is involved. As yet, the locals have been too weak to be particularly effective and frequently resort to wildcat strikes. Local bargaining has also been hindered by the jealousy of national union officers anxious to preserve their prerogatives of power.

Part of the vacuum at the local level has been filled by workers councils, which were formed to undertake joint consultation with employers. Although all workers (even if they are not union members) are eligible to vote for representatives and the councils thus far have had relatively little impact on British industrial relations, unions have welcomed the councils as a potential foothold in the local plant.

Since the councils have no power to enforce their suggestions, many employers have felt they were a good method of establishing better communications with workers in the plant. However, it still remains to be seen whether the British work councils will be replaced by stronger union locals or instead prevent their further development.

Industrywide bargaining in Great Britain started as an effort by the unions to curb competitive wage cutting during business depressions; it has continued because many of the unions believe that it enhances their bargaining power. Today industrywide bargaining is in common use in every major industry except oil refining.

Western Europe

Because the European countries in our sample are so similar in respect to bargaining units we will treat them as a group. In France, Germany, Italy, and Sweden, industrywide or national bargaining is the rule, and the union has little part in local affairs. Like Great Britain, all four countries have experienced a certain amount of "wage drift."[56] Such drift occurs because unions seek to protect the plants (especially weaker ones) in the industry by making more moderate demands. Since many of these countries have a shortage of labor, the more efficient plants have bid for workers by paying wage rates higher than those demanded by the union. Understandably many union members have begun to question the value of their unions. The lack of grievance procedure at the local level has also diminished worker interest in unions.

Closely associated with the apathy of many union members has been the feeling that regional or industrywide bargaining reduces the extent of participatory democracy, an attitude that is particularly pronounced in Sweden. We noted earlier in regard to the United States that larger bargaining units do tend to make participation by the rank and file more difficult. Unions in Europe have also been concerned with this problem because, unlike England, their shop stewards are not necessarily members of the union. Although national officers in Great Britain have sometimes been jealous of the stewards, the stewards there do at least supply a link between the national union and the union members that is often missing in Europe.

The work councils have had only limited effectiveness in both France and Italy. They have been somewhat more successful in West Germany. However, even though in Germany up to 80 percent of the councils' members are also members of a union, there has been considerable hard feeling between the two organizations. Work councils are usually forbidden to discuss any item included on the agenda for collective bargaining and unions do have some check on the activities of the councils. Nevertheless, councils have at times undermined the strike action of even the strongest German unions.

The stresses associated with broadly based bargaining in Europe have prompted some moves in the direction of decentralization. German labor unions, for example, have tried to persuade shop stewards to act as go-betweens and thus ease relations between the unions and the work councils. German unions have also adopted as their rallying cry the expression "close to the undertaking" to signify their intention to become more involved at the local level.

A 1950 French law providing for plant-level agreements had little effect for a number of years. This was partly because many French union leaders, indoctrinated in a class-warfare philos-ophy, wanted no close contacts with individual employers and partly because many French plants were so small that such bargaining was not feasible. The growing size of French firms, plus some relaxation in the ideological rigidity of the union leaders, has encouraged a shift toward more plant-level bargaining.

Swedish unions have felt the damaging effects of centralized bargaining less than the other countries although even there there have been repercussions. Centralization first became marked during World War II, was abandoned in the early 1950s and then restored after 1956. A general level of wage increase for a particular year is negotiated by the L. O. and the S. A. F.; thereafter bargaining continues at the industry level. Although the terms set within an industry are subject to review by the L. O. and the S. A. F., wage increases higher than those set by the two central bodies are not unheard of. In such cases, bargaining at the plant level determines the apportionment of the gains established by the industry negotiators as to how much will go toward improving the various items in the contract.

Israel

Whereas in many countries centralized bargaining has arisen in response to expanding industries, widening markets, and the danger of wage competition between firms in the expanding industries, Israel's highly centralized system of bargaining derives largely from the lack of large employers and the bargaining power of the Histadrut. The usual procedure is for a central bargain to be made between the Manufacturers' Association, including representatives from all industries, and the Histadrut. These two groups agree to general standards that serve as a precondition for bargaining at the industry level. Details are then worked out between the employers in a particular industry and the appropriate national union.

Despite the centralized structure of Israeli bargaining, local unions are still important. When employers are not represented in the Manufacturers' Association, bargaining in their plants is done at the local level. Even where national agreements have been made, locals in such plants have the power to make adjustments appropriate for local conditions, and locals have in some instances refused to abide by the national agreement.

India

Except in rare instances, Indian unions have been largely ineffective at the plant level, primarily because of the organizational weakness of the unions, the opposition of employers, and the fact that (as in England) a large number of unions may be represented in a single plant. Because of the unions' general ineffectiveness and the wide markets in India, there has been considerable pressure for Indian unions to engage in multiemployer bargaining. Official government policy has also encouraged movement in this direction. Sharp variations between regions in the cost of living, however, have sometimes created serious problems in setting uniform wage standards.

Japan

Although Japanese labor unions are active politically at the national level, in economic affairs they are oriented strictly toward individual enterprises. All bargaining is done at the plant level, and the issues raised vary considerably from plant to plant. As a result, union federations have little authority in Japan.

Mexico

Bargaining units in Mexico have tended to expand in size. However, a number of different unions may still represent workers in the same plant. In such situations the employer is required to make his contract with that union that has the largest membership in the plant.

Conclusions

Obviously no single trend in bargaining unit size and composition prevails in all the countries we have examined. The United States appears to be moving toward larger units (although the majority of contracts are still settled at plant level). On the other hand, in countries like West Germany, Italy, France, and Sweden, where local plant bargaining is something of an innovation, the unions are increasing attempts to enter the plants. The mixture of all sizes of units and all types of bargaining (pattern, industrywide, master contract, and single plant) that will undoubtedly be the result of current trends in the United States might eventually be matched in other Western countries.

NOTES

1. Harold W. Davey, *Contemporary Collective Bargaining,* 2nd ed. (Englewood Cliffs, N.J.: Prentice-Hall, 1959), p. 82.
2. George Barnett, "National and District Systems of Collective Bargaining in the United States," *Quarterly Journal of Economics,* 26 (May 1912), 425–443.
3. Frank C. Pierson, "Multi-Employer Bargaining," Reprint No. 4 (University of California, Los Angeles: Institute of Industrial Relations, 1949), pp. 17–18.
4. Harold W. Davey, *Contemporary Collective Bargaining,* 2nd ed. (Englewood Cliffs, N.J.: Prentice-Hall, 1959), p. 84.
5. Neil W. Chamberlain and James W.

Kuhn, *Collective Bargaining,* 2nd ed. (New York: McGraw-Hill, 1965), p. 240.

6. L. C. Chase and E. M. Moor, "Characteristics of Major Union Contracts," *Monthly Labor Review* (July 1956), pp. 805–811.

7. John T. Dunlop, *Collective Bargaining* (Chicago: Irwin, 1949), p. 27.

8. Harry A. Millis and Emily Clark Brown, *From the Wagner Act to Taft-Hartley* (Chicago: University of Chicago Press, 1950), p. 140.

9. *Ibid.,* p. 144.

10. *Ibid.,* p. 150.

11. As quoted by Millis and Brown, *op. cit.,* p. 523.

12. For further discussion of this point, see pp. 104–106.

13. Everett M. Kassalow, "White-Collar Unionism in the United States," Industrial Relations Research Institute, University of Wisconsin, Reprint Series No. 77, pp. 332–333.

14. George W. Brooks, "The Case for Decentralized Collective Bargaining," in Richard A. Lester (ed.), *Labor: Readings on Major Issues* (New York: Random House, 1965), p. 434.

15. Davey, *op. cit.,* p. 91.

16. Neil Chamberlain, "Collective Bargaining in the United States," in Adolf Sturmthal (ed.), *Contemporary Collective Bargaining in Seven Countries* (Ithaca, N.Y.: Institute of International Industrial and Labor Relations, 1957), p. 307.

17. Brooks, *op cit.,* p. 434.

18. Davey, *op. cit.,* 93–94.

19. R. F. Hoxie in "Trade Unionism in the United States," p. 201, quoted in Kenneth M. McCaffree, "A Theory of the Origin and Development of Employer Associations," Industrial Relations Research Association, *Proceedings,* 1962, pp. 56–68.

20. Max S. Wortman, Jr., "Influences of Employer Bargaining Associations in Manufacturing Firms," Industrial Relations Research Association, *Proceedings* (1962), p. 81.

21. Charles M. Rehmus, "Multiemployer Bargaining," *Current History,* 48 (August 1965), 92.

22. Mark Kahn, "Contemporary Structural Changes in Organized Labor," Industrial Relations Research Association *Proceedings* (1957), p. 171.

23. See pp. 75–76 of this book.

24. Pierson, *op. cit.,* pp. 8–9.

25. Quoted in Chamberlain and Kuhn, *op. cit.,* p. 227, from *Collective Bargaining in the Basic Steel Industry,* U.S. Department of Labor, 1961, p. 86.

26. Chamberlain, *op. cit.,* p. 261.

27. Morton S. Baratz, *The Union and the Coal Industry* (New Haven, Conn.: Yale University Press, 1955), p. 76: quotes from C. Evans, *History of the United Mine Workers of America* (1918).

28. Waldo E. Fisher, *Collective Bargaining in the Bituminous Coal Industry: An Appraisal,* (Philadelphia: University of Pennsylvania Press, 1948), p. 17.

29. Baratz, *op. cit.,* p. 51.

30. *Ibid.,* p. 79.

31. *Ibid.,* p. 78.

32. Harold M. Levinson, "Pattern Bargaining by the United Automobile Workers," *Labor Law Journal* (September 1958), p. 669.

33. Robert M. Macdonald, *Collective Bargaining in the Automotive Industry* (New Haven, Conn.: Yale University Press, 1963), p. 5.

34. *Ibid.,* p. 6.

35. *Ibid.,* p. 6.

36. *Ibid.,* p. 8.

37. *Ibid.,* pp. 311 ff. These pages include a lengthy discussion of differences in the bargaining techniques of the five auto producers.

38. Levinson, *op. cit.,* 673–674.

39. Arthur A. Sloane, "Collective Bargaining in Trucking: Prelude to a National Contract," *Industrial and Labor Relations Review,* 19 (October, 1965), 32.

40. *Ibid.,* p. 25.

41. Ralph and Estelle James, "Hoffa's Acquisition of Industrial Power," *Industrial Relations* (May 1963), p. 92.

42. Sloane, *op. cit.,* p. 21.

43. Sloane, *op. cit.,* 38–39.

44. *Ibid.,* 40.

45. "The Labor Movement," AFL–CIO, *The American Federationist* (January 1966), p. 21.

46. David Lasser, as quoted by Frederick C. Klein in "New Labor Linkup," *Wall Street Journal* (February 15, 1966), p. 1.

47. Klein, *op. cit.,* p. 14.

48. Richard Lester and Edward Robie, *Wages Under National and Regional Col-*

lective Bargaining (Princeton, N.J.: Industrial Relations Section, Princeton University, 1946), pp. 93–95.

49. *Ibid.*, p. 95.

50. Harold M. Levinson, *Determining Forces in Collective Wage Bargaining* (New York: Wiley, 1966).

51. Brooks, *op. cit.*, pp. 427–428.

52. Archibald Cox, "Labor and the Antitrust Laws, A Preliminary Analysis," *University of Pennsylvania Law Review,* Vol. 104 (November 1955), and Douglas V. Brown, "Labor and Antitrust Laws," *American Bar Association Proceedings* (August 1955).

53. Brooks, *op. cit.,* p. 435.

54. *Ibid.,* p. 441.

55. Quoted in Rehmus, *op. cit.,* p. 113. Based on: "Multiemployer Association Collective Bargaining and Its Impact on the Collective Bargaining Process," Report of the General Subcommittee on Labor, Committee on Education and Labor, U.S. House of Representatives, 88th Congress, 2nd Session, 1964, p. 32.

56. See Chapter 16.

5
The Strategies of Collective Bargaining

Bluff, bluster, and force are all out of place in collective bargaining today, if, indeed, they ever had a valid place. The objective of collective bargaining is not to see who can "win" or which side can "beat the other out," but rather to negotiate agreements which will meet the needs of the company to remain competitive and profitable, while at the same time being creatively responsive to individual interests, situations and concerns of employees.

—Clark Kerr

☐ IN the past, economists have been all too prone to neglect the non-economic aspects of collective bargaining. The reasons for this neglect are not difficult to divine and are rooted in the history of collective bargaining and the attitude of economists towards it as outlined in an earlier chapter.

Particularly in the United States, economists had little cause to occupy themselves with the issue of collective bargaining since it played such a small role in the operation of the economy. Even in such countries as England, however, where unions assumed a more dominant position at an earlier date, economists tended to minimize the importance of collective bargaining in altering the level of wages from what it would have been in the absence of union interference. Other issues in the typical contract received even scantier attention. Given this cavalier treatment of the entire subject of collective bargaining, it is little wonder that the various strategies open to unions and management alike went unexplored.

Even if earlier economists had accorded greater attention to the issue of collective bargaining, however, it is probable that they would have considered the issue of possible strategies involved in the bargaining process outside the boundaries of their discipline. Even today, many economists would reject Arthur Ross' advice to make the labor course into something more than another course in economics.[1]

Nevertheless, the techniques employed by the parties to collective bargaining play an important part in shaping the nature of the final contract and therefore quite properly should be included in any discussion of collective bargaining. Even if one accepts the belief that no amount of bargaining can overcome the natural forces of the market and that the final wage adjustment would have been much the same even in the absence of union pressure, one must admit that variations in technique can influence the form of the increase. One obvious union strategy is to seek gains where management resistance is weakest. A management determined to yield no immediate further increases in hourly wages may be induced to yield ground in the area of fringe benefits. As we shall soon see, unions have frequently tailored their demands to the exigencies of the situation and the prevailing mood of management.

In the last twenty years, the refusal of economists to include such considerations in their theorizing has been modified and bargaining theory has come to play an increasingly important part in discussion about collective bargaining. The earliest efforts in this direction were attempts (largely inconclusive) to apply the Edgeworth Contract Curve using the indifference curve approach to wage contracts. Unfortunately, it is not feasible to

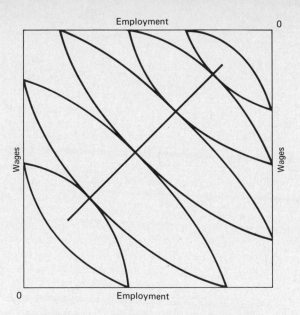

FIGURE 5.1 Indifference Curve Approach

One of the difficulties of picturing labor-management settlements in terms of indifference maps is the problem of labeling the axes. Clearly the terms employed above have different meanings for labor and management. An interesting attempt to juxtapose union indifference curves against a firm's production curves has been made by William Fellner in *Competition Among the Few* (New York: Knopf, 1949), chap. 10. Such procedure does not really bring him to a finite solution and a range for bargaining still exists.

give a lengthy explanation of indifference curve analysis, for those who are unfamiliar with it. To summarize briefly, indifference maps are drawn for both management and labor in such a way that they start from separate points of origin and their indifference curves are tangent to each other in the manner indicated in Figure 5.1. Each indifference curve represents a series of positions at which the party in question is indifferent in regard to the various combinations of rewards or goods marked on the two axes. Each point of tangency represents a meeting of minds of the two parties as to the best combination of items. By connecting the points of tangency, we obtain a "contract curve," which charts the best combination of positions for the two parties. The further away from his point of origin the position for one party is, the higher his indifference curve and the better that position is for him. Exactly where on the "contract curve" a bargain will be struck remains indeterminate. In theoretical terms, however, the scope within which there is room for agreement has been narrowed.

Although indifference curve analysis provided some aid to the economic theorist, it did little to increase understanding of how either labor or management could actually achieve a settlement. The actual process whereby bargaining resolved on one point of tangency instead of another within the range of indeterminancy was usually left to the imagination with the lame explanation that the final result would depend upon the bargaining strength of the two parties. Even such an unsatisfactory conclusion, however, represented an important departure from the earlier position that indeterminancy was unthinkable in the face of certain natural laws of economics.

Recent variations on the indifference curve approach have intrigued modern theorists like John Nash.[2] Given the normal situation, in which the union is demanding more than management is willing to pay, what compromise can the two parties achieve? According to Nash, if one assumes that the two parties are rational, that they are equal in bargaining strength, and that each has full knowledge of the tastes and wishes of the other, a solution can be found. Using the above-mentioned assumptions as a basis for his theory, Nash draws "utility frontiers" for the two bargainers and argues that it is reasonable to assume that the two parties will move to a position of compromise in which both parties will be better off than if total disagreement exists.

Although Nash's approach includes numerous mathematical refinements, representing an improvement over earlier theories (his solution is too complicated to be given in detailed form here), it fails to satisfy the student of collective bargaining on two counts. First of all, his assumptions are too heroic to meet the test of reality; bargainers do not have the perfect knowledge or rationality that he assumes. Furthermore, his solution is not predictive. It does not tell us what the outcome of a bargaining match will be, but only what it should be and how the actual solution was achieved.

Others, like J. Pen,[3] have analyzed the bargaining process in terms of the satisfaction functions that the two parties derive from different settlements and the parties' appraisals of the risk of conflict and the will of each opponent to resist.

Over a quarter of a century ago, John R. Hicks provided us with a reason and terms for settlement couched in terms of the expected duration of a strike as seen by the two parties.[4] Figure 5.2 reproduces his diagram. Note that the union's resistance curve drops sharply as it leaves the Y axis (the upper union goal), indicating that at upper levels the union is unwilling to bear a prolonged strike to secure these wage rates. As we descend the Y axis to lower wages, however, the union's willingness to make further concessions lessens and the curve flattens out. This flattening would occur in the area of true union objectives dictated by such considerations as settlements made elsewhere. Further concessions will bring sharp reductions in union satisfaction as the union is forced off its flat plateau. The line ZZ' represents a level of wages that the company deems best. This is the wage level to which the union might have to retreat if the strike were sufficiently protracted. The company's offer curve also leaves the Y axis at the point of its most desirable wage settlement or zero resistance. As the wage rate rises, the curve flattens out, indicating that the company is experiencing increasing marginal disutility. Note that the curve continues to flatten until the company reaches its point of maximum resistance. At this point a higher wage is equivalent to going out of business and no further concessions can or will be offered.

According to Hicks, settlement will occur at the point at which both sides perceive an equally lengthy strike should bargaining break down. Hicks' critics, however, have noted that his theory is not directly concerned with the bargaining process (a point Hicks himself conceded) and that the two curves are "hazy" and do not permit the determinate solution that he pictured.[5] Hicks himself also acknowledged that the estimates of the two parties might change as the strike proceeded, thus making a solution more difficult.

The next major step in bargaining analysis stems from the game theory of Oskar Morgenstern and John von Neumann.[6] Again space allows us to provide only a sketchy version of this new theory. Readers who are interested in further details should consult the suggested readings at the end of the book.

Game theory has been applied to card games like poker as well as to business situations and more questionably to diplomacy and "brinkmanship." According to game theory, each party to the game employs two basic strategies. Instead of simply seeking to maximize his gains, the rational game player seeks to follow a course that will give him a maximum return while at the same time taking into consideration the possible maximum losses to which he exposes himself. Acting on the assumption that the worst will happen (that is, his opponent will learn his strategy), the player selects a course that will yield him what is called a "minimax" or the highest minimum gain and the lowest maximum loss. Since a player has assumed that his opponent knows his strategy and acts accordingly, he selects a strategy that will result in the least damage to him even if discovered, while still earning him a maximum re-

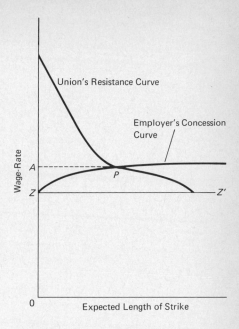

FIGURE 5.2 Concession Curves and Strike Duration

Source: John R. Hicks, *The Theory of Wages* (New York: Peter Smith, 1948), p. 143.

turn if undetected. In order to make actual detection more difficult, the player makes a series of random moves designed to confuse his opponent. The theory as devised by Morgenstern and von Neumann goes beyond the principles of statistical probability and is based on formidable mathematical reasoning.

Like indifference curve analysis, game theory has been somewhat too gamey to suit the taste of either labor or management leaders and the practical applications of this new theory to collective bargaining have been very few.[7] Therefore, although both theories may help the student even though they are not used by the collective bargaining practitioner, we must look elsewhere for further understanding. Much of the remainder of this chapter is descriptive. In it, we will explore some of the possible tactics, illustrated by actual instances of such strategies as they are employed by either or both sides.

The trick in all collective bargaining, of course, is to secure as much as possible for your side while at the same time making as few concessions as possible. Basic to all collective bargaining is the cost each side may impose upon the other if it does not secure satisfactory terms: the union can threaten a strike; employers can refuse to operate the plant entirely or possibly to continue operations by hiring substitutes for the union members. Since such action is costly to both parties, there is distinct pressure on both to arrive at a peaceful settlement. Balancing this, of course, are the costs of the settlement. Obviously the level of a firm's profits sets an upper limit to what management can concede, and the stakes of the union are equally high since it loses prestige and power if it accepts what its members regard as a poor settlement. One of the parties (usually management) may also be more concerned about the long-run aspect of the situation than the other.

Although it is a safe generalization that both parties normally seek a peaceful resolution of their differences, some important qualifications must be made. For example, a union may feel it necessary to flex its muscles occasionally to make certain that they do not deteriorate from lack of use.[8] There may even be periods when both parties are anxious to test their strength. There is ample evidence, for example, to suggest that such a desire on the part of both unions and management was responsible for the fact that the post-World War II Labor-Management Conferences called by President Truman were so unproductive. At that time, neither side was willing to proffer any concessions until it had had an opportunity to test its strength. Management was bolstered by the profits it had made during the war years; unions were encouraged by the continued rapid growth in union membership during the same period. As we shall see, a strike may occur even when both parties are reluctant to endanger their position by running the risk of one. Our analysis from this point on will deal with those situations in which both parties enter into collective bargaining in a firm hope of resolving their differences amicably.

Before dealing with the actual tactics available to the two parties as they face each other across the bargaining table, we must first examine two even more basic strategies: the timing of the negotiations and the selection of the scope of the bargaining unit.

Although in an earlier period contracts had no definite expiration date, most contracts in the United States today specify a definite length of duration. Only a few unions (the United Mine Workers is a notable example) still negotiate contracts with no fixed terminal date. In recent years only the Teamsters have expressed interest in negotiating new contracts without a definite expiration date. In Great Britain, on the other hand, virtually all contracts are of indefinite duration. The continuance of the open-ended contract in Great Britain is less a reflection of union strategy than of a philosophy of collective bargaining that involves a sharper degree of class warfare and, because of inadequate grievance procedure, a desire to have year-round bargaining as a means of improving workers' morale.

Although employers, since they are more apt to defend the status quo, may be deemed more likely than unions to favor contracts of an indefinite duration, such contracts have drawbacks for management as well. It is difficult for an employer to commit himself to terms that have no definite tenure in the face of changing market situations occasioned by the business cycle, the challenge of new competitors, and so on. These considerations tend to outweigh the fact that the union may (and usually does) treat each expiration, or contract renewal, date as an occasion for pressing for new demands.

The setting of the expiration date thus assumes considerable importance in the negotiation of any contract in an industry subject to wide seasonal variations in markets. Unions prefer to have the contract expire during the busy season when the pressure of a strike would be heaviest, while management seeks dates when a possible interruption in production will be least costly. When the International Typographical Union struck the New York newspapers in 1963 one of the major issues revolved around the determination of the newspapers' representatives to avoid a repetition of the threat of a strike during the Christmas shopping season. In earlier times when contracts had no definite expiration date, unions frequently utilized the surprise strike as a device for winning their gains. Strikes in the textile and clothing trade would be called at the peak of the industry's season when employers would be most anxious to settle in order to satisfy their customers.

If the expiration date of a contract is unfavorable to its interests, neither management nor labor lacks recourse. Although unions like to adhere to a "no contract, no work" principle, a number of them have found it expedient to violate it when the occasion demanded. Walter Reuther, for example, refused in 1948 to become involved in a strike against the auto companies. Because the season for autos had been a bad one in sales,

Reuther asked the Auto Workers to continue on the job despite the expiration of their contract. Negotiations were postponed until the following autumn when the companies were retooling for the next season and were thus in a weaker position to bear a strike.

Similarly, employers may take protective steps to ward off the worst effects of a strike during periods of high production. Management may, for example, warn customers to stockpile needed products in anticipation of a possible shutdown, as the steel companies have done several times in the past. Obviously such industries as steel can use these tactics more successfully, at least for short periods, than can industries like newspaper publishing. Whenever possible, employers have also attempted to get vital orders filled during a closedown by subcontracting them to rival plants, a practice that led unions to use the secondary boycott (subsequently handled under the Taft-Hartley Act).

Timing also plays a prominent role in such bargaining considerations as the decision of labor leaders as to which items on their list of demands to present first and the role of the strike deadline (the time limit) in facilitating negotiations, but we will discuss these facets later. We should note here, however, the significance of the trend toward longer contracts (many are now in effect for three years or more) in the United States. There is little evidence to suggest that unions have been hampered by the growth in long-term contracts. Most contracts of this type provide for automatic annual wage increases during the term of the contract or stipulate that certain parts of the contract may be periodically reopened while it is still in effect. The value of his latter stipulation to the union, however, is frequently weakened by the inclusion of a "no strike for the life of the contract" provision. The long-term contract allows both parties to benefit from the resolution of certain issues for a longer period. However, since union leaders are less likely than management to remain satisfied with the status quo, they are under greater pressure to anticipate issues that may arise while the contract is in effect during current negotiations.

The size of the teams of bargaining representatives is also important. From the union's viewpoint, the chief advantage of having a large bargaining team is that it provides more witnesses to testify to the membership that the final settlement was the best that the union could achieve. Another advantage of a large team from the standpoint of both management and union is that the larger team allows the inclusion of members who are specialists in the complexities of such issues as pension programs. In industrywide or pattern bargaining, both union and management are likely to field large bargaining teams. The 1965 steel negotiations, for example, involved 300 persons.

Serious bargaining, however, is likely to be best conducted by small groups from each side, since the process of bargaining essentially depends on the reactions of a few key leaders. Furthermore, the greater the number involved, the more likely is it that one of them will disclose the true aims and objectives of their side to the opposition.

Like variations in timing and size of the bargaining team, the choice of the appropriate bargaining unit may also render distinct advantages to one party or the other. We have previously discussed industrywide and multiemployer bargaining as seen from the viewpoint of the economy. In this section we will consider them in relation to bargaining strategy.

Industrywide collective bargaining is sometimes seen simply as a union weapon with the implication that it always serves to increase union bargaining strength. Those who take this view usually argue that this form of bargaining undermines the will of employers to resist union demands since management no longer need fear discrepancies in labor costs that result when some firms achieve better settlements than others. The employer is less reluctant to pay higher wages, it is reasoned, when he is certain that his fellow employers are in the same boat. Employers may still balk at high wage demands even if uniformly applied, of course, but in periods of high demand their resistance may in fact be somewhat reduced. This potential union advantage however, is offset by the corresponding possibility that employers will be more resistant to wage increases in periods of declining demand since they know their share of the market will not be taken by others if they face a work stoppage.

Those who contend that multiemployer bargaining enhances the union's position also offer the equally dubious argument that this type of bargaining allows the union to threaten to shut down the entire industry or an entire region and thus pressure employers to settle in order to avoid a public outcry and possible government intervention. This argument, however, neglects the possibility that this tactic may play into the hands of the employers, who will divert public wrath and the threatened government action in the direction of the union.

The argument that multiemployer bargaining always works to the advantage of the union is further weakened when we recall what the union must forego when it accepts this type of bargaining. Multiemployer bargaining denies the union the opportunity to employ whipsaw tactics. Striking only one company at a time permits great pressure to be brought to bear upon the struck company since it not only suffers the usual costs of a shutdown but is exposed to the threat that its customers may be wooed away by one of its competitors. Furthermore, in single-employer bargaining the union leader is able to select his targets one by one, and thus is able to choose the opponent most likely to make a settlement on the union's terms when threatened by a strike. Once concessions have been achieved from one company, the process can be repeated.

The effectiveness of this strategy of selectivity can be illustrated by the bargaining strategy of Walter Reuther and the UAW in the fall of 1964. Reuther chose Ford as his first target, apparently because Chrysler's economic position was still too weak for the UAW to risk endangering the corporation's future by subjecting it to a possible long strike, while General Motors was deemed too strong to be likely to concede quickly. Once Ford had settled, the pressure on the other two companies to settle was almost irresistible. In the fall of 1967, Ford was again selected as the UAW's primary target for many of the same reasons, with the additional explanation that Ford was more amenable to innovations in bargaining than the other two companies. Changed circumstances may force a change in strategy. In 1970 the UAW chose to strike General Motors. Although some of the above-cited reasons for not choosing GM still existed, union leaders were now concerned about the threat of foreign imports and felt that Ford in particular was offering more competition to the foreign small cars. For the same reason the union chose not to strike GM plants supplying parts to the other domestic automobile firms.

The reasons that prompted the UAW to reject Chrysler, which was supposedly in the weakest bargaining position as its primary target, are not immediately obvious; they are related to the nature of this type of bargaining. When the union is attempting to set a pattern for future contracts, it is likely to be less willing to make any concessions since these will be reflected in subsequent contracts as well. Thus the negotiations concerning the initial settlement are likely to be difficult and protracted. Whereas the UAW believed that Chrysler would be able to meet the terms negotiated with Ford, it felt that Chrysler might have resisted settlement had it been the initial target, and thus risked financial collapse. Although there is always the possibility that the union will see past success with other companies as evidence of an ability to secure like terms everywhere, pattern bargaining does not always bring identical results, and the union is more likely to be willing to make concessions (marginal steel firms have been given a 10 percent wage advantage) in those negotiations following the establishment of the pattern.

Because of the effectiveness of the whipsaw technique, particularly in those cases in which the employers are numerous and face a strong union, many employers have tried to band together in multiemployer bargaining units. If one plant is struck the other employers suspend operations until a master agreement has been signed with the union that covers all employers in the unit. A prime example of this tactic was the attempt of the New York City newspaper publishers in 1963 to insist upon one contract for all papers. When the unions selectively struck some of the papers (those said to be in the strongest financial position) the publishers agreed to close down all papers. The International Typographical Union vigorously denounced this action, charging the employers with a desire to frustrate collective bargaining.[9] Later the *Post* broke away from the publishers association and made a separate contract. In 1970, when the Printers succeeded in bargaining separately, a settlement was achieved with the *Times* that was then applied to the *News* and the other papers without a strike.

Multiemployer bargaining also imposes an extra cost to the union when a strike occurs. With a larger proportion of its membership out on strike, the payment of strike benefits becomes more costly. Simultaneously suspension of union dues during strikes exerts a great downward pressure on the union's revenues.

Such then are the strategies involved in setting the stage for the collective bargaining sessions. In the first chapter, we noted that collective bargaining was a continuing day-to-day process that did not end with the signing of a contract. The Federal Mediation and Conciliation Service has recommended that a program of "between crisis" talks between employers and unions would facilitate the bargaining process. Advocates of such talks see a larger and more continuous role for the mediator. Whether or not such talks will actually make settlements easier is uncertain. Clearly they have not done so in the case of the railroads. Thus far such talks have been largely confined to discussion of grievances and issues that arise out of interpretation of the current contract. Accordingly, we will limit our analysis to the strategy employed by the two parties during the period immediately prior to and during the negotiation of a new contract.

We will begin by examining a few basic institutional factors that influence the tactics of both parties, including the composition of the bargaining teams, the degree of detail present in the contract, and the nature of the record that is kept of the bargaining sessions.

Increasingly, both sides tend to send their top officials to the bargaining session. While this trend is probably explained in part by the expanding geographical scope of many contracts, early experiences with bargaining teams who had little power to make any commitment has also been a bitter lesson. Unless employed deliberately as a stalling device, a failure to send individuals with the power to make decisions to the bargaining table is likely to result in frustration and exasperation for both sides. When a single plant's contract is being negotiated, the union is likely to be represented by the local leaders. Even in such cases, however, the representatives of the national union are likely to be present and the national union may insist upon the right to ratify or reject the final contract. The role of the national officers increases as the number of plants involved increases. Where a substantial part of the bargaining is on an industrywide or a national basis (as is the case in England and many European countries), the locals may have little or no voice in the negotiations. Richard Lester mentions this as one of the problems of bargaining in Great Britain.[10]

A contract that spells out each point in great detail is more likely to be sought by both parties when an atmosphere of mutual distrust prevails. All too often, one or both parties finds that a contract that does not specify provisions for a variety of contingencies has been "perverted" by the other party. A detailed contract thus averts the endless disputes that may arise when one or both parties tries to reinterpret the contract according to its own understanding.

When one party foresees a need to

reinterpret the contract and perhaps submit it to arbitration it may insist upon a verbatim transcript of the bargaining session. Most bargainers today are wary of such faithful recordings. Both union and management have argued that such transcripts suggest and breed an air of distrust and limit the willingness to speak one's mind freely. Where, as in England, such transcripts are made available to the membership, the transcript usually arrives too late to have much meaning to the members. Many experts, including some arbitrators, question the claim that such material aids the arbitrator in his effort to interpret at some later time the meaning and intent of the contract.

Bargaining Table Strategies

We will now turn to the strategies employed at the bargaining table. Given the threat of the strike (or the lockout), what choices are available to the union's representatives? An opening gambit familiar to even the casual student of industrial relations is the high initial demand. The union will often overstate what it actually expects to win. Both the number of demands and the total cost to the company may be inflated in the initial presentation for several reasons. Many union bargainers take the position that "there's no harm in asking"; that is, the initial high demand leaves room for later bargaining without giving away too much of what is deemed essential. Since the union's bargainers are rarely in a position to know exactly what the employer is prepared to offer, the initial high demand prevents the union from asking at the beginning for less than the employer was prepared to concede. Even if the union's representatives should discover during the process of bargaining that they are in

a stronger position than they first anticipated, the unwritten rules of bargaining virtually prohibit them from increasing their original demands at a later date. How can bargaining really begin unless both parties know from the start the maximum demands of the other?

Just as an unduly high demand (in terms of cost to the company) may be set with a view to later bargaining so may a large number of demands be included with the expectation that some of them (hopefully those least essential to the interested party) can be sacrificed in order to win the others. A long list of demands may also reflect diverse interests among the union's membership. By including such items in the list of demands, the representatives are able to return a more modest settlement to the membership with the defense: "We tried our best, fellows, but we just couldn't get everything. It's a good contract and we'll try again next time."

Multiplicity of demands is also prompted by the union leader's desire to present the membership with something "new." As the years go by and wage increases continue to be repeated, the rank and file comes to expect these increases and may even credit the company with a major share of responsibility for them. If, on the other hand, the union leader can present his membership with a new and truly different fringe benefit—the union and the men who lead it are more likely to get the credit.

Since the management is unlikely to know precisely upon what terms the union will settle, the union that asks for more than it expects may be able to convince management to accede to more than the union's leaders really hoped to obtain. The success of an undetected bluff may set the stage for further successes. Management has quite often seriously misconstrued a union's aims and objectives. Providing that the "mark-up" does not become too routine an event, excessive demands may prove to be profitable.

Exaggerated demands leave room for bargaining in another sense. Management representatives who are able to cite items that the union demanded but were denied are thereby able to claim a settlement as a victory when actually it went beyond what management had planned to concede.

The union leader anxious for a peaceful solution to an existing impasse may even yield on some items that he had hoped to achieve to allow management to save face. Either union or management (sometimes both) may work itself into an untenable position from which it sees no honorable means of escape. "That's our final decision—we can't offer anything more," is a position that is sometimes difficult to retreat from unless the process of doing so is facilitated by the rival parties. Sometimes merely the appearance of a concession is necessary; at other times something more tangible is required. We will have more to say on this point in a moment.

Some have viewed the exaggerated claim as simply window dressing, arguing that the final settlement is a foregone conclusion before negotiations begin, but this interpretation seems untenable. Not only may one or both parties be uncertain as to the character of the final settlement but an immediate resolution of differences would invite (particularly in the case of the union leaders) charges of having "sold out" or acting in collusion with the opposite party. The ability to ferret out the true intended offer of the opponent is one of the essential attributes of the good bargainer, but even the most highly skilled may find this process takes time.

Sometimes union leaders will in-clude in their list of demands an item which they do not expect to secure this year, in order to set the stage for future negotiations. An innovation in bargaining demands (such as the three-month paid vacation) may, when it is first proposed, be rejected by management as too dramatic a departure from accepted norms. If similar requests have been made in the past, however, the proposal loses some of its novelty and is more likely to receive serious consideration from the management representatives.

Such new proposals may not always have the full-hearted support of the union's members. The union leader may find it advisable to submit new demands to the management because the company officials are convinced that money wages and working conditions already are very good and feel that the union is unjustified in asking for further improvements at the present moment. Because the union's members expect that each renegotiation of the contract should involve further economic gains for them, a union leader may find it necessary to use his imagination to formulate problems in areas where a more definite lack in the contract can be demonstrated. In so doing, however, his efforts to "dress up" demands in order to make a more convincing case to management may expose him to expressions of dissatisfaction by the rank and file. Even if management feels that wages are already unduly high, union members may still have an increase in take-home pay as their paramount objective. There is evidence, for example, that Philip Murray, president of the steelworkers union, had difficulty in 1949 in convincing union members to push for noncontributory pension plans instead of still higher wages. Newspaper accounts at the time indicated that only a sense of loyalty and friendship for Murray led the rank and file to support a strike on the issue of pensions.

Although union leaders probably rarely expect to achieve all of their demands, there are still limits to the tendency to claim too much at the beginning. In the first place, unrealistic initial demands may be construed by the membership of the union as a sound basis for conducting negotiations. Subsequent settlements that fall substantially below these initial demands are then likely to prove disappointing and perhaps trigger a move to reject the final settlement. One could reason, of course, that union members are well aware that the leaders are overstating their case and thus fully expect the original demands to be scaled down. The frequent rejection of a contract by the union membership, however, suggests that it has been led to expect too much from the negotiations. Similarly, management representatives may be well aware that the union's demands were overstated and take this into account in their negotiations. Furthermore, management may grow accustomed to cutting the union's demands by some set percentage, perhaps one-third, in order to arrive at an estimate of what the union is really seeking. The union leaders may then have difficulty in convincing management that they are sincere in seeking a concession that is really crucial. The public image of the union may also be damaged if it routinely seeks what seem to be impossible and unrealistic demands.

In couching his demands, then, the union leader must tread delicately. He must arouse enthusiasm for his proposals among the rank and file (but avoid getting them too set on items that may be impossible to obtain), and at the same time give management the impression that his demands must be met if he hopes to win the rank and file's approval of any settlement.

When the leader is faced with the necessity of scaling down demands because he knows that the aspirations of the members have been pushed to too high a pitch, what can he do?[11] If certain workers are demanding items that he believes management will never accept, the union leader may attempt to undermine the position of these "dissidents" in a variety of ways. He may attempt to exclude such workers from the board that formulates the union's position; the dissatisfied group may find it more difficult to get substantial changes made at the general meeting. Alternatively, the union leader may try to have some of the opposition placed on the bargaining team so that they are exposed to management's reactions and can learn how firm its opposition to some of the union's proposals actually is.

When it is impossible to exclude dissidents from the planning board and when their exposure to management's stubbornness fails to convince them that their demands are unrealistic, the union leader tries to make the best of a bad situation. He may go through the motions of presenting the union's case without much hope of winning and may use the excessive demands as a wedge to secure more from management than at first seemed likely. When he returns with a settlement that is far from their originally stated objectives, the leader may attempt to convince the rank and file through a combination of deception, blandishment, and promises for the future. The gains that have been won will be inflated in importance, while sacrificed demands will be minimized. Personal appeals for loyalty to the union and to the union's leaders who did "the best they could" can be made.

Note that the union leader must

avoid dampening the rank and file's enthusiasm for the union's case prior to negotiations with management. Whereas an inflamed membership may be difficult to handle if they are disappointed in the final settlement, their failure to support the leader solidly in his negotiations with management will weaken the leader's bargaining position.

Similarly, when a contract settlement has been made, the union leader must also exercise diplomacy in order to convince the membership that the terms represent a real victory, without creating undue resentment in the minds of management. Excessive claims of victory may suggest to management that it has given up too much and thus make future negotiations more difficult.

Other considerations limit the union's practice of asking for too much. The argument that there is "no harm in asking" is fallacious. Unless the union can present a creditable case, it will elicit no responsible counteroffer from management. The union that tells the company "pay us this impossibly large increase, or we will strike" in effect is simply serving a strike notice. Occasionally, the union will misgauge a company's profit position and overstate its demands by a wide margin. It must then either scale down the level of its demands before or after a strike (with the resulting loss of prestige among its membership and in the public eye) or witness the termination of the business. Sometimes demands are deliberately overstated when the union is dealing with a firm that it regards as marginal and a drag upon the industry. When John L. Lewis and the UMW used this tactic toward marginal coal mines, the fact that miners in these mines were thrown out of work was deemed a regrettable necessity in order to obtain better standards for the majority.

For these reasons not all union leaders agree that excessive demands represent the best opening tactic. These leaders prefer to lay their cards on the table from the beginning and press for a settlement as close to the original demand as possible. We will have more to say about this approach when we examine the management's strategy.

A third union strategy, likely to accompany the two previously discussed, is employed in order to make its demands palatable to management. This approach might be called the salesman approach or the "this won't hurt you a bit" technique. The union bargainer comes to the bargaining table loaded with statistics demonstrating (to his satisfaction at least) that the company can well afford to meet the union's demands. The company's rate of productivity increases or the record of profits are commonly cited as evidence.

The exchanging of information provides both parties in collective bargaining with an opportunity to clarify and strengthen their positions by offering evidence of the sincerity of their proposal. The union that can support its demand for a sizable increase in wage rates with solid evidence may provide nothing of an informational nature to the employer (he is probably well aware of such facts as the prevailing wage rates in the industry). However, the fact that the union is also aware of these facts may convince management that the union feels its demands are justified and is thus likely to be insistent in securing their fulfillment. When the two parties know little about each other's true position, the information provided may enable each side to judge more accurately the probable range of bargaining.

The real target of the information presented in a bargaining session may not even be the bargainer's opponent. Even if neither party has any hopes of convincing the other with his version of the "facts of the case," each may hope to convince the union membership.[12] Ultimately, of course, the union leaders are helpless without the membership's support. A membership that is unwilling to go on strike contributes little to its leaders' bargaining position. Management, on the other hand, may hope that its facts will create uncertainties among the rank and file and perhaps convince them that management is firm in its resistance to the union's demands. Management's messages may also be addressed to stockholders in an attempt to justify the management's position in the event of a costly strike. It is also possible that both parties may really be addressing the general public and/or the government. We will discuss the reasons for such appeals in more detail later.

For the union, the use of facts is not necessarily a persuasive bargaining tactic. Rarely, if ever, is a union able to provide the company with really new information, unless perhaps it concerns conditions prevailing in rival firms. Furthermore, even presentation of the overwhelming evidence in favor of the union is unlikely to persuade management. Not only are the "facts" subject to various qualifications and interpretations, but evidence of an ability of the company to meet the union's demands may not inspire any great willingness on the part of management to do so.

Perhaps the most serious charge made against the presentation of facts as a bargaining tactic concerns the manner in which such facts are utilized. Facts have been used to sell a case rather than as a means of establishing the truth. Both sides tend to select those facts that support their position and tend to ignore equally relevant information that may be detrimental to their case. When facts are used as arguments rather than as guidelines for policy decisions, the result is often to divert the discussion away from the issue in question into an argument over whose facts are best. When one set of facts is used merely to refute another set of facts, both sides frequently develop a contempt for them and give them little consideration while bargaining. The use of factual data thus becomes a hindrance rather than a help in resolving bargaining impasses.

Another variation on the "this won't hurt you a bit" technique involves the union's tacit acceptance of higher prices for the finished product or service after a settlement. Neither the Coal Miners under John L. Lewis nor the Steel Workers under David MacDonald evidenced much concern over the increases in prices to consumers that accompanied the concessions won by their unions for the members. Other leaders have on occasion treated the question of price increases in a somewhat different fashion. Walter Reuther once challenged the auto firms to prove that his labor demands were inflationary and even offered to forego wage demands if the companies would agree to a price rollback. Probably no one would have been more shocked than Reuther if the automobile companies had agreed to his offer—an offer often cited as evidence of unions' concern over inflation.

Another bargaining strategy frequently employed by union representatives is the claim that they are bargaining from weakness because they allegedly cannot control the membership and thus cannot guarantee that the contract will be ratified if it is not satisfactory to the membership. This tactic allows the bargainers to assume an air of seeming reasonableness while still insisting on the fulfillment of the union's demands. The union leaders' inability to control the rank and file may be more real than alleged. In numerous cases the membership has failed to ratify a contract worked out by their leaders and have sent them back to the bargaining table in search of still better terms. One student of the subject has estimated that as high as 14 percent of the tentative settlements handled by the Federal Mediation and Conciliation Service in 1967 were rejected by the rank and file.[13] The leaders' claims of impotence may thus become a realized fact. Although it is sometimes asserted that exhorbitant union demands come from autocratically controlled unions and that the problem would be corrected if the rank and file had more power, in general, the union leadership is probably more conservative in their demands than the rank and file. The leaders are more likely than the ordinary worker to have reliable information about the true economic position of the company and the wages and working conditions prevailing elsewhere in the industry. They are thus better able to make an accurate evaluation as to what gains can be realistically demanded. Furthermore, continued contact with management representatives is likely to arouse in the union leaders a certain sense of empathy with management's problems and perhaps even respect for management's point of view. Such identification is likely to grow stronger if the same leaders continue to represent the union for a number of years. On the other hand, the leadership, particularly at the national level, can be far more tough-minded about closing down a marginal plant than the union members (whose jobs are at stake).

Finally, of course, there is the possibility that the union leaders may grow increasingly less urgent in their demands on behalf of their membership and increasingly out of touch with its true wants. When this occurs, it is not necessarily a case of "selling out" the membership (this happens too, as some of the racketeering investigations have demonstrated). Given all of these considerations, it is little wonder that the union rank and file frequently fail to ratify the contract as negotiated by their leaders.

Union leaders who claim to be bargaining from weakness and disclaim any ability to guarantee ratification are merely using a somewhat elaborate form of the weapon that lies behind every bargaining session—the threat to strike. A leader less anxious to remain on amicable terms with management can convert the "bargaining from weakness" tactic into a strategy of power; he can in effect insist that management meet his terms or face an inevitable strike. The union leader who knows that the mood of the membership is disposed toward a strike unless the terms of settlement are completely satisfactory risks great danger by ignoring this sentiment and attempting to settle on terms closer to management's position.

Not only does the refusal of the membership to ratify a recommended contract constitute a blow to the leader's prestige, but it also endangers his power position within the union since it encourages rival factions to challenge his leadership. The key word here is "recommended." As Clyde Summers has pointed out, a contract may be rejected without loss of prestige to the leadership when management has pressed the leaders to submit it and the leaders do so without recommendation. Leaders may also submit a doubtful contract in order to test the membership's sentiments and solidarity, but this also involves the risk of loss of prestige mentioned.[14]

Furthermore, the union that repeatedly refuses to ratify contracts or engages in wildcat strikes finds itself highly suspect in the eyes of management. A management that has made what it considers to be a mutually satisfactory settlement only to find that the problem of a new contract is still unresolved will be more cautious next time in dealing with the union's leader unless he can present evidence of support for his pledge by the rank and file. Furthermore, if the union's membership discovers that its failure to ratify a contract has induced management to make further concessions, it may seek to repeat the practice in the future. While a union might be able to succeed in this strategy once or twice, any consistent repetition would result in a stiffening of management's original position.

Historically, unions have often found themselves in a weaker bargaining position than management. This situation is not uncommon today despite the widespread belief that all unions are centers of massive power. In such cases, the union may seek assistance from outside parties—the government, which is urged to investigate the unfair bargaining strength of the employers; the general public, which is asked for sympathy and support. The Textile Workers provide a good example of this practice in recent years. Such tactics are frequently born of desperation and are avoided whenever possible since they reveal the basic bargaining weakness of the union and thereby indicate its inability to force a settlement upon its opponent. Appeals of this nature are therefore usually a last resort, used only when it is already apparent to the employer that the union's bargaining strength is at most minimal.

Paralleling the variety of tactics available to the union leaders depending upon the time and circumstances are the offsetting strategies at the dis-posal of management. Just as the union's initial demands may be in excess of what it eventually hopes to win, so may management's opening terms be considerably less than those on which it plans eventually to settle. It may offer a ten-cent-an-hour wage increase, expecting to go to fifteen cents if necessary. To bolster its bargaining position, management may seek to put the union on the defensive by making the meeting of the union's demands contingent on certain conditions that the management believes desirable. The union is left to decide whether such items are mere window-dressing designed to scale down the union's initial demands or whether they are an essential part of management's counterproposal. In fashioning such demands, however, management must be careful not to touch upon especially sensitive areas; otherwise the only result may be a strengthening of the membership's resolve. There is considerable evidence, for example, that the 1959 steel strike was prolonged and the will of the union membership to fight greatly strengthened by the attempt on the part of management to secure changes in the working rules (rules regulating standards of performance that have developed on the job over a period of time) as a price for any further wage concessions.

In a variation on this tactic, the company states the maximum offer it is willing to entertain and adheres to that position irrespective of union demands or threats. This tactic has been named Boulwarism after Samuel Boulware, who initiated it as the personnel director of General Electric. Critics have been quick to point out that the tactic in effect dealt a death blow to collective bargaining since the company announced at the beginning that it had arrived at its offer by careful study and that it would not be moved regardless of any actions taken by the union. Evidently, the National Labor Relations Board and the courts questioned this tactic. In early 1965 the courts ruled that General Electric was guilty of refusing to engage in collective bargaining.

The critics have argued that by using this strategy, the company violates the whole give-and-take spirit of collective bargaining. The union is put in a position in which it has difficulty justifying its existence, since the company ignores the union and instead addresses itself directly to the workers, telling them that the company offer has been made after weighing both the needs of workers and of the company.[15] General Electric, however has contended that it is unfair to characterize its position as one of complete rigidity and unwillingness to make further concessions. Company officials maintain that they have made concessions several times when the union was able to furnish new information to justify such changes. Furthermore, the company argues, it is seeking to put collective bargaining on a more elevated plane, one based on facts, as a replacement for "give and take haggling" and periodic "nerve tests" for both sides. The decision that such bargaining was an unfair labor practice was clouded by the fact that the court took into consideration other actions taken by General Electric, such as its appeal to workers to hold a secret ballot before carrying out a strike and its attempts to provide employees with its side of the question.

By the time of the 1969–1970 dispute Boulware had left the company but the union charged that his bargaining policy lingered on. The company continued to take a stand on a decision "fair to all parties" and stick to it while the unions used the tactic of coalition bargaining to exercise greater pressure to end Boulwarism.

The result was a protracted strike and what some observers called a kind of "holy war" waged by both sides. The conflict ended with a settlement that was not fully satisfactory to either side. However, Albert J. Fitzgerald on behalf of the Electrical Workers termed it the "first negotiated settlement with General Electric in 20 years."

As the General Electric example makes evident, unions are not the only ones who come to the bargaining table armed with factual data in support of their case. Management's salesmanship efforts are likely to be a part of the day-to-day process of implementing good personnel policy. The personnel director seeks to convince the workers that the company has their best interests at heart and is doing its best to make the plant a good place in which to work. Efforts in this direction may be hampered by a number of factors, however. If the policy is not carefully worked out, it may, as in the General Electric case, expose the company to charges of unfair labor practices. Furthermore, lower echelons of management may not keep in tune with top management's desire to demonstrate a spirit of friendliness and thus reinforce the worker's tendency to be suspicious of management's motives. The union is also likely to see such a policy as a threat to its security. Even if it does not appeal to the NLRB, it may actively campaign to minimize the effectiveness of management's appeal. In addition, management is reluctant to show its books to support its contention that the union-proposed increases in wages are financially impossible, which naturally makes it difficult for management to support its case and convince the union membership of its sincerity. However, the courts have upheld a 1956 NLRB ruling that states when an employer pleads inability to pay as a reason for refusing a union's demand, he must show his books as evidence of good faith (*NLRB v. Truitt Manufacturing Co.*).

Any evaluation of the General Electric approach to collective bargaining must include answers to the following questions. Was the policy combined with other actions designed to undermine the position of the union? Is the policy of demanding more (or offering less) than you expect to get (give) basically immoral? Granted that policies like that used by General Electric are undertaken in good faith, are they based on too optimistic a view of the basic reasonableness and objectivity of both parties? Is Boulwarism really a modern form of paternalism that involves an attempt by management to determine unilaterally how much and what is good for its workers?

Let us now turn to a later stage in the negotiations. By this time, both sides have presented their initial positions and each has delivered the customary expressions of shocked amazement at the other's proposals. As bargaining proceeds, each party is faced with the dilemma of deciding how best to convince his opponent that his position is sincere and that he is willing to risk a strike if his terms are not met. Presumably, both parties have some minimum (maximum) figure in mind beneath (above) which they will not settle even if failure to settle results in a strike or a closing of the plant. The problem for each party is how to win more than this minimum amount without suffering undue costs.

How then does each opponent convince his opposite party that he is not bluffing even if he really is? Because backing away from a stated position involves difficult questions of strategy, it is more easy to defend a position that is not based on bluffing. The tactics we will describe involve burning part or all of one's bridges behind one and are thus more easily undertaken when the party really means to stick with his stated position. It should be added that the employment of the open threat ("do this or else"), although it is by no means unknown in collective bargaining, is generally considered by both parties to be in bad taste.

Although the open threat is frequently considered improper, more subtle threats are frequently employed. The use of the strike vote by union leaders either prior to or during negotiations may represent an attempt to exert a subtle form of pressure on management. Such tactics are most successful, of course, when the membership provides overwhelming support for the leader's demands, thus impressing upon management that they are willing to support a strike should the need arise. The vote by the New York City ITU membership in the spring of 1965 (1,978 "yes" and 28 "no") to support a strike provided impressive backing for the leaders' demands. The strike vote serves another purpose as well. By taking such a vote, the union publicly announces its intentions to strike if its demands are not met. Having thus committed itself, the union will find it difficult to retreat without considerable loss of face.

Management has sought to counter this strategy by seeking to include in the contract provision for a secret strike vote by the membership in advance of negotiations. These efforts, however, have been frustrated by rulings of the NLRB and the courts. Management, of course, hoped that a secret ballot might reveal that a sizable segment of the membership was unwilling to strike, thus undermining the union's bargaining position.

Although the strike vote is usually a heavy weapon in the union's hands, it may not always turn out as leaders anticipate; the failure of the Electrical workers to support the demands of James Carey in recent years is a case in point. Failure to take such a vote, on the other hand, may be construed by management as a sign of weakness. The preceding analysis also helps explain why unions express so strong an interest in the *union shop*. Union leaders argue that when the plant's labor force includes a sizable number of nonunion workers, management has a better chance of persuading some workers to continue working in the face of a union-called strike. Of course, workers who are reluctant union members may well be equally prone to flout the union's orders. Instances of this sort are by no means rare.

Like the strike vote, declarations that one's position is the only one in the public interest are also a strategy of public commitment. Either or both parties states publicly that a failure to reach a settlement in accord with its position is fraught with danger to the public. The most obvious illustration of this tactic has been the appeal of large companies for public support in their opposition to wage demands that are characterized as inflationary and likely to trigger another round in the wage-price spiral. Once management has pictured itself as a kind of Horatius at the bridge fighting valiantly to stem the tide of inflation, it becomes difficult for it to agree to the union's terms at a later time.

Each party may also take a public stand by using the news media to disseminate "facts" in support of its position to the general public. While some students of labor relations have emphasized the role of public opinion in helping to settle disputes,[16] the important point here is that the use of the news media to express a firm stand commits the party more firmly to a particular position, since again the publicity makes retreat more difficult. Furthermore, a public recital of the "facts" may help convince opponents that one is certain of the correctness of one's position, and this established validity of one's demands will assume increased importance in the opposition's eyes.

Hicks' model, discussed earlier in this chapter, indicates that the employer may be able to convince the union that he is willing to undergo a long strike for relatively small immediate savings in labor costs in order to teach the union a lesson. If management can convince the union leaders that "[t]he company is just not seeking to change the union's position in a given negotiation; [but] it is seeking to change the strategic response of the union over a long period of time,"[17] the union may revise its estimate of how long a strike the company is willing to bear upward and thus be forced to settle for something less than it had originally envisioned. Obviously, representatives of either management or unions may use similar tactics to convince their opponents that they are unlikely to yield very much from their stated position, since to do so would expose them to public embarrassment. Unquestionably, some strikes are the product of situations in which one or both parties have assumed a position from which it is impossible to retreat gracefully. In some cases, only a few pennies separate the positions of the two parties and still a peaceful resolution of the issues proves impossible.

Assuming that both parties in the bargaining process really wish to find a peaceful settlement and avoid a strike (of course, this may not be the case), the pressure for making a final offer, a reduction in demands versus an increased offer, grows as the deadline for the strike nears. Until the strike deadline is imminent, each party may hesitate to make any substantial changes in its original position for fear that its opponent would view such concessions as a sign of weakness and strengthen his resolve to adhere to *his* original position. The setting of the strike deadline thus serves two functions. In the early days of negotiations, when the deadline is still a remote threat, it assures both parties that no overt action will be taken beforehand thus guaranteeing ample time for exchanging information and views. As the deadline nears, however, the pressure to make a settlement increases. These factors help to explain why so many strikes are seemingly averted only at the last minute as the two parties bargain frantically into the wee hours of the morning.

The preceding analysis rests on the assumption that the setting of a strike deadline involves a pledge by both parties not to cease operations prior to that time. Such, of course, is not always the case. Numerous exceptions, including wildcat strikes, slowdowns, and industrial sabotage, can be cited. Furthermore, the deadline may not really exist because one or both parties is convinced that the government will take steps to defer the impending shutdown. Whether or not the government actually does so, the fact that the parties expect government intervention may lend a quite different flavor to the last moments of bargaining than would otherwise prevail.

Assuming that the deadline is real, how do the actual negotiations proceed? Even as the deadline approaches, a bargainer may be reluctant to make his very best offer since, if that offer is rejected, he has no further concessions (that he is willing to make) to offer an opponent who comes part way but still threatens a strike if further concessions are not made. As we shall see, the problem of saving face is likely to be made more difficult if further concessions are made only after a strike. Either or both parties may wish to hold something in reserve for that contingency.

Experienced bargainers are likely to develop a set of signals whereby they can inform those on the other side of the bargaining table that they are prepared to engage in a little "horse trading." In the final stages of negotiations both sides often reduce the number of bargainers, thus facilitating the transmission of such signals. An experienced bargainer will recognize such signs for what they are—an indication that the sender is anxious to make new overtures without wishing to overcommit himself. Similarly, a party can indicate that he is anxious to reach an agreement by suggesting that a particularly controversial item on the agenda should be passed over for the moment in order to concentrate upon other issues where agreement seems more probable. If a bargainer also suggests that if other items can be satisfactorily resolved the burdensome item will also find resolution, he implies that if the opposite party is willing to come to terms on other items, the item in question will be withdrawn. All these signals can be given without definitely promising anything. Efforts to arrive at a satisfactory set of terms may also be simplified when one party makes it easy for his opponent to concede. Since in many cases both parties have to return to their "constituents," they will make an effort to arrive at an attractive "package" of terms in which both parties can find reason to claim victory. Which party will initiate the overture is impossible to predict and depends on the economic circumstances and temperaments of the parties involved.

The effort to find a mutually satisfactory face-saving formula takes on even greater importance when the failure of early negotiations has resulted in a strike. Although pressure to reach a settlement increases for both parties as the strike continues, it also becomes increasingly important for each party to justify its failure to avert the strike and the attendant costs. Without some gains, however minor, it is difficult to face one's constituents. Only if the constituents themselves become disheartened and confess defeat are settlements in which the terms are exactly those demanded by the victor before the strike possible.

The strike also serves to make the assumption of a public stand by one or both parties more binding. In the early stages of bargaining, public interest is less fully aroused and firm positions taken by the parties to the dispute are therefore more easily abandoned. If such positions are repeated during the course of the strike, however, when the full spotlight of public attention is focused on the situation, it is less easy to relax a dogmatic stance.

Even under these circumstances, however, retreat is still possible, particularly if a sympathetic opponent works to make capitulation easier as well as quicker. A step in this direction may be to propose the employment of the services of a third party to act as mediator. Mediators, of course, prefer to be called upon in the early stages of the bargaining, which not only permits them to have a better understanding of the issues involved but sometimes allows them to deter the parties from taking extreme positions based on unrealistic appraisals of the situation.

The role of the skillful mediator is as difficult to describe as it is to play. The mediator's actual tactics depend, of course, on the atmosphere that prevails at the time he enters the picture. In some cases union and management representatives have literally refused to meet face to face or even to meet in the same building, and the mediators have had to commence by rotating between the two parties, listening in turn to their positions separately. In such cases, the primary function of the mediator may be simply to keep the two parties talking to him if not to each other. By lending a sympathetic ear to both parties, he may help them to work off their resentments against each other.

In later stages, the mediator can attempt to seek some definite solution to disputed issues. Rarely will he have information (for example, facts on settlements made in comparable disputes elsewhere) that is not already known to both parties. Rarely also will the mediator produce a solution that has not been previously considered by the two parties. The skill of the mediator lies in creating an atmosphere in which true bargaining can take place, one in which proposals previously rejected out of hand may now be given some serious thought. To do this, the mediator may exert pressure on one or both parties to give in at least partially on items that hitherto have been insuperable roadblocks. He may suggest informally to one party that if they yield on one item, the opposition may be willing to yield on some other point. The mediator may not report threats uttered by one party against the other if he feels that their disclosure will only serve to increase tensions. Threats may be used to encourage the granting of concessions. Finally, the mediator may act as a salesman for his own solution, attempting to convince both parties of the futility of their extreme positions.

Although the calling for mediation is sometimes avoided when possible on the grounds that it is in and of itself a concession of weakness, the mediator may serve a useful function by assuming some of the responsibility for the concessions to be made. Both parties may blame the mediator for a failure to maintain their original position. Particularly where the government is exerting great pressure on both sides for a settlement, the government representative can serve as a convenient culprit.

Less frequently have the parties been willing to seek an end to an impasse through arbitration; arbitration even of a compulsory nature is (though still not common) far more frequently a part of the industrial relations scene in other countries than it is in the United States. In this country, both unions and management tend to feel that they understand the situation far better than any outsider. Unions also view the delays involved in arbitration as dangerous to the membership's morale.

Even though there is no third party on which to lay the blame, a defeated party can always plead before the public that he "fought the good fight" and that his early position, although basically correct, was impossible to maintain in the face of the bargaining strength of the opponent. The conceding party can also claim credit for having yielded "in the public interest" even though the terms of the settlement closely resemble those against which he was warning the public only a short time earlier. Some firms have resisted union demands on the ground that the nation must be protected against inflation, and then agreed to them with the explanation that a settlement of the strike was in the public interest.

Although it is not always possible to convince anyone who is familiar with the facts that a defeat was in reality a victory, it is often possible for both sides to proclaim a victory. Thus, in 1964 the UAW after ending a month-long strike at General Motors, claimed that they had won what they sought in the form of extended seniority rights, easier production quotas, and the sharing of overtime. Simultaneously, Louis Seaton, the company's personnel director, announced that, "We haven't agreed to anything that is going to impair our responsibility to our shareholders to run an efficient business. And that's what this strike has been about." The reader is challenged to decide on the basis of these conflicting claims who really won.

Summary and Evaluation

In this chapter, we have attempted to show that the problem of bargaining involves far more than dollars and cents. While economic factors set the ultimate boundaries within which a settlement must be made (see Chapter 6 for a detailed discussion of these boundaries), considerable latitude can exist within these boundaries. Our discussion of the tactics involved in the strategy of bargaining has suggested that a wide variety of situations is possible. Because the circumstances under which bargaining takes place are so varied, it is difficult to predict the pattern of any particular bargaining session. There are too many unknowns; most important perhaps, the character and temperament of the various participants and the cost structure of the firm in question. Some businesses may prefer a devious and subtle approach; others will favor a straightforward "take it or leave it" basis. The effectiveness of these alternative approaches will depend in part upon the character and temperament of the opposition. Presumably both parties become more skilled at bargaining and more difficult to bluff as their bargaining experience increases. Whereas the bad poker player is free to continue playing the game as long as his money holds out, inept players in the collective bargaining game are likely to be speedily removed.

While both parties must develop skills in order to survive, the union leader is under greater pressure than management. He must secure a consensus from the rank and file as to their objectives as well as a pledge of their willingness to fight for those objectives. When it becomes apparent that concessions must be made, he must woo the membership to accept the new contract and convince them that it is more than adequate even though it is not all they had originally hoped for and expected.

One final comment—much of the analysis of this chapter is far more applicable to collective bargaining in the United States than to similar proceedings in other countries. In the United States both parties have been more disposed to make bargaining into a "game" than have their counterparts elsewhere in the world.

NOTES

1. Arthur Ross, "Labor Courses: The Need for Radical Reconstruction," *Industrial Relations,* 4 (October 1964), 1–17.

2. John Nash, "Two Person Cooperative Games," *Econometrica* 21 (January 1953), 128–140, and "The Bargaining Problem," *Econometrica* 18 (April 1950), 155–162.

3. J. Pen, "A General Theory of Bargaining," *American Economic Review,* 42 (March 1952), 24–42.

4. John R. Hicks, *The Theory of Wages* (New York: Peter Smith, 1948), p. 143.

5. See Bevars Mabry's defense of an earlier article of his in the "Communications" section of the *Industrial and Labor Relations Review* 19 (April 1966), 428–429.

6. John von Neumann and Oskar Morgenstern, *Theory of Games and Economic Behavior* (Princeton, N.J.: Princeton University Press, 1953).

7. One example of such a practical approach is outlined by Myron L. Joseph, "An Experimental Approach to the Study of Collective Bargaining," Industrial Relations Research Association, *Proceedings* (1960), pp. 139–155.

8. This possibility was first pointed out by John R. Hicks, *op. cit.*

9. The situation was further complicated by the number of unions involved in the pattern bargaining situation, as the various unions jockeyed for leadership position. At a later strike the ITU announced an independent position in its effort to set the wage standards. The NLRB has often frowned upon the splintering of multiemployer groups and union coalitions involved in multiemployer bargaining when a new union is involved and has been most resistant when initiative came from an employer. See Harry A. Millis and Emily Clark Brown, *From Wagner Act to Taft-Hartley* (Chicago: University of Chicago Press, 1950), pp. 150–155.

10. Richard A. Lester, "Reflections on Collective Bargaining in Britain and Sweden," *Industrial and Labor Relations Review,* 10 (April 1957), 375–401.

11. Much of the following analysis on this point was developed by Richard E. Walton, "Leadership Strategies for Achieving Membership Consensus During Negotiations," Industrial Relations Research Association, *Proceedings of the 18th Annual Meeting* (December 1965), pp. 99–110.

12. The General Electric Company has submitted as many as 246 printed statements of positions to the workers before and during bargaining over a new contract. Albert Blum, for example, takes a generally dim view of the role "facts" play in collective bargaining: ". . . collective bargaining often consists of propaganda parading as facts—a martial display put on to convince the armies of labor, management, and the public that a struggle is going on." Albert A. Blum, "Collective Bargaining—Ritual or Reality?" *Harvard Business Review,* (December 1961), pp. 63–69. In general, Blum believes most of the actions on the part of both parties are mere windowdressing since both usually know well in advance the boundaries within which a settlement will be made.

13. David I. Shair, "The Mythology of Labor Contract Rejections," *Labor Law Journal* (February 1970), pp. 88–94. Shair

argues that the problem has been grossly exaggerated, however.

14. See Clyde W. Summers, "Ratification of Agreements," in John T. Dunlop and Neil W. Chamberlain (eds.), *Frontiers of Collective Bargaining* (New York: Harper & Row, 1967), pp. 75–102.

15. For a defense of "Boulwarism," see Herbert R. Northrup, "The Case for Boul-warism," *Harvard Business Review,* 41 (September–October 1963) 86–97.

16. Neil Chamberlain, *Social Responsibility and Strikes* (New York: Harper & Row, 1953).

17. Robert R. McKersey and Richard E. Walton, "The Theory of Bargaining," *Industrial and Labor Relations Review,* 19 (April 1966), 423.

6
Wage Theory and Collective Bargaining

. . . it is a curious fact, explained perhaps by undue emphasis on a narrow price economics, that economists generally have been prone to discuss collective bargaining, the need for it, and what it can and what it cannot accomplish, in terms of wages only.

—Harry A. Millis

□ ALTHOUGH economists have been preoccupied with the relationship between wages and collective bargaining for a long time, the entire theory of wage determination is still in a very fuzzy stage of development. It is not difficult, for example, to find economists who in one breath will deny that unions are able to have any appreciable effect on the level of wages and in the next breath warn of the danger of the inflationary pressure that results from the unions' upward pressure on wage rates. The bulk of economic theorizing about wages, however, has been devoted to explaining why the efforts of unions to raise wages will prove futile. The major part of this chapter will be devoted to a review of these theories.

Malthusian Law

The Malthusian law of population is too familiar to require much explanation here. Thomas Robert Malthus warned his contemporaries of the imminent danger of overpopulation, contending that men had a propensity to reproduce themselves at a geometric rate while the means to support the expanding population could only be increased at an arithmetic rate. Therefore, Malthus argued, the population constantly tended to outstrip the means for supporting it. Only famine, disease, and war checked overpopulation and thus prevented mass starvation. In answer to early critics, Malthus later suggested that the mass practice of moral restraint might provide another solution, although he never appeared to be very convinced of the practicality of this solution.

The Malthusian doctrine was used against the unions' demands for higher wages in two ways. The first and most obvious argument stated that if workers got higher wages, they would increase the size of their families and thus endanger the nation's ability to support itself. The second argument contended that growth in the size of families would result in an increase in the size of the labor force. As more workers entered the labor market, the increased competition for jobs would drive wages down to the level that existed prior to the attempted increase by unions.

Economists who built their wage theories on the Malthusian law postulated a subsistence theory of wages. Wages could never permanently rise above the subsistence level since any tendency in this direction would soon be followed by an increase in the population. To use more modern economic language, such theorists postulated a long-run supply curve of labor that was perfectly elastic. Any increase in the long-run demand for labor could be met by the expansion of the labor supply through the growth of the population.

Although David Ricardo and others modified the grim conclusions of the Malthusian law by pointing out that the standard of what constituted subsistence did not necessarily have to remain fixed, most economists in the nineteenth century took the Malthusian warning far more seriously than economists do today. British trade unions in the mid-nineteenth century, for example, were very much concerned that the public would accept the validity of the Malthusian law and oppose the efforts of unions to increase wages. In order to reassure the public that the efforts to increase wages would not result simply in increases in the size of workers' families, the unions pointed out that they had provided their members with birth control information.

Wages Fund Doctrine

John Stuart Mill, who developed the most complete expression of the wages fund doctrine, was a disciple of Ricardo and a firm believer in the more dire aspects of the Malthusian doctrine. Nevertheless, his doctrine marked a distinct change from the simple subsistence theories of wages just outlined.

According to Mill, there was a fixed amount of capital available for the employment of labor at any given time. To secure the average wage (ignoring wage differentials of which Mill was well aware), one divided the sum of capital by the number of people to be employed as follows:

$$\frac{\text{Wages Fund}}{\text{No. to be Employed}} = \text{Wage.}$$

By transposing one obtains the equation:

$$\text{No. to be Employed} = \frac{\text{Wages Fund}}{\text{Average Wage}}.$$

This latter equation tells us how many can be employed at different levels of wages given the size of the wages fund. The implications to the economy

of an increase in wages by unions is obvious. Higher average wage rates will only result in some workers losing their jobs. Only as the wages fund increases, which is made possible by the savings of capitalists, is it possible to have higher wages and still maintain employment at a high level.

Economists sympathetic to the cause of unions were quick to attack the wages fund concept. Critics pointed out, for example, that the theory ignored the possibility that wages could be paid out of current production rather than out of a stockpile of capital accumulated at some earlier time. Although the theory continued to persist for some time after Mill's death, Mill himself eventually recanted and admitted the weaknesses of his theory.

Theory of Marginal Productivity

Many economists persist in their belief that unions can do little to affect the general level of wages because they have an abiding belief in the power of economic laws and the automatic operation of the market mechanism and cling to evidence that the economy operates in a predictable way. To admit that unions might upset the economic laws would raise questions about the accuracy and validity of the economist's reasoning, which would be bad enough in itself. However, the model of competition in the market place was satisfying to economists for another reason: It gave the best results imaginable. It is easy to understand the unwillingness of these economists to accept the possibility that unions were able to upset the economic laws.

The marginal productivity theory of wages is no exception to this generalization; one of the motives prompting its formulation was to justify the

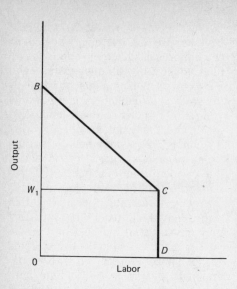

FIGURE 6.1 Marginal Productivity Theory

then-existing patterns of distribution (today the theory is used to explain rather than justify existing patterns of distribution). The first complete statement of the theory came from the famous American economic theorist John Bates Clark. To explain his theory, Clark offered the diagram shown in Figure 6.1. The curve *BC* is the demand curve for labor based on the marginal productivity gained from the employment of additional workers. Each worker is paid exactly what he is worth—the value that the additional output from his employment makes possible. A number of assumptions underlay Clark's theory; some of them were more easy to accept than others. Clark assumed the existence of nearly perfect competition, with both employers and workers seeking to maximize their income and possessing sufficient knowledge and mobility to do so. As a result, no single firm was able to act as a monopolist either in selling its products or in buying factors of production. The downward slope of the demand curve was also significant

since its slope assumed that all firms were operating under conditions of diminishing returns. Furthermore, the theory is usually stated in real terms and for the economy as an entity. Clark's theory depended on two more important assumptions. Workers were assumed to be sufficiently homogeneous so that substitutions among them could be made easily and the last worker employed was just as able (and therefore in terms of his own ability worth just as much) as the first worker employed. The fact that the last worker produced much less than the first worker did not reflect on the last worker's ability, but merely demonstrated the operation of the law of diminishing returns. Finally, the methods of production over time were sufficiently variable to permit the substitution of one factor for another.

Given the above assumptions, a number of important conclusions could be drawn. Overriding all others was the conclusion that unions (or legislatures) could not raise the wage rate without reducing the volume of employment. Assuming that the quantity of workers *OD* were seeking employment, they could all be successful only at wage W_1. Since all workers were of equal ability, the wage paid to the last one employed set the standard for all other workers as well. The forces of competition worked to ensure a tendency for the labor force to be distributed among the many firms so that the value of labor's marginal product was equal for all firms. Should wages rise above the indicated equilibrium, firms would sooner or later react by laying off workers until the marginal product of the last worker retained was just equal to the newly established wage. Because the early theorists all assumed full employment, a situation of unemployment could not long exist. Unemployed workers would seek employment and bid the wage rate back down to the point where full employment was restored.

By the same token, workers did not need any device like the union to protect them from exploitation by employers. Just as competition among workers would tend to drive wages that were above the marginal productivity level (assuming full employment) down to that level, so competition among employers would prevent wages from falling below the marginal level. Should an employer try to take advantage of his workers, they would quickly find jobs with other companies who would be glad to get them at the marginal rate.

Note also that the marginal productivity theory was couched in terms of tendencies and long-run adjustments. Opponents as well as supporters of the marginal productivity theory have been too prone to overlook the importance of both of these qualifications. Some supporters have adopted the theory as a means of demonstrating conclusively that wage increases in excess of marginal productivity level will immediately lead employers to cut their labor force. As we will see in a moment, critics have become increasingly insistent that short-run adjustments do not frequently occur in the manner prescribed by the theory. Supporters of the theory then fell back on the long-run interpretation without realizing that much of the usefulness of the theory as a determinant of wages had thereby been lost.

The marginal productivity theory also provides for the possibility of long-run adjustments in wages. Improved technology, greater worker efficiency resulting from improved standards of training, and a growth in the demand for the product can all shift the demand curve to the right. If marginal productivity is ruled in-valid in the short run and held to be applicable only in the long run, however, the precise relations between wages and the levels of employment become lost. No longer is the marginal productivity curve a fixed line in space upon which the necessary relationships between employment and wages can be computed.

Neither the wages fund doctrine nor the marginal productivity theory contended that increases in wages were impossible. Supporters of the wages fund doctrine pointed out that wages could increase as the volume of savings increased. If workers, after receiving the higher wages, would only restrain their propensity to overreproduce themselves, there was virtually no limit to the heights to which wages might rise. All of this, it should again be emphasized, could occur in the absence of any unions pushing for higher wages.

The significant fact that the theory is expressed in terms of tendencies should not be overlooked either. Supporters of the theory all too often tend to ignore the tendency qualification and write as if the relationships were cut and dried and operated in a numerically precise fashion. Critics, on the other hand, seem to assume that a tendency can be safely ignored. To them, a tendency means that it might not happen and if it might not, why worry about it?

Critics of Marginal Productivity Theory

The criticisms of marginal productivity have been too numerous and too involved to permit a detailed analysis of them within the scope of this book. The best that we can hope to do is to classify the criticisms under two general headings and indicate briefly the nature of the criticism falling under each heading.

One group of criticisms denies that the typical businessman acts in the manner dictated by marginal productivity theory. Richard Lester, for example, based on the results of a questionnaire sent to a number of business firms, suggested that employers pay scant attention to the level of their wage rates in determining the size of their plant's labor force. The executives who answered Lester's questionnaire cited the expected volume of sales as a more important determinant.[1]

Lester maintained that, when faced with a rise in wage costs, employers tried to increase prices or increase sales rather than reduce the number on their payrolls. Such action, of course, involves shifting the MP (marginal productivity) or demand curve for labor to the right. Lester suggested that businessmen avoid curtailing output because they deem their plants generally to be operating in a zone of decreasing variable costs (variable costs are those that vary with the scale of production—wages, for example). Whereas under the marginal productivity analysis a firm would expect to decrease its average variable costs when it reduces output, employers in the Lester questionnaire reported the reverse to be the case.

Lester's analysis was subjected to some stinging criticism from Fritz Machlup, who was dubious both about Lester's research methods (including the validity of his questionnaire[2]) and his conclusions as to the applicability of marginal productivity theory. Although a number of Machlup's criticisms are valid, his defense of the marginal concept does depend on a considerable relaxation in the mode of its application. Machlup conceded that the theory lacked precision in determining the volume of employment and

he increased the role expectations and uncertainty played in the theory's application. Most economists would probably agree that the extent to which other factors such as sales volume affect the marginal productivity analysis still needs further empirical investigation.

Lloyd Reynolds' analysis is similar to Lester's. Reynolds suggests that the businessman reacts to an increase in wage rates by trying to economize in all areas of operations.[3] While an increase in wages might result in some reductions in employment, the total impact of the increase would be diffused, with other factors of production also experiencing some cutback. A third point often made by critics of marginal productivity theory along these general lines is to deny that the employer really acts to maximize his profits. If an employer does not constantly seek to maximize profits, a higher level of wages may produce no discernible change in the number of workers employed. The employer's behavior in this respect is frequently attributed to a sense of social conscience. This variant of the argument suggests that employers are concerned about the suffering and misery that laying off some of their workers will cause and thus will seek to maintain the size of their labor force as long as it is humanly possible.

All theories that attack marginal productivity by contending that the employer may not react in the expected fashion to an increase in wages are predicated on the assumption that the typical employer has far more discretion in his decision making than is conceived possible under the competitive model. If the market forces are sufficiently great, the employer would be compelled to reduce employment in response to a wage increase whether he wanted to or not.

A second line of criticism suggests

that the marginal productivity theory can have no practical applicability since an employer cannot know the location of the marginal productivity curve or measure it with sufficient precision to make it usable. Even if businessmen were prone to think in marginal terms (an assumption some critics would be unwilling to make) the curve can never be translated into a usable tool but must remain only a convenient teaching device. H. M. Oliver, for example, argues that in any large corporation wage classification systems are too complex to permit application of the marginal productivity concept.[4] Some wages are based on piece rates, some on time, and some on a combination of the two. Estimating the marginal cost of an extra worker is further complicated by the existence of fringe benefits because some of these, like paid sick leave, are impossible to calculate in advance. The picture is further complicated, according to Oliver, by the frequent discrepancy between the selling and the announced list price, which makes the price of a product difficult to forecast. When allowance is made for advertising and the existence of joint products, the prospects of the businessman making a rational marginal decision with respect to wages are extremely poor.

To a large extent the validity of all these attacks rests on the question of whether or not business firms seek to maximize their profits. If it is granted that they do, a reasonably good defense of marginal productivity can be constructed. If it is argued that a businessman does not have the knowledge or the information necessary for such decisions, one can answer that he simply does the best that he can. Pushed to their logical extreme, some of these criticisms sound as if businessmen never react to increases in wages and this is obvious nonsense.

Many of the criticisms just reviewed attack the validity of the many assumptions laid down by the marginal productivity theorists. Defenders of the theory, however, argue that such attacks are irrelevant. They contend that the value of any theory lies in its ability to aid in making predictions rather than in the realism of its assumptions. The essential question then is whether or not marginal productivity theory does provide us with an insight as to how businessmen act, and it may do so even though businessmen themselves deny that they are acting in the fashion dictated by the theory.

Who is right? Hopefully, we will not sound too cowardly if we take a moderate position (thus exposing us to fire from both camps). In our opinion, the promarginalists have overstated the predictability of their theory when applied to any given market situation. At the same time, recent defenders have been too quick to deny the importance of using realistic assumptions. Although theorists must always allow for some artificiality in their assumptions in order to gain tractability, some theorists are too ready to close their eyes to these unrealities as long as the results are satisfactory, apparently on the theory "We must be doing something right" (but we're not quite sure what!).[5] On the other hand, the many criticisms of the marginal productivity theory's realism serve better as a warning to use it cautiously rather than a reason to abandon it entirely.

The story does not end here, however. Another whole series of qualifications have been advanced concerning the applicability of the marginal productivity theory. These revolve around the shape and nature of the marginal productivity curve and/or of the supply curve of labor. Unlike the objections we first discussed, these arguments do not deny the validity of the theory,

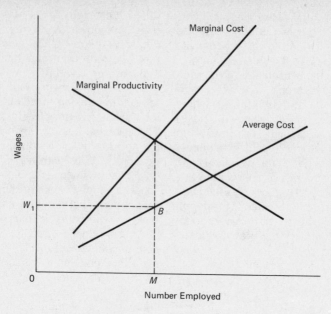

FIGURE 6.2 Monopsony

but only point out that the relationship between the wage level and the quantity of labor employed may not be as direct as has been sometimes supposed.

Many of the projected shapes of the MP curve, and the projected labor supply curve, present the employer with the opportunity to exploit workers; the efforts of unions do not distort wages away from the marginal productivity level with an accompanying loss of employment but instead tend to push them closer to competitive levels. In essence, these critics challenge the assumption of perfect competition upon which Clark founded the marginal productivity theory.

Perhaps the best-known situation in which it is possible for employers to exploit workers is one of monopsony, in which there is either only one employer or an employer who is large enough to affect the prevailing wage rate in his locale by his decision to

hire more or fewer workers. The diagram used to explain monopsony is reproduced in Figure 6.2. The marginal productivity curve is the same as that given earlier, but now there is a divergence between the average cost (supply curve) of labor and its marginal cost. This discrepancy results from the market power of the employers under conditions of monopsony. Some workers are very anxious to work and will work for say $1.00 an hour. If the employer wants to hire additional workers, he finds that he can do so only by paying a somewhat higher hourly rate, say $1.10 an hour. If still more workers are wanted, still higher wages become necessary. Since the increased wage rate will also be paid to those workers willing to work for less, the marginal cost of an extra worker becomes not only the additional cost of his own wage, but also the added amount the employer now has to pay other workers. When the

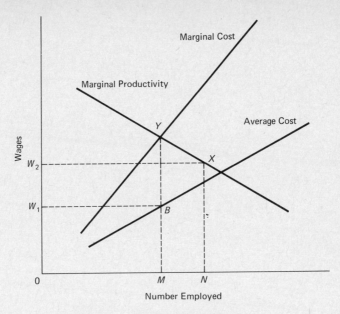

FIGURE 6.3 Union Overriding Monopsony

employer has no control over the labor input market, the supply curve of labor coincides with the marginal cost curve of labor. Under monopsony, however, the two no longer coincide, and to maximize his position, the employer hires where the marginal cost curve of labor meets his marginal productivity curve.[6] This provides him with the correct quantity of labor to employ for maximum profit. At point *B* in Figure 6.2, the intersection of the vertical with the employer's supply curve is the wage rate he will have to pay to secure that quantity of labor.

The beauty of this monopsony situation is that the union can have its cake and eat it too; an increase in wages, providing it is not too great, can result in an increase in the volume of employment rather than the normally expected reduction. Note, for example, in Figure 6.3 that if the union succeeds in raising the wages level to W_2X and removes the possibility of discrimina-

tion by the employer, the employer is faced with a perfectly elastic supply curve of labor with a marginal cost curve overlapping it. To maximize his position he will hire workers to the point where his new *MC* curve and his *MP* curves intersect. The result, as Figure 6.3 indicates, will be an increase in the number of workers he will employ, from *OM* to *ON*. Only at a wage rate above *Y* is the volume of employment less than it was before the union intervened. By removing the employer's ability to discriminate and insisting that all workers (of equal ability) be paid alike, the union can secure higher wages without necessarily reducing the volume of employment.

Although the theoretical validity of this solution has never been questioned, many have expressed doubts about the frequency with which such situations arise in real life. Unions, of course, have tended to find evidence

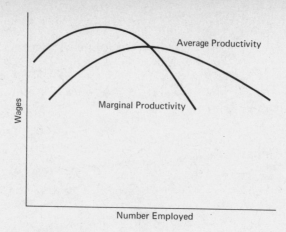

FIGURE 6.4   Average and Marginal Productivity Curves

of monopsony in every plant of any size that does not have a union. Many economists, however, doubt that the labor market is so imperfect and see monopsony as a relatively rare phenomenon.

A variation on the theme of market control is the concept of the kinky demand curve. A kinky demand curve is said to exist when the demand curve for a company's products changes slope over the range of possible prices. The situation is reproduced in Figure 6.4. Near perfect elasticity is postulated at the upper range of prices. It is assumed that a decision by the company to raise its price would not be followed by its competitors. Thus any price increase would speedily result in a loss of most of the company's customers. At lower price ranges, the reverse is true. Any effort by the company to cut prices in order to win additional customers would be quickly matched by rival firms. The result would be savings for customers but little additional sales for the firm. Unable to improve its position effectively by either raising or lowering prices, the company would tend to operate at output Q_1 and price P_1.

This analysis is relevant to our dis-

cussion of collective bargaining because the kink in the demand curve produces a discontinuity in the firm's marginal revenue curve in the manner indicated in Figure 6.4. Such a discontinuity permits the marginal cost curve to be shifted upward or downward over a considerable range without having any effect on output. (Remember that under either perfect or monopolistic competition, output is determined at the point where marginal revenue equals marginal cost.) As a result, a union bargaining with a company that has a kinky demand curve for its products can force labor costs up by an appreciable amount without disturbing the company's level of output. The tendency toward reductions in the volume of employment is correspondingly reduced.

The significance of kinky demand curves as a means to allow unions to escape from the unemployment effects of higher wages is qualified in two ways. First, the employer may still find it economically desirable to substitute other factors for labor even while maintaining the same level of output. Second, as in the case of monopsony, there is also doubt as to how frequently the kinky demand curve makes an appearance in the real world. Some economists have denied that it exists save as a figment of the economic theorist's imagination.[7]

Another line of reasoning that questions the significance of marginal productivity in wage and employment determination suggests that the demand curve for labor may be too inelastic to be important. Many years ago, Alfred Marshall in his *Principles of Economics* postulated that demand for a factor of production could be inelastic. Such a situation would develop, said Marshall, if the demand for the final product was inelastic or if the supply of substitute factors of production was inelastic. Several later economists have utilized Marshall's point that factors are not as easily divisible as the marginal productivity theory of wages suggests. These critics assume that the employer has already gone as far as possible in substituting machinery for labor; further substitution is thus impossible without massive changes in wage levels.

Marshall also proposed that the demand for a factor would be inelastic if its cost was a relatively small part of the total cost of the product produced; we will return to this point later.

Another hypothesis that has been advanced in the attack on the marginal productivity theory denies that the marginal productivity curve slopes downward and to the right in the fashion indicated in Figure 6.1. In effect, this criticism rejects the contention that the typical firm employs any factor of production under conditions of diminishing returns until plant capacity is reached,[8] and is based on the increasing returns firms experience as they expand their scale of operations. This hypothesis thus does not deny the logic of the marginal productivity theory, but rather the validity of its assumption of a static state in which increasing returns do not occur.

The question of whether or not wages are raised through collective bargaining is blurred by the claims made by both unions and employers. For once, the two parties are in basic agreement; both assert that the impact of unions on wages is considerable. Such unanimity does not necessarily prove the accuracy of the claim, however. Both unions and management have good but different reasons for asserting that unions have a substantial effect on wages. What union leader in his right mind would admit that the union provided the members with no economic benefits? While the desire for increased wages is clearly not the only reason why workers join unions, an overwhelming proportion of the membership believes that their union does win them improvements in wage levels. If they did not think so, the total union membership would be far smaller than it is. In European countries like Germany, France, and England, which have experienced a "wage drift" with many employers paying wages in excess of those specified in the union contract, there has been a substantial reduction in union membership.

Employers also assert that unions force wages upward. Unlike the union leaders, however, the employer enters this contention not as a plus item in favor of the union but as a mark against it. Management tends to stress that the union is responsible for unemployment and inflationary pressures resulting from the higher wages it has forced upon management.

Empirical Research

Given all of the conflicting views set forth by the economic theorists, plus unwillingness to accept the united assertions of union leaders and management at face value, the reader might well ask why empirical research has not been undertaken to establish the true answer. Although a number of economists have indeed attempted such research, their findings are contradictory and do not provide a final answer.

One major difficulty in testing the impact of unions on wages lies in judging the influence that wages in organized plants have on wage levels in companies that have not been organized. To what extent do nonunion employers match or even anticipate wage increases in union plants as a means of keeping the union out of their plant? One Teamster organizer, for example, reported to a local Trade Unions Council meeting that he had received a telephone call from a local soft-drink company employee that afternoon. The employee had inquired, "When are you going to come around and try to organize us again? We haven't had a wage increase in some time."

Isolating the union's influence on wages from other factors that may account for the differences between union and nonunion shops presents another major difficulty. To be valid, the comparison must involve companies in the same industry. The plant's size, its productivity, market position, and geographical location are all factors that are more difficult to control for the purpose of comparison. Inability to compute the exact worth of fringe benefits also complicates the picture.

Upon one point all students are agreed. Wages *have* experienced substantial increases in the last one hundred years. Between 1933 and 1957 alone money wages rose by over 500 percent and real wages (computed with allowances made for changes in the price level) rose by nearly 235 percent. Between 1939 and 1970 alone real wages more than doubled. The issue then is not whether or not wages have risen—they most definitely have —but how much of this increase is accounted for by the demands of unions.

One of the earliest attempts to measure the impact of unions on wages was undertaken by Paul H. Douglas (who later became a U.S. Senator) in 1930.[9] In this pioneer study, which examined six unionized and eight nonunionized industries, Douglas concluded that unions did have some effect on the level of wages but that (with the exception of the building trades) this effect was limited primarily to the early stages of the union's organization of a plant. After the initial upsurge in wages that followed the introduction of the union, the wages of union members tended to rise at the same rate as those of nonunion workers. Although Douglas noted that the building trades were an exception to this general rule, he also pointed out that for the time period upon which his study concentrated (1890–1926), real wages rose the most during a period when total union membership was declining.

Douglas did not explore the relationship between wages and employment. However, his conclusion that unions were successful in raising wages only in the early stages of their organizational effort fits into the marginal productivity theory very well provided that the principle of free competition is interpreted in a relatively relaxed fashion. Perhaps the market was functioning in a sufficiently imperfect manner (under conditions of monopsony, for example) so that workers were paid less than their full marginal productivity. Unions might then have made it possible for workers to receive the wage economists had maintained that the market assured them without any protection from unions. Once this discrepancy had been removed, however, unions faced the old economic law that ruled that further wage increases (barring changes in demand or technology) would produce reductions in employment.

Douglas' general conclusion that unions are most effective in increasing wage levels at the time they organize an employer was challenged by Arthur Ross.[10] Ross pointed out that Douglas' figures were misleading because the increases in wages were couched only in terms of percentages. He charged that this method of presentation disguised the fact that the absolute differences between the wage increases of unionized and nonunionized workers continued to exist long after the union had become a mature institution.

Ross argued quite correctly that unless one compared wage increases that had started at a common level, percentage differentials would appear much greater for those cases where wages were at a low level at the base period. To correct this flaw, Ross, whenever possible, divided the industries into three separate groups depending on the level of wages at the beginning of the period. Each group was then divided into five subdivisions based on the degree of unionization, and Ross computed percentage increases in each case. In this manner, Ross felt he had removed the error implicit in the Douglas study.

On the basis of his wage comparisons, Ross concluded that wages in the unionized industries had risen by 61 percent while wages in nonunion industries had increased by only 18 percent. From 1914 to 1926, when, according to Douglas, the well-established unions supposedly no longer had any effect on wages, Ross found the rate of wage increases in union plants was double that of the nonunion plants.

In his first study Ross concluded that "Real hourly earnings have advanced more sharply in highly organized industries than in less unionized industries, in periods of declining union membership as well as periods of rapid unionization."[11] However, he modified this formulation in three important respects in a subsequent study (with William Goldner).[12] First, he was impressed by the degree of uniformity of wage increases throughout the economy irrespective of the differing conditions under which they were gained. Second, he noted that factors other than unionization—the varying proportions of skilled workers and women and the degree of monopoly enjoyed by the firm—could also significantly affect the extent of wage increases. Finally, although Ross continued to maintain that unionization did influence the degree to which wages advanced, he now came much closer to Douglas' position that the unions' primary impact on wages came when they first organized a firm.

One of the most comprehensive studies to date was conducted by Harold Levinson, who patterned it on Ross' first study. Levinson's sample covered the years from 1914 to 1947 and included between 7 and 11 million workers,[13] overlapping Ross' sample for the years 1933 to 1947, but including several service and trade industries that Ross did not. Levinson divided his sample into a number of classes depending upon the level of wages existing at the base year. Levinson then divided his study into a series of separate time periods in order to measure the effect of unions on wages under varying economic conditions.

Levinson's major conclusion was that the effect unions have on wages varies with time and the configuration of the economy. According to Levinson, between 1920 and 1933 union members experienced significant gains relative to nonunion members. By 1947, however, nonunion members had recouped much of their relative position.

Although Levinson believes that unions have important effects on wage levels, he introduces two important qualifications. The first is that the impact of unions may vary not only from time to time, but also from industry to industry. Levinson mentions as cases in point the railroad shop-craft workers and the coal miners. Both unions were able to win better than average gains when they were strong but lost ground badly during periods of weakness. Levinson's second reservation is even more important; he concludes that government policy and changing business conditions affect wage levels more than collective bargaining does.

Levinson's basic position is that only really strong unions can change the level of wages from what it would have been in the absence of the union and even they can only do so under certain circumstances. When unfavorable economic conditions prevail or when the political atmosphere is unfriendly to unions, the position of unorganized workers and workers who are members of ineffective unions is likely to deteriorate. Only a powerful union can secure any gains against these unfavorable environmental conditions.

On the other hand, when the labor market is tight and employers are bidding actively for labor or when the government's attitude toward labor is generally favorable, Levinson contends that the powerful unions are unable to win any more for their members than can be gained by those workers without any union recognition at all. Levinson supports this contention by stressing the tendency of wage gains won by strong unions to be quickly adopted by nonunion employers or by employers faced with unions normally in a weak bargaining position. Whether employers fear the loss of their workers to higher-paying plants during periods of labor scarcity or whether they fear the possible organization of their plants during periods when the government is encouraging labor, the result is the same— wages in all sectors move up to the same extent and the superior bargaining power of the strong unions wins no differential in wages for their members.

Harry M. Douty has warned us that the frequent assumption that union wages are always above nonunion wages is subject to several important qualifications.[14] He notes, for example, that the union workers' advantage varies widely from industry to industry and from one geographical location to another. It is not at all unusual, Douty finds, for nonunion workers in the North to be paid higher wages than union workers in the South even though both groups are engaged in the same occupation. Given comparable industries and comparable situations, however, Douty concludes that union wages tend to run consistently above those paid to nonunion workers.

H. Gregg Lewis' study, *Unionism and Relative Wages in the United States,* concluded that in recent years unions had raised the relative average wage for their members by between 7 and 11 percent while at the same time reducing the average relative wage for nonunion members by about 3 or 4 percent. Lewis added that the power of unions to create differentials diminished as the rate of inflation in the country increased.[15] Accordingly Lewis' study suggested that union and nonunion wage differentials vary substantially over time. He estimated that during the past forty years the wage differential between the two varied from close to zero in the 1947–1948 inflation period to more than 25 percent in the 1932–1933 depression years.

All of the writers we have discussed thus far agree that given certain conditions, unions do have a positive effect on wage rates. All of them, by specifying favorable economic conditions or by noting the importance of other factors, have been cautious in their assessment of the impact of collective bargaining. Robert Ozanne has taken a much more positive position. Ozanne contends that other students of the question have been unduly cautious and too prone to dismiss union demands as being "filled with sound and fury which signifieth nothing."[16] Ozanne argues that other writers have been led astray by studying the impact of unions during periods when unions were too weak to achieve their goals. With the strength they have achieved during and since World War II, however, unions must be reckoned a much more potent force. Furthermore, Ozanne contends: "A second error of earlier studies has been the emphasis on distributive shares. This method is not precise enough for measuring the impact of unionism."[17] Since three-quarters of the nation's labor force do not belong to unions, Ozanne reasons that testing the over-all redistributive effects unions have on income will not tell us anything conclusive about their power to win gains for their members. We will consider the impact of unions on income distribution at more length in the next chapter.

Because Ozanne felt that previous studies had overemphasized the distributive shares approach or neglected the interaction between union plants and nearby nonunion plants, he couched his study in terms of a comparison of two time periods—one in which unions were relatively weak (1923–1929) and one when they were relatively powerful (1947–1957). Comparing the performance of wages for these two periods, Ozanne found what he termed a "phenomenal" difference. During the 1920s wages had remained virtually static, while in the period following World War II, wages rose year after year. The result was that wages for production workers in manufacturing measured in real hourly earnings rose nearly twice as fast in the second period as they had in the first period.

Ozanne believes that the post-World War II gains by unions were made in spite of market forces rather than because of those forces. Wage increases continued despite increases in the volume of unemployment. The ability of unions to overcome an unfavorable economic environment was convincing evidence to Ozanne of the increased bargaining strength of the union movement.

Brief mention should also be made of a more recent study by Ozanne of wage performance at McCormick.[18] Ozanne found that real average hourly earnings rose at 3.9 percent during the period when there was a union as compared to .1 percent when no union existed. To strengthen his argument, Ozanne makes comparisons with two other companies that were McCormick's strong competitors at the time.

Two other studies that support Ozanne's position should be cited. In line with Ozanne's suggestion that many of the earlier studies were misleading because they dealt with periods when union strength was less than it has since become, Martin Segal studied many of the same industries surveyed by Levinson but for the more recent period 1952–1958.[19] On the basis of his findings, Segal concluded that unions played a bigger role than Levinson had been willing to credit them; Segal correspondingly assigned a lesser role than Levinson to both profits and the degree of industry concentration. Segal conceded, however, that wage determination was a function not only of union but also of corporate power.

That strong unions can in individual instances do much to improve the wage position of their members has been emphasized by Frank Pierson.[20] Pierson compared the performance of wages for the years from 1947 to 1959 in six major industry groups organized by strong unions (automobiles, bituminous coal, contract construction, class I railroads, basic steel, and trucking) with manufacturing in general. In every case except automobiles, the industries with strong unions did better in terms of percentage increase in wages than did general manufacturing. Although one could quarrel with Pierson's standards and definitions of "strong," one of his major points is worthy of consideration. He points out that in three of the industries (coal, railroads, and steel) economic conditions were not those normally associated with rising wage rates—expanding markets and employment opportunities—but exactly the opposite. Pierson concludes, therefore, that it was the power of the unions in these instances that produced the increases in wages.

The late Sumner Slichter also expressed the conviction that unions do have a significant impact on wages. Slichter supported his contention less by statistical evidence than by reasoned logic. It seemed inconceivable to him that unions could win union security clauses (to which many employers are deeply opposed) and not be able to secure wage gains. Second, Slichter suggested that, in the absence of unions, wages are placed on a "take or leave it" basis by the employer and that such a standard is likely to be less responsive to the market than wages set by collective bargaining.[21]

The Opposing View

Not all economists agree with Ozanne's conclusions and many would at least voice the kind of qualifications noted by Ross and Levinson. Some would go still further and postulate that the impact on wages from collective bargaining has been negligible. Critics of Ozanne have pointed out that Ozanne's figures may be misleading because they reflect shifts in the numbers of workers involved in various occupations rather than the pressure of union demands. Statistics suggest, however, that such shifts were not important enough to produce the variation in the performance of wages indicated by Ozanne's paper. A more telling criticism may be that the two periods are not as similar as Ozanne assumes. Other variables such as the change in the role of government (minimum wages, the Employment Act of 1946, etc.) and changes in public attitude toward the desirability of steadily rising wages as a benefit of rising productivity versus declines in prices may also have played some part.

Several studies directly contradict Ozanne's findings. One of the conclusions reached by Ozanne was that unions are able to persevere in their demands despite adverse economic conditions. (Note that to the extent unemployment results from higher wages, the marginal productivity theory is confirmed.) As such he appears to assume that changes in the volume of unemployment have little impact on the wage demands of union leaders. Certainly there are a number of other economists who would subscribe to this doctrine, but a study by William Bowen suggests that union leaders are considerably more sensitive to variations in economic conditions than is sometimes suspected.[22] Although Bowen's study dealt primarily with wage-push inflation, it includes some interesting data that is also relevant to our present discussion. Bowen divided the 1947–1959 period into subperiods of contraction or expansion of the economy. In subperiods during which the demand for labor was high, wage changes for the economy as a whole and for specific industries rose much more sharply than in periods of higher unemployment. Bowen concluded that there was "no systematic difference between the behavior of wages in the more strongly unionized industries and in the weakly organized industries during the three postwar recessions."[23]

Note that Bowen by no means discounts entirely the ability of unions to force wages higher than they might otherwise be in the absence of unions. However, he believes that unions will probably be most successful in those industries where there is a high degree of concentration. "The joint effects of concentration and unionization may be greater than the algebraic sum of their individual effects."[24]

Another study somewhat analogous to Ozanne's although different time periods were used has been made by Milton Friedman.[25] To test whether or not the growing power of unions had significantly affected the movement of wages, Professor Friedman chose for his analysis three wartime periods— the Civil War, World War I, and World War II. Since in each subsequent time a substantial increase in union strength had taken place, Friedman argued that a correspondingly greater influence on wages by the unions should have been displayed. Actually Friedman found no evidence that any such transformation occurred. Wage rates appeared to rise to the same extent in all three periods.

Friedman thus concluded that, while the threat might exist in the future, there was little evidence to support the current fears about the power of unions to raise wages unduly.[26]

Presumably Ozanne would categorize Friedman's study as one of those that dealt with periods predating the full realization of the power of unions and would underscore Friedman's warnings about possible changes in the future. There is another qualification to Friedman's conclusions that needs to be made. Although the selection of three war periods assures a certain uniformity of economic conditions, in such periods employers are most likely to offer little resistance to wage demands and even to instigate upward pressure of their own on wages because of the shortage of labor. Thus, Friedman's findings may simply be a reflection of the accuracy of the Levinson analysis we noted earlier.

Another economist, Albert Rees, has stressed the strong level of demand for labor in steel as the primary factor explaining the sharp rise in wages in that industry between 1945 and 1948. Rees found that the real increase in hourly average earnings for the stated period was only half of what it was for an earlier period characterized by a rising demand for steel and a scarcity of steel workers (1914–1921).[27] As Rees points out, in this earlier period, steel workers were almost completely unorganized.

Both Rees and Friedman have raised the possibility that wages might have risen even more rapidly in the absence of unions! The logic of this somewhat startling premise rests upon the possibility that since wage increases that are negotiated by contract are fixed for a definite period, there is an incentive for employers to postpone increases, increases that might have been given more quickly to unorganized workers. Furthermore, because the presence of the union means that an employer loses his freedom to cut wages at some future time, the employer may be more cautious about granting increases.

We must express serious doubts as to the validity of this argument. The evidence, particularly in Chapter 16, concerning experience abroad suggests that employers in a tight labor market often raise wage rates above those specified by the contract in order to retain workers.

Although the authors of the preceding studies came to sharply differing conclusions, most of them used a macroeconomic approach. John Maher, on the other hand, used a microeconomic approach.[28] By studying just seven industries intensively, Maher sought to isolate the impact of unions on wages from that of all other factors that affect wage levels. Size of plant, geographical area, industry, and occupation were all held constant in comparing union and nonunion rates.

Maher found that there was no statistically significant relationship between unionism and the level of wages in five of the industries studied. In the furniture industry, Maher found a substantial differential in favor of the union workers, while in the footwear industry the reverse held true. Maher's conclusion, which he suggested might apply to other industries as well, was that the results could vary depending upon the time the study was conducted. At any given point in time, either union or nonunion wages may be gaining relative to the other depending on the economic forces at work. Like Rees and Friedman, Maher noted the possibility that contractual arrangements may slow the pace with which wage increases are introduced into the union sector during periods of inflation. He felt that this may have accounted for the fact that the level of wages in the nonunion sector of the footwear industry was higher than its union counterpart. Maher's survey of the furniture industry, on the other hand, had taken place just after the union had completed negotiating a contract. Maher noted that, given time, the union's advantage might have been substantially reduced as nonunion plants caught up.

Despite the extreme care exercised by Maher in making his study, his conclusions are subject to two important reservations. First, there is some doubt that his seven industries are representative of other industries in the economy. Furthermore, the extent to which wage increases in the nonunion sector are prompted by gains in the union sector is never identified. To the extent that union wage increases do exert this influence, the lack of a differential signifies not the lack of power of unions to raise wages, but their ability to affect wage rates in the union and nonunion sectors alike.

The Reaction of Union Leaders to the Theory of Marginal Productivity

Even if we assume that marginal productivity works exactly in the manner predicated by its exponents (that is, employers *do* reduce their payrolls in response to wage increases), it does not follow that unions will therefore be completely thwarted in their efforts to raise wages.

A number of years ago when Samuel Gompers, then president of the AFL, was asked about the aims of American labor, he summed up those objectives in a single word, "more." In their pursuit of this goal, union leaders have rarely heeded the warnings of professional economists about the inability of unions to alter the immutable laws of economics. We do not imply that union leaders have been insensitive to the danger of unemployment; the threat of unemployment is almost as foreboding a menace to union leaders as it is to the rank and file.

Even in a country like the United States where union leaders share the business community's faith in the capitalist system, there is a tendency of leaders and rank and file to see some redistribution of income as being desirable. They do not believe that such a redistribution will inevitably be accompanied by a reduction in employment. Instead they feel that, if anything, employment opportunities should be strengthened when workers (who constitute the bulk of the population) are supplied with more purchasing power. This conviction has been strengthened by the perversion of the Keynesian economics that stresses the importance of the consumption function and the need to bolster effective demand. Keynes' warning that a cut in wages might not solve the unemployment problem in the manner earlier economists had believed was reinterpreted to mean that a raising of wages when unemployment threatened would be a helpful therapy. Repeatedly in recent years, union leaders have called for boosts in wages as a means of solving the problem of persistently high levels of unemployment in the United States. Just as businessmen have been prone to overlook the income aspects of wages as a means of furbishing purchasing power, so union leaders have tended to overlook the cost aspects of increased wages. In any case, the conviction that higher wages will mean greater rather than less employment reduces union leaders' fears about pricing themselves out of the market.

Union leaders often share the conviction of those economists who believe that the demand for labor is highly inelastic. They are encouraged in this belief by the fact that this frequently appears to be the case in the short run. Any discernible long-run relationship is lost in the myriad of other changes taking place in a dynamic economy. This belief is also encouraged by the impression that labor costs represent only a small proportion of the total costs (sometimes termed the "importance of being unimportant"). While labor costs account for about two-thirds of all cost, the fraction accounted for by any particular trade union (especially if it is a craft union) may be very small. Carpenters, for example, may feel that they can safely press for high wages because their share in the over-all cost of a home is very slight. A problem, of course, arises when masons, plumbers, and painters come to the same conclusion. When all of the small fractions are added together, the labor cost becomes appreciable and one cause for the high cost of postwar housing is uncovered.

Union leaders and economists who support their actions have also developed a so-called "shock" effect of high wage demands to explain how wage increases can be effected within the boundaries of the marginal productivity theory. This shock theory suggests that high wage rates tend to make employers more efficient than they otherwise would be. Proponents of the theory attribute the rapid pace of technological innovation in the United States to the labor scarcities and high wages that have traditionally characterized this country.

The shock theory probably has greater validity historically, however, than it does when it is applied to any immediate wage demand by a union. In the latter case, the theory's application is based on a number of questionable assumptions. Most obviously, the theory assumes that management is not already doing everything possible to make itself efficient—an assumption that in the face of almost annual increases in wages implies an ineffi-ciency of almost herculean propor-tions!

Even if we assume that there was considerable room for improvements in efficiency, we still might question the theory's validity on several counts. Is the wage increase of sufficient magnitude to prompt management to change to more efficient ways? If management is prompted to take action, such action may not be as easily undertaken as it was in the past. No longer can an employer be sure that he will be able to introduce new production techniques without unleashing a storm of protest from the union. To the extent that management's actions are truly hampered, the shock effect may not evoke the expected response. Similarly, the assumption that unused means of technology hitherto untapped because their use was uneconomical are available for tapping may not be true.

One final observation needs to be made. Even if the shock theory should function in the prescribed manner, the resulting improvements in efficiency may still lead to a lowered demand for labor. Even assuming a full-employment economy, the resulting displacement of workers may be greater than the union's membership will wish to experience.

The ability of unions to press for higher wages does not rest solely on the validity of their views of wage theory, however. Thus, while unions may raise wages and thereby discourage employers from hiring as many as they did previously, unions may also seek through dismissal wages and similar provisions to make it more expensive for an employer to discharge workers. Furthermore, a union may be interested only in protecting its own membership, which it may be able to do even in the face of a general decline in employment resulting from the wage increase. Historically, unions in the United States have found it possible to restrict a union's membership by various admission practices that prevented too large a number of workers from joining the union. High dues and initiation fees, apprenticeship regulations, and the actual closing of the union rolls to all would-be members have all been used to restrict the number of union members. By controlling the size of its membership, the union is able to transfer the burden of unemployment to those who remain outside the union. Such practices, however, can only be used by skilled craft unions and are impossible for industrial unions that organize all workers in the plant.

A union may also try to achieve high wages without unemployment by encouraging the general public to buy the employer's products. The most familiar instrument for this purpose is the union label. The union label has been used with considerable success, particularly in the printing and clothing trades. We can remember an instance in which a local charity attempted to cut costs by having its tickets printed in a nonunion shop. The resulting saving was more than matched by losses the charity sustained when union people refused to buy tickets. If the union is able to win such loyalty, it may be able to raise wages and thus consumer prices without jeopardizing the employer's market for his product. Instances of unions' advertising in their union journals or even in the newspapers on behalf of a given company or name brand could also be cited.

Unions also claim that, when they are given the protection of the closed or union shop, they can protect not only their memberships, but also the employer by assuring him of top quality workers, who are more efficient and thus worth more to the employer. Since on other occasions union leaders also defend promotion by seniority on the grounds that there is little appreciable difference in quality between workers, the effectiveness of their argument is somewhat weakened. Furthermore, in the United States the closed shop is no longer legal.

A union may also be able to raise wages without its membership suffering the impact of reduced employment (at least for the short run) if it insists on the continued employment of the current labor force as a price for settlement. Even if we made the heroic assumption that the union has the power to force the employer to retain exactly as many workers as he had previous to the wage increase and to force him to continue to replace any who retire or quit, however, an unanswered question still remains. What cannot be determined and what the union cannot control is the amount of expansion in employment that might have occurred if the wage level had not risen to the level set by the union.

The marginal productivity theory as originally stated by Clark assumed the maintenance of full employment. If wages rose so high as to produce some unemployment, competition among the unemployed would drive wages back down to the point where full employment was restored. John R. Hicks has suggested that given the presence of the union, the pressure to restore full employment through wage reductions may be avoided.[29] A union may be interested in unemployment only in so far as it touches its membership. It is also possible that a union's leaders may decide that high wages for the majority and unemployment for a small minority of the union's members constitutes a better bargain than an arrangement whereby everyone is employed but at a markedly lower level of wages. This is particularly likely to be the case where a substantial program of unemployment benefits is available.

Union's Standards for Wages

In justifying their demands for ever-increasing wages, unions have employed a variety of standards. Because standards have varied according to the prevailing situation, if the different justifications were placed side by side they would often appear to be contradictory.

Although union leaders have generally been skeptical of the marginal productivity theory, they have often argued that workers' wages should reflect any increase in productivity.

In order to be able to share in the economy's gains in productivity, it would not be necessary for workers to secure higher wages. The increase in productivity could be reflected in a reduction in consumer prices, which would improve workers' real wages even though money wages remained unchanged. The unions generally reject this possibility, however, with the standard argument that large monopolistic industries would simply let the increases in efficiency be reflected in higher profits, with little or no benefit accruing to consumers.

Attempts to base wage increases on gains in productivity, however, are subject to a number of serious hazards. The most obvious problem is the difficulty of computing the rate at which productivity increases—a problem that is accentuated when measurement is attempted at the plant level.

If wages are based on some estimated annual increase for the entire economy, the result will be to freeze wage differentials into their existing patterns and make wages and labor unresponsive to changing demands in the economy. This point will be developed more completely later when we discuss government wage guidelines. On the other hand, if individual company increases in productivity are used as a guide, some workers would be granted very great increases in wages while others would achieve no increases at all. While wage increases designed to correlate an individual company's gains in productivity come closer to matching the manner in which wages would shift under the pressure of market demand than would wages geared to a national productivity figure, the resulting inequities would be tremendous. Alternatively, to gear all wages to the increase in the national average growth of productivity would leave workers and unions in industries that had experienced sharp increases in productivity dissatisfied with their share.[30]

Closely akin to the productivity standard is the union appeal for wage increases based on the company's ability to pay. In many respects ability-to-pay is simply a broadening of the productivity standard since a firm that is experiencing an increase in productivity is clearly in a better position to pay higher wages than one that is not. Even without marked gains in productivity, however, it is still possible for a firm to be enjoying a very good profit record. Few union leaders would fail to see a record of substantial profits as a sign that a firm could afford to pay its workers higher wages.

The mere existence of high profits, however, does not necessarily indicate the ability of the firm to bear a substantial increase in wages. High profits may be due to the high-risk element in the industry and any reduction in profits may seriously hamper continued operations and possible expansion. Furthermore, since profits are a highly volatile return, the union that bases its demand for higher wages on the existence of high profits may see its justification suddenly disappear.

Such changes would prove fatal more frequently than they do if it were not for the marvelous ability of union leaders to change their arguments in response to changing economic conditions.

Like the productivity standard as used by unions, the application of the principle of ability to pay would produce wide variations in wages between different plants and different industries. Both of these arguments are suited only for those unions representing workers in plants where profit margins and/or productivity gains are favorable. Unions in plants where the economic climate is less favorable, on the other hand, are likely to justify their demands for higher wages by adopting an "us too" approach. Appeals will be made to fairness and the need to maintain comparable wage standards throughout the economy.

Attempts to maintain comparable increases in various industries, however, place labor under even graver handicaps in efforts to gain those wage increases than when wage demands are based on productivity or ability-to-pay. The most obvious point is that it is likely to be far easier to secure concessions from an employer who is enjoying prosperity and is anxious to maintain continued production than from an employer who is in a poor financial position.

Furthermore, an attempt to achieve comparable wage standards creates as many if not more problems of measurability than does the use of productivity or ability to pay as standards. Variations in wages may be justifiable on the grounds of differences in the regularity of the work or of the kind of work performed. Even in the case of two plants producing basically the same product in the same industry, job titles may involve markedly different job requirements. Differences in geographic location may also explain wage variations although unions tend to be particularly resistant to any wage variations justified on these grounds.

During periods of rapidly rising prices, unions are likely to demand wage increases in order to enable workers to maintain the standard of living that existed prior to the price increases. Once again there is a problem of measurement; the Bureau of Labor Statistics has repeatedly warned that its consumer price index should not be construed as a measure of the cost of living. Variations exist from locale to locale and the extent of the change in prices depends on the individual's consumption patterns. Nevertheless, a number of unions have introduced escalator clauses into their contracts as a means of protecting members from sharp rises in prices. (An escalator clause ties wages to the price index—a rise in the latter by a certain number of points automatically ensures an increase in the level of wages.)

Reliance upon the cost-of-living increases as a justification for wage increases is fraught with twin dangers for the union. If the union demands increases in wages that just match the rises in prices, workers are securing nothing but a fixed standard of living —their real wage remains constant. If, in order to avoid this result, union leaders ask for more than the amount in wages necessary to offset price increases, they are likely to be held responsible for the spiraling prices because of their excessive wage demands.

Any reliance on a cost-of-living index as a basis for wage increases proves fatal when prices move downward. A union that has justified wage increases in terms of rising prices is hard pressed to justify continued high wages in the face of a downward trend in prices. Because in recent years the trend of prices has been almost consistently upward in all countries, however, unions have not really had to face this problem. In the few instances in the United States when escalator clauses have resulted in a reduction of even two or three cents per hour, a certain amount of grumbling by workers has been heard. As we shall see in the next chapter, unions tend to inject a certain amount of wage rigidity into the economy and the members' opposition to shifts downwards is one of the major reasons. For this reason, many of the escalator clauses are phrased so as to provide greater upward than downward flexibility; many specify a suspension in the terms if the price index moves downward more than a specified number of points.

Basically all of these standards are alternatives—each trotted out as the occasion seems suitable in the union leader's search for higher wages. The union leader is pragmatic in this search; he uses whichever argument is most appropriate at the time. This comment does not imply evidence of bad faith on the part of the union leader. His goal is a constant one— who can blame him if changing economic conditions necessitate a revision of his case from time to time?

Although union leaders never weary of repeating the adage that "labor is not a commodity," the union leader is essentially in the business of selling someone else's labor. Not only is the leader charged with the responsibility of making the best case possible for a wage increase for his constituents, but the fact that he is selling someone else's services has an additional significance.

Bargaining for wages and collective bargaining in general have become political as well as economic phenomena. The union leader must negotiate an agreement that is satisfactory not only in his judgment, but also in the judgment of the union's members. A leader who fails to produce an agreement that meets with the membership's approval is in danger of having the contract rejected by the members or having someone else succeed him in office.

Because union leaders have this responsibility to the rank and file, unions sometimes demand far more than they can reasonably expect to obtain. Rank-and-file members are sometimes too prone to regard employers as a boundless source of additional wages and to take a skeptical view when any employer pleads inability to pay. The wage theories of the economists find an even less receptive audience among the rank and file than they did among the union's leadership. While the union leader may be aware that the demands of his union are unrealistic, his responsibility to and his need to satisfy his followers may prevent him from acting in accordance with his judgment.

Unions—Political Bodies in an Economic Environment

Most labor economists would agree that the marginal productivity theory provides no unique solution for the determination of the level of wages. A number of these economists, operating on the assumption that unions do have some discretion in their wage demands, have sought to explain what economic and political considerations prompt union behavior. Sharp differences in opinion as to which factors to stress have arisen.

John Dunlop, for example, has argued that the marginal productivity theory, while it was a valid method of analyzing economic problems at an earlier time, is no longer relevant to present-day labor markets. Dunlop bases his judgment on two major points: (1) Both supply and demand play a role in determining wages and marginal productivity theory centers exclusively upon demand. (2) Wages, even within the confines of a single plant, are too variegated to be resolved in the manner indicated by marginal productivity theory.[31]

Dunlop notes that unions are not motivated by a simple urge to get more and that to attempt to explain wages in this manner is misleading. Among the variety of nonincome objectives of union wage rates may be such things as: (1) a desire to expand membership, (2) attempts to control the rate of technological change, by demanding higher wages for those dealing with new techniques, (3) attempts to get better working conditions by demanding higher wages where conditions are inferior, and (4) attempts to allocate jobs and control the rate of entrance into a trade.

Even with these alternative nonincome objectives, it is still realistic, Dunlop argues, to view unions as seeking to maximize some one thing in the same sense that the corporation tries to maximize profits. After considering the alternative goals that might be maximized (such as the highest possible wage), Dunlop concludes that unions seek to maximize the over-all wage for their entire membership. As Dunlop puts it, "The most suitable generalized model of the trade union for analytical purposes is probably that which depicts maximization of the wage bill for the total membership."[32] To understand union wage policy, Dunlop believes we must recognize that the answers will differ from time to time and "must be examined in the context of real situations; to do this we must resort to specific collective-bargaining agreements and wage conferences which constitute our primary sources."[33]

Dunlop does not picture unions as political institutions but rather as maximizing economic institutions. His views are included in this section because his views triggered reactions from a number of other prominent labor economists who denied that unions seek to maximize any one thing.

Arthur Ross rejected entirely the idea that unions were institutions with a fixed goal of maximizing wages. Dunlop was thus a natural target for Ross' attack. Ross' central thought is contained in the heading for this section —the union in his view is a political institution operating in an economic environment.[34] According to Ross, union leaders are subject to a variety of political pressures exerted upon them by their rank and file, by other unions, and by the employer. The economic environment is less important in and of itself than as a generator of political pressures with which the union leader has to reckon.

Sharply disagreeing with Dunlop and most earlier theorists, Ross maintains that the employment repercussions of wage setting cannot be determined by the union leader and therefore are usually neglected by him. Although he admits that there are occasional exceptions to this contention, Ross argues that earlier economists have tried to make the exception the rule.

A more moderate criticism of Dunlop's position has been made by Lloyd Reynolds.[35] Reynolds' picture of union wage policy resembles Ross' in many respects but places more emphasis on economic factors. Reynolds doubts whether business or union leaders set maximization of gains as a goal. According to Reynolds, union leaders are likely to follow a principle of "economy of effort." Just as some theorists have argued that corporation executives do not seek to maximize profits but only to earn sufficient profits to keep the stockholders happy, so Reynolds argues that union leaders do not seek a maximum wage, but only enough of an increase to keep the membership satisfied. Unions do not seek to maximize wages or any other quantity, Reynolds believes, because ". . . as the size of the wage demand increases, employer resistance grows steadily while the added advantage to the union as an organization diminishes."[36]

Of these three theories, Dunlop's makes the least break with earlier theory. Presumably wage maximization for all the union's members will necessitate some consideration of the employment repercussions of higher wages. Although Ross pays brief lip service to economic variables, most of his analysis appears to be predicated on the assumption that unions operate in a sellers' market and can thus safely ignore the employment situation. In an industry marked with employment problems, however, a union's leader may act more cautiously since he is unable to gauge what effect higher wages will have on employment. A study of local labor markets made by Charles Myers and George Shultz, for example, found that unions in the United States were sensitive to employment considerations during a period of considerable unemployment.[37] Unions in other countries have displayed similar sensitivity—in postwar West Germany unions were greatly concerned lest their wage demands foster unemployment.

The Institutional Market

Clark Kerr, in an often-cited paper given before a meeting of the American Economic Association,[38] suggested that the competitive models envisioned in earlier economic theory had been replaced by an institutional market populated with massive unions and business organizations. Kerr also saw an end to the dominance of economic factors in wage determination. Neither the job market nor sheer bargaining power set the wage limits, or determined where the wage would fall within those limits. As Kerr put it, "It is not so much what can be done economically which is important but what must be done politically —on both sides. Employers' associations and large corporations, as well as trade unions, have a political life which claims attention just as do the economic goals."[39]

Kerr suggests that the institutional market produces a lessening of wage differentials between plants just as postulated under competitive theory, but with an important difference. The uniform wage does not mean that the demand for and supply of labor are equal and no clearing of the market may be achieved. If it is, it is as likely to be the result of "control over entry rather than the achievement of a competitive equilibrium position."[40] In this situation the forces of demand and supply adjust to the wage rate rather than the other way around. Kerr's general conclusion is that although the institutional market is different from that postulated under competitive theory, the impact of unions on wages has been slight. Too many other institutional forces have been operating at cross-purposes to permit the impact of unions to attain very great significance. In Kerr's judgment, the economic effects of unions have been overrated.

Summary and Conclusions

The attempts of earlier economists to devise a theory of wages that would determine the exact level of wages and the distribution of employment and income have proved to be too ambitious. One would have to take a very broad definition of the term "subsistence" to believe the U.S. steelworker receiving $3.50 an hour was being paid a subsistence wage. The wages fund doctrine has proved to be equally antiquated. The marginal productivity theory of wages continues to attract some supporters but it does so less as a theory of wage determination for actual wages than as a criterion for proper wages. Most adherents admit that the proper wage (as determined by the theory) may be only infrequently achieved; they content themselves with issuing warnings of the dire consequences that will result from this failure.

How dire the consequences are likely to be is a function of the competitiveness of the market. A highly competitive industry is much more apt to pose a challenge to a union than a monopolistic one. Even after a competitive industry has been organized on an industrywide basis (thereby reducing some of its competitiveness), the union may be hard pressed to force wage concessions. Witness the case of the Amalgamated Clothing Workers who went for three years without wage increases in the early 1950s when wages in other industries were rising rapidly. Given a union of sufficient bargaining power, however, even the handicap of a highly competitive market can be overcome. The successes of the Construction Workers, the Coal Miners, and the Teamsters in recent decades provide a good illustration of this point. At the same time the Coal Miners and Teamsters have experienced the typical problems of union organization in a highly competitive industry in the past.

Just as the theories of wages and the impact of unions upon wages are confused and conflicting so is the evidence unearthed by empirical research. Until further research sheds additional light on the questions, it seems safe (if not very satisfactory) to suggest that the correct answer lies somewhere between the exaggerated fears of opponents of unions and the soothing reassurances of those who would deny that unions have any impact. One thing does seem clear—the market does not operate in a sufficiently precise fashion to assure by itself that workers of equal ability are paid equal wages. The extent and the nature of these differentials and the impact of collective bargaining upon them will be the subject of our next chapter.

NOTES

1. Richard Lester, "Shortcomings of Marginal Analysis for Wage-Employment Problems," *American Economic Review,* 36 (March 1946), 63–82.

2. Fritz Machlup, "Marginal Analysis and Empirical Research," *American Economic Review,* 36 (September 1946), 547–554

3. Lloyd Reynolds, "Toward a Short Run Theory of Wages," *American Economic Review* Vol. 38, No. 3 (June 1948), pp. 289–308.

4. H. M. Oliver, "Marginal Theory and Business Behavior," *American Economic Review* Vol. 37, No. 3 (June 1947), p. 378.

5. There are many economic theorists who would argue, however, that the true test of a theory's value lies in its ability to predict rather than in the accuracy of its assumptions. See, for example, Milton Friedman, "The Methodology of Positive Economics," in his *Essays in Positive Economics* (Chicago: University of Chicago Press, 1953).

6. Note that in referring to this as the marginal productivity curve, we are assuming that the worker is paid in units of the product he produces. To convert this curve into money we would need to multiply the marginal productivity by the marginal revenue of the product when sold. Under perfect competition, since the marginal revenue is constant at all units of output and sale, no problem is created and a simple conversion can be made. Under imperfect or monopolistic competition, however, the marginal revenue declines with an increase in the number of units so that the marginal product and the marginal revenue product curves no longer coincide.

7. George Stigler, "The Kinky Oligopoly Demand Curve and Rigid Prices," *Journal of Political Economy,* 55 (October 1947), 432–449.

8. Reynolds, *op. cit.,* pp. 294–296.

9. Paul Douglas, *Real Wages in the United States, 1890–1926* (Boston: Houghton Mifflin, 1930).

10. Arthur M. Ross, *Trade Union Wage Policy* (Berkeley: University of California Press, 1948). Sumner Slichter has made the additional criticism that Douglas' figures are really a comparison of piece rates found largely in the nonunion plants and time rates found in the union shops. (A discussion of these two forms of payment is to be found in Chapter 7.) Sumner Slichter, "Do Wage-Fixing Arrangements in the American Labor Market Have an Inflationary Bias?" *American Economic Review,* 44 (May 1954), 332.

11. Ross, *op. cit.,* p. 132.

12. Arthur Ross and William Goldner, "Forces Affecting the Interindustry Wage Structure," *Quarterly Journal of Economics* (May 1950), pp. 254–281.

13. Harold M. Levinson, *Unionism, Wage Trends and Income Distribution, 1914–1947* (Ann Arbor: University of Michigan Press, 1951).

14. Harry Douty, "Union and Nonunion Wages," in W. S. Woytinsky *et al.* (eds.), *Employment and Wages in the United States* (New York: Twentieth Century Fund, 1953), pp. 447–501.

15. H. G. Lewis, *Unionism and Relative Wages in the United States* (Chicago: University of Chicago Press, 1963), p. 5.

16. Robert Ozanne, "Impact of Unions on Wage Trends and Income Distribution," *Quarterly Journal of Economics,* 73 (May 1959), 177–196.

17. *Ibid.,* p. 179.

18. Robert Ozanne, *Wages in Practice and Theory: McCormick and International Harvester, 1860–1960* (Madison: University of Wisconsin Press, 1968).

19. Martin Segal, "Unionism and Wage Movements," *Southern Economic Journal* (October 1961), pp. 174–182.

20. Frank Pierson, "The Economic Influence of Big Unions," *The Annals* (January 1961), pp. 96–107. See also his *Unions in Postwar America* (New York: Random House, 1967), Chap. 3.

21. Slichter, *op. cit.*, pp. 330–334.

22. William Bowen, *Wage Behavior in the Postwar Period: An Empirical Analysis* (Princeton, N.J.: Princeton University, Industrial Relations Section, 1960).

23. *Ibid.*, p. 91.

24. *Ibid.*

25. Milton Friedman, "Some Comments on the Significance of Labor Unions for Economic Policy," in David McCord Wright (ed.), *The Impact of the Union* (New York: Harcourt Brace Jovanovich, 1951), pp. 204–234.

26. The word unduly is used advisedly. Friedman's position is not that unions have done nothing to change wages but only that their influences have been grossly exaggerated. "Roughly, then, we might assess the order of magnitude of unions' effect on the structure of wages by saying that perhaps 10 per cent of the labor force has had its wages raised by some 15 per cent, implying that the remainder of the labor force has had its wage rate reduced by some 1 to 4 per cent. . . . Now this is by no means an unimportant effect . . . Yet I suspect it will strike most readers as small relative to their implicit assumptions." *Ibid.*, p. 216.

27. Albert Rees, "Post-war Wage Determination in the Basic Steel Industry," *American Economic Review* (June 1951), pp. 389–404. Rees supported in another article Friedman's contention that collective bargaining holds wage increases in check. "One kind of evidence is provided by comparisons between wage movements in unionized and nonunionized sectors of the economy. These show that since 1939 most of the nonunionized sector has had relative wage increase equal to or exceeding those of the unionized sector. . . . Collective bargaining in this country produces these results primarily because it sets wages for a fixed period of time in most cases. It therefore reduces upward wage flexibility." Albert Rees, "Wage Levels Under Conditions of Long-Run Full Employment," *American Economic Review* (May 1953), p. 452.

28. John E. Maher, "Union, Nonunion Wage Differentials," *American Economic Review,* 66 (June 1956), 336–352.

29. John R. Hicks, *The Theory of Wages* (New York: Peter Smith, 1948).

30. For a careful study tracing the historical relationships between wages and productivity, see John W. Kendrick, *Productivity Trends in the United States* (Princeton, N.J.: Princeton University Press, 1961).

31. John T. Dunlop, "The Task of Contemporary Wage Theory," in his *The Theory of Wage Determination* (London: St. Martins, 1957), pp. 3–27.

32. John T. Dunlop, *Wage Determination Under Trade Unionism* (New York: Macmillan, 1944), p. 44.

33. *Ibid.*, Ch. 3.

34. Ross, *op. cit.*

35. Lloyd Reynolds, *The Structure of Labor Markets: Wages and Labor Mobility in Theory and Practice* (New York: Harper & Row, 1951).

36. *Ibid.*, p. 236.

37. Charles A. Myers and George P. Shultz, *The Dynamics of a Labor Market* (Englewood Cliffs, N.J.: Prentice-Hall, 1951).

38. Clark Kerr, "Labor Markets: Their Character and Consequences," *American Economic Review,* 40 (May 1950), 278–291.

39. *Ibid.*, p. 283.

40. *Ibid.*, p. 283.

7
Wage Patterns and Collective Bargaining

Abundant evidence now testifies that it would, in the absence of collusion, be almost more correct to say that wages tend to be unequal rather than the other way around.

—Clark Kerr

☐ THE impact of unions on the general structure of wages is by no means limited to any effect they may have on raising wages. Equally, and in some cases more, important are the efforts of unions to preserve wage standards in periods of recession and to remove what they perceive as unjustified differentials. We will begin this chapter with a discussion of the implications of the unions' tendency to increase wage rigidity. Thereafter we will turn to the effect of unions on wage differentials both within a given plant and between plants, occupations, and geographical areas. We will close with an analysis of collective bargaining's impact on the overall distribution of income.

Wage Rigidity

As we pointed out at the close of the last chapter, unions tend to resist employers' efforts to cut wages. In addition to the workers' human wish to avoid any reduction in take-home pay, the rank-and-file union members may resist all proposals for wage cuts for a variety of other reasons.

To understand fully the basis of workers' resistance to wage cuts, we must first understand exactly how a wage cut in a single plant may increase the volume of employment. As wages are reduced, labor becomes a better buy relative to other factors (assuming that the cost of these factors has not fallen by an equal or greater amount). Under these conditions, an employer will tend to substitute labor for capital. Even if he does not, a reduction in wage rates will enable him to hire a larger quantity of labor with a given amount of money. Second, the reduction in wages will reduce the employer's total costs and thus enable him to cut consumer prices. Assuming that the demand for the product is elastic, consumers will react to the lowered prices by increasing their purchases. The increased volume of sales will encourage the employer to increase his production, thereby necessitating an increase in the number he employs. Finally, the lowered wages will encourage some workers to leave the company.

Workers seldom stop to work out the above analysis, but even if they did most of them would be convinced that the process breaks down somewhere along the line. All too often in the past, before unions were powerful enough to offer any resistance, employers converted a recession or depression into an opportunity for widespread wage cuts. Sometimes the firm urgently needed to make these wage cuts in order to continue operations, but sometimes the cuts were greater than necessary and long periods of time often elapsed before the cuts were even partially restored.

Workers' suspicions of management's motives are increased when they see businessmen holding the prices of their products constant in the face of general market declines. Workers reason that if it is good business for employers to hold their prices stable, it should also be good business for workers to take the same approach with wages. Note also that when businesses hold their prices constant part of the preceding analysis of how wage cuts may stimulate employment is lost. Union leaders and union economists have been quick to cite government studies emphasizing the problem of administered prices.

Union leaders are apt to dismiss the employment-stimulating effects of wage reductions because they believe that the elasticity of the demand for labor is small. They thus conclude that any additional hiring employers may undertake in response to a cut in wages will be too modest to be of any real help. Past experience has also taught workers that wage concessions to one employer are usually quickly followed by similar or greater concessions to other employers. After such a general round of wage cutting, the over-all competitive picture remains much as it was in the first place. Furthermore, if wage cuts lead employers to expect that additional cuts will follow, employers may resist expanding their hiring until further reductions in wages have been secured.

The preceding analysis suggests that a union leader will rarely willingly offer a cut in wages. To do so is to risk the leader's stature and political popularity. No union leader ever won votes by announcing that he had just agreed to a 10 percent cut in wages! Furthermore, unions find the whole concept of wage (or other) concessions distasteful on a philosophical basis. Unions are geared to move in one direction—onward and upward on the path to greater benefits for their membership. Union leaders see this path as a steep one and their task of climbing it as too difficult for them to willingly risk any backsliding. We should also remember that the union is not necessarily interested in maxi-

mizing the benefits of all workers, but only those of its membership. If it can maintain a reasonably high volume of employment for its own members, it may leave other displaced workers to fend for themselves.

The efforts of unions to keep wages stable in the face of declining demand for labor has been said to have two repercussions. First, it supposedly worsens the problem of unemployment because it interferes with the sequence described at the beginning of this chapter. Much less prominence has been given to this charge, however, since Keynes formulated his concept of involuntary unemployment, which suggests that even completely flexible wages might not restore full employment. The other charge against the unions' attempts to maintain a certain wage level in times of economic decline is that such action gives an upward bias to wage rates. When wage rates are free to move in only one direction, each successive round of wage increases begins at a higher plateau than the preceding round. Without unions blocking wage cuts, employers would be able to roll back costs during each recession.

We feel that economists have dwelt too little on this phase of unions' actions as a means by which unions do push wages somewhat above what would be the case in the absence of unions. The danger resulting from the impact on the general level of wages from wage rigidity seems greater to us than the threat implicit in the fears expressed by some economists about the ability of unions to drive wages far above market levels. Nevertheless, several other factors must enter into any discussion of the importance of unions in increasing wage rigidity.

Even in the absence of unions, wages tend to be sticky during downturns of the business cycle.[1] Large businesses, in particular, tend to maintain stable wages as part of their program for general price stability. During periods of recession, companies may prefer to increase the pace of work and the work load rather than cut wages. An increase in the pace of work provides much the same benefits to an employer as a reduction in wages—he is now getting more work for his money than he did before. Similarly, it may be easier for the employer to secure a reduction in the piece rate (by which the worker is paid according to the amount of work he performs) than to win a cut in hourly wages. This opportunity, of course, is only open to companies with piece rates—a situation that does not prevail in the majority of American industries. Furthermore, an increasing pace of work in the face of a decline in product demand will eventually lead to unemployment.

Nor has the unions' opposition to wage reduction been absolutely complete; numerous instances can be cited where a union has accepted a sizable cut in wages as a means of keeping a firm in business. Unions may be prompted to offer wage concessions because they fear either possible unemployment or failure of the company. Alternatively, the union's leaders may believe that if they resisted wage cuts by calling a strike, the strike might be lost and the union destroyed or severely weakened.

While such exceptions are too numerous to be neglected completely, the general policy of unions is to resist wage cuts. Most students of collective bargaining agree that their impact in this direction has been considerable.

Wage Differentials

Any discussion of wage differentials must begin by distinguishing between differentials arising within the plant itself and those existing between different plants. We will look first at the various kinds of internal differences in wages and examine the impact that collective bargaining has had in each case, then turn to differences between one plant and another.

Internal Differences

Why does one worker get paid more than another one in the same plant? One obvious answer is that not all workers have the same kind of jobs. Some work is less pleasant and some jobs require special training or skills or a higher level of intelligence. Sometimes capable individuals are not given an opportunity at higher paying jobs or do not receive the same pay as others who perform comparable work. Employers may discriminate because of differences in sex or race or religion.

Negroes have been a frequent target for such discrimination; they have been the last to be hired and the first to be fired. When they are employed, they are usually given only the poorest paying jobs. Even as recently as 1968, Negro median family income was only 60 per cent of white family income. While Negro families constitute only 10 percent of all families in the United States, 22 percent of all the families in poverty in the United States are black.

Negroes experienced a rapid improvement in their economic position during World War II when the shortage of workers forced employers to open a variety of jobs that had hitherto been closed. Since the war, however, Negroes have again lost ground. Part of the discrepancy between Negro and white family income results from the frequency with which the Negro loses his job. In 1966, nonwhite workers constituted 11 percent of the labor force, but accounted for 21 percent of the unemployed and 25 percent of the long-term unemployed.[2] In recent years the unemployment rate for Negroes has been running about double that for whites. Even when employed on a full-time basis, the average Negro earns only about two-thirds the wage of the average white.

Women have also been a target for discrimination both by employers and unions. Women's wages average about 60 percent of those of males. In fact, Negro males who are full-time workers average slightly more than white females.[3]

Women have long found certain unions and certain occupations (often the better paying ones) closed to them. Despite their role in helping to organize the AFL, women have been less inclined to join unions than men. For one thing, many women tend to think of themselves as temporary members of the labor force and so are less interested in improving their jobs. Other reasons include the fact that women have been in fields largely unorganized even for males and the fact that a number of unions have placed barriers in the way of women joining. Even today, although women account for about 40 percent of the labor force and participate in it on a much more regular basis, there are only about 3.5 million women union members. This amounts to only 19 percent of total union membership.

Unions have long espoused "equal pay for equal work" and have often passed resolutions to that effect at their annual conventions. The problem for both women and Negroes has been to gain access to the "equal work." All too often both groups have been regarded as inferior workers by both the employer and the union and given the poorer paying jobs. This has been particularly true in the case of women. As time passes, it seems likely that both types of wage differentials are likely to diminish in importance as the Equal Opportunity Act is more vigorously enforced.

Skill Differentials

Although economists generally agree that there have been decreases in the percentage differential paid for varying levels of skill, they differ as to the cause of this decline. A century ago the wages of the skilled worker in this country were three times what they were for the unskilled; today the skilled exceed the unskilled by only one and one half times. A study by Harry Ober for the BLS revealed that during the forty-year period from 1907 to 1947, the spread in wages between the skilled and unskilled was cut in half.[4] There were, however, numerous variations in the size of the decline both by region and for industries within a region.

The importance of the role unions played in this decline, however, is difficult to measure because there may have been several other contributing factors. Among these factors are: (1) The fact that the flood of immigration to the United States has receded in recent years. Without the immigrants, many of whom became unskilled workers, the supply of unskilled labor has been reduced. (2) The value of unskilled labor has also been increased because the growing mechanization of unskilled work has increased its productivity. (3) Rising educational standards in the United States and other countries have contributed to a growth in the number of skilled workers. (4) A final contributing factor has been the action of the government in setting minimum wages and approving standard cents-per-hour wage increases during war periods. The fact that skill differentials have remained in the construction industry where unions have steadfastly opposed any reduction in them suggests that economic forces other than unions play an important role.

The Role of Unions and Collective Bargaining

Whatever impact unions have in narrowing skill differentials comes from two different union policies. During the 1940s and 1950s particularly, many unions tended to seek wage increases in the form of so many cents per hour rather than percentage increases. Some unions, like the UAW, because of unrest among skilled members, have reversed their early demands and are now seeking percentage increases.

Although the absolute differences in wages between skilled and unskilled may never "catch up" across the board, cents-per-hour increases for all workers tend to narrow percentage wage differentials. The same result is achieved when unions institute escalator clauses that tie wage increases for all workers to increases in the cost of living.

The union drive for a policy of internal promotions also tends to reduce wage differences between skilled and unskilled workers. First, internal promotions generally make gradations in skill less clear in workers' minds and reduce the justification for the prolonged periods of apprenticeship and training often associated with skilled jobs. Second, internal promotions tend to remove skilled jobs from the market place. An employer who trains his own skilled workers does not have to rely as heavily on the market place for his supply nor does he have to meet market prices.

Melvin Reder has supplied an important theoretical clue in this connection.[5] Reder suggests that instead of competing for workers and thereby bidding up wages, employers may choose to accept a lowering in the quality of their labor force. Whether or not they do so choose is a function of such things as the possibility of retraining, the danger of damage to expensive equipment, the existence of a "no-raiding" pact with other employers, and the existence of programs of internal promotions. To the extent that employers do lower their standards, however, the wages of workers with lower skills rise in relation to those with greater skill. Reder thus attributes the narrowing of skill differentials during periods of economic expansion to the fact that greater pressure is placed on the supply of relatively unskilled workers when employers attempt to match them to jobs calling for greater skill during a period when the demand for unskilled labor is still high.

Any attempt to determine the impact of unions on skill differentials is made more difficult because the record is mixed. Industrial and railroad unions have had the most pronounced impact in this direction. In the case of the railroads, wage differentials by skill have diminished in recent years until skilled workers receive only about 20 percent more than unskilled workers. The railroads are a rather special case, however, and much of the pressure toward equalizing skilled and unskilled rates has come from the intense rivalry among the railroad unions to enroll railroad workers.

The progress of both industrial and craft unions toward narrowing skill differentials has been uneven, with a number of factors influencing the results. For example, at the same time the UAW was pushing for equal increases for all groups (it has reversed this policy in recent years), the Steelworkers were seeking to reverse the trend and to widen the absolute differentials. Why do some unions push for equal increases for all, while others seek to maintain skill differentials? Among the forces that may influence unions to seek a *narrowing* of differentials are the following:

1. The wages of the skilled may already be very high. Thus, the union will find it difficult to justify higher wages for them without securing at least equally high increases for the unskilled. Skilled workers may remain content as long as their absolute wage advantage continues or perhaps widens.

2. In many industrial unions, the unskilled and semiskilled constitute the bulk of the union's membership. The union's officers may thus seek the wage increases most pleasing to the majority.

3. During periods of inflation, unskilled workers may be harder pressed than skilled workers in their attempts to maintain their standard of living in the face of pressure of rising prices. Consideration of equity and sympathy for the plight of the lower-paid workers may prompt the union's leaders to seek wage increases of equal amounts for all. This may partially explain why skill differentials appear to narrow most markedly during periods of inflation.

Factors that may prompt unions to strive for *maintenance* of skill differentials include:

1. The union has a strong leadership that is less responsive to the wishes of the rank and file. This factor may explain the difference between the approaches of the Steelworkers and the UAW.

2. Skilled workers may become disgruntled and threaten to form a separate union of their own unless their interests are better protected. Something of this kind prompted the UAW to modify the nature of its wage demands.

3. Employers may object to a further narrowing of skill differentials because this kind of narrowing tends to reduce the willingness of workers to undertake extensive training in order to secure higher wages. This complaint has been repeatedly expressed in England where skill differentials have been much more appreciably narrowed.[6] Although such protests were voiced by some American auto producers in the 1950s, most employers in this country have left the nature of the wage demand up to the unions and have concerned themselves more with the total cost involved.

After such a lengthy discussion, it seems almost subversive to question whether or not percentage differentials are really very important in allocating labor. Nevertheless, the question should be asked. Do workers think in percentage terms or do they view absolute differences as more important, particularly when the absolute differences are growing? Wage differentials often narrow most appreciably during periods of inflation. Do rising prices cause workers to work for wage increases that are significant in absolute terms even though the percentage improvement may be relatively small? The fact that such questions can properly be asked raises doubts as to how significant the reduction in skill differentials has been.

Whatever the impact on skill differentials of unions' demands may have been, it must be noted that unions evidently do not have any basic philosophy that leads them to make the narrowing of such differentials a set objective. The drive for uniform wage increases during periods of inflation has been prompted by the desire to protect lower-paid workers rather than by egalitarian philosophies. This ambivalence is not present in the attitude of unions toward the other types of differentials we will discuss.

Other Intraplant Differentials

Thus far we have been discussing skill differentials as if they were easily discernible and measurable so that one job could be clearly marked off from another. Jobs, of course, differ not only in terms of skill but also in terms of the amount of education, responsibility, and experience required by the job as well as the kind of work involved. On an ad hoc basis, wage differentials for different types of jobs within the plant are determined by custom as well as by market forces.

Because such methods were admittedly haphazard, many employers were anxious to uncover a more scientific means of setting wages that would not be so vulnerable to union challenges. The opportunity seemed to come with the development of job evaluation techniques, which used quasi-mathematical and statistical devices and thus lent an apparent air of precision to job evaluation. Job evaluation techniques (there are four main methods) range from a simple system that ranks one job against another to more complicated methods that award different aspects of a job points and then compare the total number of points for each job. One can get some idea of the process of job evaluation if he thinks of the Civil Service with its classification of job descriptions and eligibility requirements. Although still widely employed today, job evaluation techniques have been challenged by

the unions and are now deemed less perfect than when they were first introduced.

Union Attitudes

The attitude of unions toward job evaluation as a means of setting intraplant wage differentials has varied, depending largely on how an employer has administered the system. When the employer has been willing to consult or negotiate with the union about application of the plan, unions have tended to be favorably disposed. As William Gomberg has pointed out, unions have long used their own rough system of job evaluation in order to ensure equity in the employers' treatment of workers.[7] Job evaluation, when applied, tends to reduce discrimination in pay between workers of basically equal ability who are performing the same tasks. One aspect of workers' concept of a "fair" wage is that workers doing basically the same kind of work receive the same pay. In the clothing industries, unions have long had their own experts to help establish systems of job evaluation and job performance.

Early in the century, however, job evaluation was a dirty word to many unionists because a number of employers at that time used job evaluation as a substitute for rather than a supplement to collective bargaining. Unions were skeptical of the employers' claim that job evaluation was a perfectly objective method of determining wages and that the results were not subject to any challenge. Even today, many unions fiercely resist all proposals for job evaluation, sometimes even threatening to strike rather than accept it. On occasion, however, a specific situation will dictate a change in a union's policy of opposition. In the 1950s, for example, the Steelworkers accepted a job evaluation program in order to realign wage differentials in the basic steel plants.

Wage Incentive Programs

If employers ever had the expectation that workers would perform up to their peak capacity in return for their wages, they have long since become disenchanted. Workers and employers have seemingly always differed as to what constitutes "a fair day's work for a fair day's pay." In an effort to get workers to increase their efforts, many employers have used the device of paying a worker according to his output—the more a worker produces, the more he is paid—rather than according to the number of hours he works. Such a system of wages is often referred to as "piece rates."

Output incentive plans cover about 30 percent of the production and maintenance workers in the United States and Robert McKersie suggests that these plans certainly are not increasing and may possibly even be declining in number.[8] Even if all unions wholeheartedly supported the institution of piece rates, many companies would find them impossible to adopt. An incentive wage system can only work well under certain conditions. First, the nature of the work must be such that its pace can be determined by the worker. Where the pace is set by the assembly line's speed, a worker is forced to keep up or have his failure quickly spotted as he ties up production. By the same token, it is virtually impossible for him to work at a more rapid pace since his job is dependent on the flow of work coming to his position on the line. Second, an incentive wage presumes an ability on the part of the employer to measure ex-

actly the output of each worker. Last and equally important, it must be possible for the employer to measure the quality of the worker's production. Otherwise the worker might be tempted to increase the magnitude of his production by using slipshod production practices.

Impact of Collective Bargaining

The attitude of unions toward incentive pay has been as mixed as their view of job evaluation. The whole idea of differentials based on merit is in opposition to the basic union philosophy of equal pay for all who perform the same kind of work. At the same time, because incentive wage scales increase output, their use may revive old fears about running out of work to be done and the danger of unemployment.

In order to institute an incentive system with any hopes of success, a management must first undertake a time-study plan in order to determine a standard of production for the average worker. A rough rule of thumb is that the production norm should be set so that the average worker by exerting his best efforts can earn 20 to 30 percent more than he would under hourly rates. Unions, however, tend to suspect all studies of worker efficiency, seeing them as a device by which management seeks to raise production quotas without increasing workers' earnings.

Incentive plans are likely to yield smaller gains in output in union than in nonunion plants. If they are protected by a union, workers are more likely to form informal agreements among themselves not to overproduce. The "eager beaver" worker in the union plant may be particularly subject to social pressure from his fellow workers. Placing some limitation on worker effort is not necessarily detrimental, however. Incentive wages may encourage overcompetition among workers and lead to a production pace that is physically damaging. For example, while vacationing in the northern woods one summer we encountered one case in which lumberjacks were being paid on a piece-rate basis in terms of the number of "sticks" they completed per day. One lumberjack with a power saw set a pace of 600 to 700 "sticks" a day. At the end of a week's work, his hands had become so tight that for several days he was unable to shake hands or turn a doorknob.

Management and unions frequently disagree over the extent to which the workers will share in the increases in output produced by the incentive system. In the absence of union organization, employers often set incentive scales so that the workers get a diminished proportion of increased output. Unions have consistently opposed all such arrangements and insisted that workers share fairly in the increased yields. Managements frequently complain that the workers share all too completely in the augmented output when incentive pay systems yield wages double those of base rates. Unskilled workers on incentive pay may thus make more than their skilled counterparts working on a straight hourly basis. Management also complains that the union will attempt to extend the incentive system to cover workers for whom the incentive system is not appropriate. The Steelworkers, for example, have managed to get an incentive system applied to those working on the blast furnaces.

Another problem involves protection for incentive-pay workers whose output is reduced because of breakdowns in plant operations that are not the workers' fault. To avoid this danger, unions usually insist that the workers receive a minimum wage for the day equal to a stipulated percentage of what workers would have received on an hourly pay basis.

Even after a pay incentive scheme has been put into operation and is functioning smoothly, new technological advances or new production techniques may prompt management to seek a change in pay scales. Unions and workers are likely to regard all such attempts at revisions as efforts by the employer to institute a "speed up" in order to chisel on wage payments. Such revisions, no matter how justifiable, therefore often prove to be difficult to make.

Some employers have attempted to resolve this problem by permitting the union to participate in a joint administration of the incentive program as well as in the time study upon which the system is based. Such joint participation is confined to a minority of firms, however; most managements have too much anxiety about any possible loss of managerial autonomy to permit it. Most often management retains the right to initiate proposals for change and the union has the right to challenge the management's actions through the grievance procedure.

Incentive wage plans have their greatest chance for success when the details of the plan's operation have been clearly explained to the union's leaders as well as to the rank-and-file members. Such plans have increased in number in the last thirty years largely in response to the needs to increase output during World War II. American workers have enough of a sense of individualism to be willing to accept wage differentials based on effort as long as they are sure that no discrimination is involved and that they are being rewarded in proportion to their added effort. Piece-rate systems are far less developed in the United States than in many other countries, however.

One of the most recent forms of intraplant differentials is that produced by shift differentials; almost all of these postdate World War II. Today these differentials are virtually universal. Better than 80 percent of the companies now pay workers more for working a second shift and sometimes third-shift workers receive an even higher amount. The normal spread in the early postwar days was a 5 percent premium for those employed on the second shift and 10 percent for the third shift, but today there is an increasing tendency for both shifts to receive at least 10 percent more than the first shift. Many members of management have in fact complained that the current high shift differential has led them to cut work assignments and to refuse work that could only be accomplished by the hiring of extra shifts.

Wage Differentials Between Plants

Classical wage theory (see Chapter 6) not only provided an explanation for the general level of wages but also indicated why wide differentials in wages between plants did not exist in the long run. Since workers and employers were both assumed to be highly rational and knowledgeable individuals, the market would ensure that wages for the same kind of work would remain virtually equal. Employers would pay no more than the prevailing market wage requisite to guarantee them the necessary number of workers. Nor could employers pay any less. If they did, workers would shift to better paying jobs in other plants. This idea has prevailed into the twentieth century as the following statement by John Hicks demonstrates:

the general tendency for the wages of labourers of equal efficiency to become equalized in different occupations (allowance being made for the advantages or disadvantages of employment) has been a commonplace of economics since the days of Adam Smith . . . The movement of labour from one occupation to another, which brings it about, is certainly a slow one; but there is no need to question its reality.[9]

Note that the theory did not rule out the possibility that some differentials could exist when they were justified by the nature and quality of the work. Many years ago, Adam Smith provided economists with a wide variety of reasons why wages might differ from one occupation and one plant to another. Besides the factors we have already discussed, Smith cited allowances for differences in the cost of living from one region to another.

What traditional theory did not acknowledge was the possibility that wide wage differentials within the same occupation for workers employed in the same community could exist for an extended period. When surveys made by the War Labor Board during World War II indicated that such wide wage differentials were actually typical of the average community most economists were shocked. According to these surveys, straight-time hourly earnings in top-wage plants were often 50 percent higher than wages in low-wage plants in the same community. There appeared to be no central tendency of wages in most communities, but instead there were several separate clusters of firms paying approximately the same wage. These wage differentials appear to have persisted despite changes in the nature of the labor market. Lloyd Reynolds, for example, found wage differentials between plants to be of much the same character in 1948 as in 1940.[10]

Considerations of space do not permit us to explore all of the possible reasons why traditional wage theory has been so wide of the mark. Instead we will sketch in a few of the major factors and then devote our major attention to the impact of collective bargaining.

Any comparison of wage levels between different plants involves numerous difficulties. Job titles that read the same may involve markedly different kinds of work. All of the factors that made comparisons between union and nonunion plants difficult again come into play including variations in promotion opportunities, shift differentials, and opportunities for overtime. Variations in fringe benefits may also be important, although there is usually a good correlation between the payment of high wages and the existence of fringe benefits. The over-all magnitude of the differentials, however, suggests that they cannot be reconciled with traditional theory even if adjustments are made to take the above-mentioned factors into account.

Wage policies that employers undertake without any pressure from unions may account for some of the differentials. Employers may pay more than is necessary in order to attract an adequate supply of labor or for noneconomic reasons. Although some local labor market studies suggest that there is no appreciable difference in the quality of workers in high- versus low-wage plants,[11] employers may feel that they can attract a higher quality of workers by paying premium wages. A company may belong to a high (or low) wage industry and choose (or have) to pay wages in accordance with the norm in its industry rather than adhering to local standards. Employers may also take personal pride in running a plant with a reputation for paying top wages or they may feel that such a policy is desirable to promote good community relations.

Note also that wage differentials between plants may be the product of one of the forces cited earlier as a source of intraplant differentials. Certain plants, particularly those engaging in dirty and disagreeable work, may become known as havens for Negro workers. Because of the discrimination existing elsewhere, Negroes may flock to these plants (or industries) despite the relatively low levels of wages existing there. The very low wage that does attract the necessary supply of labor in turn confirms the conviction that this is not a proper field for white workers. Women workers have traditionally had the same experience.

Local labor market studies indicate that the bulk of workers, for a variety of reasons, tend to be immobile and unresponsive to variations in wage differentials.[12] This tendency is reinforced by the unwillingness of many employers to hire anyone already employed at another plant.

Effect of Collective Bargaining

The general effect of collective bargaining, particularly when it deals with workers in the same field, is to reduce existing wage differentials within a community. Before the turn of the century, Sidney and Beatrice Webb in their classic study of unionism noted that one of the unions' goals was the establishment of the "standard rate" or the principle of "equal pay for equal work." Another battle cry of unions has been to "take labor out of competition."

Unions see low-wage plants as a threat to the high wages and good working conditions enjoyed by their memberships. Because of the savings effected through lower labor costs, the low-wage firm may be in a position to take business away from a firm that meets the union's standards.

Although unions have actively sought greater wage uniformity, certain of their practices may actually preserve or even create diversity. One would expect that wage differentials would be most subject to union attack where they appear in plants in the same community that are organized by the same union; those members of the union who receive the lower wages might reasonably be expected to complain. However, this is not always the case. Some of the discontent may be avoided because different locals of the same national union are involved in the different plants. In negotiating for wage increases, the national union may push for a uniform increase for all companies in the industry thereby leaving existing absolute differentials untouched. High-wage firms may be encouraged by the union to retain their position even though management of those firms may have decided that they can safely abandon their traditional policy and still recruit and retain a satisfactory labor force.

Differences in wages between firms in the same community may also derive from the varying industrial composition of the firms. An unorganized plant that is new to the community may choose (but often does not) to adhere to the prevailing scales in the community—particularly if it is a low-wage community. A unionized company, on the other hand, may have to maintain the rates prevailing in the industry even though these may be far out of line with community levels. Future wage agreements in the industry may pull the firm even further out of line with local wage levels.

Industrial Differentials

Collective bargaining's impact on industrial wage structures affects both intra- and interindustry patterns. Because low-wage plants present a competitive threat in the industry, unions have a great incentive to eliminate them. The accelerating trend toward national agreements has had the effect of lessening wage differentials by contributing to changes in wage policy in both high- and low-wage plants. Low-wage plants are probably forced to pay higher wages than they would otherwise be prepared to do, while high-wage plants may pay less than the union could achieve. This effect is likely to be most pronounced where industrywide or association bargaining exists. When the labor market is very tight, employers may even pay wages in excess of those demanded by the union.

Low-wage plants, on the other hand, may find themselves paying wages that are excessive in view of their financial situation and sometimes are forced to discontinue operations. A local union may achieve the same effect by accident because the members are unaware of the seriousness of the company's financial difficulties. National officers on the other hand, may, after careful consideration, demand increases even if they realize their decision may spell financial ruin for marginal firms. While such a policy may seem very harsh to the casual observer and may evoke protests from members who lose their jobs when the plant closes, a case can be made for the assertion that a firm should not be permitted to continue operations if it can do so only by paying substandard wages.

Many students of wages in the United States believe that unions have had little effect on interindustry differentials, but there is a substantial minority who disagree. Over a quarter of a century ago, Paul Douglas, on the basis of a study of wages for the years 1890–1926, decided that the total effect of unions on interindustry differentials was small, although he found that the initial impact of the unionization on an industry's wage structure was appreciable.[13] More recently, John Dunlop has stressed the role of productivity changes in determining an industry's wage levels and has minimized the importance of unions. The core of Dunlop's views on the subject can be found in the following passage:

> The interindustry pattern of changes in average hourly earnings over substantial periods is to be explained fundamentally in terms of the following factors: change in productivity, change in output, proportion of labor costs to total outlays, competitive conditions in the product market, and the changing skill and occupational content of the industry.[14]

The dispute between Dunlop and Arthur Ross described in chapter 6 also included the question of interindustry wage differentials. Ross again placed far more emphasis than Dunlop on the importance of unions. Ross' position is partially supported by John Garbarino who reworked the studies of both Ross and Dunlop and concluded that unionization is one of three factors (the other two are the degree of concentration in the industries involved and the nature of their productivity) that affect wage differentials.[15]

Other equally distinguished experts in the field of wage determination (notably Clark Kerr, Lloyd Reynolds, and Cynthia Taft[16]) doubt whether unions have any significant effect on interindustry differentials. A study by Donald Cullen of industry wage differentials since the turn of the century suggests that the differences have remained "surprisingly stable" and that ". . . no justification has been discovered for the view that the wage structure has become increasingly rigid of late as a result of union pattern bargaining . . ."[17]

One of the reasons why there has not been more agreement on this issue is that interindustry wage differentials are influenced by so many different forces simultaneously. It thus becomes exceedingly difficult to isolate one factor, such as unionism, and measure its impact.

It is possible, for example, that such factors as differences in productivity, the nature of the product markets, or varying rates of economic growth are too powerful to be overcome by union pressure. The existence of unions themselves may be a factor in preserving differentials. Alternatively, the fact that other unions imitate pace setters such as the UAW and the Steelworkers may prevent other industries from lagging too far behind. At the same time nonunion employers may duplicate wage increases generated by unions for reasons indicated earlier. Powerful unions may be prevented from pushing wages too high in their industries because their very power encourages the formation of a strong bargaining unit on the employer side— a reversal of the countervailing power process envisioned by J. K. Galbraith.

There is still some evidence to offer in support of the belief that unions do affect interindustry wage structures. Since the various studies have not taken fringe benefits into consideration, it is possible that their inclusion might produce a greater effect than is now apparent. It is also possible that the tendency toward greater rigidity of wages in highly unionized industries (noted earlier in this chapter) may produce sizable distortions between industries during downturns in business conditions. The importance of this qualification is minimized somewhat, however, by the fact that many of the highly organized industries are dominated by large firms that tend to be slower to cut wages in any event.

Without a more precise statistical means of separating out the various opposing forces, it seems unlikely that we will be able to measure precisely the significance of collective bargaining in altering interindustry differentials. Even those who have been most convinced that unions do have some effect, however, usually concede that their impact is small—10 percent of wages or less—and often only lasts a short period of time.

One fact that strongly suggests that wage levels are set more by market forces than by union pressure is that those industries that typically pay high wages in the United States (aircraft, steel, rubber) are also high-wage industries in Canada, Great Britain, and many European countries.

The conclusion that interindustry wage differentials have been modified only slightly through union pressure, if accepted, would do a great deal to quiet the earlier alarm of those economists who believe that interindustry differentials should not be disturbed because they serve a vital function in distributing workers among the various industries. It also raises the broader question of the effectiveness of unions to raise wages at all.

Geographical Location Differentials

All of the factors that influence wage differentials in a single community are operative in the case of geographically dispersed communities. In addition, there are the differences resulting from the limitations imposed on geo-graphical mobility. Ties of family, friends, and home ownership can be added to the list of factors restricting workers' willingness to change jobs, such as seniority, fringe benefits, and other union management policies.

Traditionally, the United States has been classified into a number of regions characterized by high or low wages. The best known differential exists between the North and South, while wages are reported to be highest in the Far West. Although substantial differentials between regions still exist for certain industries such as rubber and furniture (Southern wage rates in these industries average 20 to 30 percent lower than rates in their Northern counterparts) there are many industries today where the difference is virtually or completely nonexistent. Aircraft, automobiles, coal, glass and steel are notable examples of industries where there is little or no wage differential between regions. It is important to note, however, that there may be numerous exceptions in all cases.

Wages may vary from the general industrial pattern for a region from occupation to occupation or between areas within a region.

Martin Segal's study of manufacturing industries in the North and the South revealed that during the 1947–1954 period there had been a narrowing of geographic wage differentials for 62 percent of the firms which employed 72 percent of the workers in the sample.[18] While varying widely from industry to industry, the average differential in wages between the North and the South was judged by the 1967 Handbook of Labor Statistics to be about 20 percent.

A substantial portion of the credit (or blame) for narrowing or eliminating geographical differentials within an industry can be assigned to the unions in that industry. The Segal study suggests that the North-South differential was narrowed for 70 percent of the industries that were dominated by multiplant concerns producing for national markets. Segal concluded that the fact that such a high proportion of these firms experienced a narrowing of wage differentials was due to the greater interest taken by unions in the goal of uniform wage rates, although he noted there were numerous variations between different industries.

The principal impact of unions on narrowing geographical differentials results from the adoption of industry-wide or pattern bargaining. In such cases, in which increases are equal for all firms in the industry, when there is no insistence that the low-wage firms catch up to the others, percentage differentials have diminished while absolute differentials have been left untouched. In some cases, the absolute differential has been narrowed or diminished as well (for example, in coal).

Should the reduction of geographic differentials be characterized as desirable or deplorable? Certainly numerous arguments have been brought forth to justify the existence of regional variations in wages. Differences in the cost of living are frequently cited by employers in low-wage plants as a justification for their lower wages. They argue that if their workers were paid as high a wage as workers in areas where the cost of living was higher, a real wage differential would result. Often coupled with this first argument is the assertion that the workers in the low-wage plants are actually less capable and efficient and are therefore being paid their full worth in terms of their productivity. This latter claim has sometimes been accompanied by invidious comparisons between different racial or ethnic groups. Employers paying low wages also justify themselves by claiming that they are in an unsatisfactory competitive position with respect to location of markets or raw materials and need the wage differential in order to exist.

On the whole, unions take a dim view of all these arguments, viewing all wages below the industry standard as evidence of exploitation. Differences in the cost of living are dismissed as inconsequential or at least too small to justify prevailing wage differences.

Students of wage differentials like Richard Lester have strengthened the unions' case by denying that there are significant differences in efficiency between workers in Southern and Northern plants.[19] The broadening of markets and the lessening of transportation rate differentials have also reduced some of the force of the arguments that attempt to defend the existence of low-wage plants.

The over-all effects of the narrowing of geographical differentials on the location of population and industry is difficult to determine. Some maintain that geographical differentials aid the development of certain areas because capital is supposedly attracted to these regions by the prevailing low wages. These critics see a simultaneous movement of the excess labor supply to areas where wages are higher. They contend that any artificial reduction of differentials before these two forces have had an opportunity to operate will upset the allocation of both labor and capital.

Our previous analysis suggests that the fears of these critics are exaggerated. Low wages by themselves are not a sufficient inducement to attract capital and the responsiveness of workers to wage differentials appears to be less than traditional theory has suggested.

Judging from the Canadian experience, unions have very little impact on wage differentials existing between countries. Canada is a good test since the bulk of its unions are members of internationals having their headquarters in the United States. Industries that have been organized by the same union in both countries continue to maintain substantial differences in wages. The only major exceptions are the Musician's Union, which has managed to obtain uniform wages for recordings and theater productions, and the UAW, which has had to deal with worker complaints on this score.

Income Distribution and Union Demands

Thus far we have been talking about wage differentials within and between plants. Before we turn to a discussion of developments in other countries, we need to broaden our base and examine the question of what effect, if any, unions have on the distribution of income between the three factors of production, land, labor, and capital.

Not too surprisingly, the line-up of economists who consider unions to be a significant force in raising labor's proportionate share of national income and their opponents is much the same as it was for the question of whether or not unions have a significant effect upon wage levels. When they deal with income distribution, economists have once again been more successful in voicing their opinions than they have in producing conclusive empirical evidence.

Virtually all economists agree that the share of national income going to labor has been appreciably increased during the past three or four decades. The difficulty lies in determining the degree to which unions are responsible for this changing proportion.

Many other forces may have had more significance than unions in pro-

ducing an increase in labor's share. For example, government actions such as rent control programs and monetary policy designed to maintain relatively low rates of interest and high levels of employment may have played a more important role.[20] Furthermore, labor's share in the economy is a statistical composite that includes both wages and salaries. Because our statistics are not sufficiently refined to permit the separation of these two items, it is impossible to tell whether wages or salaries have contributed most to the increase. That a rise in salaries is an important factor is evident from the decline in the number of individual enterprises (particularly in agriculture) as a proportion of total business enterprises and a corresponding rise in salaried managers. In addition there has been an increase in the number of salaried employees at all levels of government.

Beginning with Paul Douglas' study, most labor economists have held the belief (a belief supported by most of the empirical research) that unions have done relatively little to augment labor's share of income. Douglas concluded that labor shares of the national income in the period studied had remained virtually constant.

Among the best-known studies that tend to minimize the impact of unions on the distribution of income, are two separate studies by Harold Levinson.[21] Levinson found that labor's share rose by about six percentage points during two different time periods, 1914–1947 and 1929–1952. However, Levinson concluded that collective bargaining played only a subsidiary role to that of inflation and government policy in producing this increase. Unions were most successful in capturing in wage increases the relative decline experienced by rents and interest. Levinson emphasized that wage increases had not had a deleterious effect upon profits; instead profits also displayed a relative improvement during the two time periods.

Economists who are skeptical about the significance of collective bargaining in altering the patterns of income distribution point to the freedom of employers to change their prices in response to higher wages, thereby preserving capital's share. Another reason involves the likelihood that higher wages will induce employers to introduce more labor-saving machinery. The latter move, of course, by reducing the amount of labor relative to capital, also acts to check a rise in labor's share and to retain the proportionate amount going to capital.

Perhaps the strongest case for believing that labor unions do affect relative shares has been made by Robert Ozanne. Ozanne argues that the Douglas figures were accurate only for an earlier period in history when unions had little bargaining power and contends that since World War II unions have been in a position to increase labor's share.[22] In support of his position, Ozanne points to the reversal in the trend of profits after taxes. During the non-union era, profits were rising. In more recent years the share of profits in the economy has been going steadily downward.

It is possible that unions may alter the share distribution by exercising political power as well as through the collective bargaining mechanism. Clark Kerr, for example, believes that when a powerful union can insist on a program of profit-sharing or when a union can induce the government to undertake a program of price controls or steeply progressive taxation, it may succeed in increasing labor's slice of the national income.[23]

Success in this goal may actually work to the union's disadvantage. Kerr has pointed out that labor's relative share tends to fall in periods of full employment and inflation because the share of income going to profits increases during such periods.[24] At the very time when labor's share is likely to be increasing, its absolute position is deteriorating! In contrast to the instability of profits, wages tend to be relatively sticky and the intervention of unions tends to make them even more rigid. For those who remain fully employed, a depression may even be attractive, but the suffering of the unemployed and the anxiety of those who fear that they may soon lose their jobs more than offset any possible gain that may accrue to such workers.

The efforts of unions to capture a greater share of the pie may, as Kerr pointed out, lead to a shrinking of the pie itself as businessmen who are unable to escape wage demands through higher consumer prices reduce the volume of investment, again producing a reduction in the volume of employment.

Even though unions may have achieved little redistribution of relative shares, it is still possible that their existence has prevented what would otherwise have been a deterioration in labor's position. However, there appears to be no evidence to support this (somewhat Marxian) conjecture that there is a tendency for the worker's share to dwindle.

Experience Abroad

Generally speaking, the various wage differentials have been subject to greater narrowing abroad than they have in the United States.[25] One of the major reasons for this has been that other countries have placed greater reliance upon industrywide or national bargaining. Developing countries like

India constitute a special case, but here too substantial narrowing of differentials has taken place.

Great Britain

While there has been considerable narrowing of traditional wage differentials between both plants, particularly those in different geographical locations, and industries in Britain, the most striking change has been within plants. Differences between the wages of the skilled and the unskilled have narrowed appreciably in recent years and many British employers have complained that as a result they have had great difficulty in recruiting workers to those trades requiring long apprenticeships. British unions have applied the principle of "equal pay for equal work" more consistently to the cases of women and Negroes than have unions here. There has also been some shift in the share of total income going to labor, but as in the United States this probably derives as much if not more from the political activity of unions as from collective bargaining.

Continental Europe

The situation in Sweden, France, and West Germany has resembled that in Great Britain, with industrywide bargaining playing a key role. In West Germany and France, standardization of wages between plants in the same industry is enhanced by the power of the ministry of labor to extend the terms of certain agreements to companies not included under the contract. Lloyd Reynolds and Cynthia Taft assign a sizable portion of the responsibility for the narrowing of wage differentials to deliberate government policy but also emphasize the importance of built-in inflation.[26] Wage increases intended to offset rises in the price level tend to narrow percentage differentials unless the increases are also couched in percentage terms. This effect is visible in the United States and other countries as well.

Swedish unions have tried without much success to eliminate wage differentials caused by differences in skill, geographical areas, and between plants and industries. Immediately after World War II, the LO undertook with short-run success a program of "wage solidarity" designed to lessen wage differentials of all types. On the other hand, white-collar workers in Sweden, like those in most other countries, have been consistent opponents of programs to lessen wage differentials and the TCO (Sweden's white-collar union) has fought against such policies.

Differentials have emerged in recent years as plants, competing for workers, set pay scales above those established by the union. The LO's policy of "wage solidarity" has also been frustrated by the need to keep the market responsive to the need for controlling the mobility of workers.

Sweden's wage level is among the highest in Europe and Swedish unions have been given a substantial portion of the credit for this achievement. The Swedish workers' share of the national income has also risen sharply, but as in the case of the United States, the unions' role in this increase is less clear.

In West Germany, women have consistently received lower wages and have been assigned to the lower paying jobs; in recent years, however, German unions have been campaigning hard for equal pay and equal job rights for women.

Israel

Israel's wage differentials are the narrowest of perhaps any country in the world. Differences in wages between skills and occupations are particularly small, a product of both collective bargaining and official government policy. In general this situation is in keeping with the basic philosophy of Israeli workers. The narrow wage differences between the skilled and unskilled, however, have caused a certain amount of unrest among the skilled and white-collar workers. They have undertaken a series of unauthorized strikes to press for an improvement in their relative position; these strikes have prompted some readjustments. Wage differences between plants are reduced by the existence of industrywide and national bargaining.

India and Mexico

In India and Mexico, wage differentials tend to be wide. As in most developing countries, generally low levels of educational attainment for the mass of workers plus poorly organized labor markets and weak labor unions account in part for the wide differentials. Occupational differentials tend to be somewhat more narrow in underdeveloped countries except in India where prompted by differences in race or religion (caste).

One warning to bear in mind when comparing differentials between the developing and advanced countries and between countries in general is that one must allow a wide margin of error when making comparisons between industries or geographical locations, which may not be strictly comparable in different countries.

Japan

Many countries display some wage disparity between large and small plants, but in no country has this discrepancy reached the extreme proportions that it has in Japan. Wages in large plants (300 or more employees)

have often been more than triple those paid in the smaller plants. This curious dichotomy is often referred to as Japan's "dual economy." Part of this difference can be attributed to the fact that Japanese unions are comparatively strong in the large plants and virtually non-existent in the smaller plants; approximately 90 percent of the employees in the large plants are union members. Government protection is also lacking for workers in the small plants, and less than 15 percent of such workers are covered by the government's minimum wage laws.

Japanese unions have been keenly aware that the small plants pose a threat to their wage standards and have been making a strong effort to organize them for some time, but (as in the United States) the process of organization has been slow and tedious. In recent years the extreme shortage of labor in Japan has placed great wage pressure on these small plants and their wage standards have risen sharply. Much of the classic difference has thus been wiped out. This is a pattern typical of many developing countries—wide differentials between small and large plants in the early stages of development and a gradual narrowing as development proceeds.

By contrast, wage differentials between Japanese white- and blue-collar workers have always been extremely narrow. Government policy deliberately encouraged this situation during World War II, and rising standards of education have perpetuated it.

Summary and Conclusions

Wage differentials are a widespread phenomenon in the United States and differences among economists as to the impact unions and collective bargaining have on them are just as prevalent. At one end of the spectrum are Reynolds and Taft who tend to minimize the disturbing effects of unions on any kind of differentials. Even in the case of interfirm and intraindustry differentials where they feel unions have had their greatest impact, Reynolds and Taft still see competition in the product market outweighing the union's influence. They suggest that collective bargaining acts chiefly to remove some of the inequities worked by the market and to bring the actual market closer to the competitive model. Those economists who disagree with Reynolds and Taft usually focus on one particular type of differential where they feel the impact of unions has been considerable. Few, if any, have taken the position that unions have had a significant impact on all wage differentials. Most economists feel that the unions have had the least impact in altering the distribution of national income between different factors of production.

Wage differentials in other countries have in many cases narrowed even more appreciably than in the United States. Such factors as government policy and wage-cost inflation, however, appear to have been more important than collective bargaining in producing this result.

NOTES

1. Clarence Long has voiced his dissent on this score. See his "The Illusion of Wage Rigidity: Long and Short Cycles in Wages and Labor," *The Review of Economics and Statistics* 42 (May 1960), 140–151. Long concludes that "without their steep upward trend, wages are highly sensitive to economic cycles . . ." in both the long and short run. More typical is Slichter's assertion that nonunion wages are also difficult to cut. Sumner Slichter, "Do Wage-Fixing Arrangements in the American Labor Market Have an Inflationary Bias?," *American Economic Review,* Vol. XLIV, (May 1954), p. 331.

2. U.S. Department of Labor, *Negroes in the United States,* Bulletin No. 154 (Washington, D.C.: U.S. Government Printing Office, 1966)

3. See pp. 155–165 of this book for a discussion of external and internal wage differentials for Negroes and women.

4. Harry Ober, "Occupational Wage Differentials," *Monthly Labor Review* (August 1948), pp. 139–140.

5. M. W. Reder, "The Theory of Occupational Wage Flexibility," *American Economic Review* (December 1955), pp. 833–852.

6. This will be discussed in more detail later. See p. 166.

7. William Gomberg, "A Collective Bargaining Approach to Job Evaluation," *Labor and Nation* (March–December 1946), pp. 51–53.

8. Robert B. McKersie, "Changing Methods of Wage Payment," in John T. Dunlop and Neil W. Chamberlain (eds.), *Frontiers of Collective Bargaining* (New York: Harper & Row, 1967), pp. 179–180.

9. John R. Hicks, *The Theory of Wages* (New York: Peter Smith, 1948), p. 3.

10. Lloyd Reynolds, *The Structure of Labor Markets* (New York: Harper & Row, 1951).

11. Charles Myers and George P. Shultz, *The Dynamics of a Labor Market,* (Englewood Cliffs, N.J.: Prentice-Hall, 1951).

12. See notes 10 and 11.

13. Paul H. Douglas, *Real Wages in the United States, 1890–1925* (Boston: Houghton Mifflin, 1930).

14. John T. Dunlop, "Productivity and the Wage Structure," in *Income, Employment and Public Policy* (New York: Norton, 1948), p. 362.

15. John Garbarino, "A Theory of Interindustry Wage Structure Variations," *Quarterly Journal of Economics* (May 1950), pp. 282–305.

16. Clark Kerr, "Labor Markets: Their Character and Consequences," *American Economic Review* (May 1950), pp. 278–291, and Lloyd Reynolds and Cynthia Taft, *The Evolution of Wage Structure* (New Haven, Conn.: Yale University Press, 1956).

17. Donald E. Cullen, "The Interindustry Wage Structure, 1899–1950," *American Economic Review* (June 1956), pp. 353–369.

18. Martin T. Segal, "Regional Wage Differences in Manufacturing in the Postwar Period," *Review of Economics and Statistics* (May 1961), pp. 144–155.

19. Richard A. Lester, "Southern Wage Differential: Development, Analysis and Implications," *Southern Economic Journal* (April 1947), pp. 386–394.

20. See Irving Kravis, "Relative Income Shares in Fact and Theory," *American Economic Review* (December 1959), pp. 917–949.

21. Harold Levinson, *Unionism, Wage Trends and Income Distribution: 1914–1947* (Ann Arbor: University of Michigan Press, 1951) and *Postwar Movement of Prices and Wages in Manufacturing,* U. S. Congress, Joint Economic Committee Study Report No. 5. of the Study of Employment, Growth and Price Levels, 1960.

22. Robert M. Ozanne, "Impact of Unions on Wage Trends and Income Distribution," *Quarterly Journal of Economics* (May 1959), pp. 177–196.

23. Clark Kerr, "Trade Unionism and Distributive Shares," *American Economic Review* (May 1954) pp. 279–292.

24. This appears truer for early periods in our history than at the present time. Profits continue to fluctuate sharply but there has been a decline in property income accruing to rent and interest that has been at least partially matched by a rise in labor's share.

25. Irving Bernstein reminds us that even as far back as the 1920s wage differentials were greater in the United States than in Europe. At that time, Northeastern textile mills paid wages on the average in excess of 43.6% of Southern mills. Skilled workers were often paid twice what unskilled workers were paid. See Irving Bernstein, *The Lean Years* (Baltimore: Penguin, 1966), p. 67.

26. Lloyd G. Reynolds and Cynthia H. Taft, *The Evolution of Wage Structure* (New Haven, Conn.: Yale University Press, 1961), pp. 224–225.

8
Hours of Work

So long as there is one man who seeks employment and cannot obtain it, the hours of labor are too long.

—Samuel Gompers

☐ NEXT to improvements in wages, hours of work is the item that appears most consistently on any record of union demands. Although unions have always taken a keen interest in this matter, the importance of collective bargaining's role in reducing the number of hours worked is at best debatable. Some have argued that, unlike wages, reductions in hours cannot be expected to emerge from competitive forces in the market and that therefore unions and collective bargaining have played a crucial role in bringing about the reductions.[1] Others, however, minimize the importance of collective bargaining in shortening hours and emphasize instead the significant impact of government legislation.[2] Two things we do know for certain. First, the normal work week has decreased tremendously over the past century (see Table 8.1). Second, unions have worked hard to achieve that goal both at the bargaining table and through their political lobbies at state legislatures and Congress. Over the years, unions veered from one technique to another as they sought still shorter hours.

Although in 1828 New York was known as a "ten-hour town" for skilled workers, in 1830 over 81 percent of American workers still worked more than ten hours a day. A decade later, the standard work week was still seventy-eight hours—a figure that was fairly consistent with hours worked in Europe, except in Great Britain. These long hours had continued in the 1830s despite a strong effort by American unions to secure some reduction. Using the need of time for educating oneself as their theme, the drive for shorter hours had led to a ten-hour day for most mechanics and artisans. However, the depression of 1837 stopped the spread of the ten-hour day and longer hours were even restored for some workers.

During the 1840s, unions used a different argument, attempting to justify their demands for shorter hours by emphasizing that greater quality of workmanship would result if hours were reduced. The unions oscillated between efforts to win reductions through collective bargaining and appeals for legislative enactment. Their efforts to win legislative enactments at the state level bore some fruit in the immediately following years, but numerous loopholes in these state laws forced unions once again to seek improvement at the bargaining table.

Among the many things frustrating the early efforts of unions to win shorter hours, two items deserve particular attention. The first was the existence of a large agricultural sector in our economy. Farmers were accustomed to working from sunrise to sundown and had little sympathy for those who were "too lazy to be willing to do likewise." The second factor was the flood of immigrants, many of whom either came from rural backgrounds or had worked in factories in Europe where the hours were equally long or longer. Of the European nations only Great Britain in the 1840s had hours shorter than those existing in the United States. Despite these problems, slow but steady progress was made,

TABLE 8.1 Average Number of Hours in the Work Week

Year	Hours
1830	78
1850	60
1890	55
1920	50
1940	40

Source: Based on estimates made by various writers in Clyde Dankert, Floyd C. Mann, and Herbert Northrup (eds.), *Hours of Work* (New York: Harper & Row, 1965).

and by the first decade of the twentieth century the eight-hour day had become a widely established reality.

After the ten-hour day had been achieved, unions began to push for a shorter work week. Although the drive gained momentum after the eight-hour day became the norm, once again progress was slow. During the 1920s, the first real gains occurred when there was a general move toward the five-and-a-half day week and the then-unorganized Ford Motor Company announced the adoption of the five-day week. Other companies were slow to follow and a BLS survey in the 1920s disclosed that less than 6 percent of the employees in the nation had a five-day week. The forty-hour week gained general acceptance toward the end of the 1930s in response to the pressure of the 1938 Fair Labor Standards Act, which made any hours worked in excess of forty in one week subject to overtime payments. The law required time-and-one-half pay for work beyond forty-four hours for the first year, forty-two hours the second, with forty hours the maximum period at regular pay thereafter.

Since 1940, when the railroads ended their six-day week (eight hours per day), there has been no dramatic general reduction in the work week. One can name a substantial minority of trades, however, where the thirty-five-hour work week has become the accepted standard—building and construction, breweries, coal mining, electricians, longshoremen, needle trades, and printing. In a few cases (the New York City electricians, for example) the standard work week has been reduced to twenty-five hours.

Until recently, however, most unions have remained content with the forty-hour work week perhaps because their memberships seemed to have little interest in further reductions. Instead unions have concentrated on shortening the work year by pressing for paid vacations and paid holidays. Beginning in the late 1950s, however, high levels of unemployment led union leaders to agitate once again for a shorter work week. At the 1959 convention of the AFL-CIO, President George Meany called upon Congress to enact a thirty-five-hour week (five days, seven hours per day).

Arguments for the Shorter Work Week

The arguments advanced by unions to justify a shortening of the work week have changed with time. At an earlier date the justification was couched in terms of the need to make the workers better citizens and to protect their health. According to this argument, the man who spent seventy hours a week at his job not only endangered his health, but had little opportunity to be a good family man or to keep abreast of the news of the day. His right to vote lost its meaning because he had no time to study the issues.

The recent standard case for shorter hours, however, has rested on the need to protect workers from the threat of unemployment. Put in its crudest form, this argument is based on the old "lump of work" fallacy. As the name implies, this theory maintains that there is only so much work to be done. Thus, unless the work is spread around, there will not be enough jobs for all those seeking employment. The arithmetic of the theory is simple. If there are 50 million people presently working forty hours per week, let them now work for only thirty-five hours. The resulting reduction of 250 million hours of labor will create openings for more than 7 million (250 divided by 35) additional workers.

Few businessmen or economists have been convinced of the validity of this reasoning. Basic to their skepticism has been a general tendency to reject the "lump of work" theory itself. Economists deny that there is a fixed amount of work to be done, maintaining that the amount of work to be performed is related to the expanding horizons of the consumer demand.

Faced with a situation of unemployment, economists would tend to question the effectiveness of shorter hours as a palliative. The most obvious reason is that shorter hours involve an additional cost to the employer. Since the standard union demand for shorter hours is coupled with a proposal for increased wages (so that the workers' take-home pay will remain the same), the cost would be appreciable. The reduction in hours from forty to thirty-five with total take-home pay remaining unchanged would involve almost a 15 percent increase in employer costs unless offsetting developments should occur. The fact that in the absence of a request for shorter hours the union might have demanded higher wages mitigates this effect somewhat.

Even if no increase in the cost of wages accompanied the reduction in hours, it is quite possible that production costs would rise. The employer would now have to bear the costs of training additional personnel, as well

as hiring additional foremen to supervise them. In some key skills a shortage of manpower might develop, forcing employers to pay higher wages in order to attract workers possessing the necessary skills.

Furthermore, some economists suggest that reducing hours will not cure unemployment because a substantial part of the existing unemployment is structural in character. Structural unemployment involves workers unsuited for various reasons to fit current employer needs. Therefore, the argument runs, a reduction in hours can do nothing to make these workers more employable than they were before.

In addition, many employers contend that the shortening of hours is simply a device utilized by the union to ensure a greater amount of overtime or shift differentials, which enhance the amount of premium pay the workers receive and correspondingly increase employers' costs.

One last objection, which is of minor significance but still sometimes raised, is that many of the jobs created by a shortening of hours would be taken by workers who would then have time to hold two jobs. We will discuss the importance of such moonlighting later in this chapter.

Historically, the possible rise in costs to the employer has been at least partially offset by a tendency for the workers' hourly output to rise as the number of hours he worked decreased as a result of reductions in fatigue, lower accident rates, improvements in health and morale, and less absenteeism. Because so many other factors, such as technology, have also been changing, it has been impossible to measure precisely how much of the increase in hourly output has been occasioned by shorter hours. There is general agreement, however, that the offset to higher costs has been appreciable.

Because of this offset factor and because for a number of years the unions appeared satisfied with a standard forty-hour week, employers' alarm over a shorter work week was stilled. Beginning in the 1960s, however, in reaction to the high rates of unemployment in the United States (running consistently in excess of 5 percent during the 1960–1965 period) unions once again began to press for a shorter work week. This time, the thirty-five-hour week was their stated objective. In August 1962, the executive council of the AFL-CIO announced as their goal the establishment of the five-day week (seven hours a day). By this time, a number of national and international unions had already endorsed this objective, and a number of unions had already achieved it. Notable examples were the Rubber Workers, the Brewery Workers (37.5 hours), and the ILGWU, which had had half of its membership on a thirty-five hour week since the 1930s and had gained the same provision for the remaining half in the 1950s.

Unions repeated many of their earlier arguments about the effectiveness of a shorter work week in reducing unemployment. An employer who objected about the added costs was reassured with the old citations of the gains in worker productivity stemming from shorter hours.

Two points need to be made with respect to future gains in productivity resulting from a shortening of hours. First, the truer the statement is, the less valid is the union argument that a reduction in hours serves as a solution to the problem of unemployment. The original "lump of work" argument was that if each worker did less work, there would be more work available for others. However, if the reduction in hours induces the worker to produce nearly as much (or even possibly more) than he did on a longer time

schedule, the increased availability of work for others will be at least partially lost. Union leaders have often presented these arguments side by side without realizing that they are inherently contradictory.

Second, it is at least possible that further reductions in the work week below forty hours may not have as stimulating an effect on productivity as previous reductions seem to have had. The gains in terms of better health, lower accident rates, and lower absentee rates that apparently resulted when the work week was reduced to forty hours may represent the maximum possible, and further reductions may achieve very little in this direction. To the extent this is true, of course, the concern over resulting increases in costs becomes more and more significant.

Another point sometimes made by unions in support of shorter hours is that a shortening of hours will attract marginal workers, such as women, into the labor force. Possible losses in production from a shortening of hours will thus be compensated for by the larger number of workers available for employment. Whether the added numbers are likely to be of significant proportions, however, is at least debatable.[3] Furthermore, the added numbers searching for work may only serve to aggravate the unemployment problem.

From the first, employers have had little confidence in the ability of their employees to use the time away from their jobs in a fruitful fashion. Each drive for shorter hours has been met with warnings that increased drunkenness and immorality would likely result from the increase of leisure. The old proverb that "idle hands make mischief" was refurbished and applied to adults as well as children.

Unions, on the other hand, have asserted that increased leisure would benefit the entire economy. All work and no play may make jack, but it gives one no opportunity to spend it! While economists have come to stress the importance of a high level of consumer spending in maintaining full employment, unions have pointed out that a greater amount of leisure time provides the worker with a greater chance to exercise his patriotic duty to be a consumer. Judging by the amount of consumer credit outstanding, however, workers already have more than enough time to spend their paychecks. Added leisure without more pay is unlikely to raise the nation's consumption function.

In recent years, sociologists and psychologists have expressed concern over the effect that the growing amount of leisure time will have. These experts question whether workers brought up to follow a Puritan ethic that views work as a positive virtue can now adjust to a situation in which an increasingly large proportion of their days are spent away from the job. Do we need to reeducate our population so that it can make productive use of its leisure time? Will workers grow bored with their leisure and search desperately for something to do? The unhappiness of many workers who have been compelled to retire suggests that such questions are not as unrealistic as they first appear.

For most workers, however, the possibility that leisure will become an irritant does not appear to be an immediate problem. While some of the Steelworkers seem to have found their three-month sabbaticals (granted every five years to the 50 percent of the workers possessing the most years of service) unduly long, there is still opportunity for experimentation with a second vacation or even a third during the year.

Workers would probably also welcome a movement to a four-and-one-half or alternate four-day week. A news story in the fall of 1969 suggested that many workers are eager for additional time off, stating that, despite the pressure of inflation, many workers had responded to their high pay checks and the security from firing afforded by the tight labor market by regularly taking off Fridays to go fishing or pursue other personal activities.[4] Whether employers will be willing to leave their capital equipment idle for such protracted periods of time remains to be seen.

Meanwhile, a new set of voices cautioning against premature reductions in hours has come from the government. President John Kennedy and his economic advisors warned against any substantial cut in hours because of the possible detrimental impact it might have on the nation's economic growth rate. Given continued success in the government's efforts to reduce the unemployment rate, it is debatable that unions will continue to press for a general reduction in hours of work per week.

It seems safe to predict, however, that further reduction in the total number of hours in the working year are likely to continue. How much of a reduction will take place and how rapidly it will occur depends on the answers to a number of questions such as the following: How rapid will be the pace of automation and how much displacement of labor will occur? What choice will workers make between further leisure and an increased amount of goods? Will advertising remain an effective force encouraging workers to ask for more goods? How strongly will government officials oppose reductions in hours as a threat to the nation's rate of economic growth? How forcefully will employers oppose further reductions in working time because of the resulting enforced idleness of capital equipment? To what extent will employers try to make jobs more attractive to workers? What will be the trend in other countries and will our desire to exceed the Russians in all things lead us to reduce hours if they carry through their programs for sharp reductions in the work week and for longer vacations?

Moonlighting and Overtime

Many workers react to a shortened work week or extended vacations by acquiring a second job. Approximately 5 percent of the nation's workers (slightly over 3 million) hold more than one job. Whether or not this is evidence of workers' unwillingness to have too much idle time on their hands is by no means certain. Instead, workers may moonlight because they find it impossible to maintain the standard of living they deem proper in an affluent society with the income from a single job. While the shortened work week has made moonlighting possible, it does not necessarily follow that workers would not want all the leisure they have and more if their incomes were sufficiently large to permit it.

Interestingly, unions and management are both generally opposed to moonlighting, although for quite different reasons. Management fears that the moonlighter will be less productive in his job and more prone to accidents or absenteeism because he is overtired. Some managers also worry that the moonlighter may be disloyal and will either deliberately or accidentally leak confidential material to a competitor.

The opposition of unions to moonlighting is founded on three considerations. First of all, the moonlighter is difficult to organize. Indeed, he may already be a union member in a different union or local and be unwilling to pay union dues for what is often only a part-time job. Second, because the work is supplementary to his regular income, the moonlighter may be willing to work for less than the standard union wage, thereby undermining union standards. Third, the union often regards the moonlighter as someone who reduces employment opportunities for others, thereby frustrating the major reason that unions undertook a drive for shorter hours in the first place. The fact that most moonlighters work only part time and that about 40 percent of them are self-employed in their second job has not removed the stigma attached to the term by many union officials.

The relationship between shorter hours and overtime (moonlighting within the plant) is not completely clear either. At times, unions have been accused of seeking to shorten the work week in order to provide their members with more overtime. Local 3 of the IBEW in New York City, for example, has a standard twenty-five-hour work week with a guaranteed minimum of five hours of overtime. At the same time, the assurance of steady overtime may encourage workers to seek still shorter hours in order to have both more pay and greater leisure.

In general, workers and management have been more favorably disposed towards overtime than have the unions. Workers like overtime because it means a substantial increase in their take-home pay since normally overtime pays one-and-one-half times the usual hourly rate. Managers may prefer additional overtime to increasing the total number of workers because overtime enables them to spread their fixed labor costs such as fringe benefits and avoids the problem of recruitment and possible subsequent layoff.[5] Some managements also feel that overtime can be paid in lieu of a higher base wage with the hope that their overtime payments can be reduced at some future time when the labor supply is less tight. We noted in an earlier chapter the tendency of unions to increase the rigidity of wage structures downward.

Unions have been less enthusiastic about overtime largely because they fear that its use will destroy job opportunities for those seeking employment. For this reason, many unions limit the freedom with which an employer can use overtime. In the building and garment trades, for example, its use is prohibited. More frequently, contracts will call for overtime only during the peak season, when an emergency exists, when all the shop's employees are on a full-time basis, or when outside workers are unavailable.

Methods of Computation

There are various methods of computing the amount of hours, days, or weeks worked. Overtime can be based on the number of hours of work in a given day, the number of hours worked in the week, or work performed on a Saturday, Sunday, or legal holiday. Although the normal base is an eight-hour day and a forty-hour week, a number of unions have won provisions that guarantee overtime after a shorter period.

Complications arise when the weekly and daily overtime do not add up to the same amount. Suppose a worker labors for ten hours the first two days of the week. If his hours are the regular eight for the remaining three days, he will be credited with four hours of overtime whether computed on a daily or a weekly basis. But suppose that for the last two days of the week in question he works only six hours each day. While he still has overtime for his work on Monday and Tuesday if computed on a daily basis,

his weekly hours add up to the usual 40. What if anything should he receive in the way of overtime payment? The usual contract provides for the maximum protection to the worker and allows for the greatest amount of overtime possible. In the case cited, the worker would normally receive four hours of overtime.

Premium pay for work on Saturdays or Sundays is usually at the rate of one-and-one-half times and twice the hourly rate respectively. Such provisions are found, however, less frequently than are provisions for premium pay for daily overtime. Thus premium pay for Saturday work is found in 60 percent of the contracts, and premium pay for Sunday work in about three-quarters of the contracts, but over 85 percent of the contracts in manufacturing call for the payment of daily overtime.

Hours of Work in Other Countries

The forty-hour standard so familiar to American workers for the past two decades is not universally applied elsewhere in the world. We noted in the first part of this chapter that early in the last century, Great Britain had made considerably more progress toward shorter hours than had either the United States or Continental European nations. At that time, Britain's standard of sixty-nine hours bettered the United States and France by nine hours and Germany by fourteen. Today, however, the standard work week in Great Britain is still forty-two hours, although British unions have been seeking reductions to the forty-hour level. The picture on the Continent varies from country to country; most countries range from forty-two to forty-six hours as a norm. France has a statutory forty-hour work week and in textiles the week is thirty-eight hours as a result of unemployment. In the late 1960s 52 percent of West German workers were on a statutory work week of forty-two hours to forty-five hours. West German unions have been asking forty hours for all workers. As late as 1958, Sweden had a standard forty-eight-hour week, but beginning in that year hours were reduced in a series of steps to forty-five. Currently Swedish unions are aiming for forty-two-and-one-half hours.

Israel, which has prided itself on maintaining wages and working standards equivalent to those of Western Europe, has lagged behind somewhat in the matter of hours of work. The Hours of Work and Rest Law, which was still in effect at least to the late 1950s, provides a standard forty-eight-hour week for all workers and the payment of a 25 percent premium for hours worked beyond this limit. Workers under the age of eighteen are limited to a forty-hour week by law. Note that in both cases the impetus for protection has come from legal enactment rather than from collective bargaining.

Japan has a Labor Standards Law that sets the normal working day at eight hours and sets up a series of restrictions on the use of overtime. Women and men working in hazardous industries, such as mining, are severely limited as to the amount of overtime they may perform. For other male workers, the amount of overtime is left to the discretion of the representing union.

Legislative enactment is also the source of protection with respect to hours in Mexico. In general, the hours provisions there have been more successfully enforced than have regulations dealing with wages. The eight-hour day is the common standard in most manufacturing centers, in mining, and on the railroads for daytime work.

Seven-and-one-half hours is the norm for work performed at night or for situations where the work period includes both day and night hours. Double time is paid for work in excess of the standard hours with the proviso that there should be no more than three consecutive hours of overtime and no more than three consecutive days in a week when overtime work is allowed. The limitation of eight hours may be exceeded by contractual agreement of the union (or workers) and management in order to provide for free Saturday afternoons.

In recent years the actual number of hours worked per week in almost all of these countries was usually three to four hours longer than those worked in the United States because of the higher levels of employment existing abroad. Most but not all of this extra work received premium pay.

Summary and Conclusions

For a long time and in many countries unions generally have been interested in seeking shorter hours for workers. The reasons advanced in support of shorter hours have varied from time to time, but one of the most frequent arguments in this country has been that shorter hours would have a therapeutic effect on the rate of unemployment. It is for this reason that, after a number of years of being satisfied with the forty-hour week, American unions have renewed their drive for a shorter work week—this time setting a standard of thirty-five hours as their goal. The thirty-five-hour week does not yet appear to be a goal of unions in other countries. Because of the amount of unemployment, unions in this country have given both moonlighting and overtime only limited approval.

NOTES

1. Herbert R. Northrup, "The Reduction in Hours," in Clyde Dankert, Floyd C. Mann, and Herbert R. Northrup (eds.), *Hours of Work* (New York: Harper & Row, 1965), pp. 2–3.

2. Richard L. Ronan, "The Influence of Collective Bargaining on Hours," in Dankert *et al., op. cit.,* p. 17.

3. There appears to be little question, however, that a shortening of hours to make possible an increased amount of part-time work has contributed significantly to the growing proportion of women in the labor force. See Gertrude Bancroft, *The American Labor Force, Its Growth and Changing Composition* (New York: Wiley, 1958), Chap. 4.

4. *The Wall Street Journal,* October 14, 1969.

5. This has led to proposals to require double pay for overtime to make its use less tempting to employers. For a further discussion see Chapter 10 on Fringe Benefits.

9
Seniority

Seniority has become so institutionalized in our labor relations structure that the parties now generally accept it without significant conflict.
—C. Wilson Randle

☐ SENIORITY has played a far greater part in collective bargaining in the United States than it has in other countries, and its application has been far more rigorously enforced. In the United States few, if any, provisions in the typical contract provide greater protection to workers with a long history in the plant. Furthermore, despite some continuing dispute about the range of the principle's application, few items have been as completely accepted by both unions and management.

As the term implies, under a seniority system certain personnel decisions are based on the principle of length of service. Should economic conditions dictate that a plant lay off part of its labor force, those laid off first would be the ones with the shortest record of employment in the plant. Similarly, those with the longest service records would be the first to be recalled. These two basic decisions are at the heart of any system of seniority, and they are the ones most widely accepted. Seniority is associated quite properly with the union movement in this country since its general acceptance resulted largely from union demands. Demands for seniority protection were first presented in the railroad industry. Although management generally does not adopt sen-

iority programs on its own initiative, even many nonunion companies utilize the principle of seniority when decisions concerning layoffs and recalls must be made. In the absence of a union, however, adherence to the seniority system is likely to be less rigid and its application much more narrowly construed.

Unions have also pressed for the application of seniority to other questions, but here management has been more reluctant to concede. Generally, but with considerably less success than in the case of layoffs and recalls, unions have pressed for promotion by strict seniority. Unions have also sought to extend the system to other decisions, which are less important but still contribute significantly to a worker's sense of satisfaction. These include the opportunity for the worker to choose which shift he will work and the timing of his vacation. The opportunity for first chance at overtime or the right to reject it may also be of some importance, but more frequently overtime is divided equally.

Generally speaking, seniority rules do not apply to those workers who have been hired recently and are still on probation. During this probationary period, management is free to fire without prior consultation with the union and without danger of provoking a grievance. Traditionally probationary periods have extended for three months and even longer but increasingly the span has been shortened to match the union-shop provisions of the Taft-Hartley Act. Once the probationary period has been safely passed, a worker's seniority is computed from the date he was first hired, and thus includes the probationary period.

The principle of seniority is based on the belief that it is the most equitable system on which to base the decisions we have just outlined. Seniority provides protection for older workers who are faced, because of the rapid pace of modern technology, with the possibility that their skills may become obsolete. Basic also to the concept of seniority is the whole idea that a worker has a property right to his job. Just as management claims certain rights because of its control of property, so workers claim that their jobs are a property right to be protected from all challenges. Without seniority, the worker's claim to his job has little force and is subject to the whims of his foreman. Seniority is thus a vital source of protection to workers from discretionary decisions by management. Of course, seniority also provides the worker with protection from possible discriminatory action by the union.

Although old and young workers generally agree that these justifications are valid, an occasional dissenter claims that *any* seniority system is inequitable. Such dissidents stress that seniority is unfair to the younger workers who have the most family responsibilities and the fewest savings and who are, therefore, harder pressed when faced with the loss of their jobs. Minority groups in industries where seniority serves as a major factor in promotion may also have cause to complain. Herbert Northrup's study of the paper industry, for example, stresses that seniority systems have retarded the opening of advancement opportunities for Negroes in that industry.[1]

Only in those industries (construction, for example) where the duration of employment is relatively brief and where workers form an attachment to the industry rather than a particular employer does seniority play only a negligible role in layoffs and recalls. The otherwise general acceptance of seniority by management as the basis for answering the question of whom to lay off suggests that management also accepts the fairness of the principle and that management has not found it to be unduly expensive. Nevertheless, numerous problems arise in any attempt to implement a seniority system. We will discuss these difficulties from the viewpoints of management, union, and the workers.

Management's Views

Although all too many workers view any resistance by management to the application of strict seniority as self-serving, management may at times have sound bases for their opposition. Management's most serious objection to seniority is the rigidity with which unions wish to apply it. The question of rigidity is most pressing in cases where considerations of merit are paramount. Thus, while management has sometimes sought to circumvent the seniority system in order to retain workers with special skills during periods of layoff, its opposition to rigid application of seniority is likely to be more adamant when the question of promotion is at stake.[2] Before discussing promotions, however, we will first note some of the problems seniority creates for management when applied to layoffs and recalls. A minor problem is the increased amount of bookkeeping that adherence to strict seniority requires. Otherwise an error of only a few days may become the basis for a grievance. The bookkeeping problem increases in severity the longer a worker retains his seniority claim after being laid off. Unions, of course, seek to extend this period, and management seeks to shorten it. A worker's claim to seniority usually expires in six months or a year, although the terms of some contracts stipulate that a worker's name cannot be removed from the seniority list for three years or more. Management often solves this problem by allowing the union to keep the records.

More serious to management are the problems caused by "bumping" through transfer. When a worker with high seniority loses his job, he is permitted to displace someone with less seniority elsewhere within the boundaries of his seniority unit. Personnel directors have told us that as many as 700 shifts have occurred when a man with top seniority displaced someone below him and the process was continued on down the line. The disruption of work groups and losses in production that result from these shifts can become very expensive.

For this reason, management has usually attempted to narrow the scope of the seniority unit as much as possible (the usual goal is to place seniority on a departmental basis)[3] in order to minimize the number of transfers following a senior worker's reassignment. The narrower the scope of the seniority arrangement, on the other hand, the less the protection it affords to the senior workers. In general, therefore, unions prefer to see seniority established on a plantwide basis. This conflict of interest between union and management often produces a compromise whereby a worker can bump into another department, but only if a reduced percentage (often 50 percent) of his seniority in his current position would warrant his displacing someone in another department.

In the case of the railroads (which also provide a notorious example of the damaging effects that seniority has had on efficiency) the positions taken by unions and management on this issue are reversed. For a number of years, railroad management has been seeking to *broaden* the seniority unit. Two problems have been crucial in this area: One is the fact that most railroad seniority units only apply to a one-hundred-mile radius of a home base, a figure based on an earlier day's mileage equivalent of a full day's work. The other is the distinction drawn between yard and road service men. Workers refused to work outside their geographical boundaries, and management could employ road men for brief jobs as yard men only if prohibitively high penalties were paid. Furthermore, railroad unions have resisted the abandonment of disused yards because the abandonment would either displace workers or create problems of dovetailing the displaced men into other seniority systems. Pressure to broaden the seniority base in other industries has accompanied the growing fear of displacement resulting from technological change.

Frequently an impasse between the union and management on the scope of the seniority unit is resolved by varying the scope according to the application made. In the case of promotions, for example, the unit is more likely to be narrow in scope than in the case of layoffs and recalls. Within the area of layoffs, differences may depend upon whether the layoffs are deemed to be of short or long duration.

Although the effect of a strict seniority system on efficiency on the railroads has been one of the most widely publicized cases, the problem exists in other industries as well. Two particular threats to efficiency have arisen when seniority is applied to promotion. First, young workers may become discouraged from doing their best because they know that their chances of early recognition and promotion are virtually zero because of the number of men with greater seniority who are ahead of them. Second, a system of promotion by strict seniority reduces the likelihood of getting the best man for the job and thus reduces plant efficiency. Thus management has usually insisted that promotion be based on considerations of merit and ability as well as seniority. Contract clauses dealing with promotions usually state that promotion will be based on seniority where no differences in ability exist.

In defending their demand for straight seniority as the basis for promotion,[4] unions argue that in most cases differences in ability are so slight as to be almost undetectable. Unions also contend that permitting management to make promotion decisions partially a matter of discretion is to open up, albeit on a smaller scale, the whole question of favoritism and discrimination.

While the union's position is usually that the more experienced worker is the better one and hence the one more deserving of promotion, management has not found it too difficult to retain some discretion on promotions.[5] Unions have not pushed too hard largely because workers recognize the need to reward merit and are sympathetic to the desire of younger workers to get ahead. In addition, promotions at any given point in time usually involve only a fraction of a plant's labor force and so, unlike layoffs, are less likely to arouse protests.

While we are discussing the issue of promotions, it might be worthwhile to note briefly the problem that arises when a man has been promoted out of the seniority coverage. Assume, for example, that a man has been promoted to the position of foreman and that after several years a contraction in the plant's labor force eliminates his job. Although his promotion to foreman presumably indicates that he is a superior worker in the first place, he now finds that his fellow workers have been accumulating seniority during his period of service as foreman and those who were hired at the same time now have greater seniority than he has. While he may

still possess enough seniority (assuming he did not forfeit his past accumulation upon promotion) to ensure a place in the shop, he may be able to get only a relatively low-ranking position.

Some representatives of management also allege that seniority in any form is likely to lead to a plant's having an older labor force. Not only does the seniority system help to retain the older workers, but it may also drive away younger workers eager for recognition and promotion. When older workers represent a large proportion of a plant's labor force, the possibilities for lowered efficiency are obvious.

Management also charges that the existence of a seniority system tends to prevent the firing of workers even for just cause, which also contributes to lower efficiency. Management officials often allege that arbitrators are reluctant to uphold disciplinary discharges because the workers involved would lose seniority benefits. When firing regardless of the seriousness of provocation is removed from management's discretion, the effect on plant morale is likely to be serious. On the whole, however, we feel that such complaints have been overstated and that the need to protect workers has justified curbing arbitrary and excessive use of dismissal as a form of punishment.

Where seniority provides for a choice of shifts, some managements have reported that they tend to get the newer, less well-trained workers clustered on the night shift with a resulting serious discrepancy between production standards on the various shifts.

Seniority thus obviously does create problems for management. However, the accompanying advantages of improved plant relations and increased confidence of the plant's labor force in the fairness of management decisions is more than worth the costs.

Furthermore, a seniority system may enable management to assign the responsibility for difficult decisions to the union by pointing out that a decision was necessary in accordance with the prevailing seniority rules.

The Union's Views

As the pace of the merger movement quickened in the years after World War II, one might expect to find that seniority rules were a major headache to the management of merging firms. Such would indeed be the case except for the fact that management has tended to leave the problem in the laps of the union or unions involved. With the exception of the transportation and communication industries, the courts have usually ruled that the management and the union(s) are free to make any decision they choose and the worker is powerless to protest. (There were some instances during the 1930s where unions simply abolished the seniority lists for women in order to protect the position of male workers.) When no displacement of labor results from the merger, the problem is relatively simple. We will discuss the problems created when some individuals are transferred between plants later in this section.

Real difficulties, however, arise when the merger involves a reduction in the combined plants' labor force.[6] Since prior to the merger each plant had its own seniority list, the problem is how to combine the two lists in an equitable manner so that they can provide a basis to make the necessary layoffs. At first glance, a simple combining of the two lists would appear to be the simplest and most reasonable solution. This is sometimes done; however, when one company has been in operation much longer than the other, this method may result in complete displacement of one plant's labor force while workers in the other plant are left untouched. It does no good if a worker has built up ten years of seniority in a plant if most of the workers in the plant with which it is merged have fifteen or more years of seniority. Obviously, the greater the number of decisions that are based on seniority the more serious the inequity becomes for employees in the junior plant. Even if these workers manage to retain their jobs, they will still rank below workers in the other plant when important decisions based on seniority are made.

As a result of these difficulties, a variety of other solutions have been adopted from time to time, including:

1. Prorating the seniority according to the percentage of employment provided by each firm before the merger took place.

2. Granting the entire staff of the purchasing company priority over the employees of the purchased company. This method has been used in the case of mergers between newspapers.

3. Giving all of those currently working priority over those laid off at the time of merger even if some of those laid off at one plant have greater seniority than those working at the other plant.

4. Continuing the maintenance of two separate seniority lists. This is a possibility when the merged plants continue to be run as two separate entities after the merger, particularly where there is considerable geographical separation between them. Note that under this arrangement men in one plant with greater seniority than those in the other may be laid off, thus negating the value of their accumulated seniority. The rationale, of course, is that in the absence of a merger a reduction in one plant's labor force might have had the same result without arousing any protest.

A situation similar to the merger situation arises when a company transfers its production activities from one locale to another. A number of court decisions have upheld the unions' contention that workers (as workers rather than as union members) have a property claim to their jobs and that the company has a responsibility to see that these property rights are protected.

A good illustration of this principle is the attempt of the United Automobile Workers to protect its members in the face of frequent transfers of work from one plant location to another. UAW agreements call for the transfer of displaced workers who desire to move to the new plant and require that the company pay a part of their moving expenses if the move requires a shift of over fifty miles. Ordinarily, although the transferred worker has a claim on available jobs in the new plant, he loses the seniority he accumulated at the old plant. Should his position reopen at his old plant, the worker can return there and reacquire his former status or remain at the new plant. The UAW has reported that thousands have been so transferred.[7]

Sometimes the problem becomes complicated by the opposition of workers in the new plant to the transfer of workers from other plants whom they view as competitors for their jobs. In some instances, the union has organized the new plant after promising workers that there would be no transfers. When subsequent unexpected reductions in work at other plants have resulted in transfers, the original members of the new plant have charged that the union has double-crossed them and occasionally have even sought decertification. However, in such cases, the union is actually given Hobson's choice: it can break faith with one group of workers or the other. The simple but not necessarily the more honorable course for the union to have taken was to ignore the rights of the older (having more seniority) workers. The courts have ruled in a number of cases that the rights of workers can be bargained away, but that their job rights cannot be unilaterally destroyed by the employer. In one notable case, the court upheld the rights of employees to jobs in the new plant even after the plant had moved across state lines and recognized a different union. However, in this case the insistence of the union upon the protection of the workers' rights was crucial. Without it the displaced workers would have had no recognition.

Even in the absence of mergers or transfers from other plants, seniority may still create certain problems for the union. Younger workers, resenting the special privileges afforded "old-timers" in the plant, may express their dissatisfaction by creating dissension among the union's membership. Seniority may also prove a handicap in the union's efforts to prosecute a strike. First of all, seniority makes the workers who have it more satisfied with their jobs and therefore less enthusiastic about supporting a strike. Furthermore, the possibility that the employer may take advantage of the provisions of the Taft-Hartley Act and replace those workers engaged in an economic strike gives a worker with considerable seniority pause for thought about what he may lose if the strike should prove to be unsuccessful.

Views of Workers

Most workers support the principle of seniority as the best possible solution to the kinds of problems discussed earlier (particularly layoffs). Their support is largely based on their general disinclination to trust management's discretion and their inability to devise a better alternative. Thus, even younger workers, who benefit least from seniority and often are the victims of its enforcement, tend to support the principle.

The age-old principle that he who has the most seniority will be the last to be laid off has been open to some interesting variants in recent years. Where the plant's labor force has some form of guaranteed annual income or supplementary unemployment benefits (see Chapter 10), the result of layoffs by seniority will often be to leave the older, senior worker on the job working for his income while his younger counterpart will receive full pay or close to it for doing nothing. As a result, such unions as the New York Dock Workers have set up a kind of "inverted seniority" system by which the senior personnel are laid off first. Contracts that provide for three- or six-month sabbaticals for workers with sufficient seniority permit still another variation. Senior workers may choose to exercise their sabbatical rights during a period of layoffs, thus eliminating the necessity of laying off someone with less seniority. The resulting reduction in friction between "old" and "new" workers in both cases is obvious.

The type of seniority arrangement a worker deems most desirable will obviously vary from worker to worker. Some workers want a seniority system that affords them the best opportunities for promotion. Others place a premium on security and are willing to forego promotion opportunities if they can thereby reduce the risks of being bumped. A few workers have deliberately sought an arrangement that makes their jobs "dead-end" occupations. These jobs are so defined that there is no one who is above the worker. The result is that the worker is safe from bumping from above, but has no opportunity for advancement. Such arrangements can only be made where a system of strict department seniority prevails.

Unions have from time to time proposed work-sharing plans as an alternative to seniority as a means of handling reductions in the labor force. Work-sharing plans all involve a reduction in the number of hours of work for everyone without any compensating increase in pay. Instead of a few workers losing their jobs completely, while those with sufficient seniority retain their jobs on a full-time basis, the burden of unemployment is borne equally by all.

Although such programs were popular during the early 1930s, workers grew disenchanted with the idea. Technical difficulties sometimes made it impossible to arrange shifts and work assignments so that the work could be spread evenly. Even where implementation was possible, however, workers found that all too often "sharing the work" proved to be "sharing the misery." With the development of unemployment benefits under Social Security, a preference for layoffs by seniority has grown even stronger. A number of contracts do, however, call for sharing the work down to thirty-five or thirty-two hours when the reductions are to be only temporary in nature.

Perhaps the major handicap that seniority imposes upon workers is the restrictions it places upon their freedom to shift from one job to another. The worker who has accumulated a number of years of seniority with all of the accompanying privileges may find it difficult to give them up even though he is not satisfied with his present job. At the same time, channels of employment at other plants are made less attractive since at any plant with a system of seniority he must start at the bottom rung all over again.

The resulting reduction in mobility may have serious implications for the appropriate allocation of workers throughout the economy. Unemployed workers may be encouraged to remain in the vicinity of their old plant in hopes that their seniority will soon justify their recall. Some workers remain in declining industries for protracted periods when their services could be put to fuller and better use in an expanding sector of the economy.

Reduced mobility may also have serious implications for the economy during a period of national emergency. At the start of World War II, for example, considerable difficulty was experienced in persuading workers with a sizable amount of seniority to move to more essential jobs. Even in the face of the fact that there were well-paying jobs and a known need for workers in defense industries, less than one-third of the men interviewed in some forty USES (United States Employment Service) offices were willing to switch to defense jobs.

Even before the point was driven home so vividly, the government had already recognized the importance of seniority to workers. The Selective Service Act of 1940 provided for the retention and continued accumulation of seniority during the period while workers were in the armed services.

The flood of postwar local labor market studies supports the belief that seniority is an important deterrent to the shifting by workers with extended service records.[8] Although there seems little doubt that seniority does produce some reduction in mobility, its over-all impact may not be quite as great as is often suggested. The same local labor market studies also provide substantial evidence that

mobility among older, long-service workers tends to be small in any case and is reduced by a number of considerations in addition to seniority. The mobility of short-service workers may even be increased by seniority arrangements. In periods of recession, workers with short service records may quit in anticipation of layoff and in periods of prosperity they may find shifting a more rapid way to advancement than waiting out the retirement of those above them on the seniority ladder.

One final point about the impact of seniority on workers should be made. Seniority and other fringe benefits make the loss of a job through dismissal far more painful than it would in any case be. The worker who loses a job in which he has a number of years invested has lost something very valuable indeed.

Seniority Abroad

Seniority is often heralded as a means of protecting older workers against the ruthless demands of industrialism. It is ironic, therefore, that the United States, which has been notoriously less respectful of the rights of its aged than many other countries, has emphasized seniority far more than most. One of the reasons for the infrequent appearance of seniority clauses in many European collective bargaining contracts is the existence of industrywide and in some cases virtually nationwide agreements. Under such agreements, it is difficult to negotiate agreements which will meet all local requirements. Germany, for example, has no seniority provisions in bargaining contracts and historically German employers have been free to lay off whomever they chose. More recently, partly perhaps because of the influence of co-determination (the participation of union representatives in management decisions—see Chapter 12) a structure for layoffs has been devised based not on seniority but on family need, sex (married women first), and the availability of disability or retirement benefits to the worker. Where problems arise, decisions are left to the courts. Similarly, the lack of local plant bargaining precludes widespread use of seniority in France, and seniority systems there are virtually nonexistent. In France some limited appeals to the courts are possible in cases of gross inequity, but little recompense is ever made and reinstatement rarely occurs.

The lack of formal seniority arrangements in collective bargaining agreements is also evident in Great Britain. There, however, the principle of "last in, first out" is practiced more generally than in France and West Germany and unions exert informal pressure in that direction. Because they cannot rely on formal agreements, however, British unions have tended to resist all displacements and to display greater opposition to technological change than unions in the United States.

Similar variations in the use of seniority exist elsewhere in the world. In Israel provisions for seniority do exist but several other factors also serve as a basis for layoffs—family status, for example, also plays an important role. Israeli shop councils have a greater say over layoffs than the typical union spokesman in the United States and workers in Israel acquire a tenure that makes dismissal almost impossible. Similarly, Japan has had a system of seniority which provides workers with virtual life tenure. During the last 15 years Japanese unions have sought to convert this to a standard for wage payments limited to union members. Such application is confined mainly to large plants and probably does not cover more than a third of the nation's labor force.

It should be added that in a number of countries where seniority plays a small or no role in layoffs it does serve as a basis for determining wages. This is the case in Italy, Israel and the Netherlands among others.

Summary and Conclusions

The drive for job security has traditionally been a basic goal of workers. One of the redeeming features of the lord-serf relationship in manorial times was the job security it afforded the serf. Guild restrictions were another reflection of the desire of both workers and employers for security. The emergence of the capitalist system left the worker exposed to the forces of the market. American labor unions have devised the most formal and complete challenge to the capitalist's "right" to lay off and rehire whomever he chooses. Only the lifetime tenure system of Japan gives workers more job security, and few American union members, given their disposition toward free labor mobility, would willingly accept such an arrangement. Although seniority systems are sometimes found in nonunionized plants, the American system has been largely confined to union members and the unorganized workers are still subject to the employer's will.

Workers in many of the countries without formal seniority systems have sought to exert informal pressure on employers to protect workers (England) and wound up trying to protect both old-timers and newcomers. Others (like those in France and Germany) have relied on the courts to protect those workers whose rights were impaired, but this tactic has been relatively ineffective. The effort to protect the jobs of *all* workers has led unions in other countries to seek through political action governments that will undertake programs assuring full employment.

NOTES

1. Herbert R. Northrup, *The Negro in the Paper Industry* (Philadelphia: University of Pennsylvania Press, 1969).

2. Note, however, that management may be able to acquire some leeway in exchange for granting key union officers super-seniority. The union wants these men protected so that they will be able to continue to process grievances and handle union affairs within the plant during the layoff. A BLS study suggests, however, that management makes less frequent use of these super-seniority classifications than do the unions. Joseph W. Black and Robert Platt, "Layoff, Recall & Work-Sharing Procedures," *Monthly Labor Review* (February 1957), pp. 177–185. Of the 1,347 contracts studied by Black and Platt, 590 gave union officers super-seniority but only 230 gave management such choices.

3. A typical clause might read: "When layoffs become necessary because of lack of work, seniority by department shall apply; that is, the last person hired shall be the first one to be laid off."

An example of a clause that places seniority on a somewhat broader base, with some limitations, is the following: "In case it shall become necessary for the employer to lay off one or more employees, seniority rules shall apply, within classification. The employee who has been with the [company] the shortest length of time shall be the first to be laid off and in re-hiring, those laid off first shall be the last to be reemployed."

Quoted from the U.S. Department of Labor, Bureau of Labor Statistics, *Collective Bargaining Clauses: Layoff, Recall and Work-Sharing Procedures,* Bulletin No. 1189 (1956), pp. 17, 12.

4. Note that it is industrial unions who seek promotion within the plant. Craft unions are likely to be indifferent as long as promotion is made within the union.

5. At the very least, contracts may include qualifying clauses like this one: ". . . promotion to foreman, forewoman, and other positions outside the bargaining unit shall be solely a function of management . . ."

Quoted from U.S. Department of Labor, Bureau of Labor Statistics, *Major Collective Bargaining Agreements: Grievance Procedures,* Bulletin No. 1425–1 (1964), p. 10.

6. Mark Kahn, "Seniority Problems in Business Mergers," *Industrial and Labor Relations Review* (April 1955), pp. 361–378.

7. Other studies have indicated that many workers are reluctant to make the shift even when given the opportunity. See, for example, U.S. Congress, Joint Economic Committee, *New Views on Automation* (Washington, D.C.: U.S. Government Printing Office, 1960), pp. 250–253.

8. See, for example, Lloyd Reynolds, *The Structure of Labor Markets,* (New York: Harper & Row, 1951), and Howard Marshall, "Unions and Labor Mobility," *Labor Law Journal* (February 1956), pp. 83–97.

10
Fringe Benefits

We have almost reached the point where the fringe is larger than the surrey.

—Personnel director for a large printing firm

☐ ONE of the great revolutions in collective bargaining in the United States within the past twenty-five years has been the phenomenal growth in fringe benefits. The variety of benefits furnished, the amount of benefit provided each worker, and the total number of workers included—all have increased.[1]

It is difficult to list precisely what items should be included under the heading of "fringe" since individual plans vary widely from company to company and union to union. Ignoring some of the more esoteric variations, however, the benefits most frequently sought by unions are: health and life insurance, pensions (with provision for early retirement), supplements to unemployment benefits, severance pay, and paid holidays and paid vacations. Isolated cases of most of these can be found far back in American history, but they were extremely rare and were the products of unilateral decisions by the employers. Only in exceptional cases did early fringe benefits result from collective bargaining.

Notice that we did not include in our list such benefits arising from Social Security as unemployment insurance and old age and disability benefits. The omission was deliberate in order to point up the striking difference between worker benefits in the United States and those in other countries. Although, as we shall soon see, the fringe benefits listed in the previous paragraph are not unknown in collective bargaining in other countries, workers elsewhere rely far more on the government for the establishment of such benefits.

In one sense, however, our omission is misleading. Although Social Security benefits are not strictly a part of collective bargaining, unions have sometimes bargained for fringe benefits in order to pressure employers into supporting government programs. The union drive for pensions immediately after World War II was prompted in large part by a desire to raise the costs of private pensions so that businessmen would support extensions of the federal program.

Paid Vacations

We will begin with a discussion of the fringe benefit that is most widespread, the one that has shown the greatest postwar growth—the paid holiday and vacation. Since the early days of the unions, the drive to increase the amount of time workers spend away from their jobs has been a basic part of their demands. Nor is the notion that workers should be paid for that time entirely new, since the early demands for reductions in the work week were combined with demands for higher pay so that workers could afford not to work.

As we noted in Chapter 8, however, the unions' assault in recent years on the number of hours spent in the plant has been more productive in reducing the work year than the work week. Although instances of work weeks of thirty-five hours or even less are not rare, the forty-hour week is still the most widely accepted standard. The great change lies in the growth of provisions for paid vacations and paid holidays.

In 1940, for example, only about 25 percent of the workers covered by collective bargaining had the benefit of paid vacations. Today the comparable figure is about 92 percent, and the bulk of the contracts that do not contain such provisions are negotiated in industries where the duration of the contract is too brief to warrant paid vacations. Thus, 124 of the 142 contracts found by the Bureau of Labor Statistics (BLS) in 1962 to lack provisions for paid vacations were in the construction industry.[2]

At the same time that the proportion of workers receiving paid vacations has increased, the length of vacations has expanded and the period of service required for eligibility has shortened. Between 1957 and 1960, the proportion of contracts providing for vacations of four weeks or longer rose from 20 percent to 43 percent. In 1940, the 25 percent of the workers provided with paid vacations usually had a maximum period of one week, although about a quarter of them were eligible for two weeks if they had sufficiently long service records. Rarely was the vacation extended beyond the two-week limit. By contrast, today, 84 percent of all contracts provide for a maximum vacation period of at least three weeks. Only 1 percent of American workers get less than a week of paid vacation after a year of service while 73 percent get one week and 18 percent get two weeks. Only 5 percent of the workers with five years of service have less than two weeks of paid vacation, and nearly 50 percent of those workers with ten years of service have over two weeks of paid vacation. Although the list is tedious, the figures represent a great increase in enjoyment for American workers.

Paid Holidays

Although the formal observance of holidays has a long history in this country, it was rare, until recently, for workers to have such holidays paid.[3] The institution of paid holidays dates from World War II when the National War Labor Board approved the granting of up to six paid holidays per year. By 1958, only 12 percent of the workers covered by collective bargaining agreements were not being awarded paid holidays; nearly three-fifths were given seven or more (rarer) holidays. By the early 1960s the percentage granted paid holidays had risen to 95 or better. In addition to the usual holidays celebrated nationally, a number of contracts now provide that the worker will be given a holiday on his own birthday.[4]

Other Leaves

No discussion of excused absences from work would be complete without some reference to the various forms of leaves negotiated. Most frequently included in contracts are leaves for sickness, military duty, jury duty, and leaves for personal reasons such as death in the family and maternity. Most of these were not applied to production workers until comparatively recently, and often have been prompted by mandatory state laws. In the case of sick leaves and a few others, such leaves date back to the last century (for example, for the Bakers and the Plumbers). Until recently, however, such leaves were granted mainly to white-collar workers.

Sick leaves today often provide for as many as five to thirty days with or without pay; no loss of seniority or other fringe benefits is normally involved in either case. Other leaves are usually without pay but carry a similar guarantee that the worker's seniority rights will be protected providing he returns in the specified time.

Employers have not been completely happy about agreeing to leaves, even when no pay is involved, because of the possible disruption of production schedules. Employers are particularly irritated by the tendency of employees to take off Friday or Monday whenever a paid holiday fell on Tuesday or Thursday. To avoid this, employers have sought contract clauses providing for paid holidays only for those workers who worked the days immediately preceding or following the holiday providing that these were regular work days.

Shift Differentials

Like paid holidays and paid vacations and most other fringe benefits, the payment of additional wages to those workers employed on other than the regular shift is a post-World War II development. Whereas less than 50 percent of the companies paid shift differentials before the war, today the figure is close to 85 percent.

The development of round-the-clock operation of plants, which necessitates more than one shift of workers, is a product of the industrial revolution. In some industries, like steel, shutting down overnight would lead to costly delays and possible damage to equipment. In other industries the need for multiple shifts may be less urgent but is still sound financially. Many companies find it economical to make fuller use of their machinery than would be possible with a single shift, since multiple shifts allow them to average their fixed costs over a larger volume of output.

A work schedule that runs during the evening or early morning hours is probably less desirable to most workers than a regular daytime shift. It interferes with family life and places the workers out of tune with the rest of society, which is operating on a different schedule. In addition, a number of studies (largely concentrated in Europe) have indicated that night work often upsets workers' sleep and general health. It is not surprising, therefore, that unions have sought extra pay for those workers forced to labor on the second or third shift.

Most frequently, the differential takes the form of an extra few cents per hour premium paid to workers on the late shifts. The third shift has generally been paid a somewhat higher premium than the second. Differentials vary from plant to plant and industry to industry, but a 9 or 10 cents per hour premium for work on the second shift and 11 to 15 cents per hour premium on the third were most common immediately after World War II. More recently differences between the second and third shift have tended to be eliminated. (See Chapter 7.)

Somewhat less frequently, workers on the later shifts are paid a percentage increment above what they would receive if employed on the regular shift. Sometimes a higher percentage is awarded to those on the third shift, but the practice today seems to be to pay the second and third an equal percentage differential. The percentage differential rewards the higher-paid worker more for giving up his evening hours than it does the lower-paid worker. At first glance, one would think that the dissatisfaction of being placed on the later shifts would be equally great for both types of workers and that the straight cents per hour increment would be more equitable and satisfactory. Union and management officials in plants with percentage shift differentials report, however, that it may be impossible to recruit the number of skilled workers needed unless they are given this additional premium. We noted in Chapter 7 that skilled workers were often highly sensitive to any narrowing of the differential in wages between themselves and less-skilled workers. Evidently something of this nature operates in the case of shift differentials as well, since a cents per hour shift differential would slightly reduce skill differentials.

Pensions

Like paid vacations and holidays, pensions first appeared as an item in the collective bargaining contract during World War II. In fact, the drive by unions for pensions marks a major reversal of their earlier position.

Early efforts to secure pensions came in the garment trades and were quickly followed by similar demands by the International Brotherhood of Electrical Workers. The real breakthrough, however, came in 1946 when, after a bitter strike, John L. Lewis and the Coal Miners succeeded in securing a program calling for a $100 monthly pension at age sixty-two.

Unions became interested in pension plans during World War II because unions were seeking concessions from employers that would not come in conflict with the rulings of the War Labor Board. Employers were willing to grant these demands partly because court rulings had held that pensions for executives would be considered discriminatory if pensions were not provided for workers. Furthermore, because excess profits taxes were pegged at high levels, employers were able to meet the unions' demands at relatively low cost to the company since most of the expense could be written off as a tax deduction.

About 30 per cent of current pension plans were established during the ten years from 1940 to 1949.

Although the attitude of employers changed somewhat after the war, the drive of unions for pensions continued, aided by a favorable Supreme Court ruling in the Inland Steel case, which stated that pensions were a proper area for bargaining. The unions' quest for pensions was also advanced by the conclusions of a fact-finding board in the steel industry, which declared that the provision of retirement security for steel workers was an appropriate responsibility of the steel companies. The outbreak of the Korean War and the reinstitution of wage stabilization policies also encouraged the adoption of pension plans.

Although World War II marks the introduction of pensions into collective bargaining, pensions had been in existence for many years previously. Some employers had introduced them on their own as a means of improving plant relations and reducing the volume of labor turnover. It was for this latter reason that unions had denounced private pension programs as devices that tied the worker to a single employer, making it impossible for the worker to take advantage of a better job opportunity should one present itself. As we shall soon see, the same criticism has been raised against the current union-sponsored programs.

Pension programs financed by the unions themselves out of dues collected from members also predate World War II. Generally speaking, only the highly skilled trades such as the printers and the construction workers had such programs. The benefits were never very large and never provided more than minimal protection. While such plans left a member free to change employers without forfeiting his pension rights, he was still restricted to a particular trade or industry. Since pensions were limited to the highly skilled crafts, however, the volume of such occupational mobility was likely to be small in any case.

Despite the long history of pension programs in this country, the number of workers they cover at the present time is still considerably less than that covered by paid vacations and holidays. In 1964, there were about 16,000 private pension plans in the United States covering approximately 16 million workers. This means that somewhat less than one-quarter of the labor force is protected by private pension programs. Nevertheless, the pace of expansion of pension programs has been rapid; between 1950 and 1960 the coverage of private plans doubled and the United States Department of Labor predicts a second doubling by 1980.[5]

Additional evidence of the growth in pension programs is represented by the fact that the percentage of unions that had negotiated pension plans for 80 percent or more of their memberships rose from 15 to 31 percent between 1950 and 1960.

Contributory versus Noncontributory Plans

By necessity, early pension programs financed from union dues were contributory as were a large proportion of early employer-sponsored programs. When unions first began their drive for the inclusion of pensions in the collective bargaining contracts, a great debate arose as to whether the new plans should be financed partly by a contribution from the employees or whether they should be financed solely by the employers. Many employers urged the establishment of contributory plans as a means of re-

ducing the financial burden imposed on employers. Management officials also argued that contributory plans strengthened the worker's moral fiber by making him partially responsible for his own future security. Another argument emphasized that contributory plans made a lump sum available to the worker should he wish to change jobs.

Advocates of noncontributory systems stressed the financial inability of workers to make meaningful contributions and argued that such plans often led to the voluntary exclusion of many workers who felt unable to participate. The ability of the employer to treat his contribution as a tax deductible cost was also stressed. Much of the debate over this question eventually subsided and the vast proportion of pension plans established by collective bargaining are noncontributory.

Extent of Protection Provided

We must note at the outset that private pension plans will never provide protection for all workers. Even if coverage does double by 1980, less than one-half of the labor force will be served by such plans, even assuming that the labor force remains constant during the intervening years—surely a false premise in light of the fact that our labor force currently gains over a million additional workers each year. Similarly, of the present total of 10 million retired workers, only 1.2 million receive benefits from private pension plans. While the proportion is likely to increase in the coming years, it is unlikely that a majority of the retired workers will ever be served.

The participation of unions in the formulation of pension plans, however, has increased the likelihood that workers covered by a plan will actually receive benefits upon retirement.

Earlier pension plans did not necessarily provide this guarantee. Many such plans were open to withdrawal at the employer's option. Even where the employer's intentions were completely honorable, benefits were by no means assured since early plans were often unfunded. This meant that they had no financial reserves but relied on funds from current income. They thus collapsed at the first sign of economic stress on the part of the company.

Many of the early plans were devised as a means of assuring the company of a stable labor force. The worker's equity in the pension plan increased with his years of service until he could quit his job only on penalty of a serious financial loss in the form of a forfeited pension.

The early efforts of unions to secure employer-financed pensions were criticized on the same grounds. Concern was voiced that either workers would be so mobile that the protection of the pension program would prove meaningless or that workers would be held to service in one plant by a modern day version of feudal bonds. The extent to which pension plans actually reduce labor turnover has defied the efforts of empirical investigation. The most recent study under the auspices of the BLS[6] concludes that pension plans do encourage employers to further discriminate against older workers, who, if hired, would add sizably to the costs of the company's pension plan while providing only a relatively short span of years of service. Presumably voluntary quits by older workers are reduced for the reasons indicated above. Since voluntary mobility tends to be most characteristic of young workers with a short term of service in any case, the significance of this impact is reduced. Similarly, the finding that the turnover rate in plants with pension plans tends to be lower than turnover in plants without pension plans has reduced significance because plants with pension plans tend to have superior working conditions in general, including better wages and other fringe benefits.

In any case, unions have long recognized that such barriers to mobility were a serious problem and have attempted to rectify the situation by demanding provisions for vesting. Under a vesting arrangement an employee remains eligible for retirement benefits (at a reduced level) from a plan in which he was covered before he moved to another employer.[7]

Employers, of course, have almost consistently opposed vesting. Not only does vesting lessen the effectiveness of pension plans as a means of reducing turnover, but it greatly increases the cost of a pension program. Many employers who entered into pension agreements only with grave reservations counted on the high turnover in their plants to reduce the costs of such programs. A 1953 BLS study of 300 pension programs revealed that only 25 percent of the plans contained provisions for vesting and three-fourths of these were contributory plans in which the worker also pledged some of his earnings. A number of the contributory plans called for little more than the return of the workers' own contributions.[8]

By the winter of 1962–1963, another BLS study revealed that the proportion of all plans providing vesting had risen to two-thirds, with 60 percent of all workers under pension programs given vesting protection.[9] The figure is made more impressive by the fact that vesting was most frequently found among single-employer plans; about 70 percent of the plans and the workers under a single employer arrangement had vesting provisions. Multiemployer plans, usually covering all or part of an industry or a specific geographic location, account for about

7 percent of all plans. A multiemployer plan also provides some protection for the mobile worker, assuming he remains within the boundaries set forth by the plan.

Vesting is a privilege rarely granted immediately upon admission to the pension plans. Slightly over one-half of the plans with vesting privileges currently call for fifteen years of service before the worker can shift to another company and still remain eligible; a fifth of the plans, covering almost a million workers, require a term of service of twenty years or more. Less than half a million workers are covered by plans requiring less than ten years of service.

In 70 percent of the plans, which cover the same proportion of workers, a minimum age requirement is combined with the service requirement. Forty-five percent of the workers are covered by plans specifying forty as a minimum age while forty-five, fifty, and fifty-five are ages frequently specified in others. Such requirements mean that the worker who wishes to retain his eligibility for a pension finds his mobility seriously circumscribed even when vesting is provided. His freedom to move at any time and at any age is greatest under a multi-employer plan, but the boundaries within which he is free to move and still remain eligible for a pension are correspondingly limited.

How much does the typical worker who has maintained eligibility until retirement age receive in the way of benefits from his pension? Even assuming a standard retirement age of sixty-five, it is difficult to provide a precise figure since benefits will vary depending upon the number of years of service, the type of plan involved, and the level of the earnings the worker attained while employed. A safe estimate, however, is that a worker who had earned between $5,000 and $6,000 a year would, after fifteen years of service, be eligible for a pension ranging between $50 and $55 a month. Even the best plans, therefore, when combined with Social Security benefits provide a long service worker with only one-half to two-thirds of his earnings while working. About one-third of the plans give workers the option of retiring five to ten years before the normal age, usually at substantially reduced benefits.

Compulsory versus Voluntary Retirement

Management and unions have taken sharply divergent views on the question of retirement. Unions have historically pushed for early voluntary retirement, particularly where extensive layoffs are occurring, and have opposed provisions calling for compulsory retirement at a specified age. Many employers have opposed voluntary early retirements because of the added costs engendered for the program and have sought compulsory retirement at a fixed age.

In many plants compulsory retirement antedates the introduction of pension plans. In fact, many employers accepted pension plans in part because they made resistance to compulsory retirement less strenuous.

A policy of compulsory retirement has long existed in many companies because of a belief that the efficiency of a plant is reduced if too large a proportion of the plant's labor force is in the older age bracket. Most employers will admit that under compulsory retirement they lose some valuable workers who are still able to function more than satisfactorily. However, employers point out that any attempt to keep only those who are still able to work satisfactorily would create great dissension in the plant even in the absence of a union. The institution of a pension plan, it is assumed, will help remove some of the sting of compulsory retirement.

Although compulsory retirement still elicits nominal opposition from unions, their opposition is much less spirited than formerly. One factor that accounts for this change in attitude is growing concern among workers about unemployment occasioned by automation, even among those with ten or more years of seniority. A second reason is that younger workers want to see the pension funds used. They feel that they gave up an immediate increase in wages in order to secure the pension plans and that they will obtain greater job protection and better opportunities for promotion once older workers are pensioned off.

For the same reasons, unions have put increasing emphasis on the opportunity for voluntary early retirement. A BLS study in 1964 of some 15,800 pension plans revealed that 12,100 of them provided for early retirement.[10] The normal retirement age almost invariably was sixty-five; half of the plans called for early retirement at age sixty. About half of the plans, however, required the employer's consent before a worker could exercise the option for early retirement. Somewhat exceptional was the 1964 Teamster's contract. It called for $250 a month for retirement at age sixty, but with benefits scaled down to $110 per month at the age of sixty-five.

In some unions, older workers have found that the provisions for early retirement have exposed them to great pressure to exercise their option by younger workers seeking to protect themselves. This pressure for early retirement inevitably creates a certain amount of tension between old and young union members; most studies suggest that older workers are rarely willing to retire even at the normal retirement age.

The trend toward early retirement is slowed not only by the resistance of older workers but by the opposition of employers as well. Not only does early retirement reduce the amount of the annual pension, thus making it more attractive to a worker to continue working, but it inevitably increases the cost of the program for the employer. Employers have accepted the early retirement principle as a convenient way of weeding out inefficient employees, but they have been reluctant to open the opportunity to all.

Costs

The cost of pension programs is likely to grow in the years to come for several reasons besides an increase in the number of early retirements. We have already noted that the United States Department of Labor forecasts a doubling in present coverage by 1980. In the same period the number of those in the retirement age brackets will have increased, thus necessitating a growth in out payments. Unions are likely to seek added benefits, which will make existing programs, even without the inclusion of greater numbers, more expensive. Present trends in this direction include the broadening of vesting privileges, the use of variable annuities, the drive for adjustments in pension benefits to meet the rising cost of living, and the inclusion of widow's benefits.[11]

Two other aspects of the growth of private pension plans deserve brief mention. First, such plans provide dishonest elements in the union movement with an opportunity to milk pension funds for their own advantage. Evidence of the opportunities for racketeering made possible by the emergence of vast sums of money in pension and other welfare benefits has been uncovered by the McClellan Committee among others, and some corrective legislation has been enacted. Second, pension funds have become an increasingly potent force in the nation's financial markets. Insured pension funds total nearly 30 billion dollars, and the decisions of such funds to buy or not to buy have a considerable effect upon the prices of some stocks. By concentrating on blue chip stocks for investment purposes, pension funds may have helped to raise them out of line with other stock.

Health Insurance Programs

When the issue of the entrance of private industry into the field of health service first became a part of collective bargaining neither party foresaw that its implementation would have such wide repercussions. The unions' early goal of securing a substantial degree of protection for their memberships has been frustrated by the rising costs of medical care, however, as each increase in benefits has been offset by a rise in medical costs.

The growth in health insurance plans, like other fringes, has been largely a post-World War II development. Unions have pressed for them for many of the same reasons that they have pushed for pension programs. Hospital and medical insurance programs covered about 500,000 workers in 1945; by 1954 such programs covered an estimated 12 million workers and 17 million dependents. Plans for group life insurance, temporary disability, and payment for accidental death covered about 11 million workers and 500,000 dependents by 1954. This great increase resulted in large part from the pressure of unions dis-

satisfied with the meager protection provided by the federal government and from their attempt to get employers to push for expanded governmental programs.

Virtually all major unions today have some form of health and welfare program.[12] In addition to the motivations cited above, unions also recognize that there is an economy factor derived from spreading the risks over a large group. Partly for this reason, two large national unions have established their own insurance companies and a number of unions have sought to put health insurance plans on an industrywide basis.

Many of the problems encountered in our discussion of pension plans also appear in relation to health and welfare programs. Costs have been rising because of the broader coverage of the programs, both in terms of the numbers included and the extent of the benefits furnished. Estimates suggest that the typical plan currently costs an employer $500 per employee per year. Workers do not usually receive a comparable amount of protection, however. Not only is there the problem of keeping pace with rising medical costs, but the very nature of the plans makes them wasteful. Because each union prefers to organize a medical program of its own, needless and expensive duplication of facilities and bookkeeping services is involved.

Like pension plans, health insurance programs are discriminatory by the fact that they do not provide protection to all of the population. Although such discrimination is inherent in any such program secured through collective bargaining, the seriousness of the problem is, of course, enhanced by the rising cost of medical protection prompted by the programs.

Protection, including a widening application of sick leave, has been increasing, however, and one of the goals of unions has been to expand benefits as widely as possible. Two-thirds of the plans established by collective bargaining call for the entire burden of the cost to be borne by the employer, and about 60 percent of them provide for protection to the worker's dependents (88 percent of these plans stipulate that the employer pay all or part of the costs of family protection). About one-fourth of the plans provide for continued protection (usually for a maximum period of six months) for the worker in the event of a layoff.

The extension to increasing numbers of the population stems not only from the attempts by unions to extend the benefits to dependents and retired workers, but also from the tendency of nonunion employers to adopt health insurance programs on their own. As a result, the total proportion of the population covered by health plans is impressive; three-fourths of the American population is covered by some form of health insurance. The fact that 25 percent still do not receive such protection, however, points up the need for further extension so that all who need it may receive protection.

Unions have sought to combat rising medical costs in a variety of ways. When health insurance plans first became a part of collective bargaining, most of them provided for protection by the standard insurance programs including Blue Cross and Blue Shield. Recently, an increasing number of unions have tried to set up group service programs or even to establish insurance companies of their own. In New York, union officials seeking to forestall rate increases by Blue Cross have threatened to take such measures. Union leaders have also tried to exert pressure on various state government officials to induce them to veto Blue Cross appeals for rate increases.

A few unions have also been innovative in seeking to expand protection to include new areas of medical care. A number of plans now provide for medical care in one or more of the following fields: dental care, vision, maternity, and mental health. In order to offset the high cost of drugs, the Carpenters in Pennsylvania and New Jersey have set up cooperative plans among druggists.

Impact on the Economy

Health and life insurance plans raise a less pronounced threat to labor mobility than do pension plans. To the extent that they add to a worker's general sense of well-being and satisfaction, of course, they too may act to impede mobility. Unlike pension programs, which require prolonged periods of service (even with vesting) before eligibility is established, most health and life insurance programs become applicable immediately or at the very most after the worker has survived his three-to-six-month period of probation. Thus the loss of coverage due to shifting is relatively brief and the benefits do not increase with extended service.

Supplementary Unemployment Benefits

The drive for supplementary unemployment benefits (SUB) or a variation of them called the guaranteed annual wage began in 1955 under the impetus of the United Automobile Workers. While the two terms were frequently confused by the public during the heated discussions of the 1950s, a basic difference does exist. Guaranteed annual wages have a long history in the United States, although their importance has always been minor, while supplementary unemployment benefits is the system most prevalent today.

Guaranteed annual wage programs date back at least to 1894 when the National Wallpaper Company negotiated such a program with the Wallpaper Craftsmen. Other well-known plans of long-standing duration include those established by Procter and Gamble, Nunn-Bush, and Hormel. Virtually all of the early plans were established in highly seasonal industries where the employer was willing to guarantee a stipulated amount of work a year in order to be assured that a supply of labor would be available when he needed it.

Supplementary unemployment benefits, as first negotiated by the UAW with the Ford Motor Company and later achieved in the automobile, steel, farm equipment, and can industries, among others, were much less ambitious in nature. They were designed to supplement the Social Security unemployment benefits, which, with the increase in wages, had grown less and less adequate. Unemployment benefits, which in the 1930s amounted to slightly less than 50 percent of wages earned during the base year of employment, had dropped to about one-third of the worker's base wages in the 1950s. The announced goal of unions was to raise the unemployment benefit, when the state allowance and the employer contribution were combined, to two-thirds of the worker's earnings while working. In some cases, this goal has been exceeded; the 1967 Ford agreement, for example, raised the combined payments to nearly 95 percent of the take-home wage for fifty-two weeks for those who have worked over seven years.

The over-all effectiveness of supplementary unemployment benefits, however, has been weakened by a number of factors. Most significant perhaps has been their relatively limited coverage. In 1956, coverage was limited to about 2 million workers and, despite subsequent increases, coverage is still confined to a relatively small minority of the nation's labor force.

Furthermore, workers who are covered by such programs are not afforded complete protection. Protection is extended only to those workers who have a specified amount of seniority and who have been laid off for more than one week. The typical program limits the payment of benefits to a maximum of twenty-six weeks, although some agreements (the 1961 General Motors agreement, for example) have extended the period to fifty-two weeks. Furthermore, payments are limited by the size of the fund. Most of the SUB plans are based on an insurance principle. The company contributes a specified amount per worker per hour until the fund reaches a specified maximum limit. Contracts frequently specify the diversion of payments to other fringe benefits once the maximum has been attained. The fund thus constitutes a reserve pool upon which workers can draw in the event of layoff. This ability to withdraw funds, however, is usually also limited by the number of service credits (weeks) he has accumulated.

An alternative arrangement (virtually confined to the glass industry) is the so-called savings plan. Under this arrangement a part of workers' wages are withheld and put into a fund. When a worker is laid off, he can draw upon this fund. Usually a ceiling is set on the amount of the fund and thereafter the company ceases to make payments or contributes instead to other fringe benefits. Unlike the insurance arrangement, however, in which the employer's contributions are considered welfare payments, in the "savings" plan employer contributions are considered wages, thereby increasing the employees' tax burden.

Unions claim that SUB plans not only give increased protection to workers against the danger of unemployment, but also help to stabilize the economy during periods of threatened recession. The analogy is drawn with the "built-in stabilizer" effects of the unemployment benefits part of the Social Security program. Employers have countered this argument by claiming that the added costs of employing workers will lead to the utilization of fewer workers, thereby aggravating the unemployment problem. The effect of the plans on the economy in either direction has been impossible to test as a result of the relatively small number of workers involved.

SUB plans suffer from many of the same defects we noted in connection with pension and health insurance plans; for example, they tend to discriminate because only a relatively small group of workers is protected. Of even greater importance, however, is the impediment SUB plans constitute to labor mobility. SUB plans have also been condemned on the ground that they discriminate against the financially weak firms and against those which are most subject to violent oscillations in business conditions. The charge has also been made that the high level of unemployment benefits will lead workers to prefer idleness and to treat unemployment as a vacation rather than something to be avoided. The level unemployment benefits could reach without inducing workers to choose to loaf has long been questioned. The fact that some seniority systems now give the senior workers the choice of electing to be laid off suggests that in some instances that level may already have been reached.

Severance Pay

Closely akin to supplementary unemployment benefits as a means of protecting workers from the threat of unemployment is severance pay. Like a number of the other fringe benefits discussed earlier, severance pay has grown to major proportions since the end of World War II. In 1944, severance payments were a part of less than 5 percent of the contracts surveyed by the BLS. These provisions covered an unknown, but almost certainly equally small, proportion of workers. By late 1964, the proportion of contracts containing severance pay or layoff benefit provisions had risen to 30 percent of the major agreements studied with coverage for about 40 percent of the workers included in the sample.[13] Almost half of the plans in 1964 were negotiated by five unions: Steelworkers, Autoworkers, Communications Workers, Ladies' Garment Workers, and Electrical Workers. To some extent these statistics understate the prevalence of severance plans because such plans are often included in the contractual arrangements drawn up by small plants. Since these have a reputation for impermanency, they were not studied.

Severance pay agreements are often tied to SUB programs, but there is a distinct difference between the two. A SUB payment is made when the layoff is expected to be of relatively short duration, and the worker usually retains his seniority and pension rights. A severance payment, on the other hand, involves the explicit surrender by the worker of all claims to reemployment, accrued pension, and other fringe rights. Of the 525 severance plans studied by the BLS in 1964, 419 of the plans stipulated that complete termination of employment rights was a prerequisite for receipt of benefits. In some plans, workers were given a choice between layoff or severance pay.

Other prerequisites for receiving severance payment include the requirement that separation has to be involuntary; workers are ineligible if they move elsewhere in anticipation of prospective layoff. This stipulation is included in the overwhelming majority of cases. Plans vary widely as to the minimum amount of service necessary before eligibility is established, but a minimum of three years is the most familiar requirement.

The benefits also vary widely from plan to plan. Most plans provide for an increase in benefits in proportion to the worker's length of service. However, some plans give a proportionately larger benefit to workers with shorter service records. Other contracts provide greater protection to workers with long records of service by granting a greater number of weeks of allowance for each additional year of service. A few plans also recognize the greater problem of the older worker (as opposed to the long-service worker) in finding new work by granting additional pay to the older worker.

Many plans call for a minimum of one to two weeks of pay for workers with short service records. However, about half of the plans set no maximum—a worker who had served for thirty years would be eligible for thirty weeks of allowance if he were covered by a plan that provided one week for each year of service.

Severance pay plans have displayed a growing trend toward a system of funding. The 1964 BLS study noted that about three-fourths of the plans studied were still unfunded. However, the proportion of the funded plans had increased sharply, and the BLS predicted the possibility of a sharp upward move in that direction. In the event of a complete closing of a plant, the funded arrangement obviously guarantees much greater protection to the workers.

Economic Implications

Severance pay is designed to reward the worker for his past loyalty and service and to assist him in locating another job when his old one vanishes. The pressure for such protection has increased as worker concern over the impact of automation has mounted. The contention that severance pay fulfills its function of easing the transition to a new location and expediting the mobility of displaced workers, however, is subject to two qualifications. Since virtually all plans increase the amount of protection (although not always proportionately) with added years of service, such plans reduce mobility to the same extent as pensions and other fringe benefits that are similarly structured. In addition, because the worker who voluntarily quits in anticipation of a reduction in the labor force forfeits his severance allowance, a corresponding reduction in mobility is likely to result.

Over-all Economic Significance

At this point, some general observations about the over-all significance of the growth of fringe benefits in this country are in order.

When fringe benefits were first introduced, there were warnings that their institution would evoke an increased amount of government intervention in union affairs. Although this prediction did not immediately come true, a definite trend in this direction is now apparent. The Welfare and Pension Plans Disclosure Act requires that all plans involving twenty-six or more workers must be reported to the Department of Labor. Even without the headline stories of racketeering and the misappropriation of welfare funds by union officials, the magnitude of the sums involved made the growth in governmental scrutiny inevitable.

The second question involves whether or not fringe benefits are becoming a disproportionate part of the worker's income. When the issue of fringes (particularly pensions) was first raised, employers charged that they had no proper part of bargaining since the employer was being asked to pay for something for which he got nothing in return. Such benefits were sometimes termed "gratuities" and employers argued that they had no right (because of their responsibility to stockholders) or financial ability to make such concessions.

With the passage of time, it has become increasingly evident that fringe benefits are paid in lieu of, rather than in addition to, increases in wages. Even newspaper accounts of contract settlements make it abundantly clear that most settlements are package deals including a total of so many cents an hour fringe and wage increases combined. This occurs despite the fact that many fringes are difficult to resolve into a precise cents-per-hour figure. The tendency to give monetary value to fringe packages may result from the desire of union leaders to reassure the rank and file that they really got something worthwhile. Although the variation in fringe benefits between employers and industries is immense, ranging from less than 5 to over 50 percent of payroll costs, the United States Chamber of Commerce in 1959 estimated that fringe benefits accounted for 22.8 percent of total payroll costs for all industry on the average.[14] Even after allowing for some upward bias in this figure because the sample mainly involved large companies, the percentage is still impressive.

The question then arises as to whether or not more and greater fringe benefits represent a proper allocation of workers' income. Are workers anxious to obtain still more in the way of fringes if they have to forego higher take-home pay? Are workers being "sold" a set of protections they do not really want, while their hunger for higher money wages is partially frustrated? Although members of a union have sometimes seemed to be lukewarm about fringe benefits when wage demands had to be reduced in order to secure them, the growing insecurities of a complex, industrial world suggest that workers today are anxious to win added protection from such threats as automation.

Some observers, in fact, feel that the pendulum has swung too far in the opposite direction. According to this view workers are overly security-conscious and are unwilling to take the risks necessary in order to better themselves and the economy. These critics see fringe benefits as something that reinforces this trend. Many of those who voice this criticism see excessive security as something akin to immorality and fringe benefits as a corrupting influence rather than as a force for good. Howard Pyle, Deputy Assistant to the President for Federal-State Relations during the Eisenhower administration, once declared, "The right to suffer is one of the joys of a free enterprise economy, just as the right to prosper is." Presumably he would see fringes as something like pain-killing drugs. Too extensive dosage of fringes would make the recipients drug addicts and lead to a deadening not only of the pain, but of the ability of the entire economic body to function properly.

The whole problem of allocating the marginal five-cent increase has grown increasingly complicated as the number of fringe benefits has increased. Union officers have to choose between an increase in take-home pay and an increase in fringes as a means of satisfying the union's members. Furthermore, a choice must be made as to which "fringe" benefit increase should be sought at the expense of an increase in the amount of another. The problem of rational consumer choice is now very much at the doorstep of the union leaders.

Many believe that the growth of fringes poses a third danger. This danger lies in the fact that both parties at the bargaining table tend to rely increasingly on the services of outside experts. The intricate financial details involved in the establishment of health and pension insurance programs is beyond the "expertise" of virtually all union and management officials. The use of outside experts, of course, removes the rank-and-file union member another step from the actual bargaining process and is likely to breed apathy and disinterest.

Part of the responsibility for the continued high levels of unemployment in the United States during recent years has also been attributed to fringe benefits. Since many fringe benefits are a function of the number of individuals on the company's payroll rather than the number of hours worked, the reasoning goes, that part of the worker's compensation that is in the form of fringes becomes a fixed cost. Wages, as every beginning student in economics is aware, are a prime example of a variable cost. By varying the number of hours of work, an employer can adjust his total wage bill. With the growth of fringe benefits, which are a function of the total number of workers employed rather than the number of hours they work, it now becomes economically advantageous for the employer to meet his need for persons to perform additional work by employing those already on his payroll extra hours and paying them overtime rather than by increasing the total number he employs. The result, the critics suggest, is that some workers put in extensive overtime while other workers are unable to find any employment.

Some students of the problem disagree with this analysis, however. Joseph Garbarino for example, has suggested that the financial gain that employers accrue from using overtime is considerably less than is sometimes imagined and that there appears to be no upward trend in the substitution of overtime for the employment of additional workers.[15]

Fringe Benefits Abroad

Fringe benefits have played a far less significant role in collective bargaining abroad than they have in this country, the major reasons being that many of these other countries have more extensive government welfare programs. This generalization is true both for developing countries and for European nations. In fact, many of the developing countries' governments have undertaken welfare programs far beyond their financial means. In Latin America, for example, Argentina, Brazil, and Chile have all established social security programs far too generous in terms of the government's financial ability. As a result, the legislation has never been enforced properly, and some employers bear a heavy cost burden while others escape entirely. By the same token, the benefits accruing to workers are distributed just as unevenly and inequitably as in the United States under private plans.

In most European countries, holidays and paid vacations are specified by law and are not subject to collective bargaining. Similarly, virtually all pensions and health and welfare plans are government sponsored. Occasionally, as in France in the case of the Renault agreement, one can find provisions for extensive welfare benefits. The Renault agreement, which set a standard for a number of large industrial firms, created a flurry of interest at the time it was negotiated. Thereafter, interest flagged and only a handful of additional contracts were negotiated. The Renault agreement, which made elaborate provisions for vacations, pensions, and unemployment protection, was the model for agreements in some fifty large companies, many of which, unlike Renault, were privately owned. However, its spread drew to an abrupt halt partly because the benefits to employers in terms of lower turnover and better plant morale proved to be less than had been expected.

Germany has an elaborate system of social security dating back to the days of Bismarck that acts to redistribute income. Many other fringe benefits are provided for by law but a trend toward negotiated fringe benefits has been growing in recent years, with unions seeking to make permanent arrangements for benefits temporarily extended by employers in their efforts to reduce turnover. One fringe benefit that has long been widespread in Germany has been the provision of housing by employers for the workers in their plants. Today as high as 30 percent of a German worker's total wage is composed of supplementary health and retirement allowances as well as family allowances, canteens, and recreational facilities.

Israel represents an interesting blend. Fringe benefits are established by legislation and then elaborated upon through collective bargaining. The Annual Holidays Law of 1951 provides for a two-week vacation to all those who have worked for the same employer or in the same employment for at least two hundred days. In addition to his regular vacation pay, a worker receives a "rest home allowance" if he spends his vacation at an approved center. There is a wide variety of fringe benefits, ranging from paid vacations and holidays to provisions for sickness and old age.

Although the system of fringe benefits in Japan has not developed as fully as it has in the United States, many of the large plants have very elaborate programs, with little "extras" that are rarely found in this country. In large companies the travel expenses of workers to and from work are often paid and living quarters for single men and women are provided. Large companies also provide what amounts to a guarantee of permanent employment for their long-service workers. Lavish sporting facilities and holiday rest homes also are a feature of many large plants. Many unions have negotiated contracts that provide for retirement protection. As in the United States, fringe benefits have become a growing part of the total wage bill of some employers. The discrepancy that exists among employers, however, is even sharper in Japan than it is in this country.

Fringe benefit programs have developed rapidly in Mexico but are unevenly distributed among industries and plants; they are most fully developed in the larger companies. Much of the impetus toward increased protection has come from government requirements (plants employing more than one hundred workers must have fringe benefit plans) and from wage restraints imposed during the 1953–1955 inflation. Fringe benefits amount to between 20 and 30 percent of the compensation of Mexico's industrial workers.

Summary and Conclusions

Fringe benefits won through the process of collective bargaining are much more common in the United States than in other countries. This does not necessarily mean that workers in other countries are receiving less of this form of protection, since they are often covered by programs sponsored or initiated by their governments. One of the major weaknesses of privately negotiated welfare programs is the unevenness of the coverage afforded to workers. Those workers fortunate enough to have a strong union representing them are likely to secure benefits considerably more elaborate than unorganized workers or those whose union is weak. Given a major consideration such as adequate retirement income, the inequity may assume major importance. Furthermore, the worker who is currently protected may forfeit his protection if he changes employers or becomes unemployed for a protracted period of time.

Despite these and other handicaps, there appears to be a worldwide trend toward an increasing amount of privately negotiated fringe benefits and there are indications that the trend will continue to grow. Originally introduced for a variety of reasons, fringe benefits are now an integral part of the collective bargaining process in many countries.

NOTES

1. Irving Bernstein reminds us that the 1929 Handbook of Labor Statistics listed no fringe benefits except paid vacations, which only a handful of production workers received. See Irving Bernstein, The Lean Years, (Baltimore: Penguin, 1966), p. 73.

2. Frank W. Merritt, "Paid Vacation Provisions in Major Union Contracts, 1961," Monthly Labor Review (August 1962), pp. 875–881.

3. A typical paid holiday clause reads as follows:

> To be entitled to pay for a particular holiday, an employee in all cases must have completed his probationary period of thirty (30) days and have worked for the mill within the thirty days immediately preceding the holiday.
>
> (a) Subject to the provisions hereinafter set forth, employees shall be paid for the following legal holidays when no work is performed: New Year's Day, Memorial Day, Fourth of July, Labor Day, Thanksgiving Day, and Christmas Day.
>
> (b) Eligibility requirements for holiday pay shall be as follows:
>
> (1) An employee shall have completed his temporary period of employment as of the date of any such holiday.
>
> (2) An employee shall have worked all of his scheduled hours on the scheduled workday preceding and the scheduled workday following any such holiday.

4. See Abraham Weiss and Dena G. Wolk, "Holiday Provisions in Union Agreements in 1952–1953," Monthly Labor Review, 77 (February 1954), 128; and Dena G. Weiss and Henry S. Rosenbloom, "Paid Holidays in Major Contracts, 1958" Monthly Labor Review, 82 (January 1959), 20. The more recent figures mentioned earlier are derived from the U.S. Department of Labor, Bureau of Labor Statistics, Wages and Related Benefits, Part 11, pp. 60–61. A survey of contracts negotiated between 1960 and 1966 showed little change in the proportion of workers covered but did indicate that there had been two changes: (1) an increase in the number of paid holidays; (2) a reduction in the number of years required for a paid vacation. James N. Houff, "Supplementary Wage Benefits in Metropolitan Areas," Monthly Labor Review (June 1968), pp. 40, 43–47.

5. Dorothy R. Kittmer, "Health Insurance and Pension Plan Coverage in Union Contracts," Monthly Labor Review (March 1962), pp. 274–277.

6. Walter H. Franke, "Labor Market Ex-

perience of Unemployed Older Workers," *Monthly Labor Review* (March 1963), pp. 282–285.

7. Vesting privileges have usually been confined to firms in a single industry or a narrow geographical location and even where they are operative they do not permit complete freedom of movement.

8. U.S. Department of Labor, *Pension Plans Under Collective Bargaining,* Bureau of Labor Statistics Bulletin No. 1147 (1953).

9. U.S. Department of Labor, *Labor Mobility and Private Pension Plans,* Bureau of Labor Statistics *Bulletin No. 1407* (June 1964), Chap. 3.

10. Walter W. Kolodrubetz, "Early Retirement Provisions in Private Pensions Plans," *Monthly Labor Review* (October 1964), p. 1165.

11. A spokesman for the AFL-CIO at the IRRA meetings in 1969 forecast the future of union demands for pensions and other fringe benefits. Rudolph A. Oswald, "Union Prospects and Programs for the 1970's," *Proceedings of the Twenty-Second Annual Winter Meeting,* Industrial Relations Research Association, 1969, pp. 136–143.

12. A typical sickness and accident benefit clause reads:

> The Company will provide for each employee covered by this agreement, who has been in the employ of the Company at least 90 days, a policy of insurance with the (name of company) Insurance Company, providing for . . . nonoccupational accidental sickness insurance benefits in the amount of $15 per week for a maximum period of 13 weeks, starting with the eighth day of disability in the case of sickness, and the first day of disability in the case of accident.

U.S. Department of Labor, Bureau of Labor Statistics, *Labor-Management Contract Provisions: 1949–1950,* Bulletin No. 1022 (1951), p. 17.

13. U.S. Department of Labor, *Severance Pay and Layoff Benefit Plans,* Bureau of Labor Statistics Bulletin No. 1435–2 (1965).

14. *Economic Almanac 1967–1968* (New York: Macmillan, 1967), p. 84.

15. Joseph W. Garbarino, "Fringe Benefits and Overtime as Barriers in Expanding Employment," *Industrial and Labor Relations Review* (April 1964), pp. 426–442.

11

The Problem of Union Security

The central controversy is not the right to work, but the right to decide the conditions of work.
        —Willard Wirtz

The formal rationale of the union is to augment the economic welfare of its members; but a more vital institutional objective— survival and growth of the organization— will take precedence whenever it comes into conflict with the formal purpose.
        —Arthur M. Ross

□ ARTHUR Ross' statement is particularly true in the case of the United States. Unions here have dwelt on the issue of union security far more fervently than have unions in almost any other country. Few issues in American industrial relations have aroused more intense feeling on both sides than this topic. The economic aspects of the question have often been lost as the opposing sides have appealed to principles of equity, democracy, and American ideals in general in defense of their positions. We will begin our discussion of this controversial question by distinguishing some of the various forms of union security.

The most complete form of union security is the *closed shop.* Where the closed shop prevails, an employer can hire only those workers who are already members of the union. Various abuses of this form plus the fear that any union that secured such protection would thereby amass excessive power led to its being banned under the provisions of the Taft-Hartley Act of 1947. For similar reasons, the closed shop had earlier been made illegal in the railroad industry by the Railway Labor Act. It is now legal in the United States for an employer engaged in interstate commerce to grant a closed shop even should he wish to do so. Closed shops are still illegal in a number of states, including New York, for those engaged in intrastate activity. A typical closed shop clause reads as follows:

> Each employer hereby agrees to employ none but members of the union in good standing in his [establishment]. . . . Each employer agrees to hire all employees through the office of the union. The union agrees to supply each employer with competent employees within 48 hours after request therefor . . .[1]

Like the closed shop, programs of *preferential hiring* were also declared illegal under the Taft-Hartley Act. Preferential hiring systems provide that the employer will discriminate in favor of union members in his hiring whenever possible. Preferential contracts usually extend permission to employ nonunion workers whenever the supply of union workers is exhausted; these nonunion workers are frequently provided by the union with temporary work permits. In the event of a layoff, preferential contracts usually specify that these nonunion workers will be the first to be laid off. If there is lasting expansion in employment opportunities, they are usually admitted to the union.

The next most complete form of union security is the *union shop.* Under a union shop arrangement, an employer is free to hire whomever he chooses whether they be members of the union or not, but all workers must become members of the union within a specified period of time (usually thirty days). A typical union shop provision reads as follows:

All employees covered by this agreement shall become and remain members in good standing of the Union as a condition of employment. . . . All new non-union employees shall complete their affiliation and membership in the union no later than 30 days after their date of hire.[2]

The Taft-Hartley Act did not itself outlaw the union shop,[3] but one of its sections (14B) gave the states the option to outlaw it should they so choose to do. A total of twenty states currently have some kind of right-to-work laws while in six states such laws or similar legislation have been repealed. The 1965 and 1966 sessions of Congress debated President Lyndon Johnson's recommendation that Section 14B be repealed and that the power of states to rule the union shop illegal be terminated, but strong opposition led by Senator Everett Dirksen prevented Senate passage.

The *modified union shop* "modifies" the regular union shop by enabling employees in the plant at the time the plan goes into effect to remain outside the union if they so desire. All workers hired subsequent to the institution of the plan are required to become members of the union after the usual time. Such a provision is usually found in cases where a small but very vocal group of workers are strongly opposed to joining a union or where an employer feels strongly about the right of current workers to refuse to affiliate with any union if they so wish.

The *agency shop* is a form designed to meet some of the criticisms of compulsory unionism as required in forms just discussed and still render the union greater protection than it would have in the absence of any security clause in a contract. Under an agency shop agreement, payment of the union's dues is compulsory for all workers in the plant, although there is no requirement that they actually join the union. One of the merits of this alternative is that it assures the union of financial support (thus removing the union's complaints about so-called "free riders," which we will discuss shortly). At the same time the agency shop preserves the worker's freedom to join or not to join the union as he chooses. Union officials obviously also hope that workers, once they are no longer deterred by the payment of dues (since dues must be paid in any case), will be more prone to join the union voluntarily.

The *maintenance of membership* clause was first introduced during World War II as a kind of compromise between the unions' demand for the union shop or closed shop and employers' opposition to all forms of union security clauses. Under this form, the employer is free to hire whomever he chooses and to give the new employee free choice as to whether or not he wishes to join the union. All of those who decide in favor of membership in the union are bound to remain union members for a stated number of years or for the term of the contract. Failure on the part of a worker who has joined the union to remain a union member or to pay his dues for the required period is grounds for a required dismissal.[4]

An alternative to any of the forms of union security we have just discussed is the *open shop.* This term has undergone a considerable change in meaning through the years. In earlier times, the open shop was one where, to the best of the employer's knowledge at least, there were no union members in the plant. Workers were often forced to sign "yellow dog" contracts in which they vowed that they were not currently members of any union and agreed that the joining of a union would be sufficient grounds for immediate dismissal. With the legislation of the 1930s such practices became illegal and today the term open shop has a somewhat different meaning. While earlier an open shop was a plant where there were few (under cover) or no union members, an open *shop* today may be almost 100 percent organized. It is distinguished from the previously discussed arrangements by the fact that the employer has signed no agreement with the union that stipulates that all workers must join the union or pay dues. Thus there may be a small or even a substantial minority of the workers who do not belong to the union. The larger the proportion that is unorganized, of course, the greater is the concern of the union's members for the security of their organization.

Most unions that have won some form of a union security clause have also succeeded in obtaining provisions for the automatic *check-off.* Under the terms of this arrangement management agrees to withhold the dues of the union's members from their pay checks and turn that amount directly over to the union treasury. A typical check-off clause reads:

> The company will deduct out of the current net earnings payable to an employee covered by this agreement union dues and initiation fees insofar as permitted by State and Federal laws, upon receipt of and in accordance with a duly executed authorization by the employee in the form agreed upon by the company and the union.[5]

Under the terms of Taft-Hartley and state laws the check-off must be agreed to annually by the workers whose dues are deducted. The advantages to the union of such an arrangement are manifold. First, the check-off saves the union treasurer a great deal of time and trouble since he no longer needs to solicit and remind members of their dues obligation. Second, it assures the union of a prompt and regular source of funds and eliminates the problem of delinquencies. Third, the automatic deduction is a painless way of payment from the viewpoint of both the individual member and of the members charged with responsibility of collection. Dues deducted from the paycheck before it is received by a worker are missed less than dues paid once the check has been cashed and the worker has had the money in his hands. The resentments that arose on both sides in the past when the union had to set up dues barriers and refused to permit workers who were delinquent to enter or leave the plant until they paid their dues are now avoided.

As made evident by our historical sketch of collective bargaining in a variety of countries, unions in most of these countries have faced (and in some cases are still facing) a life-and-death struggle in their efforts to be recognized and to secure the protection of their members. The unions' need for security to ensure their continued existence is not unique to the United States. What *is* virtually unique, however, is the preoccupation of American unions with the various security clauses we have just outlined. In contrast, unions in many other countries devote scant attention to such clauses.[6] What factors account for this difference in approach?

First of all, employers are often strenuously opposed to granting any form of union security (this opposition is sometimes reflected in laws banning any form of compulsory union membership). Therefore, in countries where unions have been very weak it has been impossible to impose a demand for union security on management. In France and India, for example, unions have usually been too weak even to seek some form of union security.

In still other countries, unions have had such strong government support that they feel no need for greater security. In Brazil and Mexico, for example, the employer has little choice but to recognize a union that has been certified by the government. In Israel, the Histadrut is such an integral part of the government (in some cases, it is even the management) that any such guarantee would be superfluous.

Even in countries where union security is insufficient, however, unions have shown much less disposition to fight for security clauses than have unions in the United States. This apparent disinterest relates to the important distinction we noted earlier—unions in this country have never been as imbued with a sense of class consciousness as have unions elsewhere. Whereas unions abroad have tended from the first to fight for *all* workers and to raise the standards of workers as a class, American unions have tended to concentrate on the improvement of the fortunes of their own members. While it would be erroneous to charge that American unions have had no concern for the welfare of workers as a whole, it is perfectly accurate to note that when they seek to take their members "out of competition," their goal is to close job opportunities to workers who are not members of the union. The early predominance of craft unions in this country has made the pursuit of such a goal more effective than would otherwise be the case. As industrial unions have increased in importance, the conflict between ever-rising wage rates and the effect that they will have on the union's own state of health has become increasingly grave. Finally, the dilemma implicit in Arthur Ross' statement has become a reality. A union that pushes for higher wages to the point where some contraction in job opportunities occurs may experience what John Dunlop has called the "membership effect."[7] Dwindling job opportunities may lead to reductions in potential membership, thereby reducing the scope of the union's power and influence. The union thus may be torn between a desire to push for ever-higher benefits for its members and the fear that further pursuit along these lines will lead to a deterioration in its membership rolls.

When the closed shop was still legal in the United States for firms engaged in interstate commerce and when American unions were able to negotiate freely to obtain it, it was frequently combined with the closed union as a rationing device to limit the supply of labor available to the employer. Such limitations on entry have been alien to the philosophy of most foreign union movements; Japanese unions, which have secured extensive application of the union shop, rarely make use of the closed shop.

The Case for Compulsory Unionism

The fact that union security clauses are far more frequently a part of the contracts in the United States than they are elsewhere in the world does not mean that the case for them is correspondingly weakened. The concentration of American unions on the principles of business unionism and their relative neglect of political activity and the gains to be won by broad programs of social reform should not, as Selig Perlman pointed out several years ago, necessarily be condemned.[8] Given our capitalist system and the abiding support it has received from workers as well as management groups, the approach of American unions to the question of security may quite conceivably have been superior. In discussing the case for compulsory unionism, we will analyze each of the various forms from the viewpoint of their worth to the entire economy, taking into account the view of management as well as that of the workers and the union.

Closed Shop

Prior to passage of the Taft-Hartley Act, closed-shop arrangements covered a sizable minority of the organized workers in the United States: in 1946 the closed shop was involved in one-third of the nation's major collective bargaining agreements. One obvious reason that the proportion of closed shops was not larger was that employers (many of whom were antagonistic to any form of union security) simply refused to grant any demand for one. At least one-third of the employers, of course, were not that adamant. The testimony offered in congressional hearings on the Taft-Hartley Bill supports the conclusion that some employers actually favored the arrangement, since they testified in favor of the closed shop and against the proposed banning.

Employers who so testified claimed that they gained several advantages from the establishment of the closed shop, including the improved union-management relations that emerged when the union relaxed its suspiciousness and hostility toward management, and both sides became more inclined toward cooperation.

Several employers reported that the fact that they could only hire union members did not limit their ability to recruit a good labor force. Instead, the task of recruitment was reportedly made easier since an employer needed only to notify the union of his requirements and the union took care of supplying the necessary personnel. Employers dealing with the closed shop also were pleased with the quality of the workers who applied. Because the union had already screened them for ability, the employer had less need to undertake lengthy probationary periods or training programs of his own.

Since the closed shop was most widely adopted by craft unions that placed a high premium on skill requirements, the advantage to the employer of having a ready supply of well-qualified workers was appreciable. Unions in the building and construction industries, the printing trade, and the maritime and the amusement industries were among those who managed most frequently to secure the closed shop.

The advantages to a union of having a closed shop are too obvious to merit much elaboration. The closed shop represents peak security from attacks by management, raids from rival unions, or disaffection among a minority of the membership. Because the employer is entirely dependent on the union for his labor supply, the union is in a strong bargaining position with respect to wages and other employee benefits.

In attempting to defend the closed shop before the court of public opinion, however, unions have relied on more lofty arguments, as exemplified by this quotation from the September 1947 issue of *The American Federationist:*

> The closed shop is the essence of democracy, the rule of the majority . . . To say that this exercises a tyranny over the minority would be to strike at the very roots of our political philosophy . . . It is a travesty to say that to be obliged to join a union is a violation of individual freedom when, in fact, it is a guarantee of freedom from the absolute authority of the employer.[9]

For workers who are members of the union, the gains are also obvious. Members are protected from the competition of nonunion workers who might be willing to work for lower wages. On the other hand, the position of workers who are not union members and are unable to join is definitely worsened by the closed shop.

The chief advantage to the economy claimed on behalf of the closed shop is the reduction in industrial strife, work stoppages, and losses in production that is made possible by the improved relationships between management and labor.

Because the closed shop provides tangible advantages to unions, workers, and management alike in certain industries, the period immediately following the passage of the Taft-Hartley Act witnessed desperate efforts on the part of one or more of the parties concerned to maintain their previous arrangements. Both the International Typographical Union and the West Coast Longshoremen struck (to no avail) in a number of cities in an effort to undermine the legislation. The West Coast Longshoremen also tried to circumvent the intent of the law by requiring that all hiring be done on the basis of seniority; since previously only union workers had been employed, the effect of the provision was to award work only to those who were already union members.

In many jobs such as longshoring and building construction, workers only infrequently are with the same employer for more than thirty days; any effort to replace the closed shop with the union shop was thus doomed to failure. Employers in the building trades continued to rely upon the unions to furnish them with workers and permitted the unions to set their own criteria for suitability. The result again was to frustrate the intent of Taft-Hartley. In recognition of these practical problems, the section of Taft-Hartley dealing with the closed shop was amended by the Landrum-Griffin

Act in 1959 so that in certain industries it was legal for unions to refer union and nonunion workers to job openings and to require any who were not already members of the union to become members within seven days after their employment.

Those aspects of the closed shop that make it attractive to unions are sources of difficulties for employers. All too often the closed shop has been combined with the closed union in an effort to provide the union with a means of rationing the supply of labor. Workers have been kept from joining unions by a variety of devices ranging from exorbitantly high initiation fees (some ranging as high as $200) or excessively long periods of apprenticeship training to a complete closing of the union's membership rolls to all comers. As a result in some instances, the union acquired a complete monopoly on employment in the trade. Wages could be raised to higher and higher levels. When firms were driven out of business, the resulting loss in jobs was offset by the retirement of older workers. Since no new members were admitted, union members suffered little or no unemployment. Although actual cases of such events fill the books of writers who are unfriendly to the cause of unions, it is important to remember that such abuses never involved more than a small portion of all unions.

It should be noted also that the closed shop protected casual workers like the longshoremen in somewhat the same fashion that a seniority system protects workers who have remained with a particular employer. Unlike seniority, the closed shop guaranteed the worker no particular job, but rather assured him of reasonable prospects of employment in the industry.

Furthermore, one can argue that

outlawing the closed shop was not the answer to such abuses. Instead, the proper remedy would be making the closed union illegal. If unions were required to hold their membership rolls open to all qualified workers at a reasonable initiation fee, many of the evils just described would be removed. However is it correct to say that the closed shop has no function in the absence of the closed union? Given the assumption that some form of a union security clause is desirable (an assumption still to be discussed), the closed shop has been used to ration job openings, which may have an undesirable effect on those workers who are excluded. Prevented from pursuing certain channels of employment, they are forced into fields that are already overcrowded. As a result, they receive a lower level of wages than those they would have been able to obtain in fields now closed to them.

The same reasoning applies to the question of the possible ill effects the establishment of the closed shop inflicts on the whole economy. By forcing workers into fields that need them less and therefore pay them less, the pace of economic growth is slowed and a less satisfactory distribution of income results.

Thus far in our discussion of the closed shop we have not come to grips with the central issue of the union security contract—whether or not some form of compulsory unionism is desirable. All of the arguments in favor of the closed shop or some other form of union security fall on deaf ears when presented to someone who is basically antagonistic to the whole concept of workers having to join a union (or pay dues) as a price for continued employment. The state right-to-work laws (unions deem the term to be a pronounced misnomer) are based on the concept that workers should have the right to hold a job in an organized plant without having to join the union that has organized it.

Arguments Supporting the Union Shop

Union leaders who support the union shop argue that such an arrangement is both necessary and beneficial to the union. It is necessary in order to give the union security in the face of turnover in a plant's labor force. Newly hired workers may be unaware of the value of the union to them and therefore may be unwilling to join. In the event of a strike, a substantial number of nonunion members may constitute a threat as potential members of a back-to-work movement. Where no union shop exists, union members may be subject to constant urging by management to quit the union.

The union also argues that the existence of even a small number of nonunion members in a plant breeds tension and discontent among members who resent the unwillingness of a few to go along with the will of the majority. It is quite true that in some cases the feeling against nonunion members can run very high. Nonunion members have found themselves subject to social ostracism, cruel pranks (such as tire slashings), or even possible bodily harm. Although such actions are often instigated by union leaders seeking to put pressure on recalcitrant workers, the expressions of hostility may be entirely spontaneous.

Union spokesmen make much of the fact that the union shop represents the essence of the democratic principle of majority rule. When a majority of the members have declared that they do not wish to work in a plant where all workers are not members, it is only proper, they reason, that the minority abide by this decision.

Union leaders and the membership alike have been particularly vociferous about the nonunion worker who acts as a "free rider." A union is bound by law to represent all workers within its jurisdiction whether they are members of the union or not. Thus the union is compelled to press the grievances of the nonunion member and to see that his pay increases correspond to the others when an across-the-board increase is being made. Since the cost of representing a worker in a grievance and in protecting his rights is a cost to the union, free riders are stigmatized as taking unfair advantage of the situation and as being unwilling to pay their own way.

Some defenders of the union shop draw an analogy between requiring everyone to be a member of the union and compulsory vaccination. The good health of all (high wages and good working conditions) can be assured only if all work together. The implication that the nonunion worker endangers his own "health" prospects (his right to bargain for himself) when he is forced to join the union is negated by the fact that legally employers are not permitted to bargain individually with workers when a union is involved.

Note that much of the previous reasoning ignores another democratic principle—the protection of the minority. When workers are sincere in their opposition to being forced to join a union, the case for compulsory unionism is stronger and more acceptable if such workers have access to existing nonunion shops in the industry where they can find employment.

Although unions less frequently express it openly, the idea that the *union shop* enhances their bargaining power

is still an important part of their thinking. Although the closed shop, in which the employer has less discretion in hiring, perhaps has more impact on bargaining strength, there appears little reason to doubt that the union shop does enhance the union's bargaining power.

Despite the bargaining advantage the union shop awards to unions, however, many employers find this arrangement palatable because of the improved relationship between union and management that is likely to develop. Without the union shop, the union is constantly under pressure to justify its existence to its members. A union that must face continual queries of "What have you done for us lately?" may be more troublesome to an employer than a union that has been granted security. The importance of this consideration is reinforced by the high rate of turnover existing in many plants. Although the rate of labor turnover has been declining steadily in recent years, it is still not unusual to find a factory experiencing an annual turnover of 25 to 50 percent. New workers hired to replace those leaving tend to take the good wages and working conditions for granted. They may be unaware of any role the union has played in securing those benefits. In any case, the new workers will relegate what has been done to past history and in weighing the question of whether or not to join the union they may quite naturally inquire, "What's in it for me?" The employer who rejects the union's request for a union shop saying, "Let the union fight for its members," may find his factory serving as the battleground. Of course, even with a union or closed shop, the union may still sponsor ill-founded grievances as a bargaining tactic.[10] However, a management that is really on its toes can usually convert such grievances and the decisions relating to them to their own benefit. Furthermore, at the time a security clause is granted, an employer may also benefit from his ability to trade the offer of a union security clause for a reduction in other demands by the union. Finally, anything that acts to raise plant morale and reduce dissension in the labor force is naturally welcomed by employers.

Since the union shop leaves the employer with a free hand in his hiring, the possible bad effects that the closed shop has upon workers and the economy do not apply in the case of the union shop. A case has been made against the union shop, however, and we will now turn to a discussion of the critics' objections.

The Case Against the Union Shop

Critics of the union shop argue that it is bad even for the union. A union that is protected by such a security clause, they suggest, tends to grow complacent and careless. The union's interest in serving the rank and file dwindles with the assurance that members have no choice but to support it. These critics frequently go further and reason that the union should *not* be safe from raids from rival unions, which they view as a real safeguard of workers' rights. The threat of raids keeps the union's leaders responsible to the wishes of the rank and file. Alternatively, it has been suggested that if raiding is really a serious problem, stiffer legislative restrictions on the amount of raiding and NLRB enforcement of the voluntary arrangements already in force within the AFL-CIO could be enacted.

The argument that the union shop is needed in order to prevent unfair labor practices by the employer is

dismissed as being less relevant today than formerly since employers are limited by law from engaging in such practices and the NLRB has been quick to penalize violators. It should be noted that exceptions to this generalization are already apparent and that prospects in the event of a serious depression are not encouraging from a union viewpoint.

The critics of the union shop answer complaints about the inequity represented by the "free rider" in several ways. First, they contend that the union wouldn't have it any other way even if it could. No union composed of rational men would be willing to permit workers to bargain on their own even if the law permitted them to do so. The opportunities for an employer to discriminate in favor of nonunion employees would represent a serious drain on the union's bargaining power. Those who are more convinced that free riders represent an unfair burden to unions do not see this as a necessary justification for a union shop. If the free rider is a problem, they reason, why not make it illegal for anyone to be one? A legal requirement that all workers contribute a fair share toward the expenses of collective bargaining would remove the inequity without compelling anyone to become a member of the union against his will. A third line of reasoning is based on the theory that the worker who does not wish to join a union because of honest convictions about the defects of unions is more of a freethinker than a free rider. The union may be pressing economic or political policies to which a worker is sincerely opposed; to force him to join a union would be a moral wrong.

Opponents of the union shop see the issue of democracy in quite a different light than do its supporters. Critics stress the compulsory element of any union security clause and the resulting violation of individual rights. The following statement, which attacks the majority-rule justification for the union shop, is typical:

This argument [rule by the majority] loses its appeal when one considers the fact that another basic principle in our constitutional form of government is sound protection for the rights of minorities—a right the union officials are seeking to destroy in their Union Shop demands.[11]

Without questioning the sincerity of management groups who weep for the loss of the workers' democratic rights, it should be pointed out that in instances where their own powers have been questioned, management groups have been far less concerned about the democratic freedom of their workers. Union leaders also point out that not too many years ago (the 1930s) employers were insisting that all workers had to join their company unions whether they wanted to or not as a price for continued employment. The employers' past use of the blacklist is also difficult to reconcile with their current concern over workers' "right to work."

The issue of democracy in connection with the union shop is basically a value judgment that the student will have to make for himself. Questions like the following will be assigned varying importance and answered differently by different individuals. If morale is an important justification, what about the morale of those forced to join? Does the principle of majority rule apply even if the majority is a very slim one? If a worker, for religious or personal convictions, wants nothing to do with the union, should he be compelled to seek work elsewhere unless he is willing to part with his belief? Is having to join a union any more serious than having to abide by other rules of the shop or is there a distinct difference? Can the case for forced union membership be applied to the case of other organizations as well? Is there a proper analogy between the requirement that a worker must join a union as a condition for continued employment and the old yellow dog contract?

When the union shop provides the union with increased bargaining power, it may have a detrimental impact on the employer similar to that of the *closed shop.* Warnings have also been sounded that giving union leaders an allegedly freer hand to cooperate with management may lead instead to a greater coercion of the employer.

Another problem inherent in both the closed and union shop arrangement is its effect on the temporary or part-time worker. Students seeking summer employment have frequently encountered this problem. At first glance it seems unfair to require a worker to join the union when his future status is so uncertain. Unions respond, however, that these workers also have grievances that require expensive processing and it is thus only fair that they help support the union's treasury. In the case of some seasonal industries and particularly in a *closed shop,* unions have often employed permit cards. The use of such cards opens opportunities for nepotism and racketeering practices, however, and tends to reduce the incentive of the union to organize the temporary or part-time workers.

Before the passage of the Taft-Hartley Act, employers could not always be sure that their employees would be able to remain union members in good standing. Expulsion from the union, of course, under a union shop or closed shop agreement had to be accompanied by dismissal from the company. Today, only if a member is expelled for failure to pay dues or for failure to pay reasonable initiation fees does his expulsion involve the loss of his right to be employed in the plant. Although the resulting protection of workers' rights is generally desirable and particularly important in unions with weak democratic organizational structures, union leaders have complained that the present ruling works a hardship for the union. It is possible for an employer to hire workers who will be a divisive force in the union and the union will be unable to remove them from their jobs as long as they continue to pay their dues. While such instances are not unheard of, they apparently do not constitute a major problem at present.

Despite the passage of state right-to-work laws, the union shop has grown in popularity. In 1946, only 17 percent of major collective bargaining agreements contained provisions for a union shop. By 1954, the percentage had increased to 64 percent and there was a further increase to 78 percent by 1959. As the union shop became more widespread, provisions for maintenance of membership declined from 25 percent in 1946 to 7 percent in 1959.[12] Note that by adding the two figures for 1959 we find 85 percent of union members are required to stay in a union once they join it for the term of the contract.

Maintenance of Membership

The declining importance of the *maintenance of membership* clause means that we can devote proportionately less attention to its advantages and disadvantages. Since under this arrangement workers are given a free choice at the beginning, many of the arguments used against the union shop no longer are valid. No worker is compelled to join the union and those who choose to do so can remain outside its membership rolls.

Not everyone has been satisfied with the maintenance of membership arrangement. Those who object most strenuously frequently do so on the grounds that it removes a means by which union members can clearly express their dissatisfaction with the way the union is being run; when they don't like it, they can quit the union immediately. If a union's democratic processes are minimal, a member may have no other way to voice his disapproval. Under a maintenance of membership clause, members can withdraw only at the time of a new contract or during certain specified "escape" periods.

The major defect in the maintenance of membership clause, however, is that neither side (particularly the union) has found it to be a suitable permanent compromise. Unions see it as only a partial step in the direction of complete security, while management remains fearful that such a clause may tip the scales of bargaining power in the union's favor.

As a result of this mutual dissatisfaction, many unions and management groups have abandoned maintenance of membership arrangements in favor of the *modified union shop.* Thus while 74 percent of the major 1958 collective bargaining agreements were found to contain provisions for the union shop, 20 percent of them called for a modified union shop.

The Modified Union Shop

Compared to a straight union shop, the modified union shop does little either to weaken the bargaining strength of the union or to strengthen the employer's position. Even at its inception only a small number of the total workers is likely to be involved and as retirements take place the proportion of nonunion workers continues to decrease. Employers who prefer such an arrangement feel that it protects "old-timers" who may object to union membership on philosophical grounds or who feel that they do not need any help from the union because they are sufficiently secure in their positions after years of service. Its significance for the economy and workers in general is not greatly different than that of the straight union shop.

The Agency Shop

From the union's point of view, the agency shop has never been as satisfactory as the more complete forms of security. Frequently cited defects are the tendency of this arrangement to breed apathy among members and the possibility that it will open the door to raids by rival unions and subsequent decertification. Because of its more tenuous position the union has less bargaining strength than it has under a more complete union security arrangement.

Furthermore, since the Taft-Hartley Act forbids firing a worker because he has lost his union membership unless he was ejected from the union for failure to pay dues, much of the distinction between union and agency shops has been removed.

Even where unions have sought the agency shop, however, they have had little success. In 1959, less than 1 percent of some 1,600 agreements contained an agency shop provision. Part of the reason that this percentage is so low, however, lies in the fact that eleven state right-to-work laws specifically forbid the agency shop. In at least two other states, the state courts have so interpreted the state law despite the absence of a specific clause

to that effect. A Supreme Court decision has upheld the right of state courts and legislatures to so act. The Teachers union has been the most notable group interested in the agency shop in recent years.

The Check-off

Employers who are unwilling to accept the union shop rarely agree to the check-off. Even in a union shop, however, the application of the check-off to every worker is not automatically guaranteed. Section 302 of the Taft-Hartley Act provides that the employee must give his permission before the check-off can be instituted. Despite this legal restriction, the popularity of the check-off has increased tremendously during the past three decades; contained in 20 percent of the contracts in 1942, it has mounted to slightly over 70 percent in recent years.[13]

Criticism of the check-off has been less strident than that directed at the forms of union security we discussed earlier. The major reservation has been that nonpayment of dues may be a way by which a union member can express his dissatisfaction with the union's leaders. This argument is weakened by the fact that a failure to pay dues, with or without a check-off, is the one ground for expulsion from the union that can be converted into a dismissal from the job.

Decertification

It should be borne in mind that none of the above arrangements gives a union permanent security. Workers who have voted to accept a union are not thereby locked into that union for all time. Under the terms of the Taft-Hartley Act, an employer, another union, or a group of 30 percent or more of the employees in the bargaining unit can request the NLRB to hold a decertification election. The usual rule is that at least a year must have passed since the last election. If a majority of the workers vote against the union, it is decertified and declared no longer representing the workers in that bargaining unit. The use of the appeal for decertification by employers, particularly during strikes, has been a subject for sharp criticism by union leaders.

Taft-Hartley and State Right-to-Work Laws

Detailed consideration of the right-to-work laws is beyond the central concern of this book. Since they do impose a serious limitation on free collective bargaining because they prevent an employer from granting a union shop even should he choose to do so, however, we will examine briefly the motives underlying their passage and the results that have been produced.

If one examines the list of states that have enacted right-to-work legislation,[14] one finds that it contains a heavy concentration of states that are rural, in the South, or both. Unquestionably many state legislators were concerned about the excessive power of unions and the threat to workers' freedom resulting from forced membership in unions, and the passage of the Taft-Hartley Act allowed them to take serious action. States that were relatively nonindustrialized probably also felt that the passage of legislation controlling the power of unions would attract new industries.

Like the Taft-Hartley Act itself, right-to-work laws have most seriously hampered weak unions in their efforts to carry on effective bargaining; they

have had much less effect on strong unions. Where the union does not have the full support of the workers—whatever the reason may be—the right-to-work laws have enabled the employer to undermine and in some cases to uproot the union. The laws are applied when the state authorities receive a complaint—such complaints are obviously more likely to be forthcoming from employers who feel they can be successful in fighting the union.

Most studies suggest, however, that despite dire predictions to the contrary by union leaders, most unions have been less seriously hampered than might be expected. Many employers of craft trades in right-to-work states have continued to rely upon the union as their primary source for the recruitment of needed workers, making the laws in some cases unenforceable. Similarly, there has been a tendency for large multiplant companies to abide by the spirit of the union shop clause when it has been negotiated in other plants in the company. Prosecutions by the attorneys general have been hampered by the inability to assemble sufficient evidence to support a case. Unions have thus found that the laws expose them to harassment and leave them uncertain as to what repercussions might emerge from various actions, but on the whole do not deliver any mortal wounds.

Security From Raiding by Rival Unions

In addition to protecting the union from attack by management, union security clauses also provide the union with a safeguard against attack by rival unions.

Where the union security clause is used to protect the union from management attacks, the normal expectation is that the interests of the workers and the union will be identical. The Wagner Act was itself predicated on this assumption, plus, of course, the idea that the unions would be responsive to the interests of the workers they represented.

Even in the early days of the NLRB administration of the Wagner Act, however, it soon became evident that a union security clause could provide a union with valuable protection from attack by rival unions. Furthermore, it was clear that NLRB decisions regarding appropriate bargaining units might have important repercussions with respect to the health and security of a given union. Because management has often sought to weaken a union by attacking the contract's union security clause, workers have had to view all challenges to the security clause as management inspired. Where the management has accepted a given union, however, and come to work closely with the union's officers, a union security clause may serve chiefly to keep the union's members or at least their pocketbooks safely in the union's power. Given a strong security clause, any rival union finds itself almost completely frozen out. As a result, the rank and file may be unable to overthrow the union's leaders even though the members are openly dissatisfied with the union's operations.

NLRB decisions during the past three decades have acted both to strengthen unions from attack by rivals and to diminish the extent of union security from actions by rival unions and management alike. The board has ruled that multiplant and even multiemployer bargaining agreements are subject to challenge by a rival union only if the entire bargaining unit is involved. In other words, a rival union cannot succeed by winning converts in a single plant if a multiplant agreement is in effect; it must secure the support of a majority of the entire bargaining unit.

Long-term contracts also reduce the frequency with which rival unions can challenge the current leadership. The recent NLRB decision that protects a union from challenge for three years instead of the previous two-year period adds to the security of the union that is already established in the plant.

The effect of these decisions is offset by the NLRB rulings that exclude sizable fractions of a plant's labor force from the bargaining unit. The board has required separate elections for technical or office workers. The impact of this ruling is seen in the aerospace industry, where 40 percent or more of the workers in some companies were not included in the bargaining unit. When such a sizable fraction of the plant's labor force is excluded, the winning of a union security clause may be a hollow victory.

The Nature of Union Security Elsewhere in the World

When we turn to a discussion of union security in other parts of the world, we find that unions and management advance many of the same arguments that they do in the United States but that the attitude of the government often differs markedly from the American case.

Great Britain

There are no legal limitations in Britain on the right of unions to seek union security clauses and the issue, particularly with reference to the closed shop, has been a subject for much heated debate since World War II. The debate began in 1946 when the

Trades Union Congress adopted a resolution part of which read as follows:

A union which has the responsibility of maintaining fair wages and working conditions must also have the right to determine, according to the circumstances in the particular case, whether or not it is wise or safe to tolerate non-unionism and therefore permit the presence of actual or potential blacklegs . . .

In Great Britain, the unions' interpretation of what union security is and the means by which they hope to achieve it are somewhat different than in the United States. British unions have sought to make all the workers in a plant members of some union but not necessarily of the same union. In their drives to ensure 100 percent union membership, unions have exerted pressure upon employees rather than on employers and few formal contract provisions for union security exist. Pressure on non-union workers to join takes the form of a refusal of union members to work with nonunion workers. Pleas have been made for the protection of the right of the minority not to have to join a union in order to work. The unions have in turn asserted that the majority has a right not to have to work beside nonunionists.

Although the question has been debated extensively in Parliament in recent years, there has been no official government policy with respect to union security since the repeal of the 1927 Trades Disputes Act in 1946. The absence of a government policy cuts both ways—even the yellow dog contract is still legal in Great Britain.

Most writers feel that it will be a long time, if ever, before British unions display the same degree of interest in efforts to compel workers to join a particular union that unions in the United States do, although some

scholars profess to see the beginnings of a trend in that direction. At the moment about 39 percent of British union members are in closed shops; the closed shop is particularly prevalent in shipbuilding, mining, longshoring, and printing. Whether or not any further expansion will occur is impossible to determine at the present time. In part the answer will depend upon whether or not jurisdictional disputes will continue to play as small a role in British industrial relations as they have in the past.

Continental Europe

As we indicated earlier, the question of union security has not had the same political and legal implications in Europe as it has had in the United States. In Europe the legal treatment accorded security clauses varies widely from country to country. In Sweden, the legislature has deliberately avoided extending to workers the right to remain unorganized; the general feeling is that this right does not exist. In France, on the other hand, the right to refuse to join a union is firmly upheld. The situation in West Germany is more complex. The issue is still unresolved at this writing, although a few collective bargaining contracts do contain provisions for the union shop.

The agency shop is becoming increasingly popular in a number of European countries. According to van de Vall, union leaders in Western Europe see fluctuations in membership as a good barometer of the union's popularity with its members.[15]

India, Israel, and Japan

Further evidence of the richness of variety is provided by a few more brief examples. In India all forms of union security are virtually nonexistent. Until the Payment of Wages Act of 1936 prohibited employers from withholding any part of workers' wages, plants in a few well-organized industries (textiles, for example) used the check-off.

The relatively infrequent occurrence of either the union shop or the closed shop in India is explained not only by government and employer opposition but also by the reluctance of unions to support these programs. Most union opposition appears to rest on two counts: (1) the fear that the employer will somehow use the union security clause to freeze out rival unions less to his liking or that the clause will be used to protect unions favored by the government; and (2) a rejection of the union security clause on principle as harmful to workers and the labor movement alike.

The absence of security clauses has handicapped Indian unions, and many of them have had trouble collecting dues from their members. Some unions have attempted to solve this problem by paying one of the officers a percentage of the dues he collects as a device to encourage collection.

In Israel approximately 85 percent of the workers are union members, and an overwhelming majority of them are members of the Histadrut, paying their dues directly to it. In turn, the Histadrut assigns them to the appropriate national union in terms of their trade or profession. Little concern, therefore, has been shown about union security clauses. Japanese employers have bitterly opposed both the union shop and the checkoff.

Mexico

Of all the countries in Central and South America, only Mexico has legislation specifically approving the doctrine of compulsory unionism. Most of the other countries have legal guar-antees protecting the right of unions to organize, but their laws also specifically bar any requirements that workers join unions.

Mexico permits with some modifications both the union and the closed shop. The latter is found more frequently in large industries. Unions are permitted to sign exclusive bargaining contracts with an employer but those workers who are employed at the time of the signing of the contract are not required to join the union if they do not wish to do so. Once a worker is a member of the union, however, he faces possible loss of his job should he either quit the union or be expelled from it.

Summary and Conclusions

Four general conclusions can be drawn from the material presented in this chapter:

1. Most governments today endorse the principle of unionization and guarantee the right of unions to organize and to bargain. Great Britain is an interesting exception to this general rule; unions there, however, are so well established that they do not need this protection.

2. The question of union security clauses is still very much an issue of contention in the United States and numerous arguments continue to be presented for and against its institution.

3. Despite bitter cries of protest and repeated efforts to repeal Taft-Hartley, United States government policy is relatively liberal compared to that of other countries. Of those countries with which comparisons were made, only Mexico, Sweden, Israel, Great Britain, and Japan were more permissive.

4. Unions in other countries have been much more relaxed about the issue of union security as it has been

defined in this country. They have sought increased union membership, but not necessarily in any particular union.

Two major features of the trade union movement in many of the countries we have studied have been the well-known apathy of many of the unions' members and the tendency of the total membership to decline in numbers in the postwar years. Whether union security clauses will protect unions from these twin dangers or instead reinforce them remains to be seen.

NOTES

1. Theodore Rose, "Union Security Provisions in Major Union Contracts, 1958–1959," *Monthly Labor Review* (December 1959), pp. 10–49.

2. U.S. Department of Labor, Bureau of Labor Statistics, Bulletin No. 1142, *Labor Management Contract Provisions, 1952: Prevalence and Characteristics of Selected Collective-Bargaining Clauses.*

3. See Chapter 3 for a further discussion of governmental attitudes toward the union shop. In the early years of Taft-Hartley an election was necessary before an employer could grant the union shop, but this requirement was later abandoned.

4. A typical maintenance of membership clause reads as follows:

All employees who, 15 days after the date of certification by the NLRB that all of the provisions of the LMRA [Labor Management Relations Act] have been complied with by the union, and that the union has been authorized pursuant to the provisions of such act to enter into a maintenance-of-membership agreement, or who, 15 days after the date upon which it becomes legal to enter into a maintenance-of-membership agreement without such certification, are members of the union in good standing in accordance with the constitution and by-laws of the union, and all employees who thereafter become members of the union, shall as a condition of employment, remain members of the union in good standing for the duration of the agreement.

Any employee who wishes to withdraw from membership in the union during the above 15-day period may do so by written notification by registered letter to the union.

Theodore Rose, "Union Security Provisions in Agreements, 1954," *Monthly Labor Review,* 78 (June 1955), 654.

5. Theodore Rose, "Checkoff Provisions in Major Union Contracts," *Monthly Labor Review,* 83 (January 1960), 31.

6. See below, pp. 220–222.

7. John Dunlop, *Wage Determination Under Trade Unions* (New York: Macmillan, 1944), p. 46.

8. Selig Perlman, *A Theory of the Labor Movement* (New York: Macmillan, 1928).

9. Quoted from George F. Jansen, "The Closed Shop is not a Closed Issue," *Industrial and Labor Relations Review* (July 1949), p. 547.

10. See Sumner H. Slichter, James Healy, and E. Robert Livernash, *The Impact of Collective Bargaining on Management* (Washington, D.C.: Brookings, 1960), p. 40.

11. General Electric, "Compulsory Unionism—A Failing Issue: Part I," *Relations News Letter* (April 5, 1963), reprinted in *The Personnel Administrator* (November–December 1963), p. 8.

12. Theodore Rose, "Union Security Provisions in Major Union Contracts, 1958–1959," *op. cit.,* p. 13–49.

13. Theodore Rose, "Checkoff Provisions," *op. cit.,* pp. 26–31.

14. The following states had enacted right-to-work laws as of March 1967: Alabama, Arizona, Arkansas, Florida, Georgia, Iowa, Kansas, Mississippi, Nebraska, Nevada, North Carolina, North Dakota, South Carolina, South Dakota, Tennessee, Texas, Virginia, and Wyoming. Louisiana has enacted an agricultural right-to-work law.

In Delaware, Hawaii, Indiana, Louisiana, Maine, and New Hampshire, there has been subsequent repeal of right-to-work laws. See U.S. Department of Labor, *Growth of Labor Law in United States* (Washington, D.C.: Government Printing Office, 1967), p. 217.

15. Mark van de Vall, *Labor Organizations* (London: Cambridge Press, 1970).

12
The Issue of Management Security

In order to implement the twin objectives of building the organization and promoting the economic well-being of the members, union leaders are constantly driven to acquire more and more control over jobs, and are thus compelled to encroach upon what company executives conceive to be the area of vital managerial functions.

—Frederick H. Harbison and
John R. Coleman

□ COLLECTIVE bargaining by its very nature restricts the boundaries within which a manager or his representatives are free to act. From its very inception, collective bargaining has been designed to protect the worker from unilateral decisions by the employer that are detrimental to the workers' welfare. Thus insistence that decisions concerning wage payments, layoffs, dismissals, vacations, and retirement be subject to union challenge has been a familiar part of virtually all collective bargaining agreements. Historically, the focus of union interest has concerned personnel management and it is in this area that unions have constituted the greatest challenge to management's freedom of action. Questions concerning personnel have grown increasingly broad with the passage of time, and management now sees challenges to its "right to manage" arising in other fields as well. Thus it is not surprising that management has grown increasingly concerned about the preservation of its authority, and it seems fair to say that management has resisted all encroachments on its authority with considerable vehemence.

Management Authority in Earlier Times

In almost all industrialized nations there was an early period when no worker dreamed of challenging the authority of his boss. Anyone who became dissatisfied with the treatment he received was free to quit and seek work elsewhere, but adequate protection in a given position was unthinkable. Management's rights were founded on the rights of private property. As Charles Beard has pointed out, our Constitution was written largely as a document designed to protect property rights and any challenge to the rights of property was considered un-American and undemocratic. As we saw in Chapter 3 much of the early opposition to unions was founded on the allegation that they represented a threat to private property.

Early economists provided a fine theoretical support for this position. Private property was inextricably linked with the free enterprise system and the market economy. Any action that threatened the freest exercise of property rights thus constituted a menace to the entire system. For this reason the English classical economists were notorious opponents of legislation designed to improve working conditions in the factory and to protect the health of women and child laborers. Economists like Nassau Senior espoused the "last hour" theory of work, contending that profits were made only during the last hour in the day's labor. Given this basic premise, any proposal to shorten the working day was horrifying in the extreme; it threatened every employer with immediate financial losses and bankruptcy.

As originally developed, the case for the unlimited rights of private property revolved around the concept of individual ownership. The emergence of the corporation and the accompanying increase in the amount of business property held under the corporate form failed to change the basic philosophy. In 1819 the Supreme Court under the leadership of John Marshall decided in the Dartmouth College case that a corporation had the rights of a legal person to hold property and to have its contracts enforced.

Fortified by this Supreme Court decision, the defenders of management's authority now shifted ground slightly. No longer was it ownership per se that justified the exercise of power by management; instead the fact that managers were trustees acting on behalf of the stockholder owners provided the justification. In order to carry out their responsibilities as trustees, the argument now ran, managers must be given a free hand to run the company as they saw fit.

Meanwhile, back at the plant, the industrial worker remained virtually helpless to protect himself. Adam Smith's early warning about the superior bargaining position of employers was virtually ignored as later economists constructed a model of perfect competition where workers were willing and able to better their condition by shifting from one employer to another. Assuming a normal state of full employment, early theorists neglected the potential for exploitation that derived from the workers' fear to move because of what Selig Perlman has termed a sense of "job scarcity."[1] Because of the relative scarcity of labor and resulting high wage levels in the United States,

American workers never experienced the degree of hardship attendant upon industrialization in England and in other countries. Even in the United States, however, the foreman was often a harsh taskmaster with whom workers had to curry favor as he dispensed layoffs, promotions, and fines, often capriciously.

In their efforts to protect their memberships from these dangers and to improve living standards for workers, it was inevitable that unions challenge management's authority. Furthermore, in a complex industrial society almost every management decision has some ramifications that affect those employed by the company. Thus it is natural that the areas in which unions seek some voice in management's decisions continue to expand.

In earlier times, management had sought to avoid this danger by having as little to do with unions as possible; they were more willing to offer concessions to their workers in order to satisfy them than they were to recognize and bargain with a union. With the passage of the Wagner Act in 1935, however, employers were legally bound both to recognize and bargain with a union that had won majority support of the unit involved. As unions increased in power, they sought more and more to check management's autonomy and to seek a voice in those decisions that affected their membership. Their right to do so was supported not only by the reversal in legislative attitude exemplified by the Wagner Act but also by the changing attitudes of the courts.

In an earlier era the courts, including the Supreme Court, had ruled that various pieces of legislation designed to protect the rights of workers were unconstitutional. These decisions were based on the grounds that such legislation interfered with management's right to hire and fire and thus endangered property without due process. *Adair vs. U.S.,* which overturned the section of the Erdman Act that had banned yellow dog contracts, and *Coppage vs. Kansas,* in which the Supreme Court following the Adair case ruled a Kansas ban on yellow dog contracts also illegal, are prime examples of the attitude of the courts during the early part of the twentieth century. Businessmen who had witnessed the ruling that the National Industrial Recovery Act (NIRA) was unconstitutional were rudely shocked when the Supreme Court upheld the Wagner Act, which required management to bargain with their workers' duly elected representatives.

As the United States moved into World War II, the issue of management autonomy lost some of its significance under the pressure of war production, but with the end of the war the question assumed new prominence. In an attempt to avoid a postwar breakdown in production, President Harry Truman in 1945 called for a National Labor-Management Conference. At this conference, a management committee dealing with "management's right to manage" listed twenty areas in which management's decisions should go unchallenged by unions. Included in this list were such questions as the location of the plant, the plant's layout, the products to be produced, and the equipment, materials, and inventories to be used. The committee also recommended that in such areas as discharges and the application of seniority management should have the initiative but the union had the right to challenge its decisions. The union representatives, however, objected, asserting that union leaders should not be restricted by any fixed boundaries in their bargaining with management.

Negotiations at the conference broke down on this and other points and the whole issue was left unresolved.

Milton Derber has suggested that three major arguments are used by those who support increased union challenges to management's rights and union attempts to share in the control of the plant.[2] First, it is argued that giving workers or their representatives some voice in how the factory is being run contributes to a more democratic industrial system. The second argument is that workers have a contribution to make to management; the plant will be more efficiently run if they help share in the decision-making process. The third major argument is that the opportunity to share in management decisions makes work more satisfying and rewarding for the worker. This last point is advanced by those who are concerned about the alienation of workers from their work and who seek a partial solution through collective bargaining.

Beginning with Neil Chamberlain's book *The Union Challenge to Management Control,* there has been a revival of interest in the question both in academic and business circles. Management officials have viewed with growing alarm the continuing expansion in the union's challenge to management's rights fostered by the increasing power of the unions and the sympathetic treatment of the unions' position by the courts. Of particular concern to management has been the 1960 decision of the Supreme Court in *United Steelworkers of America v. Warrior and Gulf Navigation Co.* in which the court ruled that subcontracting was subject to arbitration despite terms of the existing contract to the contrary. This decision, by throwing a whole area of management decision-making open to union challenge and possible revision by an arbitrator, has raised fresh fears in management's minds. Management has sought protection by attempting to include in their contracts a management rights clause, which reserves certain powers exclusively to management.

Such clauses have taken one of two forms. Some spell out in great detail the specific areas in which management retains sole jurisdiction, while others are less detailed, simply reserving decision-making to management on all items not specifically mentioned in the contract. Management officials have debated among themselves the merits of these two alternate phrasings. Supporters of the more detailed approach argue that it reduces the possibility of misunderstanding or misinterpretation and serves as an educational device by reminding union members of those areas that are properly (in management's view) in management's exclusive jurisdiction. Proponents of the more abbreviated version argue that its shorter and more general phrasing actually provides more protection because it minimizes the danger of possible omissions from a more comprehensive list and presents a less overt red flag of challenge to union leaders. This last reason also provides the rationale for those management officials who prefer to omit either type of management rights clause. These managers maintain that all powers not delegated to the union automatically accrue to management and that any effort to spell them out is likely to be viewed by the union as a challenge to its security. This group sees the inclusion of such clauses in the contract as another source of conflict between the two parties since they will be subject to constant renegotiation in future years. Nevertheless, management rights clauses appear more frequently in contracts today, largely because of a desire by management to limit arbitrators' and courts' decisions.

Management's Causes for Concern— Are They Overstated?

It is not difficult to fathom management's reasons for alarm over the alleged trend toward union intervention in management's affairs. It is only human to prefer a situation in which one is free to act as one thinks best without having to be accountable to someone else for one's actions. Today the initiative for action still lies with management, but management now finds its decisions increasingly challenged by union leaders. Furthermore, this challenge comes at a time when management already finds many of its basic actions hampered by government legislation or by concern over public opinion. The old days of laissez-faire are over and a "public be damned" attitude becomes increasingly difficult to maintain even for those who have no social conscience to bother them.

Many of these checks are healthy when viewed from the vantage point of the economy, but to the average businessman they can be very annoying. One of the most exasperating features of limitations imposed by government and public opinion is the inability of the businessman to do anything about them. When we keep this fact in mind, it is easier to understand why management has tried so hard to block the attack by the unions, against whom it feels it may have some hope of defending itself.

Some critics of management have dismissed management's fears as being unduly magnified, while others suggest that they damage management's effectiveness. Those who have taken the first position argue that management's powers were never intended to be absolute and that it would be dangerous if they were. Unions, it is argued, have no desire to "run the plant," but are simply checking those management actions that have repercussions on workers. Except for the classic case of Walter Reuther's challenge to General Motors to cut automobile prices, unions have not challenged management's decisions in the areas of pricing and marketing and finance. Even in Germany, where union officials have served on the boards of directors, executive decision-making has not been seriously limited. Instead the labor representatives on the boards of directors have, for the most part, concentrated their attention on labor issues. In Great Britain, unions have imposed more serious handicaps on management efforts to attain increased efficiency. The situation is made somewhat more complex and presents more difficulties because British unions have no formal seniority system. The unions there are thereby more conscious of the possibility that technological change could lead to possible displacement of workers.

To support their contention that management is unduly concerned over the union challenge to its control, critics offer as evidence the phenomenal record of productivity increases in the United States that began two centuries ago and continues today. If management were really being seriously hampered, critics ask, would such increases have been achieved and, more important, would they continue to occur?

Even in areas where management has suffered the greatest challenge to its authority—control of its personnel—it still retains considerable autonomy. While an employer of a union-organized plant no longer can fire on sheer whim, "just cause" dismissals have been consistently upheld by arbitrators even when challenged by the union. Instances of disloyalty or gross insubordination are always grounds for discipline and frequently cause for dismissal. Garnishment of wages can also be a basis of dismissal provided that management has given prior publicity to the fact that it is a cause for dismissal.

"The long arm of the job" does not reach into the worker's life away from the job quite as extensively as it used to. The right of the worker to get drunk on his own time is nowadays unquestioned except to the extent that it reflects upon his ability to do his job at the plant. Moonlighting or the holding of a second (usually part-time) job is a basis for dismissal if the employer has posted a notice forbidding it or if the job is in the service of a direct competitor to the employer.

Whether the proscribed activity of a worker takes place at the job or away from it, the company must be able to back up its charge with solid evidence before it can be sure that it will be upheld by an arbitrator in the face of a challenge by the union. Even strong suspicions of theft, in the absence of tangible evidence to that effect, does not furnish an employer with the right to fire a worker. In light of the damage to a man's working career in the face of dismissal for such reasons, the insistence that a man is "innocent until proven guilty" seems to be a desirable check on management autonomy.

Those who belittle management's fears also point out that management retains the initiative even in those areas where unions have challenged management's power. Management can still institute new changes; the only difference is that where these changes can affect employees, the union must first be consulted and its approval secured.

A good illustration of the issue in question is the matter of plant relocations. Management has always held that the selection of a plant's site and the decision to relocate is exclusively management's affair. The obvious union answer to this is that anything that so drastically affects the lives of the workers in the plant is properly a matter of union concern as well.

Unions have, of course, been particularly sensitive to plant relocations because of their past experiences. As Leo Wolman suggested, plant mobility was a familiar tactic in early employer opposition to unions.[3] When threatened with union organization, an employer would often simply move his plant elsewhere. Examples of the "runaway" shop can still be found today (although they are a relatively rare occurrence), but the NLRB has consistently found the action to be an unfair labor practice and has ordered either that the company return to its original location or that it employ the workers at the new plant and pay their moving costs.[4] A more recent decision involving a major textile plant has even forbidden the closing down of one plant while other company plants were kept open, when the intention of the closing was obviously to undermine the union.

Many other considerations besides a desire to eliminate the union play a prominent role in the decision by management to relocate a plant. Such factors include changing markets centers, changing sources of raw materials, and the attempts of states and local communities to attract plants by offering companies such financial lures as low taxes and low-rent factory sites. The mounting pace of technology, which has made many old plants obsolete and reduced the significance of considerations of fixed capital, has enabled management to take advantage of such opportunities when they arise.

Since many managers feel that their contract with the union has been signed under duress and that their relations with the union are based on coercion, they feel less compunction about rupturing their relationship with the union than they would about breaking a long-standing arrangement with a customer or with a supplier.

The union has been successful in challenging the legality of such moves, however, when management held no discussion with union leaders prior to the move and when no protection was provided for the employees. The most important source of such protection has been the insistence by unions that the seniority lists that applied in the old plant should provide a guiding rule for employment in the new plant also. Whenever possible, unions have also sought to protect workers who preferred to remain where they were by asking for a grant of severance pay designed to help them in their search for a new job. In order to avoid granting of severance pay, management has sometimes sought clauses in their contracts specifically freeing them from all such responsibilities. Despite the restrictions outlined above, companies are still free to move and a number of them relocate yearly.

Another argument advanced by those who question the seriousness of management's loss of control to the unions is that management never had any such "right"[5] to complete autonomy. Those who pursue this line of reasoning argue that workers always had the "right" to challenge management's decisions, but until recently did not have sufficient economic strength to do so. Management's error lies in assuming that its autonomous powers were "rights" because they previously went unchallenged.

Finally, the argument is made that management gets back *quid pro quo* for many of the "rights" it surrenders. Not only does consultation with the union assure a more peaceable and amicable relationship between the two parties with few strikes and grievances, but also the union may be able to make positive suggestions for implementing management's plans. The result may be to increase management's profit margin as plant efficiency is increased.

Management's Views

Many of the preceding arguments are dismissed by management representatives as unrealistic or discredited because they are put forth by experts who have never "had to meet a payroll." Management thus continues to express apprehension over the unions' intrusion on its rights, and advances a number of reasons in addition to the human reluctance to relinquish power. As might be expected in an economy that places a premium on operating efficiency, one of management's major arguments is that the unions' challenge represents a threat to efficiency. Two aspects of this argument deserve particular attention. First of all, any requirement that certain decisions can be acted upon only after consultation with the union and after appropriate arrangements have been made with it inevitably produces a time lag. When the union has little to lose and much to gain by stalling, a satisfactory resolution of the issues in question may require a considerable amount of time. Occasions do arise when, from manage-

ment's viewpoint, speed is of the essence. Once a move has been decided upon, the competitive situation may demand that prompt action be taken. The need to consult with the union, an irritant in and of itself, becomes even more of an annoyance when valuable time is lost.

Second, management officials also argue that union restrictive practices and work rules hamper efficiency to a greater extent than is sometimes suggested. The diesel firemen, the stand-by musicians, and the bogus typesetters are the examples of union-sponsored inefficiency most familiar to the public. Other instances that come readily to mind are the limits placed on the size of paintbrushes or the number of bricks to be laid in an hour.

Featherbedding practices have two sources of inspiration. They arise basically from the worker's concern about the general availability of work. Workers, believing that there is a limited supply of work to be performed (the "lump of work" fallacy), seek means to assure that they receive their share. Years ago, Sumner Slichter called unions a conservative force in the American economy, and his label has an obvious application to our current discussion. Secondly, workers tend to resist innovation and changes in production technique for the very simple reason that any such change may constitute a potential threat to their security. Many workers are left uncertain as to what the new technique will involve and, even in the face of management's reassurances, are inclined to be suspicious of how the proposed change will affect them.

The preceding discussion also contributes to our understanding of the basis for jurisdictional disputes. Jurisdictional disputes that arise when different types of workers lay claim to the same job, each asserting that the work in question lies within its jurisdiction, are the product not only of the union's desire to protect its strength but also of the workers' fears of losing their jobs. By a process of compromise and bargaining, jurisdictional lines may eventually be drawn. In a dynamic economy any such settlement can only be short-lived, however; changes in technology and reorganizations of plant layout inevitably raise fresh questions as to which group of workers should have jurisdiction over the new jobs. Furthermore, some of the new jobs are likely to be composed of a blend of tasks previously performed by two or more quite distinct sets of workers. The commonly proposed union solution—assigning a different worker to each different task —is unlikely to win much support from a management that originally proposed the changes as a means of increasing efficiency.

Even management officials who are sympathetic to the problems that technological change creates for workers are likely to stress the primacy of their own problems and the need to foster rapid economic change in order to stay competitive. In a fiercely competitive society, the race belongs to the swift, and the "also rans" are likely to find themselves disqualified from further competition by financial loss. The problem has been accentuated by the increasing ability of producers in other countries to compete with American companies.

The growing ability of foreign producers to meet us on our own terms has been fostered by two major changes in the international scene. First, there has been a growing relaxation of trade restrictions by the United States government. Foreign companies can usually reach our markets without the barrier of exorbitant tariffs or other devices for restricting trade. Second, foreign producers, who had

typically been inferior to their American counterparts in productive efficiency, have since World War II come closer to matching and in some cases even surpassing American standards. The reasons for this dramatic reversal stem from the destruction wreaked on European factories during the war. When these factories were rebuilt, many of them used the most modern technology and the most efficient layouts available. Except in England, foreign labor unions have either willingly cooperated with the introduction of the modern techniques or been too weak to resist them.

In stressing the danger to efficiency inherent in sharing control with the union, managements argue that they must be able to make decisions quickly and without prior consultation if the operation of their plants is to remain flexible and capable of being adjusted to rapid changes in the industrial scene. While there may be a tendency, for reasons indicated earlier, for management to overstate the problem, there seems little reason to question the sincerity of the alarm expressed. What is striking is that this cry comes from managements in countries where the record for efficiency is good; in countries where performance is less satisfactory, the outcry from management is less pronounced.

More questionable perhaps than management's concern about the unions' threat to efficiency are its philosophical objections. We have already pointed out that some management groups state that unions are improperly taking away certain rights and privileges traditionally reserved to management. Whether or not such rights were inalienable or indeed whether they were even rights or merely expressions of economic power is surely a debatable point. Many management representatives prefer to adopt the doctrine that such rights are a proper part of a system of private property. Many go further and justify their power in terms of their new positions as trustees, claiming that they have a broad responsibility not just to the stockholders, or even to the stockholders and workers combined, but to the entire economy. In order to carry out this heavy responsibility, they claim, it is necessary for power to be centralized in the hands of those few who are responsible for seeing that the firm is run for the interests of everyone. Although management usually states this argument in somewhat subtler terms than we have used, the message essentially constitutes a blatant endorsement of paternalism.

Accompanying the belief that certain powers properly rest in the hands of management is an innate suspicion of too much power in the hands of the unions. Since in any democratic society a good case can be made for the diffusion of power and the elimination of any concentrations, how can power in the hands of management be justified, while power held by unions is suspect?

Even in today's world of billion-dollar corporations, business executives like to think of themselves as living dangerously. They liken themselves to captains of ships trying to stay afloat on the rough waters of competition. Only if their power to command is absolute can they prevent the ship (the business firm) from foundering. Judged by current market practices, however, this appears to be a faulty analogy. Business leaders do have the power to pour oil on the troubled waters and the restrictive practices of unions have been all too frequently patterned after examples set by business enterprises. The very concept of the businessman as a trustee with some discretion in his choice of whom to protect belies the notion that he is completely helpless before the onslaught of market forces.

The businessman's often-expressed fear that unions are obtaining too much power has a pragmatic as well as a philosophical base. Since an increase in power for one group is likely to be achieved at the expense of another group, much of management's concern is based on the fear that union power will be used to weaken or possibly destroy management's power. While much of management's fear of union power is thus self-protective in origin, management also argues that the forces in the economy that hold its own power in check do not often apply to labor unions. Because they are largely exempt from antitrust action, unions are able to develop a number of restrictive practices that, if practiced by a company, would be in clear violation of the antitrust laws. American businessmen are philosophically wedded to the concept of a competitive market. Any actions, other than their own (for which a justification can always be found), that threaten the competitive model are classed as dangerous. Having demonstrated on occasion their willingness to be critical of their fellow businessmen, it is little wonder that they fear the growth in power of a group whose interests are generally quite different from their own.

One other aspect of the manager's fear of the union challenge to his right to manage involves the position of the foreman. Although once the foreman as a lower-level representative of management ranked supreme in his bailiwick and his orders were seldom if ever subject to challenge, he has increasingly lost stature in industrial relations. The attack on the foreman's position has come from two directions—from above, with the establishment of personnel officers, and from the workers below. Personnel officers and industrial relations experts now play an increasingly large role in companies of any significant size. These new positions were created in order to improve a plant's labor relations and to solve some of the internal disputes between lower levels of management and the workers that came into the open when the workers won union representation. These offices have been reasonably successful in achieving this goal, but the formerly unchallengeable stature of the foreman has suffered in the process. Today the foreman's decisions are subject to constant challenge from below and to review from above.

When the upper echelons of management are anxious to cooperate with the union, foremen sometimes find themselves caught in a crossfire. Their orders may be constantly challenged by the union's stewards, who appeal the foreman's every decision to upper management. At times, unions have even sought the firing of foremen charging that they were poor supervisors who mistreated or discriminated among members of their work crews. Foremen who have difficulty adjusting to the idea of working with subordinates rather than having subordinates work for them may find themselves a target for dismissal rather than instigators of the dismissal of others.

Perhaps because of the obvious inequities that existed under an arrangement where the foreman reigned supreme, management for a number of years while busy fighting off the union, took relatively little notice of the effect that the changing conditions had on the morale of foremen. For the plight of the foreman is not limited to the problems we have just outlined. Management has always thought of fore-

men as members of the management team and has been opposed to seeing them organize. "To organize foremen would be to organize management itself" has been the cry. Again, foremen find themselves caught in a squeeze between upper management and the workers below them. In an earlier day, the position of foreman often provided an opening wedge to positions in the upper ranks of management. Today, however, the educational requirements established for management in most large companies preclude the foreman from rising very far upward in management's ranks. At the same time, a foreman often discovers that the workers below him are making wages that come alarmingly close to his own. Furthermore, the line worker through his union may have secured greater protection in the form of seniority, supplementary unemployment benefits, and so on than has the foreman.

How a foreman reacts to these various pressures depends on the individual in question, the nature of the bargaining situation, and the attitudes of upper management and union leaders toward the position of foreman. In many plants good relations and apparent harmony exist between the upper strata of the union and the management and a breakdown in relationships at lower levels. Such breakdowns are sometimes attributed to the insincerity of one or both parties or to a breakdown in communications between upper and lower levels of management. Another explanation is that the difficulty sometimes arises because the foreman is unable to adjust to the changed situation and resists the new policy of collaboration. Although the impact of the union challenge to the prerogatives of foremen has not figured prominently in the literature on management rights, top-level management has become increasingly aware of the problem and has taken steps to restore foremen (through various forms of pay and security arrangements) to a position of greater status. Unions also are not unaware of the difficult position in which many foremen find themselves today. The UAW steward manual, for example, points out:

> The foreman is in a difficult middle, between the production workers and top management. He cannot decide company policy; orders come down to him from higher management, and whether he agrees with them or not, his job is to see that they are carried out.

How Management Rights Are Lost

In view of the firm management opposition we indicated in the preceding sections, it is reasonable to inquire how and why management permitted any loss of autonomy at all. The loss of managerial autonomy basically had three general causes: (1) forces have emerged over which management has had little or no control; (2) certain decisions or actions have had far wider repercussions than were originally thought to be possible; and (3) strangely enough, some managerial powers have simply atrophied because management failed to exercise them.

Perhaps the most obvious example of a largely uncontrollable power undermining management prerogatives is the union itself. Unions feel it necessary to "police" an expanding class of managerial decisions in order to render meaningful protection to their members. We began this chapter by observing that, from the first moment they enter into collective bargaining with an employer, unions are challeng-

ing his previous "right" to hire, fire, and pay his employees whatever the market will bear. Accepting this as an important and essential first step, unions have felt the need to go further and monitor other management decisions as well. The National Labor Relations Board has generally taken a broad view when passing upon the questions of what constitutes a refusal to bargain and what areas are an appropriate subject for bargaining.

Although unions initiated the challenge, they have been supported in their efforts not only by the NLRB and other executive bureaus, but also in more recent years by important court decisions. We discussed in some detail earlier the support given the unions by the NLRB and the courts in the matter of plant relocation. The unions have similarly been upheld in their right to participate in decisions involving subcontracting, in which a plant assigns work to other companies or to subsidiary plants. As in the case of plant relocations, subcontracting may be undertaken by management either as a deliberate means of undermining the power of the union or for perfectly legitimate reasons. In either case a major goal is to cut costs by improving operating efficiency. For example, aspects of a job assignment may call for the use of personnel or equipment not regularly employed in the plant. To hire people and purchase equipment that would see little or no subsequent service would be wasteful. It is far more economical and efficient to farm out the assignment to a company that already has the necessary equipment and personnel. Needless to say, a decision to subcontract is subject to the strongest union challenge when the company has previously done the work itself or when the subcontracting firm performs the work at the first plant's premises, constantly reminding workers of its presence. Tension will also develop when the company doing the subcontracting work is organized by a union different from the one in the home plant.

As the specifications of many production contracts in an increasingly complex technological world have grown more and more complicated, the need to have part of the work done elsewhere has increased. Other factors have also speeded the increase in the volume of subcontracting. In some instances, the growing complexity of the work has fostered jurisdictional disputes that management has sought to escape by subcontracting. The growing proportion of production contracts that are defense contracts has also put a premium on speed in meeting the deadline specified in the contract. As things now stand, although a union is invariably upheld in its right to prior consultation, the right of management to subcontract given prior consultation with the union has usually also been upheld.

As a result, the number of cases involving the issue of subcontracting has risen sharply. A study by G. Allan Dash showed that while during one twelve-year period (1947–1959) only sixty-four such cases were reported, a more recent three-year period (1960–1962) provided reports of fifty some cases.[6] The upsurge in the number of subcontracting cases subjected to arbitration, thereby increasing the potential for subsequent reversal of management decisions by a third party, results not only from the amount of subcontracting currently taking place but also from a historic Supreme Court decision. In the case of *United Steelworkers of America v. Warrior and Gulf Navigation,* the Supreme Court ruled in 1960 that subcontracting was subject to arbitration despite provisions in the then-existing contract to the contrary. In so ruling, the Supreme Court reversed the contrary holdings of the lower courts. The Supreme Court's ruling held that such items as arbitration were so fundamental a part of the entire bargaining process that the union had the right to press for a resolution of the grievance by arbitration. In upholding the arbitrator's decision, the Supreme Court held that the decision was within the province of the arbitrator and should not therefore be challenged by the courts. A blanket endorsement of the expertise of the arbitrator was thus assured.

Although the decision was solely concerned with the issues of subcontracting, the manner in which it was promulgated suggested to an alarmed management that the decision might be applied to a wide range of future decisions under arbitration in which final authority would also be removed from management's hands and left to the judgment of an outside party. Some arbitrators have also been dismayed at the wide latitude they have been granted and have urged a policy of caution and restraint upon both unions and managements. It is still too early to judge how sweeping the impact of this decision will be, but past experience with similar situations suggests that things are rarely as revolutionary as they may at first appear.

The second reason for loss of management powers involves decisions that are seemingly minor and harmless at the time when they are made but sometimes prove to have wide ramifications at some future date. For example, many contracts include a provision giving the workers, whenever possible, a choice as to the dates of their paid vacations. Companies, having once made this concession, find it impossible to institute a uniform vacation period during which the entire plant shuts down. Another apparently innocent decision that may have future repercussions is the decision to solve some thorny question through the use of a study committee. When management and the union have been unable to reach agreement on a particular question, immediate settlement is often deferred while a joint committee studies the problem. In its anxiety to reach some sort of settlement, management fails to realize that the appointment of a study committee at least partially binds management to act upon any recommendations the study committee may make. Similarly, a management that agrees to permit either partial or total union participation in formulating plant rules may later find it virtually impossible to change rules that have proved to be inoperative.

The third reason for the loss of management authority is the failure of management to exercise its power. Arbitrators have sometimes ruled improper sudden efforts to tighten discipline or to enforce rules that had not been implemented for a long time. The arbitrator's line of reasoning has been that while the rule itself was perfectly proper and well within management's exclusive jurisdiction to decide, failure to enforce it for a period of time had misled workers into believing that the rule only existed on paper. It has been ruled that a sudden effort at enforcement, because it may change the nature of the job, is illegal.

Similarly, managements have found it necessary to make more rapid decisions as to the suitability of a new worker for continued employment. No longer can management be certain that it will be upheld in its right to discharge a worker on grounds of inability to perform satisfactory work when a year or more has gone by since he was first employed. In fact, the thrust of the body of arbitrators' decisions makes it a distinct likelihood that the union will be able to challenge any such decision successfully.

The Union Position

Once it has forfeited or been compelled to relinquish some of its authority, what can management do to win back its lost power? In order to be able to answer this question, we must first look at the union's position in a bit more detail. Unions tend to reject the thesis that there is any specific set of boundaries beyond which they should not trespass in their bargaining with employers. Since from the very beginning of collective bargaining unions have heard complaints that their demands were improper, they have grown hardened to the accusation that their activities encroach upon the legitimate powers of management. Both in this country and abroad union leaders can remember a day when the proposed shortening of the fourteen-hour day was attacked on the grounds that the proper length of the working day was a management decision alone.

Basically, unions subscribe to the notion that the scope of bargaining is also subject to the bargaining process and that particular issues must be decided upon a case by case approach. Unions argue that many of the cases cited by management to the public as horrifying examples of management's inability to control its own plant and win improvements in efficiency are misleading. In many cases, union leaders point out, the alleged restrictive practice began as a concession voluntarily tendered by management in order to secure some other concessions that it was anxious to win. A foreman may agree to permit workers to quit early or to have a longer noon hour in order to get the workers' consent to periods when they will be forced to work at top speed. It is not surprising that the union regards such practices as payments for return favors and feels that management is trying to have its cake and eat it too when it seeks the removal of various work rules.

The unwillingness of unions to define set parameters for managerial authority should not be interpreted to mean that unions are seriously considering taking over management's functions on a mass scale. Most union leaders in this country are well aware that the process of running a business is complicated and tricky and they have no desire to assume such a burden. The experience of unions in countries like Great Britain has discouraged many American unionists who had aspirations in that direction. British unions have found that it is far easier to play the role of critic than to share responsibility for decisions that prove to be unpopular with the rank and file. Particularly during the period in the 1940s and again in the 1960s when the Labour Party was in power, British union leaders found it difficult to convince workers of the desirability of displaying restraint in their wage demands in order to assist the Labour Party in its efforts to correct the balance of payments.

Union leaders in this country argue that most key managerial decisions involving financial policies, plant organization, work assignments, and the content of jobs are usually left to management. In personnel matters (and occasionally with respect to the topics on the above list), unions have challenged management decisions. In virtually almost every case, however, the initiative for action remains in the hands of management. Union officials also point out that arbitrators have not always upheld the union's challenge to management action. Where a union

has challenged management's attempts to increase the amount of work assigned to each worker, arguing that such assignments would lead to reductions in efficiency, arbitrators have upheld the freedom of management to make decisions, even wrong ones. They further ruled that, even if the union should prove to be right, there still would be no basis for overruling management.

Unions also argue quite properly that practices designed to restrict output are widespread among unorganized workers as well as unionists. Various studies by observer-participant teams suggest that workers seem to have a concept of their own as to what constitutes a "fair day's work" and refuse to extend themselves beyond this point.[7] Fears of endangering the incentive system or displacing some workers from their jobs because of the belief that there is only so much work to be done also play a role. At times the efforts on the part of workers to frustrate the management's search for greater efficiency bear all the earmarks of a game. While union efforts to restrict output are inevitably more organized in nature and thus more effective, it would be a mistake to think that restrictive practices are solely a product of union machinations.

Management even gains some benefit from the fact that union restrictive practices are more formally organized; for example, the employer can deal with a known quantity (the union) when he seeks relief from such impediments.

Ways Management Can Protect Itself

Management's position is by no means hopeless and numerous proposals have been advanced to help management protect its "rights." Management's problem is of a twofold nature. First, it must avoid any further surrender of authority. To this end, management can seek a number of changes in the collective bargaining agreement and the manner in which it is enforced. For example, management can request a "no strike" provision in the contract, which ensures that any grievances that may arise while the contract is in force will be solved in a peaceful fashion. Reversing a 1962 decision the Supreme Court held in 1970 that federal courts could enforce no strike clauses. While the union will still have the right to present grievances in response to management's actions, it will not be able to threaten management with a shutdown each time a company policy is questioned. In order to avoid further erosion of its authority, the management should also avoid all mutual consent clauses or prior consultation clauses since they limit management's power to initiate action. The union's right to challenge the action need not be jeopardized by removing its right to prior consultation. Note here the distinction between prior notification and prior consultation. Arbitration awards have frequently reversed management decisions on the grounds that the union was not given advance notice of the intended action; prior consultation was not required.

If a union uses a consent clause as a means of hamstringing management by repeatedly withholding consent, the handicap to management is too obvious to require elaboration. Where the union is less obdurate, however, it too may have cause to regret the existence of a consent decree. Suppose, for example, that a management must "consult" with a union before taking disciplinary action. Would a union ever wish to put itself in a position of approving of such an action?

Management can also do much to protect itself by making sure that the foremen do not unintentionally give away any of management's rights. Management can do this by insisting that foremen abide by the strict rules of the contract and give management the benefit of the doubt in debatable cases. Not infrequently a foreman will be asked to excuse an unjustified (by terms of the contract) absence or lateness or some similar minor infraction on the part of the worker. Should the foreman do so, however, his decision may serve as a precedent for subsequent union grievances when similar situations later arise elsewhere in the plant.

Finally, management can often save itself much future grief by being sure that the terms of the contract are clear at the time of negotiation. There is an understandable tendency on both sides to gloss over seemingly minor issues at the time when the major issues that have been delaying a settlement are finally resolved. Fuzzily worded clauses, however, may provide a union with an unexpected opening wedge for challenging management's actions at some later date. While a management is wise to seek a contract that is as clearly worded as possible, a certain degree of discretion is needed to avoid going to the other extreme and spelling out every possibility in painful detail.

The second part of management's problem is how to win back its freedom to make needed changes once it has lost it. How is management to go about regaining its lost authority? As an example of what management cannot and should not do in this direction, we can cite the action of the steel companies during the 1959 steel strike. Most observers felt the union had only lukewarm support from the workers for its demand for higher wages. However, when management suddenly interjected the issue of work rules as a condition for settlement, the union capitalized on this issue to stiffen the resolve of the membership. After a long-drawn-out strike, the union won sizable increases in wages and management was forced to abandon its proposed revision of the work rules.

Not all efforts at freeing management's hands to make sweeping changes and introduce new techniques have been as unsuccessful. For example, striking success was achieved in the West Coast longshore industry by a contract negotiated in 1960. Management was able to remove a number of irksome limitations on the size of the work crews, the appropriate weight for a sling, and the need to have ships' cargoes unloaded onto the dock rather than directly loaded on the appropriate means of transportation. In order to gain these advantages, employers were forced to make sizable concessions in the form of increased wages and expanded pension plans with provisions for early retirement at age sixty-two. When work shrinkages develop, there is also provision for compulsory early retirement at higher rates of retirement pay.[8] Workers were classified into three separate groups with a guaranteed weekly wage for those classified as fully registered. Those designated as B men and those classified as casuals receive lower proportions of the available work. What, in effect, management did in this case was buy back some of the power that for one reason or another it had previously surrendered.

In the bituminous coal industry management also offered to share the gains from increased productivity occasioned by the introduction of new technology with the workers in the form of higher wages and increased fringe benefits. Management thus gained a much freer hand in operating the mines. Critics have even charged that the Mine Workers gave the mine operators too much discretion in laying off workers and that the resulting shrinkage in employment for miners more than offset the gains won for those still employed.

Other illustrations of instances where management has succeeded in securing greater freedom of action at the price of higher wages and other concessions to those displaced can be found in the agreements made by Kaiser Steel and the Armour meat-packing company. From the workers' viewpoint, however, neither of these has been a complete success. The Kaiser contract, which set up an elaborate profit-sharing arrangement, has led workers to protest that they are not sharing fully in the gains when profits lag. The Armour contract established a $500,000 automation fund to aid workers who had been laid off, but the company has not succeeded in placing discharged workers in new positions. A similar program established by the Xerox Corporation for the retraining of displaced workers was more successful because of the tremendous expansion experienced by Xerox in the 1950s and 1960s.

Where the resulting displacement of workers is likely to be great and where management feels it cannot afford to offer much in recompense, the efforts by management to secure union cooperation are likely to meet with scant success. In general, arbitrators have been extremely reluctant to approve actions undertaken by management solely in order to reduce costs if no protection was given to the job rights of workers as well. Arbitrators have taken this attitude when the company in question was in serious financial difficulties.

On the other hand, the union's resistance to change is likely to be strongest in the case of large companies. Many small companies with serious financial problems have found the union willing and anxious to cooperate in helping them to continue operations. In some instances, such as the clothing industry, the unions have been a source of borrowed capital. Under such circumstances, the issue of management prerogatives has been subordinated to the pressing financial need and management has accepted consultation with union leaders on all proposed changes. Once again, the company has paid a price for securing union cooperation—the termination of unilateral decision making. We should emphasize, however, that such instances are comparatively few in number. Most management groups have been too fearful of the consequent loss of their prerogatives to be willing to participate in such arrangements except as a last resort.

Furthermore, when large corporations have been involved, unions have often been suspicious of pleas of financial stress and they have been reluctant to make revisions in work rules. The plight of the American railroads is an interesting case in point. The unions have almost consistently refused to acknowledge that any but a very few of the railroads are in serious financial difficulty. Even when they do admit the seriousness of the railroad's plight, they contend that the problem is of management's own making. Even before the Presidential fact finding board and the subsequent partial resolution of the dispute, however, railroad management, in the face of fierce opposition from the unions, had succeeded in reducing the number on its payrolls by several thousand. The moral is obvious—a tenacious management that persists in its efforts to undertake certain actions can often succeed even in the face of stout opposition from the union.

The Problem in Other Countries

The standard assurance often given by foreign visitors to American managers is "You don't know how lucky you are. Think of your problems if you had to face the interfering union leaders in other countries." Unions in other countries, particularly in Europe, have traditionally had a reputation for seeking to challenge management's authority. The most obvious explanation for these repeated challenges lies in the strong socialist background of many of these unions, which is expressed by their overt hostility to capitalism and private ownership. Catholic social doctrines that preach worker representation by legislation as a God-given right and the early traditions stemming from the guilds have also contributed to the unions' tendency to challenge management.

Although foreign labor unions are often charged with a greater tendency to challenge management's autonomy, the evidence suggests that on the contrary the actual challenge is often minimal. Furthermore, the threat generally comes from works councils rather than from the labor unions. Since in the late forties and early fifties codetermination was frequently cited by management as the epitome of union encroachment upon management rights, we will begin with a discussion of this phenomenon as it developed in West Germany.

Codetermination in West Germany

Codetermination was already in practice in the German steel industry when it was granted legislative approval in 1951 and extended to coal. In 1952, additional legislation restricted the practice to those areas of coal and iron mining and steel manufacture where it was already in existence.

Under codetermination, the supervisory board of directors of a plant consists of five representatives elected by the union, five elected by the stockholders, and an eleventh director who is supposedly neutral but is actually selected by the stockholders. In addition, there is a three-man manager board (one manager each for production, business, and labor), and of these three, the labor manager is selected by the unions. Although codetermination thus apparently represents a formidable union intrusion into management territory, the actual impact on management authority has been relatively slight. The eleven-man supervisory board rarely splits along management-labor lines; instead, it usually submits unanimous decisions. The committees of the supervisory board are usually constituted so that the labor representatives have a majority on those committees dealing with labor issues, while management controls the other functions. Much the same division of work applies to the actual task of managing. The labor manager rarely participates in the decisions of the other two managers, but he is generally given a free hand in his own area. The plant is essentially run by these managers since the supervisory board rarely if ever takes an active role in management.

On the whole, codetermination has proved to be less of a challenge to management than originally feared. Trade secrets have not become common knowledge and decisions have usually been unanimous (of course, the extent to which both sides have had to compromise to achieve this unanimity is unknown). However, management in the United States continues to oppose the admission of any outsiders to the board and to resist proposals for cumulative voting. It seems safe to assert that any repetition of the suggestion by Philip Murray

(past president of the CIO) that the CIO should seek codetermination would still make American management's blood run cold.

Works Councils in France and Elsewhere

Most students of West Germany's industrial relations agree that one by-product of codetermination is the growth in Works Councils, organizations established to give workers a voice in the daily operations of plants. Works councils exist in many European countries besides Germany, and in some countries like France and Italy they are sponsored by the government. These works councils are quite distinct from the labor unions, which bargain on an industry-wide basis and which have little or no contact with workers in local plants. Partly because of government sponsorship, works councils experienced widespread growth when they were first organized. In the 1950s 30 percent of Holland's industry had works councils and the comparable figure in France was 75 percent. After the first flush of success, however, many of the councils became inactive and today play only a minor role. Arthur Ross estimates, for example, that not more than a third of the French plants have organized committees and that even where they exist, the committees have little impact on management.[9]

In cases where the councils have successfully challenged management's control, it is more appropriate to call it a labor rather than a union challenge, although the unions have on the whole welcomed works councils as a means of reaching workers at the plant level. The relative lack of success of works councils does not necessarily mean that European workers do not endorse them in principle or do not want a greater voice in management affairs. It may very well be that workers in those countries with works councils have simply grown discouraged because the councils can boast of only relatively small accomplishments.

Just as American managers have managed to stave off many threats to their autonomy, so European managers have succeeded in perverting works councils to serve their own ends. By refusing to grant the councils information or by providing the information too late for the councils to take effective action, European management has succeeded in weakening them substantially.

Although the works councils have become moribund in much of the private sector in France, in the nationalized French industries labor's role in management is pronounced, with the trade unions sitting on the board of directors much as they do in West Germany.

Great Britain

Great Britain represents an interesting and complex blend. There is a considerable amount of interference by unions in management affairs in some areas and a complete lack of any challenge in others. The idea of union participation dates back to the nineteenth century and stems from the socialistic views of British labor. The nationalization laws passed after World War II provided that the nationalized industries be run by experts. The Soviet experience after 1918 had convinced British labor leaders that management was not in fact a simple process that anyone could perform. As a gesture toward the idea of worker participation in management, the nationalization laws provided opportunities for consultation. Similar arrangements were also instituted in the private sector. The opportunities for

consultation have been of small importance, however, and the Trades Union Congress (TUC) has continued to maintain that a "union cannot sit on both sides of the bargaining table." In the summer of 1968 headlines indicated fresh interest in labor participation in the management of the steel industry, but it is too early to predict how meaningful this will be.

On the surface British unions also participate very little in personnel policy and they have publicly disclaimed any desire to interfere with management's right to discipline workers except when there was clear evidence of discrimination because of union membership. Nevertheless, a sizable proportion of British strikes are prompted by dismissal issues, and one observer has declared that the American manager has far more freedom to dismiss a worker than has his British counterpart.[10]

As stated earlier, England is something of a special case. In many respects, it represents to many American managers a hideous example of what can happen when unions have too great a voice in management's handling of personnel. In addition to being threatened with possible nationalization whenever the Labour party is in power, British management has been affected by the drive by British workers for greater security in two other ways. First, the costs of the welfare state have in part fallen on the shoulders of business leaders. Second, British unions have been particularly resistant to shop changes that entail any loss of jobs. The British population, even after allowing for differences between methods of computing the volume of unemployment, have been far more sensitive than Americans to the threat of unemployment. Witness the riot before the houses of Parliament in the spring of 1963, a demonstration that protested unemployment at a time when the British unemployment rate, even after adjustment, was considerably below our own. The sentiments of the Luddites in the early nineteenth century have not been completely dispelled in Britain.[11] Further evidence of this concern are the "productivity agreements"—national agreements made by British unions whereby arrangements are made on an industrywide basis to link productivity gains and wage gains. At the same time room is left for featherbedding practices where they are deemed essential to protect workers from unemployment.

Israel

Although Israeli labor unions have played a major role in their country's economy from the time modern industrialization began after World War II, even they do not dramatically affect management. Except for the formality of joint production councils in all plants employing more than fifty workers, the extent of worker participation is roughly equivalent to that in the United States. Milton Derber found more worker participation in those plants owned by the Histadrut, the Israeli labor federation, but even there management was left surprisingly free.[12]

Mexico

In marked contrast to most of the other countries in this study, Mexican management has been able to retain its rights and is still often free to act in a highly autocratic and paternalistic fashion. In many Latin American countries, management has been even more successful in this regard than in Mexico. Paternalism and authoritarianism are the key words in any description of Latin American managers whether they be native or foreign born.

Government laws rather than union interference are responsible for any limits on management's freedom of action. Grievance procedures and arbitration, major sources of management concern in the United States, are virtually unknown in other countries. Unions elsewhere tend to rely on direct action (e.g., the threat of strike) or shift the responsibility to works councils. This is not always the case, however.

Summary and Conclusions

We have suggested that American employers have little more latitude in their actions than do their counterparts elsewhere in the world. While American unions have been more willing to accept the principle that technological change should serve as a fulcrum toward economic progress than have unions in some other countries, and although collective bargaining has been left much more in the hands of unions and management with less governmental controls in this country than abroad, American unions have more frequently challenged management's rights than have unions elsewhere. The danger to managerial authority implied by recent arbitration decisions in the United States, however, is far more real in countries that have a system of compulsory arbitration.

In comparison to the United States, other countries' grievance procedures and arbitration have attained only a relatively low level of development, and this fact represents a major difference between the challenge of unions to management here and elsewhere.

Here and in most other countries many of the major areas of decision making (for example, financial policy, choice of product, and methods of production) are still largely in the hands of management. In the field of personnel, management still retains the power to take the initiative, but it must now face the possibility that the union may challenge its decisions. The outburst of experimentation with union participation that followed World War II has for the moment died away. If one believes, as the authors do, that workers have a property right in the possession of their jobs, the role of the union in challenging management when it endangers these job rights seems both inevitable and desirable. The experience in Russian factories immediately after the revolution in 1918 suggests that someone must serve as leader, if complete chaos is to be prevented. The right of leadership in a democratic society, however, should not involve the right to take actions that may jeopardize the welfare of hundreds or even thousands of others.

Although the outburst of excitement about union participation in management affairs appears to have died down somewhat at the moment, three factors augur a continuation of the trend toward more and more union challenges both in the developing countries and those that are at present more fully industrialized. The first is the greater support for democratic principles in the field of industrial relations. The second factor is the growing educational standards of workers; this facilitates their intelligent participation in management decisions. The third is the world-wide trend toward increased use of economic planning in order to achieve a more rapid and steadier pace of economic growth. Where there are at least some elements of economic planning, the participation of labor in managerial decisions comes much more easily.

The concept that management has certain rights that are absolutely sac-rosanct is already suspect. To forestall further challenges to its authority, management, at the minimum, will have to prove that such challenges result in a serious loss in efficiency. Until it offers sufficient proof (and it has not yet done so), it cannot expect immunity from union challenges.

NOTES

1. Selig Perlman, *A Theory of the Labor Movement* (New York: Macmillan, 1928). Perlman argued that much of the character and action of unions could be explained on this basis.
2. Milton Derber, "Labor Participation in Management: Some Impressions of Experiences in the Metal Working Industries of Britain, Israel and the United States," Industrial Relations Research Association, *Proceedings of the 17th Meeting,* 1964, pp. 261–269.
3. Leo Wolman, *Ebb and Flow in Trade Unionism* (New York: National Bureau of Economic Research, 1936), 86–87.
4. See Hopwood Retinning Co. Inc. case (No. C–237) in which NLRB ordered reopening of former plant; decided January 15, 1938. See also J. Klotz & Company case (No. C–829), decided July 20, 1939. The company was ordered to pay transportation of workers to new plant or pay for workers' weekly visits to relatives living in city where old plant was located (plant had moved from New York City to Pawling). See also Schieber Millinery Co. case (No. C–1436), decided August 22, 1940. The company was ordered either to bring back plant or pay moving expenses of workers.
5. Eli Ginzberg, Ivar Berg, John L. Herma, and James K. Anderson, *Democratic Values and the Rights of Management* (New York: Columbia University Press, 1963).
6. Study by Dash, cited in Marcia L. Greenbaum, "The Arbitration of Subcontracting Disputes: An Addendum," *Industrial and Labor Relations Review* (January 1963), p. 221.
7. See, for example, Donald Roy, "Quota Restriction and Goldbricking in a Machine Shop," *The American Journal of Sociology,* 57 (March 1952), 427–442; and Donald Roy,

"Efficiency and 'The Fix'; Informal Inter-group Relations in a Piecework Machine Shop," *American Journal of Sociology,* 60 (November 1954), 254–266.

8. See Chapter 15, pp. 298–300.

9. Arthur M. Ross, "Prosperity and Labor Relations in Western Europe: Italy and France," *Industrial and Labor Relations Review* (October 1962), p. 79.

10. Frederic Meyers, "Job Protections in France and Britain," Proceedings of the Spring Meeting of the Industrial Relations Research Association in *Labor Law Journal* (July 1962), 566–575.

11. The Luddites were groups of English workmen who, following the example of Ned Ludd, destroyed some of the machinery to prevent the spread of technology. The Luddites blamed the existence of low wages and unemployment on these machines.

12. Milton Derber, "Worker Participation In Israeli Management," *Industrial Relations* (October 1963), p. 57.

13
Grievance Procedure and Grievance Arbitration

. . . as a stabilizing and humanizing force in our industrial society, the grievance machinery has made a most significant contribution.　　　—John H. Coleman
The handling of workers' grievances on the job is perhaps the single most important function of modern unionism.

—Jack Barbash

☐ DESPITE the eulogies for grievance procedure cited above, a fully developed system of grievance procedure is of comparatively recent vintage in the United States and grievance procedures exist in only a rudimentary stage in most other countries. Before we explore the reasons that explain why grievance procedure developed so slowly both here and abroad, we will first pause to define some terms.

Thus far in this book our discussion of collective bargaining has centered almost exclusively on the process of agreeing on the terms of a new contract. If all contracts were written in heaven and all the participants acted like angels thereafter, there would be no further need for bargaining until the time for the negotiation of a new contract arrived. Since both possibilities are likely to remain remote, some machinery is needed to resolve issues not clearly (to the satisfaction of both parties) covered by the contract.

Leaving a more detailed analysis of grievances and their causes until a bit later in this chapter, we need only note at this point that in our terms, a griev-

ance exists when either party to the contract (including the workers represented by the union) feels that he is being treated unfairly. In more strict legal terms only those dissatisfactions involving a breach of contract can be properly defined as grievances.[1] Note that our definition, in contrast, is a very broad one. It includes the possibility that management as well as workers may wish to present grievances and that the grievance may or may not have its source in the contract.

It is important to note at this point the fundamental distinction between rewriting a contract and adjusting grievances arising under an existing contract. The negotiation of a new contract is basically a legislative matter. By contrast, grievance procedure is a judicial or administrative matter and normally deals with the interpretation of the current contract, rather than with attempts to write a new one to replace it. Inevitably the union (and sometimes management) seeks to stretch the contract so that it will better reflect its own views, but such efforts still involve *broadening* rather than *rewriting* the current contract.

Because it is impossible to foresee all contingencies at the time when a contract is drafted and because some ambiguities of language are almost inevitable, some adjustment machinery is helpful. The problem of interpreting the contract and settling disputes that may arise during its life is usually handled in the United States today by the insertion in the contract of a clause providing for the handling of grievances. Such clauses are a basic part of satisfactory collective bargaining and every bit as important as the drafting of the original contract. The best contract in the world will prove unsatisfactory if it is improperly administered.

Reasons for Slowness of Adoption in the United States

If grievance procedure is so important, why has it had relatively slow acceptance both here and abroad? The history of collective bargaining (see Chapter 1) supplies us with part of the answer. In earlier times, employers wanted as little to do with unions as possible and usually consented to bargain with them only when compelled to do so. Management viewed the bargaining process as basically distasteful, a task to be completed as rapidly as possible with a minimum of acknowledgment of the union's existence. Not only was the concept of continuous collective bargaining (which is implicit in the grievance process) likely to accord too much recognition to the union for management's tastes, but it also constituted a threat to the prerogatives of management. In the early days, any worker who challenged the foreman's authority in any way was regarded as being guilty of the grossest form of disloyalty. Grievances thus represented a direct challenge to the bosses' "right" to command.

When management refused to have anything more to do with unions than was absolutely necessary, union leaders responded by failing to distinguish between those situations calling for the negotiation of a new contract and those requiring adjustments within the terms of the existing one. As a result minor grievances were often nursed under cover for some time, with the resentments involved frequently erupting into a strike or a work slowdown.

Because of the obvious costs involved to both parties from such breakdowns, grievance procedure began to appear more and more frequently toward the end of the nineteenth century and in the years preceding World War I. The grievance settlement machinery that proved so successful in both the anthracite coal and the clothing industries set the model for other industries to copy.

Gradually, both labor and management came to recognize the distinction between a dispute arising over the interpretation of some particular aspect of the contract and the negotiation of a brand new contract. Management, however, for the reasons we have just mentioned, continued to drag its feet. Even after the passage of the Wagner Act (1935), which required an employer to recognize any union organizing a majority of his workers, managers refused to accept fully the principle of grievance procedure.

The part of grievance procedure that many employers have found least palatable is the provision for arbitration. Grievance arbitration involves the voluntary agreement by the two primary parties to submit to a third party whose decision is binding any issues involving the interpretation and enforcement of the contract that they cannot settle between themselves. In the past the decisions of the arbitrator were sometimes subjected to further testing by the courts, but such challenges are extremely rare today. A typical clause calling for arbitration might read: "It is agreed that should any dispute arise in any plant of a member of the association that such dispute shall be adjusted with the employer without loss of time. If this is impossible the dispute shall then be referred to the joint arbitration board . . ."[2]

Managers who object to such clauses claim that to surrender the right to final decision to a third party clearly violates property rights. "What right does an outsider have to make decisions with which we have to live and for which we have to pay?" is the query raised by many employers.

The pressure for uninterrupted production occasioned by World War II led the War Labor Board to insist that employers adopt arbitration as a solution to their grievance difficulties whenever it proved necessary. Although protests against the requirement of arbitration of unsettled grievances are still heard periodically today, the battle has been virtually won. Over 90 percent of all contracts call for arbitration as a final step in the grievance machinery.

Most students of industrial relations would agree that movement in this direction was inevitable and desirable even in the absence of war-time production needs. If no arrangements for arbitration exist, the only alternative may be unresolved disputes that continue to fester and promote hard feelings on both sides. Of course, arbitration should be resorted to only sparingly. A grievance procedure is working at its best when the vast majority of the cases are resolved by agreement between the two parties directly concerned. Inevitably, however, the two parties are sometimes unable to resolve an issue by themselves and in such situations the aid of an outside party becomes essential. Management has continued to try to protect itself from undue outside interference by stipulating certain areas that are to remain exclusively within management's domain and thus are not subject to grievance procedure or to bar decisions in these areas from challenge by arbitration.

Types of Grievances

As we indicated earlier, management has sometimes used grievance procedure to register its complaints against either the union or certain workers. Management-initiated procedures, however, represent only a fraction of the thousands of grievances processed each year. By the nature of the process, it is management that executes or puts into operation the various clauses in the contract. Management is therefore necessarily the target, rather than the originator, of most of the grievances.

Given the thousands of factories in operation in this country and the millions of workers employed in them, it is not surprising that an almost endless variety of grievances are filed nearly every working day. However, since many grievances resemble each other rather closely even though the details may vary from case to case, our discussion will focus on certain large categories and ignore the minor differences that can both fascinate and exasperate the student of grievance procedure.

One general classification distinguishes those grievances that arise out of the contract itself from those that involve complaints not directly germane to the contract. Management representatives that employ a strictly legal approach to grievance procedure are inclined to dismiss the latter as improper subjects for joint management-union adjustment. Grievances that arise out of the day-to-day frictions that are an inevitable product of group relations are deemed by these members of management to be an improper subject for negotiation.

The dividing line between those grievances that are properly subject to bargaining and those that are not is extremely elusive. In contrast to those who would draw an arbitrary line between those grievances that are applicable to the contract and thus negotiable and those that are disqualified, other students of grievances maintain that all grievances are a manifestation of unrest and discontent and should be subject to joint consideration.

It seems apparent that both positions are too extreme. Obviously, a contract would settle nothing if any and all possible grievances were to be entertained regardless of whether they had any bearing on the existing contract. Nevertheless, very real grievances that involve no interpretation of the contract *do* arise. To dismiss all such grievances summarily is to invite a different but no less real brand of chaos. Increasingly, therefore, management has come to recognize the propriety of admitting both types of grievances to formal grievance procedure. For those grievances that fall outside the boundaries of the contract, however, management has frequently insisted that there be no recourse to arbitration. Thus, unless the grievance can be settled by mutual consent, the final decision rests with management. In the absence of a specific no strike clause, however, the union in turn is free to press the issue by calling for a work stoppage if it feels that the issue is of sufficient importance.

The refusal of a management to permit such grievances to go to arbitration does not represent as much of a stumbling block as might be expected. In the case of such issues, frequently all workers want is an opportunity to be heard. Once they have had a chance to register their complaint and have gained an audience, the decision, no matter which way it goes, becomes relatively unimportant.

The grievances we have been discussing thus far are those that lie outside the purview of the contract either because the issue is one that would never be subject to contractual agreement or one (particularly in the case of new contracts) that simply had not been considered at the time the contract was negotiated. In this way, grievances provide ammunition for future sessions when a new contract is being considered.

The bulk of grievances in a plant that has been unionized for some time involve interpretations and applications of the existing contract. Questions of proper pay (particularly overtime), promotion, and the application of seniority to questions of layoffs and recalls, transfers, vacations and holidays are all subject to constant challenge. The issue that is most frequently the subject for grievance procedure, however, is discipline. Was disciplinary action actually called for, and, if so, did "the punishment fit the crime?" A variety of actions that are judged as evidence of misconduct by management may be seen in a different light by the union. Alternately, the union may feel they should be excused because of extenuating circumstances. The term "misconduct" is broad enough to cover acts ranging from the use of foul and abusive language to a foreman or other workers to engaging in fights with superiors or fellow workers. Gambling, loafing on the job, participating in wildcat strikes, or engaging in unauthorized union business on company time are all likely to expose the worker to disciplinary action.

In order to avoid pleas of ignorance, management often provides the newly hired worker with a printed code stating the conduct expected of workers while they are on the premises. Seldom are the penalties for violating the code prescribed in such documents, however, and the question of just punishment may still arise.

In an earlier day the power of the foreman to dictate any kind of discipline he thought proper, including discharge, was rarely challenged. Today, a foreman seldom does more than initiate a discipline, and even minor penalties are often challenged by the union and appealed to higher levels of management.

While management officials sometimes complain that their control over the plant's labor force has been severely hampered by union challenges to disciplinary action, arbitrators rarely uphold a challenge to a disciplinary case without good and sufficient reason.[3] The added security protection from arbitrary treatment that grievance procedure affords the workers more than offsets any problems that it creates for management. This is especially true today. The increasing scale of operations means that in many industries three or four firms dominate the industry and account for 75 percent or more of the employment in that industry, thus reducing alternative job opportunities in these industries. Furthermore, the loss of one's job today in a great many cases involves a forfeiture of pension rights and other fringe benefits. For a worker with a long term of service, such benefits may amount to a sizable amount of money. In addition, the loss of seniority rights is no trifling consideration.

Many grievances arise over the question of the applicability of the general provisions of the contract to a specific situation. Are there ameliorating circumstances that justify condoning or treating in a less severe fashion an action that on the surface is a clear violation of the contract? Such grievances arise from two different sources. Sometimes a clause in a contract is left deliberately vague at the time of negotiations in order to avoid a breakdown in the bargaining process. Neither side wishes to risk a strike over this particular issue, and in effect the disagreement is postponed until a later date. With the passage of time, the questionable clauses become a subject for fresh dispute with the union claiming one interpretation and management claiming another. What does a pledge to consult with the union before workers are laid off because of technological change involve? If a worker is laid off, was he laid off improperly if management informed the union beforehand but made no effort to find an alternative solution (alternate employment)?

Secondly, no matter how precise the wording, however, there may still be difficulty in applying the general rule to a specific case. In general, management representatives, particularly in large or multiplant companies, are inclined to interpret the contract in a rather strict and legalistic fashion. Past experience has shown them that if they grant an exception in a special case, the union may subsequently insist that the exception become the new rule. Large companies are always wary lest discrepancies in the enforcement of rules between one plant or department to another provoke endless controversy in the future.

Sometimes a grievance may appear to be a minor complaint, yet represent a far more serious dissatisfaction. A complaint about the administration of the contract may be a superficial manifestation of a discontent that runs much deeper, one that, if left untreated, will erupt into open warfare at some future time. The skilled grievance adjustors on both sides must be alert to these symptoms and avoid dismissing too quickly grievances that at first glance appear to have no merit.

On the other hand, some grievances that appear to have no foundation prove, on closer examination, to be exactly what they seem—unjustified. Such "dogs" arise from time to time and they may even be advanced to the upper stages of the grievance settlement procedure and placed at the doorstep of an arbitrator (at a financial cost to both parties) for resolution. Why do such cases, which have no hope of being won, appear, let alone survive several stages of appeal on the grievance ladder? Generally speaking, any substantial number of such cases can be taken as evidence that the union's leaders are inexperienced or simply lack good judgment. Sometimes, however, such grievances may be pressed even when the union's leaders are aware that they have no chance of winning. Even though it may be impossible to settle a dispute to the satisfaction of the workers in question, the leaders may fear that failure to seek a settlement will expose them to criticism from the union's members. Presentation of unjustified grievances may therefore be a form of "buck passing"; the union's leaders simply let someone else inform the complainants that they really have no case at all. Although the complaining worker may remain dissatisfied, his resentment will be focused against the management or against the arbitrator. The leaders can always assure him that they did the best they could on his behalf.

Some union leaders will seek to increase the number of cases they win by deliberately pressing more cases than they have any expectation of winning. Suppose a leader has five legitimate grievances to present and he hopes to win at least three of them. He may reason that if he submits a total of eight grievances—three of which are really "dogs"—the management or the arbitrator may be unwilling to decide too many cases against him and thus decide one of the close ones in his favor.

Such reasoning is based on the assumption that grievance officials and arbitrators tend to split the difference between the two parties. While such tactics may occasionally work for a short time or with a particular arbitra-

tor, eventually they are likely to reflect on the leaders' discretion and ability to present grievances properly. The cry of "wolf" when presenting a grievance is unlikely to prevent it from being recognized for the "dog" that it really is.

Functions and Benefits of Grievance Procedure

Granted that the primary function of any grievance machinery is to protect the rights of workers, it is important to note that a good grievance procedure provides management with many important advantages as well.

First of all, management does on occasion use the grievance machinery to register complaints against the union or against a group of workers. The union is the more frequent target since ordinarily management can resort to direct disciplinary action when workers are performing in an unsatisfactory manner. Sometimes when discipline cases have been difficult to win, however, management has resorted to grievance machinery for relief. Charges pressed by management against unions fall into two categories: (1) complaints that the union has failed to abide by the contract's union responsibility clause or (2) charges that the union has been maligning management and misrepresenting its views to the workers.

In addition to direct use by management of grievance machinery, the existence of such a procedure provides management with other, more frequently available, benefits. Since no contract negotiator can conceivably anticipate every contingency that may arise during the life of the contract, grievance machinery provides a means of solving new problems as they arise. The grievance machinery may be particularly helpful to a management that wishes to institute changes in production techniques without risking a deterioration in the morale of the plant's labor force. In such cases the machinery can be utilized to clarify the needs of the management with the issue presented as a problem-showing process.

Grievance machinery is really a system of communications extending from the bottommost layers of the plant to the top and back down again. As such, it provides management with a listening device into the heart of the plant. To the extent that a management avails itself of this listening device, it is in a better position to anticipate problems and read the mood of the labor force. By the same token, management is better able to judge the kind of job its supervisory personnel is performing. How many grievances does a given foreman have lodged against him? What are the merits of these grievances? How skillful and efficient is he in resolving these grievances? The answers to these and similar questions all provide valuable clues to the management in its efforts to find methods of running a more efficient plant. In order to obtain the answers to such questions, many companies keep both detailed grievance records for each foreman and records of the total number of grievances as well as the number won and lost for the entire plant. The problem with keeping too close a record on each foreman is that a foreman may be tempted into making settlements at the first stage in order to maintain a good record of quick resolution of grievances. Some of these quick settlements may later prove inimical to management's interest.

Last, but far from least, is the contribution a responsive grievance machinery makes to good plant morale and harmonious industrial relations, which modern management recognizes as important factors in securing high levels of output. To the extent that grievance machinery helps to reduce absenteeism, high labor turnover, and other symptoms of low morale among workers, it can be regarded as making a positive contribution to management's goals. Union Stewards and officers also become better aware of management's problems and may be less ready to dismiss its arguments as mere propaganda.

Similarly, a well-oiled grievance machinery may work to the advantage of the union. Not only does grievance machinery bring home vividly to union members the value of union membership (and the apathy of many union members toward their union is well known), but it keeps the union's leaders in touch with the wishes of the rank and file and alert to problems that are creating unrest. If the union's leaders know what workers are currently thinking and are thus able to seek relief for their complaints, the leaders are at an obvious advantage. Otherwise, they may be exposed to the threat of a wildcat strike and the charge that they cannot control the union's membership. Wildcat strikes are as often a protest against the union as they are against management.

Steps in the Grievance Procedure

We have suggested that a wide variety of problems are likely to produce grievances; to some extent there is a similar profusion in the arrangements provided in different plants for handling whatever grievances may arise. Small plants are likely to be less formal in their arrangements than are large ones. In the small plant, many grievances are raised and settled without ever having been committed to writing. Most large plants, on the other hand, require a written statement even at the time the grievance is initially submitted to the foremen for consideration. In small plants the foreman is likely to have greater power to make decisions on his own without consulting upper layers of management. As indicated earlier, some plants provide that all issues upon which the two interested parties are unable to agree will be resolved by arbitration while an increasingly smaller number still make no provision for intervention by a third party. Probably a substantial majority provide for arbitration in most instances but reserve certain issues exclusively to management's jurisdiction.

In most large plants and in many small plants an aggrieved worker will take his complaint up with his local shop steward. Shop stewards are union officials elected by the union members to represent them in grievance cases. Most contracts provide that a shop steward may be absent from his work place for a specified amount of time without loss of pay while carrying on union business. A large company like General Motors may spend between $2 and $3 million a year on wages for shop stewards, wages paid for their work in settling grievances. Because a smoothly functioning grievance machinery that uses the stewards depends on their experience and training, most contracts provide super seniority for the shop steward as well as other top union officers irrespective of their actual length of service.

A number of recent studies of local unions in operation, however, suggest that the worker with a grievance often bypasses the shop steward and takes his complaint directly to the union's president.[4] Some union members "start at the top" because they are convinced that nothing gets settled in the preliminary stages anyway. In some cases a distrust of the capabilities of the shop steward is also involved.

Although variations in procedure are numerous and a particular plant or union is likely to display highly individual characteristics, it is possible to outline the most familiar steps in the process of seeking a resolution to a grievance.

When a worker (or a group of workers) feels, for whatever reason, that he has been unfairly or improperly treated, he is ready to take the first step. Assuming for the moment that the scene is a factory and that there is a shop steward system, the worker would take his complaint to the steward who is his representative. A typical large plant will have one shop steward for every twenty to fifty workers. If the steward decides that the complaint is a legitimate one, he will present the problem to the foreman in charge of the worker involved. Depending on how formal the grievance procedure is, the steward may make either an informal verbal presentation or (less frequently) a written statement. A management that insists that all grievances be presented in written form quite frequently does so as a means of holding down the number of grievances presented. Many personnel directors believe that a worker and his steward will be less likely to complain about a petty issue if they are forced to put their grievance on paper.

Upon receipt of the grievance, a foreman may take one of several courses. He may be willing to settle the question to the satisfaction of the aggrieved worker without consulting others. Alternatively, he may feel that the grievance involves an issue that he believes that he has no authority to decide. He may also feel, after discussing the question with the worker and the steward, that the grievance is unjustified and so refuse the request for an adjustment.

Sometimes, when a worker has had a chance to blow off steam and has heard the foreman's reasons for the disputed decision, he may decide to let the issue die at that point. In one way or another, the bulk of all grievances (over 75 percent) are resolved at this initial stage. In many of the remaining cases, the worker and his steward will appeal the decision of the foreman.

Customarily, the next step is for an unresolved grievance to be forwarded to a plant grievance committee composed of an equal number of union and management officials who are experienced in handling grievances. Depending upon the size of the plant and the number of grievances normally handled, this committee meets with more or less frequency to handle all questions presented to them. An alternative plan, often used in smaller plants, is to have those issues unresolved by the foreman forwarded to the chief steward and the plant's personnel director.

When work is performed outside a factory, as in the construction trade, the workers' grievances are often handled for them by the union's business agent. Sometimes he will handle a grievance at both the local and upper levels. He may also turn a grievance over to one of the other officers of the union if an appeal from an adverse decision is to be made. Whatever the intermediate stages may be, there is always the possibility that the two sides will continue to disagree. When this happens, the final step of submitting the dispute to the decision of an outside third party is likely to be made.

Grievance Arbitration

Even companies that enjoy the best union-management relationships sometimes encounter problems to which neither side is able to offer a mutually satisfactory solution. It is in such situations that the services of an arbitrator are vital.[5] Although the importance of providing for arbitration as a last resort has been apparent throughout this chapter, we should again emphasize that we feel arbitration should be used as a means for resolving disputes only when all else fails. Arbitration is most successful when employed sparingly; too heavy dependence upon it tends to undermine the rest of collective bargaining.

Grievance Arbitration Machinery

Representing the union and presenting the grievance initiated by the union is usually the responsibility of the district staff officer accompanied by the shop's grievance committee and the appropriate shop steward. Appearing for the company are often staff members from the office of the vice-president of personnel relations. Increasingly both sides are likely to retain one or more lawyers.

How Arbitrators Are Chosen

Since World War II both labor and management have increasingly come to rely on the decisions of outsiders to resolve issues upon which the two parties cannot agree. Most of these arbitrators are lawyers, law professors, and economists. Many are either members of the American Arbitration Association, a private non-profit organization, or on the lists of available arbitrators maintained by that organization. In large companies the arbitrator(s) may be designated in the contract.

Companies and unions employ different procedures in selecting an arbitrator. Some prefer to have a tripartite board on the theory that there is safety in numbers and with such a board, the possibility of bias is reduced. The tripartite board includes representatives from the two interested parties—labor and management—plus a third neutral. Frequently the neutral party serves as chairman. When he is unable to reconcile the views of the other two, he may be called upon to cast the deciding vote. Partly for reasons of cost, partly because of increased confidence in the dispassionate judgment of arbitrators by both unions and management, and partly because the three-man board is more cumbersome (more disagreements occur), there has been a steady decline in the use of such boards and increasing reliance on the decisions by a single arbitrator. The tripartite board often leads to internal bargaining among the board members prior to rendering a decision.

Even among those who employ a single arbitrator, variations exist. Some companies prefer to utilize the services of a single arbitrator who retains the post as long as he continues to be satisfactory to both parties. The retention of a given arbitrator on a semipermanent basis has several important advantages. First of all, it eliminates the headaches involved in deciding upon a new one (a point to which we will shortly return). The more frequently the need for arbitration arises, the more important this advantage becomes. A related advantage is that when a selection is made with a view to the long run it is likely to be more carefully made and prove ultimately to be more satisfactory to both the union and management. Furthermore, a semipermanent arbitrator has an opportunity to become familiar with the problems of the industry and the particular firm and union that he is serving. It is argued that this familiarity with the past history of previous disputes gives him a sounder base for rendering his decisions.

At the same time, assuming that the arbitrator is consistent in his judgments where the facts are the same, both the union and management become able to predict in advance what his decisions are likely to be. This may save time, trouble, and money by preventing the processing of unnecessary cases. In standard cases, both the union and management may circulate arbitration decisions in order to keep the plant's work force and the foremen alert as to what may be expected.

Sometimes, however, the case load may become too heavy for a single arbitrator even though he is employed on a full-time basis. Firms and unions faced with this situation often retain one individual as their regular arbitrator and arrange for two or three standby arbitrators to be available when the pressure of the case load becomes too great for the regular man to handle alone.

There are a sizable number of firms and unions, however, that prefer ad hoc arbitrators. This provides them with at least the opportunity to select a new man each time even though they may not exercise this option. One or both parties sometimes fear that a permanent arbitrator will come to be limited too much by preceding judgments and feel that if he has made a series of verdicts in favor of one side, he must now make some decisions in the opposite direction. The probability that such a development results from the choice of a poor arbitrator rather than from the permanent arrangement apparently does not convince these companies and unions that the risk is worthwhile.

Although ad hoc arbitration is still considerably more common than more permanent arrangements, it is important to note that the latter is particularly characteristic of those firms and unions where a strong mutual respect and trust prevail and a healthy working relationship exists. Rarely, if ever, do companies that have adopted a permanent arbitrator system return to an ad hoc arrangement. Furthermore, many firms and unions using an ad hoc arrangement reemploy the same individual time after time. Since even a permanent arbitrator can be dismissed whenever he proves unsatisfactory to one of the two parties, the difference is not as great as it first appears.

When an ad hoc system is used, the two parties may draw up a list of names of individuals who are judged qualified for service. From these lists a master list is compiled and one or more (if it is to be a three-man board) are chosen. More frequently today the two parties ask the Federal Mediation and Conciliation Service or the American Arbitration Association to nominate a group from which the union and management can choose.

Role of the Arbitrator

Once they have chosen an arbitrator, what may the two parties expect from him? Ideally, the union and the management should make it clear to the arbitrator what they want in advance. Thereafter the good arbitrator will serve in that capacity and that capacity alone and will not seek to impose upon the two parties gratuitous advice or service. Some companies and unions, for example, may want an arbitrator who will also serve as mediator and attempt to resolve the differences between the two parties without having to make a binding decision on his own. More frequently, however, all that is desired of the arbitrator is that he hear the two presentations and then render a binding decision.[6]

When the arbitrator has been called upon to resolve some issue relating to the contract (the usual case), he should confine himself to rendering a decision within the framework of the contract in question. It is not up to him to pass judgment upon the wisdom of the contract. Even when a contract violates his standards of justice and offends his common sense as an industrial relations expert, he should keep such thoughts to himself. His sole task is to interpret the contract as it reads to the best of his ability.

Since discipline cases make up such a large proportion of the total number of grievances, it is not surprising to find that about one-third of all the grievances going to arbitration involve the issue of discipline. Depending upon the contract, an arbitrator may either find that there was or was not cause for discipline or he may be free to reduce the penalty if he feels it is too heavy.

Some contracts seek to tie the arbitrator's hands by preventing him from altering the penalty. His only function is to decide whether or not discipline was called for in the circumstances in question. If in his judgment they were, he in effect upholds management. Management then has the right to assess whatever punishment it thinks is appropriate. While such clauses are designed to prevent arbitrators from interfering unduly with the rights of management, the result is often the opposite of that intended. An arbitrator who feels that the punishment inflicted by management is far in excess of what is proper in view of the relatively minor nature of the infraction committed may be tempted to hold that no infraction at all has been perpetrated. Whatever the degree of freedom of judgment granted to the arbitrator, however, the rule in all discipline cases should be that the burden of proof rests with the employer.

The Legal Basis for Arbitration Decisions

With the exception of a brief period in the state of Kansas, compulsory arbitration has never been favored in the United States as a means of establishing the terms of a new contract or for settling a disagreement over an existing contract.[7] Once the two parties have voluntarily agreed to submit their differences to an arbitrator, however, they surrender their right to take exception to the verdict. Some large companies and unions have signed agreements whereby both pledge never to appeal to the courts, but thus far such agreements are in a distinct minority.

Even prior to the Taft-Hartley Act, employers and unions had already agreed that only in exceptional cases would they appeal an arbitrator's ruling to the courts. Appeals might be made in cases where the arbitrator was found to be guilty of fraud, where he permitted misconduct at the hearings, or where he was influenced in his decision by fraud on the part of one of the two parties to the dispute. Court appeals could also be made where the arbitrator's decision exceeded the jurisdiction of the contract, violated public policy, or failed to resolve some of the issues in question.

Under the terms of the Taft-Hartley Act an agreement to submit grievances to arbitration is legally enforceable in the courts. Thus either party can now appeal to the courts to compel the other party to use grievance arbitration procedure.

A series of Supreme Court decisions in the late 1950s and early 1960s have opened the door to much wider court enforcement of arbitration decisions. It is still too early to determine the full effect of these awards, but already they have been both hailed as strengthening the character of arbitration and attacked as granting arbitrators excessively broad powers. The three cases decided in June 1960[8] (known as the "arbitration trilogy") greatly increased the power of a union to insist on the services of an arbitrator even though the company maintained that the issue was not subject to arbitration or refused to abide by the arbitrator's decision.

Even in the absence of court pressure there has been a marked trend in the direction of voluntarily making use of the services of an arbitrator from the beginning. The advantages of arbitration in the form of lessened formality and greater speed of settlement combined with the desire of both parties to have a hand in the selection of the decision-maker all account for this trend.

Since no one, including an arbitrator, can please all of his clients all of the time, a series of unfavorable decisions is likely to lead one party to demand the selection of a new arbitrator.[9] Employers argue that an arbitrator is too lax or too sympathetic to the union's point of view. The authors can remember hearing a personnel director of a large industrial plant moaning after he lost an arbitration case, "I should have known that no one from [a leading industrial relations school] would give us a fair break. They're all pro-union up there." Employers also fear that the arbitrator will make his decision too all-inclusive or hand down one decision that will set a precedent for other cases that may in actuality be quite different in character. Many employers have agreed to arbitration of grievances only after the union has accepted a no strike ban for the term of the contract. Unions are also suspicious about the dispassionate and unbiased character of arbitrators' decisions. It is, therefore, a tribute to arbitrators that their services have come increasingly into demand and that so few of their decisions are challenged by either side.

What Constitutes a Good Grievance System?

We will conclude our discussion of grievance procedures in the United States by noting some of the characteristics that distinguish a good grievance system from a mediocre one. First of all, a scarcity of grievances may be just as much of a danger sign as an overabundance. A lack of formal grievances may be a symptom that the union is unwilling or unable to do its job, that workers distrust or fear the grievance procedure, or that the system operates so poorly that both sides are unwilling to employ it.

To those who tend to think of unions as mischief-makers who are anxious to stir up trouble at every opportunity, it may come as a shock to learn that unions sometimes ignore the complaints of their members and actually fail to process a number of grievances. In the majority of cases, a union's unwillingness is based on the knowledge that the grievance is unjustified. Sometimes, however, a worker who is unpopular with the union's leaders will find himself at a disadvantage when he tries to get the union to take up his cause. At other times, a grievance may be taken up by the union only to be abandoned at a later stage. One reason that this may happen is when the upper layers of management and union officials engage in logrolling—some grievances are settled on the union's terms for the price of having other grievances dropped. The worker whose grievance has been dropped, however, finds little consolation in the fact that a fellow worker won his.

Until recently the worker whose grievance has been thus bypassed has had little recourse. When the worker has appealed to the courts he has generally been advised that his complaint is properly with his union and that he should work within the union to correct the fault. Under the Taft-Hartley Act, workers have the right to petition for the settlement of a grievance on their own; when the management is unwilling to go against the wishes of the unions, however, the worker has been helpless.

It is quite possible that the Landrum-Griffin Act will induce unions to take cases to arbitration that would previously have been dropped. The unions presumably fear that if they do not they will be charged with not properly representing the interests of individual members.

The first and most obvious criterion of a successful grievance procedure is whether or not it works fairly and equitably. Everyone who has a legitimate grievance should have an opportunity to express that grievance. It is just as improper if friendship with a steward or a union president is necessary to win a hearing as it is if friendship with the foreman is a prerequisite for equitable treatment.

Not only should grievance procedure be available to all workers, but it also should assure as speedy a resolution of the problem as is humanly possible. Any grievance worthy of processing deserves prompt settlement. Until it is resolved, it remains an irritant and handicaps the smooth functioning of the plant's operations.

One way to achieve prompt resolution depends on both the foreman and the stewards being well trained in their duties. Many more grievances could be settled at the initial stage of the process if these men really knew their jobs.[10] We noted earlier that there is a tendency in some plants to bypass the first stage because the foreman has no power to make decisions. Understandably management is fearful lest a foreman unwittingly make a concession that would have plant-wide repercussions. However, if the foreman were better trained to handle grievances, this fear would subside and many more disputes could be settled at the initial stage.

Delay and procrastination are particularly characteristic of the upper stages of the grievance machinery. When it is at all feasible it is advisable to specify a time limit during which responses to a grievance must be made. Settlement of grievances that go to arbitration consumes more and more time. Arthur Ross in a study of arbitration awards that compared the years 1945–1946 to 1955–1956, found that the average time for settlements increased by 50 percent during the time period studied.[11] By 1956 it took on the average over 200 days to reach a settlement. To the authors' knowledge, no comparable study has been made recently, but our experience suggests that the time lag is still enormous. Various explanations have been advanced to account for this lengthening gap between initiation and settlement, but the most important reason is probably the increasing emphasis on the role of legalism in arbitration procedure. As we use the term "legalism," we mean excessive preoccupation with the strict rules laid down by the contract and with

court procedures to implement those contracts.

While a certain amount of legalism, particularly in large plants, is inevitable, the authors are convinced that the great majority of cases involve special circumstances which make for heavy reliance on a body of precedents as a means of assuring uniformity. All too often, however, precedents cannot really be applied to all cases. Attempts to apply them only slow the pace of settlement.

The same advice applies equally well to those international unions that insist on a legalistic approach. Quite frequently their insistence results from a fear that they will lose some of their control over the rank and file if too many grievances are settled between the steward and the foreman. Although this may be an important consideration for the international, a broader perspective suggests that what benefits the workers is a more important objective.

We can summarize much of our preceding discussion in this sentence: Grievance machinery works well when the two parties really work at it. "Working at it" means maintaining a mutual respect and a willingness to listen to each other's viewpoints and compromising when compromise is necessary. The best-oiled grievance machinery in the world will function poorly if the two parties continually throw sand in the gears. Both parties must be willing to accept decisions that go against them even when such decisions involve issues very dear to their hearts. One party or the other will sometimes refuse to abide by the arbitrator's decision or exert improper pressure to win his point. Union members sometimes engage in wildcat strikes, work slowdowns, and other harassing tactics designed to put pressure on management to settle on the union's terms. Since management's acceptance of grievance machinery up to and including arbitration is sometimes predicated on a quid pro quo agreement by the union not to strike over such issues, management exasperation at these tactics is understandable. Management, on the other hand, may stall and delay in order to frustrate the grievance machinery. The result of any of these obstructive maneuvers is to destroy in part or entirely the reason for establishing a grievance machinery in the first place.

Furthermore grievance machinery should not be used by either party as a means to secure concessions that he had not been able to win at the bargaining table. The distinction between negotiating a new contract and the administration of a current one should be rigorously maintained and any deliberate attempt to blur it should be regarded as a perversion.

Grievance Procedure Abroad

Although grievance machinery is not unknown outside the United States, elsewhere in the world it has been developed far less fully than it has in this country. The existence of industrywide bargaining, the lack of contracts of the unions in individual plants, and a failure to distinguish grievance procedure from new contract negotiations largely account for this phenomenon.

Great Britain

After the United States, Great Britain's grievance machinery (or lack of it) has attracted perhaps the most scholarly attention. Although both unions and management in Great Britain are philosophically disposed toward the settlement of grievances at the plant level because they feel any grievance settled at the national level may produce a solution ill-suited to the industry as a whole, grievances often do get processed to the upper level where there is often interminable delay. A relatively simple matter may take months to resolve simply because there is no satisfactory machinery at the plant level. Local union officers are sometimes appointed to their office by the national unions and so are less responsive to the mood and desires of the local's rank and file than if they were elected.

The British pride themselves on the close local contact and cooperation between the two parties and the absence of lawyers and legal paperwork. They see a resort to arbitration as a confession of failure on the part of both parties and try to avoid it as much as possible. Arbitration is thus used far less frequently than in the United States for the settlement of grievances. On the other hand, the prevalence of industrywide bargaining and the need for England to maintain production in order to compete in world markets have made economic warfare between labor and capital extremely costly, thus encouraging the use of arbitration in settling disputes arising over *new* contracts. In Great Britain (and elsewhere in Europe) there is no clear distinction between grievances and new contract proposals. Employers are subject to bargaining over new contracts at any time since contracts have no definite expiration date.

As a result, there has been, particularly in recent years, a rash of wildcat strikes, which have interrupted production and caused bitterness on both sides. Few outside observers would deny that the British industrial relations scene would be greatly improved if Britain adopted a system of grievance machinery similar to that existing in the United States.

Continental Europe

What we have just said about Great Britain applies with even more force to the handling of grievances on the European continent. In England the shop stewards are not only numerous (there are over 200,000 of them) but they are an integral part of the unions and elected to their posts by the union members. It is these stewards who have led many of the wildcat strikes developing on a local level.

The continental unions have been even more opposed to plant bargaining than have the British unions. As a result, there is even less opportunity for the airing of grievances. In France there is no plant procedure for the settlement of such disputes, and most grievances wind up in the French labor courts. These labor courts have not been a complete success and have been the cause of considerable grumbling by both unions and management. (This is true in West Germany as well.) Both parties complain of the expenses involved and the often lengthy delays in decisions. The decisions of the labor courts are often subject to review by the country's higher courts. The judge is therefore likely to be overly conscious of the legal aspects of the case and he is prone to ignore the human elements or the peculiarities of the particular case in question. Outside observers see the party against whom the verdict is rendered having greater difficulty accepting defeat than he would in a grievance case processed American style. Consequently, appeals from original decisions are likely to be frequent.

In both France and Italy, works councils have been set up to compensate for the absence of unions in the plants, but in neither country have these councils been very effective in representing the workers.

Of the continental European countries covered in this book, only in Sweden do the unions delineate sharply between new contract negotiations and grievances arising under an existing contract. Provision is made for various stages of grievance machinery including district mediators and arbitrators and labor courts.

West German grievance procedure resembles that of Sweden, but is less well developed. In West Germany grievances are handled by works councils rather than by the union and strikes over grievances are forbidden by law. About 80 percent of the workers belong to both a works council and a union so there is considerable continuity. Nevertheless, the leaders of the German unions have tried to get the unions into the plant and find the councils a stumbling block toward progress in that direction.

Israel

Israel has a fairly complete system of grievance procedures. The procedures resemble those in the United States, although Israeli contracts tend to spell out procedures at the local or plant level less fully than American contracts. The lack of formal procedure at the lowest level has figured prominently in criticisms of the Israeli labor system. The responsibility for the settlement of grievances lies with the personnel director or plant manager and the workers' committees. A grievance that is not settled in the plant goes to the local bipartite committee, which consists of representatives of the Manufacturers' Association and the Histadrut. If the case is not settled at this point, it is referred to the Histadrut central committee. If this too fails, the final step is arbitration either by a three-man board or a single arbitrator.

In enterprises run by the Histadrut,

the procedure is somewhat different for grievances that cannot be settled at the plant level. The first step is an attempt at settlement between the personnel director and the local labor council secretary. If unsettled, the central personnel director of the Koor (as a Histadrut enterprise is called) and the secretary of the National Committee of the Histadrut Workers would negotiate. Final decisions are made by the head of the Industrial Workers Division of the Trade Union Department of Histadrut.

India

Considering that unions in India are in a relatively early stage of development, it is not surprising that formal systems of grievance procedure occur only infrequently. Ordinarily an aggrieved worker takes his complaint directly to his supervisor or to top management (often the Indian supervisor's hands are tied much like the American foreman's). If he fails to receive satisfaction, the worker can appeal to the local government labor welfare office. Some of the stronger unions are instituting grievance procedures along American lines. A number of plants have workers' committees that are composed of an equal number of union and management representatives and are set up to settle any grievance involving several workers. On the whole, however, these workers committees have not been very successful mainly because neither the unions nor employers have been very enthusiastic about them. The lack of a satisfactory grievance procedure and the failure to distinguish grievances from items subject to negotiation at contract renewal time have led to a number of strikes over issues that would have been settled in the United States through regular grievance procedure channels.

The failure of grievance procedure in day-to-day operations contrasts vividly with the elaborate provisions for it under India's First Five Year Plan. The plan called for all employers to post in their plants information on the ways in which workers could express their grievances to the employer. To implement the grievance procedure, the plan recommended the establishment of a system of shop stewards. In addition, the plan called for the creation of the workers' committees and envisioned them as "the culminating step in the grievance machinery."

Japan

In those Japanese plants where unions play an important role, there are joint councils of labor and management that deal primarily with grievances. A national mediation service established by the Labor Relations Adjustment Act of 1946 handles those problems not solved at the plant level. Cases that are not resolved at this level are referred to the Central Labor Relations Committee, which is the supreme mediation agency. A separate arbitration procedure has been established for government employees.

True collective bargaining came to Japan only after the end of World War II. Considering this, the Japanese have made great progress in the development of collective bargaining. For a short period after the war a "production control" system existed under which workers could take over the plant and run it until management had met their demands or satisfied their grievances, but this system quickly proved to be unworkable.

Mexico

Grievance procedure in Mexico is a curious blend of informal relationships and a formal machinery established by the government. Whether or not there is a good system in an individual plant depends primarily on the personalities involved and the relationships existing between the leaders of the union and the company. The government has provided machinery to settle labor-management disputes and grievances of all types are frequently processed through provincial labor departments. Many of the grievances coming before the government boards involve the issue of discharge. Employers must agree to grievance arbitration when it is requested by workers.

Summary

If one believes, as we do, that the achievement of a smoothly operating grievances system is a major step toward better industrial relations, it is necessary to emphasize that most countries have a long way to go before they match the arrangements established in the United States. It is in the area of grievance handling that the United States provides the best example of good industrial relations to other countries.

American grievance procedure is by no means perfect, however. Lengthy delays occasioned by excessive legalism, lengthy transcripts, and tripartite boards have made grievance procedure more expensive in recent years whenever arbitration has proved necessary. Even with these defects, however, grievance machinery in the United States has operated with remarkable smoothness and dispatch.

NOTES

1. A typical clause limiting grievances to the terms of the existing contract is the following:

Grievances, within the meaning of the grievance procedure, shall consist only of disputes about wages, hours of work, and working conditions, as provided in this agreement; and about the meaning and application of this agreement; and about alleged violations of this agreement.

Quoted from U.S. Department of Labor, *Grievance Procedures,* Bulletin No. 1425–1 (1964), p. 7.

2. *Ibid.,* p. 6.

3. This is true even though the arbitrator may be inclined to disagree with the way management handled the situation or with the penalty assigned. The question of proper penalty, however, is often removed from the arbitrator's hands.

4. See, for example, Leonard Sayles and George Strauss, *The Local Union* (New York: Harper & Row, 1953).

5. The Teamsters provide the major example of a union that makes no provision for grievance arbitration. Many Teamster contracts provide for a strike if the two parties are unable to agree on a way of resolving the dispute. Hoffa sought to avoid the establishment of precedents in this fashion, but used the power to strike sparingly perhaps because he feared compulsory arbitration. It should be noted, however, that many regional and local agreements negotiated by the Teamsters do carry provisions for arbitration if the local joint employer-union committee so agrees. Many locals in the steel industry have sought the ultimate right to strike over grievances not settled to their satisfaction. The UAW also permits its locals the option of striking over local issues.

6. In most cases, the arbitrator is well advised to keep his relationship with the company and the union on as straightforward a basis as possible since extremely few arbitrators (Professor George Taylor of University of Pennsylvania would be one exception) have the gifts to play a multidimensional role.

7. Against the wishes of both management and labor but because neither party was willing to concede its position in the dispute, Congress in mid-1967 enacted a compulsory arbitration arrangement for the railroads, applicable only in this case. The subsequent decision was unsatisfactory to railroad management, but at this writing

they have decided not to appeal to the courts.

8. *United Steelworkers of America v. American Manufacturing, 363 U.S. 564; United Steelworkers of America v. Warrior and Gulf Navigation Co., 363 U.S. 574;* and *United Steelworkers of America v. Enterprise Wheel and Car Corp., 363 U.S. 593.*

9. A good case in point was the ouster of Harry H. Platt by the UAW at the Ford Motor Company. Mr. Platt's position as arbitrator for the company and the union, which was contingent on acceptance by both parties, became inoperable after the union requested his resignation on the eve of contract negotiations between the UAW and Ford in the fall of 1967. The union's request for Platt's resignation was presumably triggered by a decision rendered by Platt in favor of the company over the issue of subcontracting.

10. International Harvester in recent years has been putting great emphasis on oral settlements by foremen and stewards as the first step as a means of making its grievance procedure work better.

11. Arthur M. Ross, "The Well-Aged Arbitration Case," *Industrial and Labor Relations Review,* 11 (January 1958), 262–268.

14

The Strike—A Breakdown and Continuation of the Bargaining Process

"A strike . . . comes to be regarded as a failure of collective bargaining, while one of the most accepted tests of successful collective bargaining is the length of the period during which no strikes or lockouts have occurred . . ."

—U.S. Senate, Committee on Labor and Public Welfare

☐ LABOR unrest appears to be inevitable. Clark Kerr has observed that "one universal response to industrialization . . . is protest on the part of the labor force as it is fitted into the new social structure."[1] The strike, in the United States and Canada at least, is an accepted form of industrial conflict and an often-needed means for expressing the discontent and protest of the labor force. Industrial change brings labor unrest, and the strikes of organized labor in the United States are the result of industrialization, and not simply a phenomenon of unionization. On the other hand, the form of business unionism that has arisen in the United States has shaped the industrial conflict within the country and unions have adopted the strike as a means of pressing their demands. The meaning of the strike depends on the nature of the organization using it.

Initially we will confine ourselves to strikes in the United States and then observe the role of the strike in other economies. In all countries the strike involves the cessation of work, but it differs from the quit in that it

is a collective action and does not represent a decision on the part of workers to leave the company permanently. The strike involves a refusal to obey (that is, workers fail to obey orders to perform the duties assigned to their jobs), and it is an open expression of aggression. The workers, by going out on strike, are pitting their strength or their "staying power" against that of management. They are serving public notice of their inability to come to an agreement with management. The "classic" strike is one that occurs following the breakdown of collective bargaining between employers and workers.

Function

The function of the strike or threat of a strike is to bring economic pressure to bear on both sides to settle their disputes. The strike or the threat of one is therefore really a part of bargaining. Because the threat of strike is meaningless unless the threat at least occasionally becomes the reality, strikes do continue to occur, with each side blaming the other for the resulting cessation of operations. Because of inability to assign responsibility for the interruption of operations to either side, the U.S. Department of Labor no longer uses the classifications of strikes and lock-outs (which occur when management decides to cease operations temporarily due to a dispute with labor). Instead, the statistics cited monthly by the Bureau of Labor Statistics relate to *work stoppages,* which include all cessations in operations that result from industrial dispute. Responsibility for the stoppage is not assigned to either party.

A strike threatens management with the loss of profits and orders. When the workers fail to take part in the productive process, finished goods are no longer available for sale. Not only do profits disappear, but customers may make permanent arrangements for alternate sources of supply or for substitute goods. Inventories are depleted, perishable materials may spoil, and plant and equipment may become obsolete. The costs of stopping and resuming production are particularly obvious in the case of the steel mill (the banking of fires, etc.). The picket lines that usually accompany the strike will, if recognized, keep other, nonstriking workers from their jobs, stop delivery of raw materials and supplies, and prevent distribution of any product from the plant.

To the union, the cost of the strike appears in the reduced income available for their workers. Some national unions maintain strike funds from which benefits on a limited scale can be paid to the strikers. During a prolonged strike, when available strike funds are depleted, the national or international may, after a vote, assess the working members across the nation to maintain the strikers. (This occurred during the 1963 New York City newspaper strike.) In a few states, unemployment insurance can be paid to striking workers after a certain length of time.

During a strike, each side attempts to improve its bargaining position vis-à-vis the other. The union, for example, uses the picket line and the boycott to accomplish this. The boycott, a group refusal to buy the products or to work on the products of the firm, is called primary if it is against the products of the firm struck. This action is legal, under current legislation, but the secondary boycott, against products of a second employer (an action designed to influence the struck employer), is illegal. One effect of the strike is to draw public attention to the situation and the union or management may capitalize on this public attention to claim that the other party is guilty of undemocratic or unfair practices. Such charges have been disseminated by word of mouth, and on occasion (during the 1959 steel strike, for example) both parties have used advertisements on radio and television and in the newspapers to charge that wages were too low in proportion to the cost of living or that profits were too low in proportion to the amount of capital invested.

The company may attempt to improve its bargaining position by continuing production through the use of strike breakers or, where possible, supervisory personnel. The blacklist is illegal and the company must rehire its strikers if the NLRB determines that the company was unfair, but management frequently threatens the future of its striking workers. Strikers face eviction from company-owned homes or the cancellation of credit from banks sympathetic to management.

Both union and management must assess the costs of the strike to their side and balance them against the costs of compliance with the offers or demands of the other side. Aside from the most obvious economic factors, other factors may have to be taken into account. Management, for example, may willingly accept a strike in order to use up a large inventory. The union, on the other hand, may feel that the income its membership will lose through the strike is outweighed by the discipline and sense of unity of purpose the membership will gain. Each side might decide to hold out as a matter of principle. It is often observed that in strikes, as in wars, there may be no relationship between intensity and the importance of the issue. (Of course, the true importance of the issue may not be apparent to the outside observer.)

Psychoanalysts have tried to look beyond economic explanations, which they believe are symptoms rather than causes. They are prone to interpret the strike in Freudian terms, viewing it as a rebellion against the father (management), society, and the industrial situation. All of these forces restrict the individual's impulses and thereby create aggression. Psychoanalysts of the Freudian persuasion also view individuals as identifying themselves with the group (the union) in their egos. Those who rely on Alfred Adler suggest that perhaps strikers are in fact overcompensating for a feeling of inferiority.[2]

Most observers, however, support the thesis that economic motives are the main underlying causes of strikes. However, the specific economic factors that cause strikes today are different from those of the early years of the unions. In the decades before the right of collective bargaining was protected by law, the majority of strikes were concerned with the question of unionization. In more recent years, first wages and hours, then fringe benefits, have become the major issues at stake.

Neil Chamberlain has pointed out that a strike jars the public, not because it threatens economic loss, but because the public fears social unrest and is disturbed by the thought that in this age of computers we cannot manage man's relations with man.[3] But the purpose of the strike in the American economy is to achieve industrial partnership, not to produce a revolution. George Shultz has listed a number of factors relevant to the role of conflict in our economy.[4] In the first place, conflict is a widely used method for producing generally desirable results in our society. Secondly, vitality on the part of both management and labor is desirable. To quote William Graham Sumner: "The other social interests are in the constant habit of testing the market, in order to get all

they can out of it. A strike, rationally begun and rationally conducted, only does the same thing for the wage-earning interests."[5] Related to the vitality of management and labor is the need for responsibility on the part of both parties. Shultz's final point is that the conflict is the price of free collective bargaining. We will return to this point later.

Classification

Strikes classified according to goals and the techniques used include the *economic strike* and the *sympathetic strike.* The economic strike is the most typical strike in the United States, one precipitated by the worker's desire for economic improvement. All the pressures we have just discussed come into play on the two parties involved. Today, the economic strike occurs at the end of contract when the parties cannot arrive at new terms for the sale and purchase of labor.

Sympathetic strikes are illegal because the economic well-being of the workers involved is not in question. In a sympathetic strike, workers of one union strike against their employers because another union is having a dispute with a different management. Workers participate in a sympathetic strike in the obvious hope that their employers can bring some pressure to bear on the employer who is the target of the original strike. The two sets of employers need not in any way be related.

The *sit-down strike,* one of the tactics introduced by the CIO in the 1930s, has also been termed illegal by Senate resolution and by Supreme Court decision (*NLRB vs. Fansteel Metallurgical Corp.,* 306 U.S. 270, 1939). In this type of strike, the striking workers occupy the plant, refusing to allow nonstrikers to enter and thereby effectively blocking the use of strikebreakers by management. Although the top officers of the CIO never officially approved of the sit-down technique, more than half a million of their workers were involved in such strikes during 1936 and 1937.

The *slowdown* resembles the sit-down strike in that the striking workers protest in a manner that prevents nonstrikers from taking their places. The pace of the work is slowed, but the worker still appears on the job and ostensibly performs his duties. Often the slowdown is not detected by management until production figures for a specific period of time are available and can be compared to previous time periods. With the advent of assembly-line production and automation the slowdown has become less and less effective.

The slowdown was sometimes used as a strike technique by workers when they did not have the approval of their union. In the same category are *stay-aways,* which involve workers simply not coming to work on a specified day. The most important category of unauthorized strike techniques, however, is the *wildcat strike.* As the name implies, a wildcat strike is a sudden, unannounced strike of the union membership without official union approval. Often the strike occurs at a time when the union could not legally strike, that is, during the contract period. Such strikes may be shorter in duration than the average strike because the main purpose of the strike is to register a protest and its unofficial nature makes it impossible for the union to grant strike benefits. In Great Britain some unofficial (wildcat) strikes do become quasi-official since the union's executive committee may determine to pay dispute benefits.

Observers often characterize the wildcat strike as leaderless and un-

planned. It is true that the leaders of the wildcat strike are not elected officials of the union and that notice of the strike is not given to management and the government. Sociologists, however, point to very definite leadership patterns, sometimes referred to as spontaneous leadership, and note that planning does go on in advance. In some cases the union leadership may not only have been informed but actually have backed the plans unofficially, particularly in cases when a strike would be illegal.

What produces the wildcat? Obviously it is an expression of aggression. But this aggression may be directed in several directions. It is possible that the workers are concerned with a "perishable" issue,[6] one on which action must be taken immediately without waiting until the expiration of the contract. The workers' aggression might also be directed against the dilatory manner in which workers' grievances are dealt with:[7] in this case the dissatisfaction of the workers is directed at the union as well as management. A wildcat strike may arise over issues not ordinarily discussed by the union and business leaders. Perhaps the issue has never even been mentioned at the bargaining table. This too is a direct slap at the recognized union leadership.

Eldridge and Cameron have listed several objections to the wildcat strike.[8] Sociological objections are based on Elton Mayo's concept that cooperation is essential in social health and the concomitant desire for regularizing collective bargaining procedure in order to avoid the sharper forms of social antagonisms. Administrative objections include the attitudes of the union officials themselves. To the degree that the wildcat strike was directed against them, or at least took place without their approval, how much power have they lost? Will they be able to gain it back? What effect has the strike had on the status quo? Economic objections to wildcat strikes include the question of the impact on the economy as a whole. Can the country afford this "luxury"? How can the loss be measured? Are the strikers replaceable? Can these objections be balanced by the fact that the strike acts as a cathartic on the workers (if it does in fact have this effect), making them that much more agreeable (and therefore productive) in the future? The final classification encompasses moral objections. Are these workers pursuing their own selfish whims without regard for the plant as a whole, and are they breaking a contract to which they had, at an earlier date, agreed? In seeking to evaluate all of these various objections, it is necessary to keep constantly in mind the issues over which the strike was called.

Strikes are also classified according to their causes, rather than the techniques used by the strikers. After the recognition of a union as the bargaining agent once it had won an election was assured, and after the formation of the CIO, the question of jurisdiction assumed major importance in the American economy. It was now possible that more than one union might logically cover a given group of workers. In such cases, the unions, each wanting to build up its strength, would compete for membership; the result frequently was the *jurisdictional strike*. Such strikes have also arisen from disputes over which union shall represent the workers. Stringent restrictions on such strikes were included in the 1947 Taft-Hartley Act. Furthermore, the merged AFL-CIO in 1955 accepted as one of its functions the settlement of jurisdictional disputes without resort to strike by either rival union.

Rivalry between unions, of course, cannot be legislated away. The continued existence of such rivalry at least partially explains the intensity of feeling in some situations over what appears to the outsider to be a minor economic issue, for example, a 2 cent wage increase. The union that is currently recognized feels that if it cannot win the promised gain for its membership, the members might turn to the rival union.

The *general strike* is rarely found on the American scene (although there have been occasional instances in American cities). As the name indicates, the workers of the city as a whole go on strike in this type of strike. Such a strike is most often a political maneuver designed to show the power of organized labor and to demand certain governmental reforms. When a large segment of the economy is nationalized, the general strike may be used by workers as a device to secure higher wages from their employer, the government.

Arthur M. Ross has developed a useful classification of strikes into revolutionary, organizational, and business unionist. The revolutionary unionist sees the function of a strike as a tool or medium for organizing the workers and alerting them to their common problem, their common needs and goals. By striking together they can obtain some identity as a group. The strike also has an agitational motive. It allows neither side to become too complacent or too satisfied with the status quo.

Thus postwar strikes in France were conducted in a highly sophisticated context. They were at one and the same time a protest on the part of the rank and file against the deterioration of living standards, a means of pushing forward the domestic propaganda program of the Communist Party, and a response to the problems of Russian policy in Western Europe.[9]

Organizational strikes in this country differ from those carried on by business unions once they have become well established. At the time of organization, emotions run high and the incipient union group is not at all disciplined. With representative elections the organizational strike is no longer necessary. John R. Commons pointed out that violence was inversely proportional to the degree of organization. As we pointed out earlier, business unionism, once recognized, does much to shape the pattern of industrial conflict. Ross describes this phenomenon at length.[10] Under business unionism, the conduct of the strike is rationalized. Strategy is important and erratic, unplanned moves are not made by the men who are professional union leaders. Discipline of the rank and file is maintained. The union can rely on the membership for support in a dispute with management, and the leaders also know that when the contract is signed the workers will go back to work for its duration. Business unionism has adjusted itself to the political and economic customs of the society. In other words, it is not revolutionary. The union bargains with management on specific issues but does not debate management's right to manage. The strike is planned and executed in such a manner as to minimize damage to industry, inconvenience to the community, and loss of public support for the union.

In discussing the wildcat strike, we noted that occasionally union officials stood behind such a strike when the union could not legally engage in a strike. This statement implied that union officials are concerned with the legality of the strike action. This is an important, if not well-defined, area.

The participants in the strikes of half a century ago would scarcely recognize the typical strike scene should they happen to visit it today. The goon squads, the hired strikebreakers, and the use of the shotgun and club, all expressions of the old violence, are mostly things of the past. Occasionally an act of violence will erupt during the course of a strike, but more frequently management serves coffee to those on the picket line and erects rest stations to protect the strikers from the inclement weather.

Legality

The right to strike has continued to be an inherent part of the American labor scene: the first recorded strike in the United States was in 1791. However, neither common law nor the Thirteenth Amendment confer the absolute right to strike. Instead, the right to strike comes from an interpretation of our developing law and is based on two assumptions.[11] First, there can be no true bargaining between an employee acting alone and his employer. Second, collective bargaining would be sterile and ineffective without the right of management to lock its workers out and the right of unions to strike. By the late 1950s, the interdependence of economic interest of all those engaged in the same industry was commonly accepted. J. M. Clark called the right to strike the alternative to serfdom and emphasized that there must be an absolute right to strike.[12] Those who agree with Clark's position would hold that any laws that weaken the parties' power of economic coercion constitute government compulsion.

The Taft-Hartley Act (section 13) states that none of its clauses may be construed in such a way as to interfere with or impede or diminish the right to strike except as specifically provided for in the act. The exceptions are familiar: the emergency procedure, secondary boycotts, an uncertified union, jurisdictional disputes, and the provision that through NLRB action management can obtain an injunction. (This latter provision narrows the impact of the Norris-LaGuardia Act.)

The obviously illegal strike is one that is in violation of the contract. The union, when agreeing to a contract, accepts the terms therein and agrees not to strike for the duration of the contract. The no strike clause in a contract is itself a source of conflict and of prolonged adjudication.[13] The striker in a legal, economic strike has his rights to his job protected by law.

> . . . employees who participate in legal and peaceful economic strikes only lose their status as employees when their jobs are permanently filled. Unfair labor practice strikers have almost an absolute right to reemployment and do not lose their jobs even if they are replaced by other workers. In fact, the employer is legally required to put these strikers back on their jobs if they make an unqualified application within a reasonable time, and if they are not guilty of committing violence during the strike. On the other hand, any employee who engages in an illegal work stoppage or unlawful concerted activities loses his employment status, and if he returns to work he does so as a new employee. The employer is justified in discharging such employees and refusing them reinstatement unless he is guilty of committing an unfair practice which caused or prolonged the strike, or waives his right to discipline by soliciting the strikers to return to their jobs. . . . However, while the participating of the union in slowdowns, using harassing techniques which are harmful to the employer, and the engaging in other illegal strikes are not protected by the law, they do not violate the good faith bargaining requirement outlined in Section 8(b)(3) of the [Taft-Hartley Act].[14]

In general, a strike is considered to be an unfair labor practice strike if it is precipitated in part by the unfair practices of the employer, even if economic reasons or issues contribute to the work stoppage. Strikers entitled to reinstatement must make the request. They lose all rights, regardless of findings of the NLRB, if they engage in violence.

Effects

The effects of a strike on the economy of the community and the nation, of course, vary from one occasion to another. Since no generalizations can be made, the possible economic effects can best be illustrated by a case history.

The case in point concerns the contract between the American Federation of Grain Millers and the grain elevator operators in Duluth, Minnesota and Superior, Wisconsin, that expired June 30, 1964. The Duluth-Superior harbor, although ice locked for several months of the year, had had enough shipping to be ranked as the fifth largest port in the United States. The amount of shipping increased when the port became a seaport when the St. Lawrence Seaway was completed in 1959. Although ore shipments from the Mesabi Range have declined in recent years, grain shipments have been increasing because foreign ships are now able to load from the grain elevators that store grain brought in from Minnesota and North Dakota by train. In 1958, 127,478,000 bushels of grain were handled in the port; in 1963, (after the opening of the seaway) the total bushels handled was 193,247,000. The area appears from time to time on the list of depressed local labor market areas, owing to the seasonal nature of the shipping and the decline in ore production.

Within a week after the strike began, the railroads servicing the area announced an embargo on shipments of all grain, soybeans, and flaxseed into the two ports. This move came at the height of what had signs of being a record-breaking year for the grain shipments. Four hundred and fifty Grain Millers were on strike, and another one hundred "free-lance" grain truckdrivers were unable to work. The primary concern of the grain-producing communities was finding storage space for the new grain as it came in. Normally, the storage facilities would be vacated as the government-owned grains (previous season's unsold grain) were moved out through Duluth-Superior. The alternative to a strike solution was to force farmers to store their own product or to put the new crop on the open ground at the local storage facilities. In all the grain-producing states, the state governments gave the terminals authority to issue receipts for grain stored on the ground for lack of space.

Efforts on the part of local businessmen and government officials to have the Taft-Hartley Act emergency procedure invoked were turned down on the grounds that the port grain strike did not have nationwide impact. The following official statement was made by Secretary of Labor Willard Wirtz on August 7, 1964: "Although the administration has urged a prompt resumption of negotiations leading to a settlement, it does not appear that there is a legal basis for further government action. I cannot recommend to the President that a board of inquiry be appointed under the Taft Hartley Act because it seems unlikely that this strike will imperil 'the national health or safety' as that phrase has been interpreted by the courts."

As the strike wore on, the Wisconsin Grain and Warehouse Commission laid off sixty to seventy of its men, and efforts were made to move more grain boats out because the port stay was costing them from $1,200 to $2,000 a day. Figures on the number of workers in other lines of work laid off as a result of the strike are inaccurate because some of the men wanted "to save their unemployment benefits for the winter months." The railroads informally offered to ship grain at lower rates than usual out of Duluth and Minneapolis to other Great Lakes ports. This offer particularly appealed to owners of grain temporarily stored in freight cars waiting in Duluth yards all ready for unloading. It did not appeal to the exporters because such a solution would have meant still another addition to their costs.

Grain shipments for the month of July amounted to 563,329 bushels, compared to 16,201,618 bushels for the preceding July. The number of ships that were diverted to other ports and the number of carloads of grain shipped east by railroad remained a matter of speculation.

Early in August the head of the Duluth local applied for unemployment compensation contending that the strike had become a lock-out (because management had not gone along with the union's offer to accept arbitration). Wisconsin workers did not file because under the laws of their state they were ineligible for compensation whether the dispute was judged to be a lock-out or a strike.

By the time a new contract was agreed to (after a strike of six weeks), twenty foreign vessels were tied up in the harbor. The strike had already cost their owners some $700,000 to $800,000, a figure that excludes what the vessels could have earned if they had been engaged in other trade. The actual loading of the ships is done by the International Longshoremen's Association (ILA), which had honored the picket lines, with the Grain Millers moving the grain into the terminals. Within hours after the settlement all other groups were back at work and the twenty ships moved into the available berths. Loading would take ten to fourteen days to complete but there was plenty of grain on hand. The reaction of wheat elevator managers in Minnesota and North Dakota was that the settlement had come too late. They already had made other arrangements during the forty-two days of the strike. The generally accepted belief was that prices would be lower. As one manager observed, "Any time you lose a competitive advantage, you lose a price advantage. It will cost the state money that never can be gotten back."

The total cost of the grain strike to the firms and workmen directly or indirectly involved was expected to top $1.5 million. In addition to the losses to shipowners we have already quoted, an estimated fifty to sixty grain cargoes were lost, representing a dollar loss of $115,000 to $330,000 in stevedoring charges and agents' fees. The loss to ILA members could not be estimated because many ILA workers were kept busy handling general cargo. The loss in Grain Millers' wages was estimated at $700 per man or a total of about $250,000. Others who lost income during the strike included members of the Wisconsin and Minnesota grain inspection and weighing departments, railroad men engaged in manning trains carrying grain, grain truck operators (many of them private individuals maintaining their own rigs), truck stop services, tug operators, and mooring line handling crews. The cost of grain storage in railroad cars in the port approximated $10,000 a day. Local merchants indicated their involvement by taking out newspaper ads and their sales must have suffered. Unestimable was the long-run impact on the commerce of the cities.

The interest of the public in the strike must now be discussed. The public, of course, is made up of in-dividuals who have their own vested interests at stake; in this case, the relevant public included the farmers, who needed their grain shipped, the merchants, who wanted money circulating in their community, and the good citizens, who wanted the reputation of their port maintained. What part public agitation played in the settlement of this strike is unclear, but the public did express its views—in letters, telegrams, and newspaper advertisements.[15] The public involved in this case were residents of a city and a region. The nation as a whole did not suffer. Only if wheat importers had turned to Canada or to other sources that were free of labor unrest would the national picture have changed. The question of damage to a local economy or to the national economy is, then, one facet of the public's concern. If the market for wheat were tighter and if wheat were not a surplus crop, the public might have been aroused because the strike threatened the nation's health. Public inconvenience only partially accounts for such public concern. Strikes in such industries as steel or the railroad strike represent a threat to national security because they impair the defense program, and thus engender public concern on this basis. Possibly a grain tie-up, if prolonged enough, could arouse the final public concern—the fear that the strike will have an ill effect on the nation's prestige and on its foreign policy. This assumes, of course, that wheat exports are an important adjunct to our foreign policy.

As the case of the Grain Millers' strike in Duluth and Superior illustrates, the impact of a strike may be great even though only a relatively small number of workers are involved. The impact of the tugboat operators strike on food deliveries in New York City is but one of a number of similar cases in point. A strike does not have to involve an entire industry and thousands or hundreds of thousands of workers in order to be a costly affair to a sizable segment of the public.

The task of measuring the cost of strikes is a difficult one and precise figures are not available. How close the New York City Retail Board came in estimating the cost of the 1965 newspaper strike at $40 million is impossible to determine. The best we can do is sketch some of the factors that will make a given strike more or less costly to the general public, to management, and to the strikers.

From the point of view of the general public, the two dominant features that determine the cost of a strike are the length of the strike and the availability of the product or service involved, including the existence of close substitutes. Quite obviously a strike involving even such essentials as public transportation or a public utility service can be borne more easily for two or three days than for two or three weeks. If the strike involves curtailment of only part of the supply either because the firm continues to operate or because it has provided its outlets with sizable stockpiles or because alternative products are still available, public distress will be correspondingly reduced. Often members of the consuming public will suffer less from out-of-pocket costs than from the inconveniences resulting from the strike. The airline strike in the summer of 1966 involved more costs in the way of inconvenience and disappointment for many travelers than it did increased dollar costs.

Customers of the struck firm, however, who depend upon it for the continuation of their own businesses may be badly affected by the strike. In some cases they may even be forced to suspend operations themselves. If their actions in turn prompt layoffs that reduce sales elsewhere and so produce still further layoffs, the secondary repercussions of the strike may be very great, prompting the government to declare it a national emergency. The larger the strike and the greater the number of workers involved, the more likely it is that these secondary ramifications will become important. It is in anticipation of such results that strikes have sometimes been proclaimed national emergencies before their impact has had much chance to be felt.

The cost to the company of a strike depends on four main variables: current operating level of the plant at the time of the strike, existence of large inventories, the ability of the firm to continue operations despite the strike, and coverage of the firm by strike insurance. A firm that is operating considerably below full capacity prior to the strike may find the strike relatively painless, at least in the initial stages, because it may provide a period in which to work off excessive supplies of the product. Any lost production can then be recouped after the strike by returning to capacity production.

For the past twenty-five years, strikes have normally entailed a closing down of the plant for the duration of the strike. More recently, however, thanks partly to the introduction of automated equipment, a number of firms have found it possible to maintain output in the face of a strike. Little is known about how successful many of these ventures have been. The Kohler company claimed that it continued to operate at a profit throughout the prolonged strike by the UAW, but this contention has been hotly disputed by the union.

Strike insurance may reduce a company's costs considerably. The New York newspaper publishers had an insurance fund that paid to each paper $13,000 for each weekday lost and $26,000 for each Sunday. Total maximum protection was $650,000 for each paper and $2,750,000 for all the papers covered by the insurance plan. Insurance plans are expensive, however, and rarely cover a company's full losses in the event of a shutdown.

The costs to workers of a strike are a function of the availability of alternate jobs, government unemployment benefits, and union strike benefits. In a small company town where few other employers are available, the worker who is on strike for a protracted period will be unable to seek employment at another company. In a large city like New York, on the other hand, a number of part-time or short-term positions may be open to him.

The rule regarding the payment of unemployment benefits to strikers varies from state to state. Many unions have strike benefits that pay the worker half or more of his regular salary and help him meet living expenses while he is out on strike, but these benefits run out in a prolonged strike.

Obviously, a strike also takes a toll on the nerves and dispositions of both management and the strikers (not to mention the public), and the severity of this problem increases with the passage of time as the financial costs of the strike continue to mount. It is this combined financial and psychological pressure that leads eventually to the capitulation of one party or the other.

Trends in Strikes

The Duluth and Superior Grain Miller's strike was chosen as the subject of our case study in order to show the continuous impact a strike has on the economy of an area, even though relatively few workers are on strike. However, discussion of any particular strike is misleading in that it tends to overlook the fact that 99 percent of all contracts are signed without a strike. The time lost in strikes in the United States today is something like one-quarter of 1 percent of total man-days. This figure represents approximately one-fiftieth of the time lost through unemployment. Any evaluation of the economic effects of strikes must also take into consideration the fact that most goods and services prove to have fairly close substitutes and many manufacturers tend to have sizable inventories of finished goods.

Domestic observers have predicted cuts in the American strike rate and compared trends in the United States with strike trends in other countries. Our first task is to discover the observable facts of the American economy. (See Table 14.1.) About fifteen years ago, Robert Dubin made a forecast of stability in the trend of strike activity and the data since then have tended to bear him out.[16] His forecast was based on a belief that group behavior becomes stabilized through institutionalization and a conviction that the individuals and groups involved develop an investment in institutionalized behavior. He further theorized that on fundamental issues (those not yet a part of collective bargaining) in collective bargaining the amount of conflict in union-management relations is inversely related to the disparity in power between the company and the union.

Strike activity in the major industries has shown a decline and this in turn pulls down the average. Strike patterns vary from one industry to another because of the nature of the work (hazards involved, etc.), political forces (degree of organization of employers), and the amount of cohesiveness present among masses of workers. Obviously two- or three-man shops are more difficult to organize

TABLE 14.1   Work Stoppages Resulting from Labor-Management Disputes[1]

Year	Number of Stoppages Beginning in Year	Workers Involved in Stoppages Beginning in Year (Thousands)	Man-Days Idle During Year Number (Thousands)	Percent of Estimated Working Time
1945	4,750	3,470	38,000	0.31
1946	4,985	4,600	116,000	1.04
1947	3,693	2,170	34,600	.30
1948	3,419	1,960	34,100	.28
1949	3,606	3,030	50,500	.44
1950	4,843	2,410	38,800	.33
1951	4,737	2,220	22,900	.18
1952	5,117	3,540	59,100	.48
1953	5,091	2,400	28,300	.22
1954	3,468	1,530	22,600	.18
1955	4,320	2,650	28,200	.22
1956	3,825	1,900	33,100	.24
1957	3,673	1,390	16,500	.12
1958	3,694	2,060	23,900	.18
1959	3,708	1,880	69,000	.50
1960	3,333	1,320	19,100	.14
1961	3,367	1,450	16,300	.11
1962	3,614	1,230	18,600	.13
1963	3,362	941	16,100	.11
1964	3,655	1,640	22,900	.15
1965	3,963	1,550	23,300	.15
1966	4,405	1,960	25,400	.15
1967	4,595	2,870	42,100	.25
1968	5,045	2,649	49,018	.28

[1] The data include all known strikes or lockouts involving 6 workers or more and lasting a full day or shift or longer. Figures on workers involved and man-days idle cover all workers made idle for as long as 1 shift in establishments directly involved in a stoppage. They do not measure the indirect or secondary effect on other establishments or industries whose employees are made idle as a result of material or service shortages.
Source: *Monthly Labor Review,* April 1970.

than the shop employing 200 to 300 workers, and therefore fewer strikes could be expected in small shops. Another factor is the increased use of strike substitutes. The ballot, for example, if guaranteed to all workers, can change their attitudes and allow them a way to express their opinions. Bargaining in good faith can have the same effect as can the assurance of union security. (It is interesting to note that strike activity has increased in those states where union security is threatened by state right-to-work laws.) Richard Lester has cited the "technological obsolescence of the strike," referring to the effects of automation on the willingness and ability of workers to strike. When a shop that previously employed many workers has been reduced to two men by the introduction of automated machinery what will happen to the *esprit de corps* that until now has been an essential requirement for unionization? How can men working individually feel the unifying bond of common problems that could lead to a successful strike? How can a handful of workers consider going on strike when they know that they can be easily replaced by supervisory personnel and that the strike might have no economic impact at all?

Automation is not alone responsible for increasing the disutility or at least the decline in the utility of a strike.[17] The very fact that both parties are increasingly prepared for such action has decreased the economic impact of the strike. Since 1947 legislation has provided that the NLRB be notified sixty days before the end of the contract if agreement on new terms has not been achieved. Once it has been thus forewarned of the union's sentiments, management can plan its inventories and iron out shipping problems. It can even provide its customers with alternate sources of supply in advance. The unions, which are in any case in much healthier financial condition today than they were in the early days, can strengthen their strike funds and begin to line up community support for their position.

Despite Dubin's prediction of a decline in strike activity, an examination of Table 14.1 reveals that strike activity has *increased* in the last few years. Increasing inflationary pressure combined with high corporate profits prompted this increase. Even if the long-run decline in strike activity is resumed, some economists will still find cause for concern in the increased duration of strikes. At least part of the explanation for the increased

duration of strikes undoubtedly lies with the increased strike funds and healthy treasuries we have just mentioned. The unions can afford a prolonged walkout if it is necessary to gain their ends. Management can tolerate longer strikes for two reasons. First, strike insurance schemes are available that ease the economic impact of the strike. Second, in a world of increasing technology it becomes easier for management to quickly make up back orders when the plant is in operation again. Certainly the union workers are not averse to earning overtime pay after the strike is over. The increased duration of strikes may also relate to the fact that today most contracts are long term (twenty-four to thirty-six months). Perhaps within this longer period more complex (and correspondingly difficult to settle) issues arise. Furthermore, both parties, realizing that the contract will not be reopened for negotiation for a prolonged period, may pursue their goals more vehemently. Some economists have also hinted that there is another change in strike trends that is a cause for concern, the fact that strikes *during* contracts are increasing in frequency.[18]

Foreign Strike Patterns

Arthur M. Ross and Paul T. Hartman in 1960 produced an invaluab!e study of strike trends in other countries with free labor movements.[19] They note a general decline in strike activity since the late 1930s. This decline is really the result of two trends—a "withering away" of the strike and a transformation of the strike into an instrument of political protest. Statistics for the fifteen countries studied are compared, and Ross and Hartman point out that the most relevant are the comparisons of strike activity to the number unionized. The authors are realistic enough not to rely completely on statistics: ". . . although statistical measures conceal much of the variety and complexity of human affairs, they do indicate what is characteristic, prevalent and significant."[20]

Ross and Hartman classify the countries studied under four headings according to the particular pattern they show. In all cases, however, the same "leading influences" in strike activity are explored. These influences are those that are amenable to comparison as well as being the most relevant as explanations for strike activity. The stability of organized labor is one of these leading influences: How old is the labor movement? How stable is union membership? (Ross and Hartman point to a plateau in union growth in many countries besides the United States since 1947.) The question of leadership within organized labor is also important: Are there conflicts, rival unions and so on? How strong is the communist influence on labor? Stability of labor-management relations is another issue of importance: To what degree are unions accepted by management? To what extent is there consolidation of the bargaining structure? Organized labor's political activity is examined too, for sometimes gains in this direction satisfy the demands of the members. Is there a labor party as such and if so has it participated in the government? The final leading influence is the role of the state in collective bargaining. To what extent does the government define the terms of employment? To what extent does it step in to settle disputes, and what are the procedures and policies for dispute settlement? Ross and Hartman used this theoretical framework to go far toward explaining the varying patterns of strike activity. With this thesis we certainly agree.

Great Britain

Into the first Ross-Hartman classification (North European pattern, first variant) are grouped the United Kingdom, Denmark, the Netherlands, and Germany. In these countries there is a nominal propensity to strike and strikes have a low to moderate duration. For example, in Great Britain the average time lost as a result of strikes is one-half day per worker compared to two days per worker in the United States. Unions in Great Britain are matched by employer associations of long standing. In Great Britain, as in the other four countries, there is a labor party that has participated in the government, and the government itself participates in the collective bargaining process. When the Labour party has been in power in Great Britain, at least, the unions have apparently not felt obligated to show particular restraint in their demands and actions.[21] Each of the countries in this group has quite different organizations. There are a great variety of structural forms in England, which also has the safety valve of the unofficial strike (70 to 90 percent of all strikes), the protest by union members against the action and decisions of their leaders (we would call it a wildcat strike). Most such strikes are led by the stewards rather than by the union's top leaders. In some industries there are work councils, which regulate the terms of employment. Finally it should be noted that strikers have no protection under English law and are subject to discharge for striking, although they rarely suffer this penalty.

West Germany

West Germany, like Great Britain, also has union stability, a surprising fact when one remembers that collective bargaining was suspended from

1933 to 1945. West Germany is a special instance because there the employer associations are relatively strong and the workers are comparatively docile. In each plant elected works councils administer agreements, settle grievances, and, incidentally, weaken the union. At the same time codetermination has reduced the number of strikes in the steel industry.

Sweden

The North European pattern, second variant, is exemplified by Sweden where strikes are infrequent but those that do occur are long. The significant difference between Sweden and those countries representing the first variant of this pattern is that in the former the government does not interfere in labor disputes. A one-week advance notice of a strike or lockout is required in Sweden. There are eight official national district mediators, and one of these must be called in before either a strike or a lockout can be instituted. If his efforts fail, however, no further government intervention results.

Strikes are magnified in Sweden because of two considerations. In the first place, both sides have strike insurance that protects them at least in part from the crippling costs of a huge strike. Second, the tendency toward industrywide and even nationwide bargaining means inevitably that a large number of workers will be involved. Even where the unions have sought to engage in "spot" strikes, employer associations have almost invariably responded with an industry-wide lockout to avoid "whipsawing."

France

Quite different characteristics are displayed by the countries grouped by Ross and Hartman into the Mediterranean-Asian pattern; France, Italy,

Japan, and India. In these countries, the number of strikes is very high, but the duration of each strike is short, sometimes measured only in hours. The most common characteristic of these four countries is the weak, unstable nature of the relatively young trade unions. As a result, labor relations are weak and unstable and the content of bargaining is minimal. The unions lack the financial resources to support a prolonged strike and they are continually weakened and confused by dissension from the left. Frequently, labor protest is directed against the government—strikes become demonstration strikes.

France has one of the older labor movements of this group but it has been plagued with rivalries for leadership between communists, socialists, and Catholics. The bargaining pattern is not clear; somewhat broader than plantwide, it is not industrywide. Collective bargaining is concerned primarily with wages because the government has regulated the terms of employment since the 1930s and because employers are strongly organized against union activity. Government regulation has covered hours, paid vacations, and a minimum wage high enough to have an effect on all wages. Social charges, family allowances, and the like are determined by the government, which also plays the role of entrepreneur. Thus it is not surprising that French strikes are more in the nature of political demonstrations than tests of economic power.

Japan

The Japanese labor movement is particularly new, since it is a product of the Allied occupation. Legislation during the occupation and further legislation in 1947 restricted collective bargaining and strikes so that most strikes have been political demonstrations. Japan has enterprise unions, which cover all workers in a company regardless of their occupation, as opposed to national unions. Thus there can be no such thing as industrywide collective bargaining and every conceivable labor movement ideology is to be found represented in Japanese unions. Peak union membership was reached in 1949–1950 but membership fell off afterwards as campaigns were waged against communism. Despite the decline of communist influence, demonstration strikes have been frequent, but the unions remain weak politically. In Japan bargaining until recently has been limited in scope, concentrating primarily upon bonuses, retirement problems, and rights of permanent employees. The unions are weak financially and some of the employers have regained the upper hand. There has been a resurgence of union interest in wages in more recent years. Between 1950 and 1956, the Japanese economy averaged 600 work stoppages a year. Since 1960, however, the figure has risen to over 1,000 annually, and many of these have had increased wages as their objective.[22]

India

The resemblance of India's strike pattern to the Mediterranean-Asian group has declined somewhat since independence. There are a large number of strikes, but in India they tend to be of longer duration than in the rest of the group. Pradeep Kumar, a contemporary Indian observer, correlated labor unrest to the state of the economy: during the First Five Year Plan there was prosperity and industrial peace; during the Second Five Year Plan, there was inflation and unrest.[23] Kumar also observes, "In India, generally speaking, a large number of strikes are conducted for political reasons disguised as economic purposes and although the trade unions are not so financially well off as in the United States, the duration of the strikes is longer than in many advanced countries."[24] Kumar also relates the length of strikes to the financial well-being of the union. Ross, observing that Indian unions are weak financially because they depend on contributions rather than on dues, points to other reasons for long strikes. Among these are the Indian tradition of civil disobedience, which makes a strike more acceptable, extreme inter-union rivalries (primarily rivalries exist between the Congress Party supported INTUC—Indian National Trade Union Congress—and the Communist Party dominated AITUA—All India Trade Union Association), and the fact that the Indian is so accustomed to abject poverty that the loss of his wage for a period is more supportable.

Certainly some of the reasons for disputes derive from the fact that no Indian union is assured of a position as an exclusive bargaining agent and from the caste system, with its social barriers and traditions, an important element in the consideration of many contemporary Indian problems. Most management officials are totally unconcerned with personnel problems and hence are hostile to labor organizations. Many strikes can be traced to what would be grievances in the United States: for example, workers may strike against a discriminatory discharge, against management language that injured their sentiments, against the transfer of workers, or against harassment by management.[25]

The Congress Party is not a labor party, but the trade unions did constitute the labor arm of the independence movement. Party leaders have become members of unions in an attempt to promote industrial peace.

The government has attempted to cut the strike rate by adjudication, but in 1960 only 3.2 percent of all strikes were settled in that manner. Conciliation and mediation through the government were more successful, accounting for 39.2 percent of the settlements. Voluntary arbitration is not too important for the country as a whole, but it is the keystone of the industrial systems of states like Maharashtra and Madhya Pradesh.

United States and Canada

Ross and Hartman group the United States and Canada together in their final category as countries that experience long and frequent strikes. Although the government policies of these two countries differ, they are grouped together because the practices of unions and employers are frequently the same. Canada uses elaborate conciliation procedures, generally involving delay periods, compulsory mediation, and recommendations by conciliation boards. The reasons for the American-Canadian strike pattern include (in brief): relatively recent occurrence of mass unionization, interunion rivalries (where these have abated the number of strikes has dropped), decentralization of collective bargaining, lack of a dominant labor party in either country, and a permissive attitude by the two governments toward lengthy economic tests of strength.

How much of the future strike pattern of the United States can be forecast from the examination of the patterns of other countries? A reexamination of the major influences on strike patterns is revealing. In so far as an older, highly organized union organization tends to promote industrial peace, we can predict no reductions in strikes from this direction. With the union of the AFL and the CIO

there was less reason to talk in terms of conflict in ideology or rival leadership, but with the new ALA more unrest may result. Stability of labor-management relations, an important factor in the reduction of strike activity, is also increasing in the American scene. More and more employers are coming to accept unions as bargaining agents for the workers. However, there is no labor party in the United States that might replace an interest in economic gains with an interest in political gains. Furthermore, the government does not take an active part in collective bargaining, compared to governments of countries following the North European pattern (first variant). Ross and Hartman thus conclude that the United States may see an eventual decline in strike activity, but the level will not reach the lows experienced in the United Kingdom, the Netherlands, Denmark, and West Germany.

Israel

Of course, many countries do not fall into any neat classification. For example, Israel, despite the newness of the country and its institutions, mostly enjoys industrial peace. This phenomenon results from the great strength of the Histadrut relative to the employers as well as the fact that employers generally must pay strike benefits if they lose the strike.[26] Interestingly enough, the years in which strike-caused production losses were highest in Israel were years in which there was conflict within the Histadrut.

Mexico

The environment for strikes in Mexico depends on the government's attitude, which ranges from deep hostility to open permissiveness and encouragement. Except in the case of public employees, where the period is

TABLE 14.2 Number of Work Stoppages and Time Lost

Country	Year	No. Econ. Active	Year	No. of Disputes	No. of Workers	No. of Work Days Lost
Australia	1961	4,225,096	1966	1,273	394,851	732,084
France	1967	20,269,000	1967	1,675	2,824,000	4,204,000
Germany (West)	1966	27,161,000	1967	n.f.	60,000	390,000
India	1961	188,675,500	1966	2,210	1,205,570	10,494,000
Israel	1966	948,400	1966	282	88,616	155,975
Italy	1966	19,653,000	1967	2,658	2,244,000	8,568,000
Japan	1966	48,910,000	1967	1,214	733,000	1,830,000
Mexico	1960	11,332,016	1965	663	14,137	n.f.
Nether.	1960	4,168,626	1966	20	11,188	12,647
Sweden	1965	3,449,900	1967	4	100	400
U.K.	1961	24,616,620	1967	2,116	734,000	2,787,000
U.S.	1966	80,164,000	1967	4,595	2,870,000	42,100,000

Source: *Yearbook of Labour Statistics* (I.L.O., Geneva, 1967); *1969 Handbook of Labor Statistics* (Bureau of Labor Statistics, Washington, 1969).

ten days, a union must notify both the employer and the government conciliation service of its intent to strike six days in advance. Unions are forbidden to strike for higher wages purely in response to rising prices but they can engage in sympathy strikes.

If the government declares a strike to be legal, the employer is free to hire substitute workers only to the extent necessary for purposes of plant safety. Furthermore, the employer must continue to pay wages to the striking workers. If a strike is declared illegal, on the other hand, the employer is relieved of all payments to the strikers and can seek to hire others. Since unions have little in the way of strike funds, the question of suspension of wage payments is a serious one.

Between 1949 and 1957 Mexico experienced about 200 strikes per year. There was a sharp jump to 740 in 1958; thereafter a plateau of about 380 a year was maintained. About 58 percent of the strikes are settled between the two parties. The rest are terminated by government cease-and-desist orders or by formal conciliation and arbitration proceedings.

As in the United States, union recognition has dwindled in importance as a major source of strikes in recent years in Mexico. (For a statistical account of above discussion, see Table 14.2.)

Attempts at Solution

As we have already mentioned, there are conflicting opinions about the burdens strikes impose on the American economy. Even if the belief that strikes will diminish in number is accepted, particular concern still exists over the effect of a strike on an industry involving the national defense. In 1947 this concern was reflected in the national emergency procedures included in the Taft-Hartley Act. Evidence of a continuing concern is apparent in the criticisms of this procedure and the suggestions for its improvement. Criticisms of the Taft-Hartley procedure (to summarize, the procedure is accused of being too rigid, too limited, and too predictable), will be explored after we outline the main provisions of the act itself.

The Taft-Hartley Act provides that the President, if he fears that a strike or lockout that will constitute a national emergency is imminent, can appoint a board of inquiry to prepare a written report on the facts of the dispute. This board is not empowered to make recommendations. After reviewing this report, the President may direct the Attorney General to seek an injunction from the appropriate district court to prevent the strike. If this court agrees that there is a danger to the national health and safety, it will issue the injunction. During the next sixty days business proceeds as usual while the Federal Mediation and Conciliation Service tries to mediate the dispute and both parties "make every effort" to resolve the dispute voluntarily. With the issuance of the injunction, the board of inquiry is reconvened and at the end of the sixty days it reports to the President on the state of the dispute and management's last offer. Within the next fifteen days, the NLRB holds a secret ballot on this offer, and within the succeeding five days the Attorney General is directed to seek the discharge of the injunction. Thus, if no settlement is achieved within the eighty-day period, the parties are free to go ahead with the strike. At this point, the President reports on the proceedings to Congress and makes any recommendations that he may feel are relevant.

Criticisms of Taft-Hartley have ranged from charges that it is too forceful to claims that it has insufficient power, depending upon whether the source of the criticism was a spokesman for labor or for management or a labor relations expert. Adding to the confusion is the substantial disagreement among the labor "experts."

The "experts" do virtually agree, however, that the provision for a secret ballot on the employer's final offer should be eliminated. Contrary to the expectations of the formulators of that provision, union members have consistently and overwhelmingly rejected the "final offer." Experts contend that the ballot does nothing except harden positions on both sides. These observers express more disagreement on the subject of whether or not it would be advisable to have the fact-finding board appointed by the President make its finding public. Although this would place considerable pressure on the recalcitrant party to accept the recommendation, some experts are concerned about the very power this would give the board and the President. Finally, a number of experts maintain that the procedures provided for under Taft-Hartley are too inflexible and that the President should be granted several alternative ways to approach the problem. Although all the Presidents since Truman have exercised their option to ignore the Taft-Hartley Act and pursue some other course (including doing nothing), a number of critics argue that the President is not truly free to act as long as the terms of the Taft-Hartley Act serve as his primary option.

Union representatives tend to concentrate their fire on Taft-Hartley's provision for the use of the injunction. The injunction obviously has unpleasant historical connotations. Furthermore, unions argue that it is unfair to them because it gives management another eighty-day period during which working conditions remain unchanged. Union spokesmen who feel that the imminence of a strike is a necessary catalyst to effective bargaining by management argue that there is little incentive for management to settle during this period.

Spokesmen for management have been less critical of Taft-Hartley than have those for labor. The reservations of the former focus on the fact that a real emergency may not be averted under the terms of the act. Of twenty-four cases where Taft-Hartley has been invoked in a national emergency situation, eight cases resulted in strikes after the injunction expired. The fact that seven of these were in shipping or longshoring (one was in coal) provides cold comfort to those who reason that it could just as easily happen in more vital industries in the future. Thus management frequently sees the need for a law designed to curb the power of unions still more.

Alternatives to Strikes

Some critics are concerned not with the danger of shutdown of a defense industry but with the concept of a strike itself. These observers contend that the strike is a primitive form of conflict and that it might well be replaced in a more sophisticated society. Suggestions for progress from one writer include first of all deciding which of the issues precipitating the strike can and should be resolved by other methods.[27] The equality of power of the two parties should be coincident with the public's image of this equality and public policy might be changed to reflect acceptance of unions.

Many critics of the Taft-Hartley would agree with the idea of Neil Chamberlain's "bag of tricks,"[28] without necessarily subscribing to all of the tricks contained therein. Chamberlain's point is that government should have a variety of measures at its disposal so that there will be some question in the minds of labor and management about what it will do. Any measure used too frequently is deemed likely to be ineffective. Chamberlain tests his tricks against two criteria: Will the flow of essential goods and

services be maintained? Will voluntarism (the notion that workers should rely exclusively on unions to promote their interests as wage earners, not on the government) be maintained?

The measures mentioned by Chamberlain or others include mediation, which is the advice of a nonpartisan person or group who has explored the situation. The major problem, of course, is that acceptance of mediation is voluntary and so the method will not work in the toughest cases. The appointment of a fact-finding board that will make the results of its inquiry known publicly relies on the power of public opinion and may weaken voluntarism if there is strong moral pressure applied. The use of an injunction, or a second one if the Taft-Hartley procedure has already been employed, satisfies those who want to maintain the status quo but does nothing to solve the problem. Government seizure has often been discussed and it has occasionally been practiced in time of war, but this technique makes it possible for the government to play favorites and could have serious political implications. How can voluntarism be protected in such a situation and how can the seizure be kept temporary? In a sense, this method, like the injunction, simply postpones the problem, since it contributes nothing to getting either party to agree to terms. In addition, seizure presents new problems: issues arise involving how much the employer should be compensated and how much wages should be paid.

The suggestion of compulsory arbitration raises a variety of problems. This method differs from mediation in that both parties must accept the solutions proposed by the nonpartisan expert(s). The flow of essential goods and services may be maintained but voluntarism is certainly lost. How serious should a dispute be before it warrants such a severe measure? How can the nonpartisan group come to a decision? Chamberlain notes that the nonpartisan group has a harder role than the role of the public service commission. Once the decision has been made and publicized, will it be enforceable? Compulsory arbitration could also become a political question with appointment to the arbitrating group being subject to political pressure. Certainly once both sides to the dispute lose their freedom, they may give up making any attempt to settle their own problems.

Perhaps the greatest amount of uncertainty as to government action could be introduced by providing for referral of the problem to Congress when the President finds no other solution, since Congress would be acting in the pressure of the moment. Moreover, such a decision might well be one that Congress would prefer not to live with.

Little attention has been paid to an alternative procedure proposed by Neil Chamberlain as well as other prominent labor economists (e.g., E. Wight Bakke, LeRoy Marceau, Richard Musgrave, George Goble).[29] This procedure is known as the nonstop-page strike (sometimes called the statutory strike) or the nonstrike. Each man has varied the details of this procedure, but the essentials remain the same—both sides to the dispute would forego the cessation of work but would suffer predetermined economic penalties. Labor would forfeit a part of the wages and management would forego profits and perhaps bear additional expenses. Critics have asked how the parties can agree to the terms of such a strike when they cannot settle on a contract. Some proponents of the nonstrike have answered this by suggesting that it might be a procedure that could be invoked by the President in an emergency situation. The problem of guaranteeing that the workers will work at capacity when receiving, for example, half their usual wages, remains. If management penalizes a worker who has slowed down will it be accused of discriminating against a strike leader? Why would such a strike not be interminable when the pressure of public opinion is absent?

All such plans call for a refund of forfeited wages and profits if the strike is settled within a certain time. At the end of each time period, then, there would be particular pressure to settle. One of the chief economic pressures on management is missing here. Profits are lost but customers are not. Problems of hiring new personnel at all levels would have to be faced. Who would want to take a job at a penalty rate when regular paying jobs might be available?

Scholars and government officials in other countries have also been working on the problem of strikes, but most of the techniques they have proposed have been at least suggested in the United States. Many countries on the European continent have devised a system of labor courts to resolve disputes arising under existing contracts, but these have developed mainly because of deficiencies in the grievance machinery.

Certainly the most dramatic departure from the American experience has been made by those countries utilizing compulsory arbitration. England (for a period during World War II), the Scandinavian countries (Sweden excepted) and Australia have all had for varying periods of time a system of compulsory arbitration. In the winter of 1969–1970 the United States (with approval of Congress and the President) adopted a program of compulsory arbitration for the railroads.

Most students of collective bargaining agree that compulsory arbitration is likely to weaken the effectiveness of free collective bargaining. Either or both parties may hope to obtain more from the arbiter's decision than they can from the bargaining table. They may thus fail to enter wholeheartedly into bargaining but simply hold out for a decision by an outside party. Many of these same criticisms have been raised in those countries where compulsory arbitration is in effect. Critics there still argue that it should be abandoned or reserved for essential industries or for cases of true national emergency. Periodically, a particularly vexing strike in the United States brings forth calls for compulsory arbitration, but the calls soon subside once the strike has ended.

Conclusions

Are strikes a necessary part of free collective bargaining? For the last century American opinion has been divided between two extremes. On one side are those that maintain that the injunction is slavery; their opponents claim that industrywide strikes demonstrate the monopoly that organized labor has attained.

Regardless of where in this range of opinion one places oneself as an economist, one must note the incontrovertible fact that the nature of the strike is changing. While the strike is still used as a bargaining technique, the emotional content of the strike has declined. The strikers are assigned to position and fulfill their tasks as they fulfill their jobs. There have even been instances of management's serving coffee to the placard carriers, illustrating the acceptance by both parties that this is just a further technique of bargaining.

This change, of course, brings a decrease in violence in its wake. The really violent strikes in the United States occurred before the right to organize was protected by law, when both sides still felt something was to be gained by militant aggressiveness. Now the union matches management in its "businesslike" approach to bargaining.

There seems to be no basis for a forecast of a continued decline in strike activity in this country. The short-run unemployment threat posed by automation will be countered by strong protests until some successful formula can be worked out. Perhaps in countries where economic conditions (England's dependence on foreign trade, for example) virtually dictate the need for uninterrupted production, the strike, except as a wildcat protest, may continue to decline in importance.

NOTES

1. Quoted by Arthur M. Ross and Paul T. Hartman, *Changing Patterns of Industrial Conflict* (New York: Wiley, 1960), p. 5.
2. Joel Morris, "The Psychoanalysis of Labor Strikes," *Labor Law Journal* (December 1959), pp. 833–844.
3. Neil W. Chamberlain, "The Problem of Strikes," *Proceedings of New York University Thirteenth Annual Conference on Labor* (1960), pp. 423–424.
4. George P. Shultz, "Strikes: The Private Stake and the Public Interest," in Richard Lester (ed.), *Labor: Readings on Major Issues* (New York: Random House, 1965), pp. 463–464.
5. William Graham Sumner, as quoted in E. Wight Bakke, Clark Kerr, and Charles W. Anrod (eds.), *Unions, Management, and the Public* (New York: Harcourt Brace Jovanovich, 1960), p. 248.
6. J. E. T. Eldridge and G. C. Cameron, "Unofficial Strikes: Some Objections Considered," *British Journal of Sociology* (March 1964), p. 21.
7. Alvin W. Gouldner, *Wildcat Strike* (Yellow Springs, Ohio: Antioch Press, 1954), pp. 89–91.
8. Eldridge and Cameron, *op. cit.*

9. Arthur M. Ross, "The Natural History of the Strike," in Arthur Kornhauser, Robert Dubin, and Arthur M. Ross (eds.), *Industrial Conflict* (New York: McGraw-Hill, 1954), p. 31.

10. *Ibid.,* p. 32–33.

11. Henry Mayer, "Strategy of the Strike," *Labor Law Journal* (August 1960), p. 762.

12. As quoted by Mayer, *op. cit.,* p. 754.

13. Ivan A. Ezrine, "Nadir of the No-Strike Clause," *Labor Law Journal* (November 1957), pp. 769–816.

14. Walter L. Daykin, "The Legal Aspects of Strikes," *Labor Law Journal* (August 1960), pp. 752, 765.

15. The classic statement of the belief that the pressure of public opinion can be a potent force in resolving strikes can be found in Neil W. Chamberlain, *Social Responsibility and Strikes* (New York: Harper & Row, 1953).

16. Robert Dubin, "Industrial Conflict: The Power of Prediction," *Industrial and Labor Relations Review* (April 1965), pp. 352–363.

17. James L. Stern, "Declining Utility of the Strike," *Industrial and Labor Relations Review* (October 1964), pp. 60–72.

18. Joseph W. Block, "The Strike and Discontent," *Monthly Labor Review* (June 1963), p. 646.

19. Ross and Hartman, *op. cit.*

20. *Ibid.,* p. 41.

21. Sterling D. Spero, *Labor Relations in British Nationalized Industry* (New York: New York University Press, 1955), p. 50.

22. Robert Evans, Jr., "Shinto: Japanese Labor Spring Wage Offensive," *Monthly Labor Review* (October 1967), p. 23.

23. Pradeep Kumar, "Strikes in India," *The Economic Weekly* (October 3, 1964), p. 1603.

24. *Ibid.,* p. 1605.

25. Van Dusen Kennedy, "The Role of the Union in the Plant in India," *Industrial and Labor Relations Review* (December 1955), pp. 258–259.

26. Irvin Sobel, "Israel," in Walter Galenson (ed.), *Labor in Developing Economies* (Berkeley: University of California Press, 1963), p. 240.

27. Stern, *op. cit.,* p. 68.

28. Chamberlain, "The Problem of Strikes," *op. cit.,* pp. 421–448.

29. For a current appraisal, see Stephen H. Sosnick, "Non-Stoppage Strikes: A New Approach," *Industrial and Labor Relations Review* (October 1964), pp. 72–80.

3

Collective Bargaining and the Economy

15

Automation and the Threat of Unemployment

No one but a fool or a man who has been displaced from his job would oppose the miracle of technological change.

—Anonymous

The solution of the problem of technological change and unemployment is not to prevent automation or slow down technology, but rather to move toward improving the flexibility and the adaptability of the labor force.

—Ewan Clague

□ SINCE time immemorial most men have been torn by two conflicting attitudes toward their work—a dislike of their jobs and the fear that they might lose them. Unemployment, for at least short periods, can result from a variety of causes including technological change. It is not surprising, therefore, that a substantial part of unions' efforts have been directed toward protecting workers from this danger. As we shall see shortly, however, all too often collective bargaining has been helpless to protect workers from the crisis of unemployment.

There are five main kinds of unemployment: seasonal, frictional, structural, cyclical, and technological. *Seasonal unemployment* is often an important attribute of certain lines of work that, for one reason or another, can only be done during certain seasons of the year. We are all familiar with the irregularities of work in construction and certain kinds of agriculture, but we are still startled when we find that a prosperous resort city like

Atlantic City is classed as a depressed area during the winter months. Weather also plays a major role in the seasonal character of iron ore shipping on the Great Lakes.

Unions have tried to combat seasonal unemployment by attempting to push up wages in such trades so that a worker's annual take-home pay is adequate even though he is forced to endure weeks or even months of idleness. In addition, unions that help employers recruit workers often have been able to relocate workers in other cities during slack periods in their home communities.

Frictional unemployment exists because United States plants still experience a sizable amount of turnover in their labor forces. Furthermore, each year an additional 1 to 2 million workers enter the labor market. On the whole, the actions of unions probably do more to complicate the lives of the frictionally unemployed than to help them. Unions normally seek seniority provisions covering layoffs and promotions by length of service. While these provisions protect workers already in the plant, they make the position of newly hired workers less tenable. The high rates of unemployment among teenagers, for example, can probably partially be attributed to these union rules.

Structural unemployment in some ways resembles long-term frictional unemployment, but it is that and more. Structural unemployment involves changes in the structure of the economy. When there is rapid growth in some industries and decline in others workers may be unable to make the required shifts between industries in response to changing demands for labor. Workers may fail to shift because they lack the necessary skill or education to fill the new jobs or because they are unwilling or unable to leave their present geographical locations. Some of the latter instances are more properly referred to as unemployment connected with residence in a depressed area.

Many of our comments about the actions of unions with respect to frictional unemployment are equally applicable to structural unemployment. Provisions like seniority make shifting by the structurally unemployed more difficult. Furthermore, unions are sometimes charged with pushing wages too high in expanding fields, thereby lessening the demand for labor and decreasing the number of job opportunities in those areas. Unions, however, do try to protect workers from displacement due to structural changes by their demands for severance pay and for retraining programs (paid for by the employer) that will fit workers for new jobs when their old ones disappear.

Historically, *cyclical unemployment* has perhaps been the major source of alarm to workers. Even after three decades of comparatively high levels of employment in this country, many workers still remember the thirties when as much as 25 percent of the labor force was without work. Because downswings in business cycles wreak heavy damage on business as well as labor, labor has been unable to secure much by way of protection from cyclical unemployment through collective bargaining. The best that unions have been able to achieve is strict observance of seniority for layoffs and recalls, which protects the older workers with a long service record. Where plants have been compelled to halt operations completely, even such limited protection becomes meaningless.

Older than the fear of cyclical unemployment and equally closely identified with capitalism is fear of *technological unemployment.* Early in the nineteenth century English loom workers rioted and smashed the new machines that threatened the old ways of production. The workers' continuing fear of modern technological developments is a compound of anxiety that they will be displaced from their jobs and a general dread and suspicion of anything new. Any change in production routines is disturbing because it creates uncertainties in the worker's mind as to whether he can meet the requirements of the new job (physically or mentally) and whether he will now receive less pay or be required to do more work for the same wage. It is not surprising, therefore, that unions have always taken a keen interest in all such proposed changes and have sought to protect their memberships as best they can.

It is not true, as some writers seem to imply, that unions have always taken a negative attitude toward technological change. Union leaders have from the first recognized many of the benefits to be derived from the use of machinery and their attitude has never been one of unflagging resistance to change. In the 1880s, for example, Samuel Gompers welcomed technological change and hailed its benefits to workers. Later, however, he reversed his position and almost wrecked the Cigarmakers Union by his opposition to new equipment for rolling cigars.

John L. Lewis provides the prime example of one of the most sweeping embraces of modern technology by a labor leader. During the late 1940s and in the 1950s, Lewis welcomed modern coal-mining machinery as a means of raising the coal miners' standard of living, and he worked with management to crush all resistance by workers to the new methods. The cost in terms of displacement of miners was a heavy one, however. Since 1958 between 12 and 15 percent of the miners have been out of work. Mechanization is not responsible for all this unemployment. (The coal industry has been declining for some years as a result of competition from other fuels.) Nevertheless, fear of mass unemployment has been the primary reason that unions have tended to be cautious in their acceptance of new techniques.

Nearly a quarter of a century ago the late Sumner Slichter, one of this country's most distinguished industrial relations experts, suggested that there were three main methods open to unions in handling the problem of unemployment created by technological change.[1] The first possibility for the union was a policy of opposition—the union could refuse to permit the machines' entry into the plant. Even where unions were powerful enough to compel an employer to abide by this ruling, however, their efforts, according to Slichter, were doomed to ultimate failure. Other plants that were either not unionized or organized by different unions would eventually come to adopt the new equipment. Sooner or later, the company that failed to introduce the new equipment would find itself at so severe a competitive disadvantage that the union would either have to yield in its opposition to the technological improvements or the firm would be driven out of business. Either way the end result was inevitably the triumph of the machines and if this meant a displacement of workers, then a policy of opposition could do nothing to prevent it in the long run.

It is not difficult, however, to find unions that have enforced work rules designed to limit the pace of innovation. Classic illustrations can be found in the building trades where unions have limited the width of paint brushes or refused to employ paint sprayers. Unions have refused to work on prefabricated construction units, requiring that parts preassembled at the fac-

tory must be disassembled and then reassembled at the job site. In the 1920s the Hosiery Workers Union limited a worker to the care of a single machine, even though nonunion shops regularly specified two machines per worker. In the long run, however, in both cases the unions have had to yield substantial ground in precisely the manner predicted by Slichter.

Two points should be emphasized here. First, opposition to technological change is by no means limited to unionized workers. Unions simply organize, formalize, and enhance the cohesiveness and coordination of featherbedding practices[2] that are used by unorganized workers. Second, although Slichter was right in arguing that complete opposition to technological change is doomed to eventual failure, unions can have considerable success in the short run in holding up change and may even frustrate effective use of technological innovation for protracted periods. As we will see later, resistance to automation may be more difficult for unions to maintain even in the short run.

A second possible union reaction to the threatened introduction of machinery is competition. In this instance, according to Slichter, the union would not only offer to forego future wage increases, but would accept wage reductions while agreeing to work harder as a price for the employer's rejecting the proposed technological change. Once again the efforts of the union are doomed to eventual failure. The increases in productivity in rival companies made possible by their adoption of the change will make it increasingly difficult for the workers in the plant without the new equipment to compete effectively. Either they have to agree, as the machinery demonstrates its efficiency elsewhere, to accept lower and lower wages and work harder and harder until their jobs are no longer really worth preserving, or they resist further concessions. In the latter case, they expose their employer to the same economic jeopardy noted with respect to the policy of outright opposition.

The only policy with any real long-run chance of success, said Slichter, was a policy of control. Controlling the process of introducing technological change can involve either a slowing of the pace of introduction to enable workers to make adjustments to its impact or the provision of assistance to displaced workers or some combination of the two.

If the pace of technological change is not too rapid, the process of turnover in the plant's labor force will reduce the need to displace workers. As workers quit or retire, they are simply not replaced, thus diminishing the need to lay off workers as the volume of employment shrinks.

Even when technological change does not decrease the total number of jobs or possibly even increases it, job requirements may be changed so radically that many old jobs will be eliminated and replaced with new ones. The union's control over the introduction of machinery includes its insistence that currently employed workers be given an opportunity at the new positions, even if they have to be retrained in order to be employable. In the past some of the craft unions established their own training programs, but increasingly in recent years unions have insisted that employers bear the cost of retraining workers. As early as the end of the nineteenth century, the ITU won for its members the right to learn the linotype at standard union rates.

Where some displacement was inevitable because the number of jobs was reduced or because some workers (usually the older ones) felt inadequate to meet the demands of the new equipment, unions have sought to protect the displaced workers in a variety of ways. Severance pay designed to help support the worker while he is between jobs and to aid him (with moving expenses, etc.) in his search for a new one has become an increasingly popular item in collective bargaining agreements. As we noted in an earlier chapter, opportunities for early retirement under company pension programs have also grown in popularity.

The judicious exercise of such control by the union can clearly help workers to ease the pains of transition from old methods of production to new ones. Equally obvious is the fact that if the reins of control over the introduction of new production methods are not solely in the hands of management, the pace of introduction will be slower and more relaxed.[3]

Agitation against technological change has experienced a resurgence since World War II in response to the introduction of automation. The word automation means so many things to so many people that our discussion must logically begin with an outline of the processes that are most frequently lumped together under the general heading of automation.

1. The mere mechanization of the handling of material at an accelerated pace, including the use of hoists, cranes, conveyor belts (including pneumatic tubes for the transportation of materials by air pressure) as well as newly designed tractors and forklift trucks, has sometimes been cited as an example of automation. Although great increases in efficiency can be obtained by these means, they represent a less dramatic departure from past forms of mechanization than other forms of automation.

2. The linking together of conventionally separate operations by the use of automatic lines of operation is also

included under the heading of automation. Sometimes the machine stations are kept separate, but the material passes automatically from one machine station to another without the need of human intervention or direction. This process is sometimes controlled by tape with directions given by computer. There have also been some attempts to integrate these hitherto separate steps by using a single huge machine that can by itself process the material through the various stages.

3. By the use of a series of feedbacks, automated equipment is now able to check automatically on the quality of the goods being produced. Not only does this raise the plant's standards of quality control, but it also eliminates the necessity for human inspections of this type since the system can be set up so that the machine can correct itself automatically if any errors are found.

4. Perhaps the most dramatic and best known form of automation involves the use of the computer. The computer is capable of storing vast amounts of information and recalling it upon command. Furthermore, mathematical problems that previously took a team of mathematicians years to complete can be solved by a computer in the fraction of a second. Computers can also be employed for routine office tasks like payroll processing. It is, in fact, in the area of office work (which has also experienced the greatest increase in work demands) that the most dramatic effects of automation have been felt. Without the modern computer, today's paper work, which is already staggering, would have completely swamped many offices.

More significant to industrial workers has been the gradual introduction of the computer into the factory. Computers are now being used in fields such as chemicals and electrical power. The various component parts of the plant's equipment feed data to the computer with respect to their operations. This mass of information is then compiled and assessed by the computer, which then feeds back to the component parts instructions for their more efficient use. The last variation has perhaps the most revolutionary implications for production standards in the near future.

Automation, in whatever form, presents us with two basic questions. Does automation pose more of a threat to workers' job security than technological change has in the past or is automation nothing more than a continuation of technological progress that began with the industrial revolution? A second question, less frequently asked but still important, is directed at the unions. Does automation pose new and greater problems to unions and collective bargaining than the earlier forms of technological change?

Those who distinguish automation as something sharply different from technological change in the past do so on several grounds. First of all, they emphasize the speed with which automation is being introduced. Although the concept was worked out considerably earlier, computers were not really introduced in the private sector in the United States until 1954. Nevertheless, today there are already between 15,000 and 20,000 computers in use in banks, insurance companies, and government offices, as well as in industrial firms. Technological change in the past has been manageable, this argument runs, because workers have had time to make adjustments to the new requirements prescribed by the machines. Today, by contrast, the pace of automation is so swift as to leave no time for adjustments. Masses of workers will be displaced from their jobs and will be unable to find work elsewhere. According to these scholars, the problem is compounded by the tremendous upsurge in our labor force brought about by the entry of the bumper crop of postwar babies. The proportion of the American labor force over 25 in 1969 was only 77.3 percent. Some economists even go so far as to say that the rash of young workers conceals the gravity of the problems since many of those who would otherwise enter the labor force decide not to do so because no jobs are available. The extended period of education partly (but only partly) offsets the upsurge in our population of recent years by keeping young people from entering our labor force. The increase in the labor force since the 1960s has been three times as fast for teenagers as it has been for the adult population.

There can be no question that in selected industries the impact of automation on employment has been startling. Instances of a reduction in a plant's labor force by 60 percent or more have not been unheard of, leading to stories of a not too distant day when the completely automated factory will take over and all human supervision of machinery will become unnecessary. At an earlier date the glass blower craft was rendered virtually extinct by the invention of the automatic glass blower in 1917.

Even if automation does not eliminate the need for the bulk of production workers, a variation of the theme runs, we will face a need for a far more highly trained and intelligent labor force than is currently available. The task of retraining workers may be so great as to be virtually impossible. Even if it is attempted, it may prove unsuccessful because many workers, particularly the older ones, will be unwilling or unable to learn the skills required.

Automation is accused of presenting a third major threat to the economy. In a variation on the old "secular stagnation" theme of the 1930s, the suggestion is made that automation will permit us to produce more goods than we really need or want. Holders of this view see J. K. Galbraith's "affluent society" turning into a nightmare in which an endless supply of goods for which there are no customers arrives at the nation's marketplaces. All three of these views are so widely held, particularly by workers, that we will analyze each one separately.

Judging by the figures shown in Table 15.1, the growth of the nation's overall productivity rate is somewhat less startling than some of the more alarming forecasts would lead us to believe. While there has been some increase in recent years amounting to about one half of one percent, the gain is less than would have been expected given the fantastic stories of automation's capabilities. Furthermore,

TABLE 15.1 Rates of Change per Year in Output per Man Hour 1919–1969

Years	Total Private	Manufacturing
1919–47	2.2%	3.0%
1947–63	3.2%	2.7%
1947–60	4.5%	4.3%
1950–60	2.7%	2.0%
1960–63	3.5%	3.7%
1960–61	3.3%	2.6%
1961–62	3.9%	3.4%
1962–63	3.5%	3.1%
1963–64	3.8%	3.7%
1964–65	2.8%	2.1%
1965–66	2.8%	2.4%
1966–67	(Series was revised this year)	
1967–68	4.4%	4.3%
1968–69	1.2%	.6%

Source: Walter W. Heller, "Employment and Manpower," in Stanley Lebergott (ed.), *Men Without Work: The Economics of Unemployment* (Englewood Cliffs, N.J.: Prentice-Hall, 1964), p. 10; Department of Labor.

the span of time is too brief to be certain that the increase is a permanent one.

In addition, there are several reasons for believing that the pace of adoption of automation will continue to be slow even in the absence of overt union opposition. First of all, many firms are simply too small or have layouts that are ill suited for extensive automated processes. Even where it is technically feasible to structure the work so that it proceeds in an orderly flow that is adaptable to automation, the costs of doing so may be prohibitive. Some of the more gloomy prophets seem to imply that what is technically feasible is automatically economically appropriate, but this is by no means necessarily the case.

Even where automation is both technically feasible and economically promising, it still may not be adopted immediately. Not only do the forces of inertia slow down the pace of change, but also it often takes a long time to recast a plant's operations even after the basic decision to do so has been made.

In light of these forces acting as a drag on the pace of automation, it is not surprising to learn that the predicted "bandwagon effect," in which competitive pressures irresistibly drive employers to adopt the new techniques overnight, has not materialized. As George Terborgh has noted in his book *The Automation Hysteria,* a recent BLS survey showed only fourteen out of thirty-six industries even mentioned computer control of production.[4]

While all of this is reassuring, there are two reservations that need to be made. Although a gain in productivity of 1 percent or less looks small, it represents a tremendous increase percentagewise when the annual increment has been about 3 percent, and its implications may be far more significant than they appear to be at first glance.[5] Furthermore, one could argue that switches to automated procedures in the future will occur at exactly the same time as the numbers arriving in the labor market are doubling, thereby making future adjustments more difficult to achieve.

Economists have always been inclined to dismiss the fears of workers and others who fear permanent displacement of men by machines. Only a handful of economists—many of them under the influence of Karl Marx —have foreseen the creation of an industrial reserve army of the technologically unemployed. Economists have minimized the danger of unemployment from technological improvement for three major reasons. First, it is generally believed that machines, by creating many new products, create as many (or more) jobs as they destroy. Consumers are viewed as having an unending demand for additional consumer goods, and the machine is seen as a way of bringing more goods to consumers at lower prices.

Second, the overall elasticity of consumer demand is assumed to be sufficiently great to produce more than proportionate increases in the quantities purchased as the new technology through lowered costs makes lower prices on consumer goods possible.

Those who fear the effects of automation argue, however, that this new breed of technology is different from the earlier forms on two counts. First, they contend that it entails a far more complete displacement of workers than previous technological change did. The fact of the matter is, of course, that not only has technological change been going on for a long time, but so has technological displacement of workers. The second argument is that automation, unlike earlier forms of technology, brings with it no new products like the automobile or the television set. Therefore, it not only does not stimulate new rounds of consumer spending as earlier forms of technology did, but it does not prompt extensive secondary investment. The economists' second defense of automation—that it expands output through lowered prices—is countered by noting that the early stages of the industrial revolution occurred when the economy was far more competitive and prices more responsive to changes in costs.

Economists use a third argument to reassure those who worry that machinery will displace human labor. According to this "comparative advantage" thesis there will always be a wage rate at which it will be profitable to maintain the full employment of both human beings and existing capital equipment. If wages are sufficiently flexible downwards, full employment of the factor of human labor can always be ensured. This argument, however, easily leads to the position that labor unions are to blame for unemployment. Unemployment results, according to this argument, not from the destruction of jobs due to technological change, but from union resistance to reductions in wages. Unskilled and semiskilled workers are priced out of the market and go unhired by management because of the high wage demands.[6]

Much has been written about the inability of great numbers (perhaps even the overwhelming majority) of our workers to meet the mental and skill requirements of an automated age. Workers who are incapable of obtaining Ph.D.'s in electrical engineering will be obsolete! Once again, however, there is surprisingly little evidence to support these fears. It is obviously true that there will be an expanded demand for highly trained technicians to install and provide detailed servicing of the new equipment, but some of the scholarly studies[7] suggest and many union leaders complain that automation does little to raise the skill requirements demanded of the average worker. There is even some anxiety lest it actually reduce those requirements. Thus far, however, unemployment seems to have hit most heavily those with little education.

For most of mankind's history, the possibility that men might someday be able to produce so much of almost everything that they would have difficulty finding a market for their output has seemed a remote dream. Does automation make this possibility less of a dream? Predictions about a superfluity of goods, like those concerning mass layoffs, seem somewhat premature. Just before we became unbearably complacent about our position as "affluent Americans," Michael Harrington reminded us of the "other" America, in which 20 percent or more of our people still lived in poverty. Until we have managed to lick the problem of poverty, it seems foolish to talk of being able to produce more than we are able to consume.

Even if poverty were eliminated, there seems little reason to believe that consumer wants will not continue to increase as the means of satisfying those wants expands. The proportion of disposable income going to savings has remained remarkably stable through the years. Consumers may have a "dependence" on advertisers as J. K. Galbraith alleges,[8] but they also appear to be remarkably adjustable to rises in their living standards.

Even though automation may have a far less damaging overall effect on the volume of employment than has been sometimes forecast, there can be little question that its impact will be disturbing to those workers who are forced to change jobs or to acquire new skills. The problem will be the greatest where current employment is in isolated geographical areas (for example, in coal-mining regions), but the overall impact should not be minimized. One labor expert had estimated that in the 1960s, 2.3 million jobs a year would be affected by technology and that in the course of the decade nearly 24 million jobs would have been eliminated or altered.[9] What plans have unions formulated (by discussion and interaction) through collective bargaining to cope with these changes?

Recalling Slichter's outline of common union answers to technological change, the first thing we note is that the policies of opposition and competition are even more futile against automation than they were against earlier forms of technological change. Where introduction is feasible, the gains automation produces by way of reductions in cost and increases in output are too great to be resisted. No group of workers could possibly compete by working harder and accepting lower wages. By the same token, the pressure to introduce the new methods will be too great for a union to be able to resist their introduction completely. Unions have been left, therefore, with the task of devising means of making the transition to automated techniques as easy for their members as possible. We will cite the terms of three recently negotiated contracts as evidence of the kinds of settlements unions have been seeking.

The West Coast Longshore Agreement

Labor strife has been a familiar part of the industrial relations scene for the West Coast longshoring industry. Between 1935 and 1950 there were nearly twenty port strikes, averaging better than one a year, and 300 days of coast-wide strikes. It was something of a surprise, therefore, when in the 1950s the two sides decided to sit down together and negotiate seriously in an effort to resolve their differences. One of the major differences was the issue of technological change. Employers denounced the then-current work rules as archaic and union leaders demanded protection from displacement for workers in the industry.

The first fruits of these talks came in 1959 when the two parties agreed that during the coming year, while additional data was being assembled, management was to be given a free hand in introducing all desired mechanization. The price for this freedom was steep; management agreed to pay $1.5 million to the union workers and to guarantee the jobs of all fully registered (Class A) workers. For the time being all restrictive work rules were to remain in effect.

As negotiations continued, employers began more and more to favor a "buying out" of the restrictive work rules rather than a "sharing of the gains" to be anticipated. It was clear also that employers were seeking more than just the right to introduce mechanization. They wanted to end all restrictive work practices as well.

The union's final selling price when agreement was reached in late 1960 was not low. Management agreed to pay to the workers in addition to the original $1.5 million, $5 million per year for the next five and one half years, or a total of $29 million. All fully registered Longshoremen are guaranteed thirty-five hours of work opportunity per week; this amounts to $111.65 per week per protected worker. If not all workers are needed, they are still paid. Alternatively, if they are eligible for retirement, they can be retired early. A man at the age of sixty-two with the required twenty-five years of service can retire on a pension of $220 per month. This pension continues at that amount until the worker reaches sixty-five, when the pension reverts to the regular pension of $115 per month.

In return for these concessions, management received a free hand in introducing technological change and the right to eliminate all restrictive work rules. Furthermore, the necessity of having to employ unnecessary Longshoremen was eliminated.

The Kaiser Steel Plan

The Kaiser Plan evolved out of the 116-day nationwide steel strike of 1959. During the course of the strike, Kaiser Steel developed a plan that called for the resolution of those issues currently in dispute and for the establishment of a tripartite committee headed by George Taylor, a noted labor mediator. It was agreed that both parties would give the study as much time as was necessary and that neither party would prejudge any of the proposals until the entire package had been determined. The Kaiser Plan was rejected by the other steel companies, and as a result Kaiser signed a separate contract with the Steelworkers.

Like the West Coast Longshore agreement, the end result of the Kaiser plan was to give management a freer hand in introducing technological change and in weeding out restrictive work practices. Unlike the first plan, however, Kaiser agreed to share the gains with employees—increased profits from whatever source are to be apportioned to workers at a rate of 32.5 percent. The agreement guaranteed that workers would receive wage and benefit increases at least equal to those granted elsewhere in the industry. While both labor and management officials reported favorable early

results from the plan, there has been considerable grumbling heard among the union's rank and file.

Armour Meatpacking Plant Plan

The third plan we will discuss developed in an industry beset by rapid mechanization and a sharp decline in the industry's labor force in the decades since World War II. During the four years 1955–1959, employment in the meat packing industry dropped nearly 20 percent (by some 36,000 workers). The abandonment of many old plants as well as mechanization played an important role in this decline. When plant renegotiations opened in 1959, the union presented a list of demands designed to provide the workers with greater job security. Included on this list were demands for a shorter work week, a one-year notice of plant shutdown, and greater severance pay for workers who were dismissed. After several weeks of negotiations, however, the union accepted Armour's counterproposal to establish a $500,000 automation fund.

This new fund was established to finance a prolonged study of the economic conditions in the industry—by a tripartite group known as the Automation Committee—and to make recommendations on the basis of its study. The $500,000 kitty was to be financed by the payment of a one cent per hundred weight of meat contribution by the company. Unlike the plans previously discussed, the fund was not designed to provide immediate and direct benefits to workers who were laid off. Some benefits have been paid but these have been on an ad hoc basis, and the primary intent of such payments has been *to study* how effective a particular form of aid might prove to be. Thus at various times displaced workers have been given moving expenses to enable them to move from a plant that was being closed to another Armour plant or they have been offered help (including retraining) in locating jobs elsewhere in the area. The most successful experiment to date has involved an extensive retraining program preparing displaced workers for other careers in the company, elsewhere in the industry, or in entirely new jobs.

A number of other firms in various industries have also been cooperating with their unions in working out solutions to displacement problems. Retraining, severance pay, and early retirement provisions are among the most frequent solutions found. At the same time, the workers who have kept their jobs have usually been assured of some share in the reductions in costs resulting from the new equipment.

Although these devices will continue to play an important role in the efforts of unions to protect their members,[10] we can expect other proposals to be made. Recently, for example, the UAW and the United Steelworkers have been expressing interest in the recommendation made by the Presidential Committee on Technology, Automation and Economic Progress that salaries be substituted for wages in order to assure workers greater stability of take-home pay. Although the stated goal of the union leaders thus far has been to assure factory workers of a week's (or a month's) pay irrespective of the actual number of hours worked during the specified period, there has also been talk of expanding the supplementary unemployment benefits into a true guaranteed annual wage. Clearly a weekly or monthly salary arrangement would provide workers with little protection against layoffs, but a yearly guaranteed

salary would provide important temporary protection against displacement. Management has expressed strongly worded opposition to even a weekly wage. However, this was one of the central issues of the Ford strike, and the union largely won its point.

In the major steel plants a plan was in effect as of August 1, 1969 whereby workers suffering a loss of pay because of technological displacement or other reasons would be assured of earnings for the quarter in question equal to 85 percent of their earnings in the average quarter of the previous year.

The plan was prompted by the move to new processes such as the substitution of the basic oxygen furnace for the traditional open hearth furnace. The new furnaces produce more steel with fewer workers. The resulting reassignments, even though no immediate unemployment occurred, might, without the new plan, still cause workers to lose as much as 60 cents an hour in wages. Because of the difficulty of determining who was suffering pay reductions because of technology, the plan was broadened to cover all employees who experienced pay reductions, whatever the reason.

Another popular solution in union circles has been the proposal to shorten the normal work week. We noted some of the problems involved in this solution in Chapter 8, but certainly, as added benefits from automation in the form of lower costs accrue to the employer, workers should be able to win their share of these gains in the form of reductions in working time. Such reductions have been desirable in the past and there is nothing sacred about the forty-hour work week. However, a premature reduction of hours, one accompanied by a simultaneous attempt to maintain or increase take-home pay, must be avoided, or inflationary pressures will result.

Other Implications of Automation for Unions

Although unions are most concerned about the possibility that automation will displace workers, automation also may have other important consequences. For example, the introduction of automation is likely to weaken the bargaining strength of a union. To the extent that automation eliminates many of the more dirty and disagreeable tasks, workers are less likely to be dissatisfied and so experience less pressure to join the union. Automation has also been associated with an upsurge in the proportion of white-collar workers in the labor force, and historically at least white-collar workers in this country have been difficult to organize.

Automation stimulates two other developments that are likely to be unfavorable to union organization. First, workers in an automated plant are less likely to share common problems and the bonds of a common job. In an automated plant each worker is likely to be involved in tasks quite different from those performed by his fellow workers in the plant. His sense of comradeship, identifying himself with fellow workers faced with the same problems, is thereby reduced. In addition, in many automated plants each worker often works in isolation from his fellows. The opportunity to swap gripes and discuss mutual problems is greatly reduced when your nearest fellow worker is several hundred feet away.

Union bargaining strength may also be reduced because automation diminishes the effectiveness of the strike. Strikes may be less feasible, not only because workers may be less cohesive, for the reasons just indicated, but also because in many automated plants, key management personnel (foremen as well as higher management) can maintain operations for some time even in the face of a strike. Examples of continued production even after the union has called for a shutdown can be found in the oil and chemical industries and in the telephone companies. In addition, unions may be discouraged from calling strikes by the fear that the company will use the strike periods to introduce more automated equipment, thereby possibly producing still greater displacement of union members.

Changing work patterns in the plant prompted by the introduction of automated techniques may create numerous administrative headaches for the union. Job classification systems may have to be completely redone with corresponding revisions of seniority lists. Jurisdictional lines that have been carefully preserved for decades may be wiped away overnight. Pay differentials based on variations in skill as well as incentive pay schemes may no longer be applicable, while meantime new variations in pay differentials will have developed. Complaints from workers concerning such changes will have to be ironed out lest they create resentment against the union as well as management.

Finally, unions may be confronted with the spectacle of the entire plant being closed down and a new plant built elsewhere. The introduction of automation often makes an existing plant so obsolete that the alterations required are nearly as expensive as the construction of an entirely new plant. With the possible expanded use of atomic power in the future, plants hitherto severely restricted in their choice of locations because of their need for power may find they have wide options in their choice of location. Similarly the use of automation will reduce the need of some companies to locate near plentiful sources of cheap labor. The greater mobility of plants will challenge unions to ensure the jobs of workers employed in the old plants and necessitate organizing new workers at the new location. The basic fact is, however, that for many of the problems wrought by automation unions have no real protection. Collective bargaining is simply not able to cope with mass layoffs or the destruction of skills built up over long years. The middle-aged, skilled worker who suddenly finds his trade abolished may need more help than either the union or the company can offer him, and the older worker who has the opportunity to retire early at an enhanced pension may really wish to continue work but be unable to do so.

For this reason, unions have moved outside the area of collective bargaining and into the political arena. It is beyond the scope of this book to detail all the actions taken by Congress and the President partly in response to the urgings of unions. We will note in passing that there have been numerous committee hearings on the subject, a report by a federal commission on automation, and such legislation as The Manpower Development and Training Act, which was designed to provide programs to retrain workers to meet the changing needs of the economy.

Gains From Automation

Thus far we have been writing as if workers had everything to lose and little to gain from automation. We must now pause briefly to examine the other side of the ledger. First of all, union members are also consumers and in the latter capacity they reap the benefits of lower prices and better quality products made possible by the use of the newest technological equipment.

Automation also grants benefits on the job as well as away from it. Many of the jobs eliminated by automation involved the heaviest and most irksome forms of work. Whether or not jobs in automated plants will prove to be less tedious and more interesting is, however, a moot point. The evidence thus far provides a mixed verdict. Those who argue that the new jobs are more exciting point out that the worker now has greater responsibility and more independence. Those who disagree stress the isolation of many automated jobs and the excessive boredom involved when the worker essentially does nothing for long periods except watch the machine operate.

Automation Abroad

In many of the European countries the introduction of modern technological developments has occurred more smoothly because of the relatively low levels of unemployment existing there for the past decade and a half. As a glance at Table 15.2 will demonstrate, many of these countries have been able to maintain levels of unemployment considerably below those experienced in the United States. Unemployment in Europe has remained close to 2 percent during this period. Unions in these countries have thus been under less pressure to resist automation because workers have confidence in their ability to find jobs.[11]

In most of the European countries, unions have been less concerned

TABLE 15.2 Percent of Civilian Labor Force Unemployed in Selected Countries[1]

Year	France	West Germany	Italy	Sweden	United Kingdom	United States
1950		7.2		2.0	1.2	5.2
1951		6.4		2.4	0.9	3.2
1952		6.1		3.5	1.4	2.9
1953		5.5		2.5	1.3	2.8
1954	1.6	5.2	8.7	1.8	1.0	5.3
1955	1.4	3.9	7.5	1.3	0.8	4.2
1956	1.1	3.1	9.3	0.9	0.9	4.0
1957	0.8	2.7	7.4	1.2	1.1	4.2
1958	0.9	2.7	6.4	2.3	1.7	6.6
1959	1.3	1.9	5.4	1.8	1.7	5.3
1960	1.2	0.9	4.0	1.1	1.3	5.4
1961	1.1	0.6	3.4	0.8	1.1	6.5
1962	1.2	0.5	2.9	1.3	1.6	5.4
1963		0.8	2.5	1.4	2.6	5.7
1964		0.7	2.7	1.1	1.7	5.2
1965		0.6	3.6	1.1	1.5	4.5
1966		0.7	3.9	1.4	1.6	3.8
1967		2.1	3.5	1.8	2.5	3.8
1968		1.6	3.5	2.0	2.5	3.6

[1] Because of different methods of estimating unemployment the figures for the European countries are not strictly comparable with each other or with the figures for the United States. Figures in most of the European countries should probably be increased by a half a percentage point each year to make them comparable to U.S. statistics. Furthermore, the national figures conceal important internal differentials; the United States has not been the only country with depressed areas. For example, the unemployment rate in Scotland has often run close to 4 percent while the figure for Great Britain was less than 2 percent. Oskar Morgenstern has pointed out the inconsistency of such figures even within the United States. See his *On The Accuracy of Economic Observations* (Princeton, N.J.: Princeton University Press, 1956), p. 226.
Source: *United Nations Yearbook.*

about automation not only because of the steps taken by the national governments to assure full employment,[12] but also because their laws prescribe many of the protections negotiated through collective bargaining in the United States. Such items include retraining allowances, notice of dismissal in advance, severance pay, and early retirement.

In general, where similar programs do exist in the United States, the benefits paid are likely to be much lower (when compared to the pay received by the employed worker) than those granted in the European countries.

This is true, for example, both for our retraining and Social Security unemployment benefits.

Because union leaders and management officials alike in European countries have been far less wary of governmental interference in industrial relations than their counterparts in the United States, collective bargaining agreements in those countries spell out far less carefully procedures for layoffs. Furthermore, seniority tends to be applied on an improvised basis. It should be noted, however, that when layoffs do occur in these countries, the workers often react with strikes and disruptions in production that would have been avoided in this country.

The distinction between the ways European and American unions approach the problem of automation can be made clearer if we list some of the specific things European unions *do not* do: (1) They do not place any great emphasis on shorter hours as a cure for unemployment. Shorter hours have instead been used as a means of attracting workers to disagreeable trades like mining. (2) They do not stress seniority as a means of protecting workers in the case of plant transfers. Transfers from one plant to another within a company are much rarer in Europe than in the United States. (3) They do not insist on severance pay. Only Great Britain has much of a severance pay program. Although there are instances of severance pay in continental countries like France, the practice is far less widespread than in this country. (4) They do not worry about the destruction of skills. This results from the fact that European unions tend to be more completely organized on industrial rather than craft lines.[13]

Compared to American unions, European unions *do* place far more emphasis upon advance notice of layoff. Minimum time periods for notices of intention to lay off are prescribed in Great Britain and West Germany. Some unions, like those in Sweden, are strongly opposed to all forms of work sharing.

Modern technology was ushered in immediately after World War II when the European countries were rebuilding, and it was natural to include the most modern and efficient equipment available. Some of these countries have also benefited from extensive investment programs undertaken by American companies wishing to capitalize on foreign markets.

Incidentally, even those European workers with limited training and educational background have shown themselves able to adjust to automation. In fact, one of the striking things about technological advance in Europe is that it has been achieved despite the fact that its workers have a somewhat lower level of educational attainment than those of the United States. Technological change has had a small impact (in unemployment) on this group compared with our experience.

Obviously one can find wide discrepancies between countries (West Germany and Great Britain) and within countries (France and Italy). If we consider the less developed nations such as India and Mexico we find even greater internal contrasts. Economists have even continued to debate whether or not, given India's already large volume of unemployment, rapid industrialization is a desirable way to speed economic growth. In Mexico, which has been experiencing a very rapid pace of economic growth in recent years, about 50 percent of its population is still engaged in agriculture. As in many of the developing nations there are no reliable statistics as to the amount of unemployment in Mexico, but it is generally believed to be low, but with substantial amounts of underemployment. Mexican law requires the payment of severance pay whether the worker is fired or laid off for lack of work after he has been employed for thirty days.[14]

The unions in all these other countries have not been completely free of fear of automation—even the West German unions have expressed doubts from time to time. Much of the opposition, however, comes less from the fear of spreading unemployment than from the fear that new changes will threaten time-honored shop rules. This latter motive, for example, has been particularly important in explaining the resistance of British unions to innovation.

Summary and Conclusions

Historically many critics have tended to count unions as the foes of economic change and technological progress. We have seen that this is a partial truth. Unions in this country have not been inimical to technological progress as long as the rights of their members were protected.

Although we have seen that attempts to cope with the problem vary from country to country and from union to union within a given country, there are certain standard protections sought by unions against all forms of unemployment. Among these, we have noted provisions for consultation, study committees, advance notice of layoffs, separation pay, transfer rights and allowances for moving expenses, and funds for retraining. The real issue is how far these protections can be extended before they stifle the incentive to introduce change. At the same time it should be borne in mind that national unions in this country have done an important service in educating the rank and file to accept the value of technological change.

We have suggested that the shrill cries of alarm emanating from some spectators of the contemporary scene (both union and nonunion) are premature and excessively pessimistic. This is not to suggest that no one will be hurt by automation. The programs that unions have been devising to provide retraining, early retirement, and severance pay will help to ease the transition. The lesson from abroad, however, is that the best therapy is the maintenance of a high level of employment and economic growth.

Responsibility for the achievement of these goals inevitably rests with the government.

NOTES

1. Sumner Slichter, *Union Policies and Industrial Management* (Washington, D.C.: Brookings, 1941), Chaps. 7–9.

2. Featherbedding, as such practices are frequently called, is stimulated by technological change but is not solely the result of it. Certainly, one of the largest incentives for engaging in featherbedding is the fear of job insecurity prompted in part by the old "lump of work" fallacy. However, other forces also underlie the practice of featherbedding. Closely allied but quite distinct is the workers' fear of a "speed-up," where they are forced to do more than they believe to be a fair day's work. The introduction of new machinery and production techniques always raises doubts in workers' minds about their continued ability to maintain or regulate the required pace of output.

To a greater extent than is sometimes appreciated, featherbedding may also be a product of union and worker concern over health and safety standards. Not only may the new equipment be dangerous to operate unless proper precautions are taken, but the added pace and strains accompanying its use may be injurious to the health of workers in the long run even though in the short run no ill effects can be detected.

A final consideration is the model provided by the management of a plant. If managers appear to be taking numerous vacations and spending a disproportionate amount of time away from the business on the golf links or in other recreational activities, workers tend to resent it and wonder why they "should kill themselves" on the boss's behalf.

3. Perhaps the most marked fear of management about automation is the danger it will open the door to union and government interference in business decisions.

4. George Terborgh, *The Automation Hysteria* (New York: Norton, 1966), pp. 42–43.

5. According to the National Commission on Automation, the average rate of increase of output per man hour, excluding agriculture, was 2 percent before World War II and 2.5 percent after it. *Report of the National Commission on Technology, Automation and Economic Progress* (Washington, D.C.: U.S. Government Printing Office, 1966), pp. 2–3.

6. See, for example, Yale Brozen, *Employment and Unemployment: The Problem of the 1960's* (Washington, D.C.: U. S. Chamber of Commerce, 1961).

7. James Bright, "Opportunity and Threat in Technological Change," *Harvard Business Review* (November 1963), pp. 76–86.

8. See John K. Galbraith, *The Affluent Society* (Boston: Houghton Mifflin, 1958), Chap. 11.

9. Seymour Wolfbein, *Employment, Unemployment and Public Policy* (New York: Random House, 1965), p. 15.

10. In each of its recent contracts the UAW has strengthened provisions for severance pay, early retirement, and "preferential hiring." The Ford Motor Company reported that as a result of its preferential hiring arrangements 27,000 workers who had been laid off got jobs in other Ford plants between 1951 and 1960.

11. The governments of these countries have been more willing to assume responsibility for full employment than has our government. Traditional conservatism plus fears about our balance of payments deficit and cost-push inflation have hampered strong government action in this country. Government activity to assure full employment in other countries has gone beyond fiscal and monetary policy, however. Sweden, for example, has an elaborate program for encouraging the mobility of unemployed workers and for helping them in their search for new jobs.

12. The techniques undertaken to assure full employment have varied widely from country to country. In Great Britain, for example, there has been great emphasis on bringing jobs to workers by providing financial inducements to influence the location of industry. This program has not been a marked success, however, and Britain has been forced to subsidize the relocation of workers. Sweden, by contrast, has largely confined its efforts to moving the workers to the jobs. Both countries have had regional areas where the local unemployment level was several times higher than the national level, making their efforts to attain full employment more difficult. Other countries such as West Germany have not experienced these regional discrepancies. See Joint Economic Committee of the Congress, *Economic Policies and Practices,* Paper No. 8 (Washington, D.C.: U.S. Government Printing Office, 1966).

13. Much of the preceding was based on Arnold R. Weber, "Manpower Adjustments to Technological Change: An International Analysis," in Solomon Barkin, William Dymond, Everett M. Kassalow, Frederick Meyers, and Charles A. Myers (eds.), *International Labor* (New York: Harper & Row, 1967), pp. 132–157.

14. Mexican law governing the awarding of severance pay is more complicated than this statement suggests. Almost inevitably the case is referred to a board of arbitration or conciliation. Only in extreme cases involving violence, disclosure of trade secrets, or similar misdeeds is the employer free to discharge the worker without severance pay. However, even in such instances the worker is usually entitled to a review of the decision.

16

Inflation, Economic Growth, and Collective Bargaining

No longer are wage movements explained in the main by the demand for labor. More and more, wages are the result of wage policies of trade unions and more and more they are a determinant of prices rather than being determined by them.

—Sumner H. Slichter

Other than in war emergencies, government efforts in industrial, non-Communist countries to limit wage and price increases by direct or selective means have been distinguished chiefly by their disappointing results.

—Frank C. Pierson

☐ ALTHOUGH collective bargaining has been the target of criticism from its very inception, assertions that collective bargaining imparts an inflationary bias into a growing, full-employment economy are of recent vintage. It was not until the 1940s that the terms "cost-push" and "wage-push" inflation as applied to unions began to figure prominently in the analyses of economists.

The phenomenon of sharp rises in the level of prices was, of course, well known at a much earlier date and appears in the earliest studies of economics as a subject. Prior to World War II, however, the economists' standard diagnosis for the rises in the general price level was that they resulted from the existence of too much money seeking too few goods. Inflation was the responsibility of the monetary authorities and the government because they permitted excessive amounts of money and credit to circulate in the economy.

A simple "cost-push" theory of inflation has always been a part of the layman's diagnosis of the problem of rising prices. From early times, the profiteer and the hoarder have always been assigned a heavy portion of the blame for any rise in prices. Note, however, that here the culprit was the businessman and merchant and not the unions. Note also that most economists tended to discount the disruptive effects of the hoarder and speculator and even assigned them a useful role in the economy.

Part of the reason, therefore, why unions did not stand accused earlier was that most economists were confident that in the case of inflation they had already uncovered both the correct cause and the proper therapy. Even the jumps in the consumer price level in the immediate postwar period, which in this country and elsewhere were quite sharp, could be explained by traditional theory.

In the months immediately following the end of World War II, the United States government showed little hesitancy in removing price and wage controls. The government's haste can be partially explained by a general longing to get things back to normal as quickly as possible and a general frustration and resentment over government controls. Such controls, which had worked much better than many had anticipated, had, despite (and because of) their success, been an irritant to workers, businessmen, and consumers alike. Although some observers issued dire warnings about the inflationary dangers involved in a premature removal of all wage and price controls, even economists were not as vocal in their denunciations as might have been expected.

A great many economists at that time were concerned about the likelihood that the economy would suffer a sharp depression as the result of the conversion of production from a wartime to a peacetime basis. The goal of "sixty million jobs" envisioned by Henry Wallace in a book by that name was seen by many economists of the period as a goal worth seeking but unlikely to be won. The memory of the depression of the 1930s was too fresh in economists' minds to permit them to see that pent-up consumer demand had the potential to buoy and over-expand the economy.

There was a sharp rise in wages and prices following the relaxation of wage and price controls. Between 1945 and 1948 the level of the consumer price index increased 35 percent. Although the general wage increase followed the pattern set by the steel and automobile agreements in 1946, which provided for an increase of 18.5 cents per hour, primary responsibility for the rising prices was not assigned by most economists to the demands by unions for excessively high wages. Instead, economists continued to rely on the old quantity theory of money.

Symptomatic of the fact that economists and politicians as well as the general public were concerned over the dangers of deflation rather than inflation in the immediate postwar years was the passage of the Employment Act of 1946. This legislation, which established the Council of Economic Advisors, underscored the fact that the federal government had assumed responsibility for the assurance of full employment. This position marked a sharp departure from the traditional government policy, which was based on the assumption that the economy always tended toward full employment and would speedily restore itself to that position if it were only left alone. As observers began to realize the possible implications of a

government commitment to a program designed to sustain full employment and a rapid pace of economic growth (primarily in the last two decades), they began to explore the significance to the price level of wage determination under collective bargaining. Those who charged that the government was failing to pursue a course designed to assure a more rapid pace of economic growth and full employment are now answered with the claim that any greater effort to do so would expose the American economy to the dangers of a runaway inflation. Statistics demonstrating that our rate of growth was unsatisfactory judged by the record of most other industrial countries were matched by figures showing the alarming decline in our stock of gold and the widening gap in our balance of payments.

The terms "cost-push" and "wage-push inflation" began to enjoy increasing popularity among economists and businessmen; they have often been used as a new and alternative way of explaining some inflationary periods. Although there are numerous subtleties and variations, the idea behind wage-push inflation is basically very simple. Because of their enhanced bargaining power, unions are able to force upon employers wage increases in excess of gains in productivity. Faced with rising costs that threaten his profit margin, the businessman passes the added cost along to the consumer in the form of a higher price. The union now finds that its wage increase has been wiped out by increases in the cost of living. It therefore returns to the bargaining table in search of another wage increase. The stage is then set for a round of price increases followed by further wage demands, and the spiral continues ever upward.

Although theorists of wage-push inflation stress the relationship between levels of productivity and levels of wages, their conclusions are different from those set forth by the original supporters of the marginal productivity theory of wages.[1] These latter theorists assumed that if wages were pushed too high, the result would be unemployment and a downward pressure on wages until full employment was once again restored. Today's wage-push theorists deny that wage increases will result in sufficient unemployment to reduce wages again because they see the government standing ready to undertake appropriate action to avert any such increase in unemployment. As we shall see, the questions of how much unemployment is necessary to check wage-push inflation and what is proper government policy have been topics for vigorous debate among economists.

A detailed discussion of how the government can set about avoiding unemployment is beyond the scope of this book. It suffices to say that both monetary policy, which controls the amount of money and credit available, and fiscal policy, which stimulates or reduces the amount of spending in the economy by adjustments in the amount of government spending relative to government revenues and by variations in tax policy, are the major weapons at any government's disposal. When unemployment increases unduly, the Federal Reserve on its own initiative can ease credit by various methods. The Treasury can increase spending and lower the level of taxes, although its actions, of course, are subject to prior approval by Congress.

Supporters of the wage-push theory are also quick to point out that labor unions have consistently championed an easy money policy by the Federal Reserve and have been ready to urge the government to take steps through its fiscal policy to forestall any increase in the volume of unemployment.

There has been substantial dis-agreement about what constitutes full employment. How full is full has been almost as difficult a question to answer as how high is up! Definitions have ranged all the way from Lord Beveridge's famous dictum that full employment exists only when there are more jobs than there are men to fill them[2] to the more conservative estimates of some businessmen that we should be satisfied if the economy consistently maintains an unemployment rate of no more than 5 or 6 percent. Although economists today still disagree, probably most of them would settle for 3 to 4 percent as being reasonably full. Unions have consistently pushed for as low a figure as possible. They were highly critical of the Eisenhower administration because it tolerated a 6 to 7 percent rate of unemployment without taking vigorous action.

Because the government stands ready to expand aggregate demand whenever it seems necessary in order to avoid increasing the amount of unemployment, businessmen have no difficulty converting their increased wage costs into higher prices for their products. In view of this fact, many economists have serious doubts about whether the three goals of full employment, rapid economic growth, and a stable price level can be achieved so long as free collective bargaining exists.

An examination of the statistics in Tables 16.1 and 16.2 clearly demonstrates that wages have been rising more rapidly than increases in productivity. Wage increases in the years since World War II have averaged 3.1 percent per year for the economy as a whole, while productivity increases have averaged 2.5 percent per year. As we will note in some detail later in this chapter, this fact by itself does not provide conclusive proof that unions are responsible for the price

TABLE 16.1 Indices of Labor Productivity

1958 = 100

Country	1955	56	57	58	59	1960	61	62	63	64
U.S.	95	95	98	100	104	106	108	113	117	120
U.K.	96	98	99	100	103	107	109	110	114	119
France	90	94	98	100	102	110	114	120	124	
Germany	90	94	97	100	106	113	118	122	125	133
Israel	88	94	95	100	109	115	119	123	135	142
Japan	87	93	97	100	116	130	148	154	171	187

Source: International Labor Office.

increases that have occurred since the end of World War II.

There seems little hope of accelerating productivity gains sufficiently to offset future wage pressures. The standard methods of increasing productivity by introducing new technology, improving plant layouts and management supervision, stimulating workers to greater effort, relocating workers in more efficient plants and industries through the market mechanism, and using better-quality materials have long been known to management and economists, but the long-run record of increases in productivity has been consistently less than 3 percent annually. While new technology is likely to be introduced at a more rapid pace in the future, it seems doubtful whether the national average of annual productivity gains can be accelerated sufficiently to match wage increases if they continue at their recent pace. Furthermore, the continuous maintenance of high levels of employment will assure the perpetuation of some inefficient firms and the employment of some inefficient workers who would otherwise be excluded from the market and their continued presence will exert a depressing effect on productivity.

One of the most serious problems in trying to relate wages to gains in productivity is to decide which index of productivity to employ. If the composite national figure (which we referred to earlier) is used, numerous problems arise, which we will note below. Or are wage increases to be geared to the varying increases in productivity (always assuming that they can be measured) associated with different plants and industries? If it were strictly adhered to, this formula would produce extreme differentials in wages, far wider differentials than have ever been countenanced in any market system with or without collective bargaining.

In actual fact, unions in industries where productivity gains have been most rapid have succeeded in winning very handsome wage increases. Even where the wage increase in such an industry is not in excess of the increases in productivity for that industry (this has not always been the case), the resulting wage bargain may set a pattern for similar wage increases in industries and firms that can ill afford to pay them. At various times, one industry (the steel industry or the auto industry, for example) has established a formula that subsequently has been applied to firms in completely different industries. While the amount of the increase has not been identical for all firms and all industries in the economy, enough similarity exists to justify the use of the term "pattern setting."

TABLE 16.2 Earnings in Manufacturing

Country and currency unit	C O D E	S E X	By hour (H), day (D), week (W) or month (M)						
			M. Male	F. Female		MF. Both Sexes			
			1963	1964	1965	1966	1967	1968	1969
France (Franc)	H	MF	2.65	2.84	3.00	3.18	3.37	3.78	...
Germany, F.R. (D. Mark)	H	M	3.77	4.10	4.49	4.80	4.99	5.19	...
(D. Mark)	H	F	2.59	2.80	3.09	3.33	3.45	3.60	...
(D. Mark)	H	MF	3.46	3.74	4.12	4.42	4.60	4.79	...
Japan (000 Yen)	M	MF	30.2	33.1	36.1	40.5	45.6	52.7	...
Mexico (Peso)	M	MF	1 135	1 239	1 324	1 385	1 468	1 544	...
Sweden (Krona)	H	M	7.91	8.57	9.45	10.26	9.88	10.46	...
(Krona)	H	F	5.71	6.31	7.08	7.85	7.76	8.26	...
(Krona)	H	MF	7.29	7.94	8.78	9.60	9.30	9.87	...
United Kingdom (Pence)	H	M	88.7	95.5	105.0	110.8	116.0	123.8	...
(Index)	W	MF	100	105	109	114	118	127	134
United States (Dollar)	H	MF	2.46	2.53	2.61	2.72	2.83	3.01	3.19

General note. The figures generally relate to earnings of all wage-earners. They normally include bonuses, cost of living allowances, taxes, social insurance contributions payable by the employed person and, in some cases, payments in kind. They normally exclude social insurance contributions payable by the employers, family allowances and other social security benefits.
Source: *International Labour Office.*

Consideration of this line of reasoning suggests that those supporting it do not necessarily accept the thesis that unions have a marked effect in improving the position of their members over that of nonunion workers. It is possible that unions exert sufficient influence to impart an upward bias to the entire wage structure with an accompanying inflationary pressure, even though they may not be able to raise union wages relative to nonunion scales.

Another phase of union negotiations over wages that has been frequently criticized as having an inflationary impact is the unions' demand for escalator clauses. Over 4 million workers in steel, autos, and other industries are covered by contracts that adjust wages to variations in the cost of living. Such clauses usually specify that there will be a 2 to 3 cent increase in wages for every point increase in the consumer price index. Critics make the obvious point that in chasing the rise in prices, unions are only further adding to costs and thereby adding to the inflationary spiral.

Thus far we have emphasized those aspects of union demands for higher wages that augment costs and thus produce inflationary repercussions. Another charge frequently made is that the higher wages bolster workers' purchasing power, thereby making it easier for businessmen to offset their rising costs by raising their prices. Without the added purchasing power made possible by the increased wages, the argument runs, the higher prices would meet stiffer buyer resistance and would prove impossible to maintain.

Those who have been reluctant to assign full blame for inflation to unions but who still feel unions must share some of the responsibility have sometimes pictured unions as a kind of triggering mechanism that ignites the spark in an atmosphere that is laden with inflationary powder. According to this view, the stage is set for the start of an inflationary spiral when shortages have been building up in certain areas, an excessive amount of money and credit is in circulation, and the levels of consumer and investment demand are high. Open price rises do not begin, however, until some direct action such as a demand by unions for a pay hike sparks a sudden rise in prices elsewhere in the economy.

The resulting price rises may be far in excess of that necessitated by the wage increase itself. Corporations may have delayed passing slowly increasing costs on to the consumer by raising prices because of uncertainty about the response of rivals, fear of public reaction and possible government investigation, or a sense of social responsibility and an unwillingness to start the inflationary ball rolling.

For whatever reason, the unions' demand for higher wages is followed by a sharp general rise in prices. Inflation may continue for some time since businessmen can now rationalize their price increases on the ground that they were forced into them by union demands.

Opposing Views

Some economists have been unwilling to assign to the unions even limited responsibility for inflation. These scholars rest their case on two general arguments: (1) Wages would have performed in much the same manner even in the absence of union pressure. (2) Unions are really passive recipients of unwise monetary and fiscal policy that presents them with the opportunity to get wage increases for the asking.

One of the best-known expositions of this point of view was set forth in a 1950 article by Walter Morton.[3] According to Morton, the basic problem of postwar inflation was caused by the backlog of demand for consumer goods that had gone unsatisfied all during the war combined with the large amounts of liquid funds available to consumers in the form of savings accounts and war bonds. Wages did rise, said Morton, but this was a *result* of rising prices rather than a *cause* of rising prices. Morton contended: "There is no reason to believe that prices would have risen any less if labor unions had been weak or nonexistent."[4]

Morton also examined the dilemma posed earlier in this chapter—Is it possible for full employment, stable prices, and free collective bargaining to exist simultaneously for any protracted period of time?

Morton's answer to this query was a firm "yes." The problem, he said, was that the monetary and fiscal authorities had been overly concerned about unemployment and too ready to step in and heap fresh fuel on the fire whenever the economy appeared to be running out of steam. Given a government guarantee of full employment, wage-push inflation was indeed inevitable. It was perfectly natural for labor and union leaders to seek higher wages, but pressure from this quarter would be irresistible only if the government stood always ready to stimulate the activity of the economy still further.

If the monetary authorities were determined to hold firm, any group, including unions, that sought more than their productivity increases justified would be soundly punished by experiencing sharp rises in unemployment. The only proper way to cure this kind of unemployment was for the group in question to accept appropriate downward adjustments in wages.

Morton qualified this statement, however. He distinguished between two kinds of unemployment situations and stipulated the appropriate fiscal policy to be applied in each case. When unemployment was general throughout the economy, it was a signal for the government to undertake appropriate spending and tax policies. When unemployment was confined to a select group of industries, however, it was probably an indication that wage rates in those areas had been pushed too high. Under such circumstances, Morton believed, the government should be very wary of taking any corrective action. If the government declined to take action prematurely, management would learn from experience that its attempts to pass higher prices on to consumers would result in a substantial loss of sales. To the extent that these increases in prices had been prompted by union wage demands, management would thereafter be more resistant to pressures for excessive increases in wages. Similarly, union leaders would become more cautious in their demands once they discovered firsthand that excessive wage increases bore a heavy price in terms of unemployment for union members.

Morton concluded that if the monetary authorities were willing to adopt a policy designed to ensure stable prices, it would be possible to reach all three goals—full employment, stable prices, and free collective bargaining. In the past monetary policy, not unions, had been responsible for inflation; unions had done little more than take what had been far too generously offered them. If the pickings were made less easy, unions would learn to live by the new rules and would resist seeking wage increases that would foster wage-distortion un-

employment. Surely, Morton reasoned, proper action by the Federal Reserve Board was far preferable to the establishment of some kind of wage control board or some other device designed to weaken the labor movement needlessly.

Although Morton's article has been often reprinted in whole or in part and has become a standard part of the critical literature dealing with wage-push inflation, there are several strong reasons for not accepting his analysis at full face value, and several less valid criticisms.

The first objection to Morton's thesis is natural, although it can be easily answered. If Morton is right, these critics say, how is it possible to explain the large number of strikes and the substantial amount of unrest that occurred in the immediate postwar years? After all, if wages would have risen to the same extent in the absence of union pressure, what was all the fuss about? Why didn't business leaders simply accept the unions' demands for wage increases without putting up so much resistance?

To refute this argument, we must recall the uncertainties about the exact settlement and the strategies of collective bargaining discussed in Chapter 5. As we pointed out in that chapter, the various game theories devised to analyze bargaining situations are far more useful in explaining how a final resolution of the issues may have been achieved than in predicting in advance what the ultimate settlement figure will be. Even if the two parties are fairly certain of the outcome in advance, a difference of only a few cents may be the source of bitter dispute, particularly in industries that are acting as pattern setters for other firms in the economy. It is not too surprising, therefore, that in the years immediately after World War II the fiercest struggles and the greatest need for government intervention occurred in industries such as steel and coal.

A more serious criticism of Morton's thesis is that it more accurately depicts the causes of inflation from the end of World War II to 1950, when his article was published, than it does the situation prevailing in more recent years.[5] Throughout the latter half of the 1950s and the first part of the 1960s, the United States had undesirably high levels of unemployment. (The level was in excess of 6 percent much of the time.) Nevertheless, wages not only did not decline, they continued to advance. Morton's major point—that unions only took what would have been coming to them in any case because of excessive monetary demand—seems to stand contradicted by this later evidence. Instead of falling into line and ceasing to demand large wage increases for fear of the resulting unemployment, union leaders turned the existence of unemployment into a justification for higher wages. Unemployment, they proclaimed, resulted from inadequate purchasing power occasioned by the maldistribution of income, i.e., income going into the hands of those who didn't spend. It was important, therefore, to increase wages in order to ensure the sale of all of the goods currently being brought to market.

Many economists have refused to believe that unions would respond to the threat of unemployment in the fashion envisioned by Morton, insisting that his argument amounts to little more than saying that the monetary and fiscal authorities must accept the fact that they cannot permit employment to approach a level too close to "fullness" without exposing the economy to inflation. Gottfried Haberler's comments are typical of this view:

Suppose monetary and fiscal policy had been more vigorous, . . . as Pro-

fessor Morton recommends. Is it not certain that unemployment would have appeared? Professor Morton denies that because he thinks that labor unions would have meekly given up, or modified sufficiently, their drive for higher wages. My guess is they would not have sufficiently moderated their demands for higher wages unless a considerable volume of unemployment had restrained them.[6]

Some not altogether precise empirical studies suggest that reductions in the rate of unemployment beyond a certain percentage lead to inflation. A. W. Phillips, for example, in a study of the history of English prices from 1861 to 1957 found a close relationship between wage levels and the volume of unemployment.[7] Wages tended to increase by no more than the gains in productivity, leaving the price level unchanged, as long as the unemployment rate remained at 2.5 percent or above. When the rate of unemployment fell below that percentage, however, marked upward movements in wages developed. To have productivity gains reflected in falling prices with wages remaining stable, Phillips said, appeared to require a level of unemployment of about 5.5 percent.

Although many interpreted Phillips' findings as evidence of the necessity of making a choice between full employment and stable prices, two points should be noted. The rise in wages (and hence prices) as full employment is reached does not appear necessarily to be the result of union action and, thus, in part reinforces the Morton thesis. Furthermore, the 2.5 percent that Phillips advanced as the danger point is well below the target set by many economists for the American economy.

A more recent study in the United States, by Paul Samuelson and Robert Solow, suggests that a striking change has occurred that alters Phillips' conclusions. Whereas in earlier periods an unemployment rate of only 2 to 3 percent was required to hold wage increases in line with gains in productivity, the necessary rate of unemployment in post-World War II years was about double that figure.[8] Samuelson and Solow's conclusion was that to hold wage increases to the 2.5 to 3 percent figure attributed to annual increases in productivity, it would be necessary to permit a rate of unemployment of between 5 and 6 percent. Conversely, if an unemployment rate of 3 percent was to be the nation's goal, a rate of price increases of 4 to 5 percent might have to be experienced annually. Although these estimates were, by the authors' own confession, admittedly crude and although a 3 percent rate of unemployment is perhaps too ambitious a target, the fact that two of the nation's leading economists (who could not be readily identified as antiunion in viewpoint) offered this conclusion gave other economists considerable pause.

An equally pessimistic conclusion has been reached by William G. Bowen. On the basis of a similar but somewhat more elaborate survey than the one conducted by Samuelson and Solow, Bowen concludes that it would require an unemployment rate of about 9 percent in order to maintain wage increases at the 2.5 percent increase in productivity experienced by this country historically.[9] Note again, however, that the 2.5 percent figure is considerably more conservative than the 3.25 percent employed by the Council of Economic Advisors in setting wage guidelines in the mid-1960s. (See the discussion of guidelines below.)

A similarly gloomy prognosis has been made by George L. Parry on the basis of an elaborate statistical study of the recent figures. Fitting equations to the postwar U.S. quarterly data, he concludes that in order to have kept price change between 1960 and 1966 at zero while maintaining a profit rate of 10 percent (after taxes) on stockholders' equity, a 5 percent rate of unemployment would have been necessary.[10]

Given the above empirical findings, in our judgment the original Morton thesis dismisses too lightly the power of unions to secure wage increases even in the face of substantial unemployment. However, it does have therapeutic value to the extent that it warns economists against placing excessive blame for inflation on the shoulders of unions. There are substantial reasons to question many of the arguments cited earlier to support the position that unions are a major source of inflationary pressure. Let us now examine some of these points more closely.

Careful consideration of escalator clauses, for example, suggests that even if widely adopted (about 4 million workers in this country are so covered today), such clauses may add little to inflationary pressure. The usual argument, of course, is that escalator clauses permit unions to keep wages more closely in step with rises in prices, making for a more immediate push on costs and thus on prices. It is by no means clear that this is necessarily the case. Without the protection of an escalator clause, the union might attempt to anticipate future rises in prices by asking for more at the time the contract is being renegotiated. Conversely, if the union is assured that the question of wages can be reopened should price rises materialize, it may settle for less at the time the new contract is signed.

Economists like Milton Friedman, who believes that the pace of wage increases is actually slowed down through collective bargaining because of the longer duration of negotiated contracts,[11] would argue that escalator clauses may push wages up somewhat more rapidly than they otherwise would rise under collective bargaining, but that the comparison would be less alarming if the wage increases were compared to those in markets where unions were nonexistent. Obviously, the logic of this position holds only so long as one accepts the conclusion that unions do not have any appreciable effect on wage levels.

Those who are apprehensive that union demands for sizable wage increases will endanger price stability by triggering a series of price adjustments elsewhere in the economy may also see escalator clauses as something of a safety valve. To the extent such clauses allow wage increases to come more gradually with less abrupt and dramatic suddenness, the impact of such increases in producing offsetting adjustments elsewhere may be reduced.

Another argument suggests that wage increases stimulate inflation because they strengthen the purchasing power of workers, who are in lower-income categories and thus have a higher propensity to consume. This argument, however, has been weakened by recent empirical research about the character of the consumption function. Most evidence now suggests that there is relatively little or no difference between the marginal propensity to consume of upper- and lower-income persons. If this is true, the entire argument dissolves, since the money taken from employers to pay the higher wages reduces the power of employers to consume.

In an earlier chapter we noted that wages tend to become increasingly rigid downward because of union resistance to all efforts to reduce wages. This tendency is important relative to the impact on prices because each new round of wage increases starts from a higher plateau than existed for the preceding round. Although escalator clauses frequently call for the suspension of the relationship between wages and prices when prices move downward by more than a few percentage points, even this slight downward adjustment does provide a greater degree of flexibility than would otherwise exist.

The importance of wage rigidity enhanced by collective bargaining as a factor contributing to inflation has been stressed by Charles Schultze. Schultze's theory can best be described as a blend of the old demand-pull theory of inflation and the new cost-push variant. According to Schultze, shifts in demand from one sector of the economy to another are the initiating cause of wage and price increases. Schultze suggests that inflation may arise not only because of general overabundance of demand relative to the overall supply of goods, as the early quantity theorists had suggested, or because of initiating pressure from below in the form of excess wage increases, but also because of a sudden increase in demand in a particular sector of the economy.

The sudden upsurge in demand in one sector of the economy has an inflationary impact on the entire economy for two reasons. First, rises in one sector tend to be copied elsewhere in the economy; rising demand brings a resultant rise in wages. Second, in those industries where demand is declining, there is unlikely to be much downward adjustment in wages or prices because of union resistance and business pricing practices. The phenomenon is not new, says Schultze, but achieved increasing importance with the growing effort to ensure full employment.

The magnetic effect of rising costs in particular sectors of the economy on the general level of costs is not a novel phenomenon. But the recurrence of sharp and prolonged general depressions was generally sufficient to break through these rigidities and enforce a reduction in the most sensitive prices and wages.[12]

Note that while Schultze does not contend that unions are directly responsible for inflation because of their pressure for higher wages, his theory rests heavily on the assumption that unions do substantially increase wage rigidities. As Schultze points out, sudden shifts in demand from one sector of the economy to another are not new and a smoothly operating market mechanism, by establishing appropriate adjustments in wages and prices elsewhere, should make the transition, as it has been many times in the past, relatively painless. Thus, to the extent that unions interfere with the process of adjustment by resisting wage cuts, they still must shoulder some of the blame for inflation.

To what extent have unions been guilty of interfering with the efficient operation of the economy, thereby diminishing real output and the supply of goods and services that would otherwise appear on the market? As suggested previously, unions are accused of promoting inefficiency by (1) reducing labor mobility, thereby preventing workers from shifting to more productive jobs, or (2) impeding production through the use of various featherbedding techniques. Although space does not allow us to deal with these charges in any detail, it should be noted that some experts in the field contend that the impact of unions is not very serious in either direction.

It is true, for example, that labor turnover has been steadily declining for the past several decades, but the extent to which this decline can be attributed to labor unions is uncertain. Unions are said to restrict mobility because they have successfully demanded strict seniority systems and programs of fringe benefits, which not only increase the workers' satisfaction with their current jobs but also may discourage workers from making any move because of the loss of benefits involved. Reductions in wage differentials as an incentive for movement have been a third major reason for declining labor turnover. All of these reasons are subject to some qualification, however. Almost any plant, whether it is unionized or not, has to rely on some variant of a seniority system. One must remember that employers are much more anxious to reduce turnover than are unions. The growth of vesting for pension plans, the relatively low amount of the present benefits, and the small number of workers currently collecting benefits all suggest that pensions weigh as heavily on workers' minds when contemplating a move as is sometimes feared.

Similarly, most observers agree that featherbedding has excited more attention than it really deserves and that, compared with unions in many other countries, American unions have been quite receptive to change.

Proposed Solutions

Depending upon how serious one regards the problem of inflation to be and how great one believes the role of collective bargaining to be in that inflation, one or more of a wide variety of solutions has been advanced. Those who believe that price stability must be preserved at all costs may be willing to sacrifice some amount of growth or employment or to place serious limitations on unions and collective bargaining. Others, who are more friendly to the cause of unions and who worry about unemployment and/or lack of growth, may be willing to permit the economy to suffer some degree of consistent inflation. The clearest statement of the latter position was set forth by the late Sumner Slichter.[13]

Slichter's Thesis

Slichter's view was that none of the proposals designed to deal with the problems of wage-push inflation were likely to be successful. However, Slichter believed that other economists had exaggerated the seriousness of the problems involved in a moderate annual increase in prices (1 to 2 percent).

One fear is that a mild or slight rise in prices may, if permitted to continue, suddenly burst into a galloping hyper-inflation where prices rise 10 to 20 percent or more a year. According to Slichter, however, as long as we remain alert to this danger and are willing to employ our monetary and fiscal weapons when necessary, such an outbreak need never occur.

A second possibility is that inflation will hit heavily persons with fixed or low incomes. (Often the two groups are the same.) Social Security recipients, pensioners, civil service employees, teachers, and a host of others are said to have fixed incomes that do not respond readily to rising prices. Any rise in prices thus erodes part of the value of their income. A popular examination question in economics is the request for an evaluation of the statement that "Inflation is the most regressive of all forms of taxation." Here too, Slichter was less worried than his fellow economists, arguing that most groups today had found ways to get their incomes adjusted to rising prices. Teacher exerted pressure on their school boards and Social Security recipients contacted their Congressmen to get payments increased whenever there was a rise in the general price level.

Slichter also denied the possibility that a gradual inflation might reduce the incentive to save and thus handicap capital formation, pointing out that in recent years, although there has been a steadily rising level of prices, the total volume of savings has been greater than ever.

Slichter did not assign total responsibility for inflation to the demands of unions. Other factors such as the level of government spending, aid to underdeveloped countries, and the rapid pace of technological change had to share the blame. Neither did he give his unconditional blessing to inflationary price increases even though they remained gradual. The problem, said Slichter, was not that the cost of inflation was zero, but that the costs of fighting it were greater than the costs of inflation itself. The costs to society of continuously battling a slight wage-push inflation were greater than those incurred by permitting it to continue on two counts. First, those hurt seriously by gently rising prices were likely to be a smaller proportion of the society than those who would be injured if the government took corrective action. Second, Slichter saw inflation as the price the economy had to pay for continued economic growth and high levels of employment. Surely, he reasoned, the distortions and inefficiencies resulting from gently rising prices were less than those produced when economic growth was slowed and unemployment permitted to increase.

Slichter's suggestion that a little inflation may be less harmful than other possible alternatives has won relatively little support from his fellow economists or from businessmen and government officials, most of whom continue to regard inflation as a deadly disease. There are some who, if a choice had to be made, would prefer a stable price level to either full employment or a steady pace of economic growth. Perhaps the majority who disagree with Slichter's analysis, however, feel that his conclusion that nothing can be done save make the best of a bad situation is overly pessimistic. These economists feel that it is possible to sustain full employment and satisfactory economic growth without rising prices. Let us now evaluate some of the methods proposed for achieving this goal.

We have already noted that many economists find the old weapons, tight monetary and fiscal policies, unsuitable to deal with the new breed of inflation, which stems not from the pull of excessive demand but from the push of rising costs. Of course, some economists, including Walter Morton, still argue that others have given up too readily on monetary and fiscal policy.

Perhaps the most drastic alternative proposal has been the suggestion that direct controls over wages and prices should be imposed. Although such controls were rapidly abandoned at the end of World War II, Congress has several times since then toyed with the notion of reinstating the President's power to enact such controls, if necessary, on a stand-by basis. Unions might be permitted to seek wage increases and businessmen to advance prices within the limits set by the government (presumably by the Council of Economic Advisors), but increases above this ceiling would be illegal.

The country's experience during World War II does not augur well for the success of a long-term program of such controls during peacetime. Even under the pressure of patriotism, controls were voided numerous times

during the war by sizable exceptions. If voluntary compliance is not forthcoming, the government's enforcement officials are faced with the sticky question of what recourse to take if a union refuses to abide by their ruling. In a democratic society it is difficult to compel hundreds or thousands of workers to work against their will or to assess financial fines against them or their union. Even if such a policy is completely successful, the implications for free collective bargaining are obvious.

Believing the problem to be primarily a question of excessive union power, some writers have proposed subjecting unions to antitrust legislation as a means of reducing their power to drive wages upwards. Those who urge such programs profess to see a similarity between the monopoly power of business and its ability to set administered prices and the monopoly power of unions and their ability to set artificially high wage rates.

Considering that American labor unions have a long history of exposure to antitrust prosecutions, it is little wonder that all such legislation is instinctively opposed by labor leaders and union members alike. At the same time some businessmen and economists have become so alarmed by their own descriptions of union power that they see no other satisfactory remedy available than the close shackling of that power.

An appraisal of the propriety and effectiveness of applying the antitrust laws to union power is complicated by the fact that proponents envision varying applications of such laws. One proposal has been to limit the various union featherbedding techniques that are said to restrict production. As we pointed out earlier, however, not all economists are agreed that featherbedding is a major problem. While some legal checks on the more flagrant cases of featherbedding might be desirable, such cases are relatively few, and it is difficult to see how much such restrictions would accomplish by way of checking inflation.

Most proponents of antitrust legislation for unions, however, probably have in mind some measure designed to deal directly with the bargaining strength of unions. To do this, they would undertake a program of breaking up large unions much in the same manner as antitrust laws have been used to break up large businesses. It has frequently been suggested, for example, that bargaining should be limited to a single plant, a restriction that would prevent the massive displays of strength by unions that accompany industrywide or regionwide bargaining.

The evidence from Chapter 4, however, suggests that industrywide bargaining has not played a major role in pushing wage rates higher than they otherwise would be. On the contrary, experience both in this country and abroad suggests that responsibility for preserving jobs in marginal firms throughout the industry tends to make a union's leaders more cautious in their wage demands when they are engaged in formulating an industrywide agreement. On the other hand, the experience in the American construction industry should dispel the illusion that fragmented bargaining offers any magic panaceas for the problem of exorbitant wage demands!

The proposal to limit bargaining to a single plant would quite clearly reduce the union's bargaining power vis-à-vis the multiplant billion-dollar corporation. In fact, it would not be unreasonable to ask whether such measures might not render a union virtually impotent.

Additional problems are suggested by our experience with the antitrust laws as they have been applied to business. Tacit collusion between rival firms has presented major problems in the application of antitrust laws. Almost certainly this same difficulty would arise if bargaining were restricted to a single plant. What types of cooperation between the local and the national union would be permissible? How could support to the local plant by the parent company be avoided, and if it could not, would not aid by the national union to the local have to be permitted? If all cooperation between lower and upper levels of both companies and unions were banned, how could legal evidence of violations be obtained? All of these questions suggest that limiting bargaining to a single plant, if not inoperable, would at least be much more difficult to enforce than is sometimes envisioned.

A program of wage guidelines, which was designed to be somewhat more politically palatable and less autocratic in its implications than wage controls was pursued by the Johnson administration during the mid-1960s. A discussion of this program will indicate the problems involved in any proposal to curtail severely the bargaining strength of unions. The idea behind wage guidelines was very simple. The Council of Economic Advisors (CEA) announced the expected increase in productivity for the entire economy for a given year (set at 3.2 percent in 1966) and this served as a rough upper limit to wage increases negotiated that year.

The first complete statement of the idea was contained in the January 1962 *Economic Report* of the President. At that time the Council of Economic Advisors suggested that:

The general guide for noninflationary wage behavior is that the rate of increase in wage rates (including fringe benefits) in each industry be equal to the trend of overall productivity increase. General acceptance of this guide would maintain stability of labor cost per unit of output for the economy as a whole . . .

President John Kennedy attempted to implement this program of guidelines for both labor and business, an attempt that cúlminated in his famous struggle with the steel industry. It was natural that President Lyndon Johnson, known for his talents as a "friendly persuader," should continue to follow a program of guidelines.

From the very beginning, the guidelines were under heavy attack from a number of economists, businessmen, and labor leaders. Although the council's statement had noted that the principle of holding wage increases to the general rise in productivity should be ignored in instances where a rapidly expanding industry found itself unable to recruit a sufficient supply of labor or in areas where wages were presently extremely low, critics argued that the guidelines tended to perpetuate the status quo in wage differentials and would restrict the amount of price flexibility. Flexibility in both wages and prices is needed in a market economy to adjust production and the use of various factors of production. Economists, who in general are suspicious of all artificial restraints imposed on the market, felt that the guidelines were ineffectual and damaged the efficient functioning of the economy.

Some critics expressed alarm that the ineffectiveness of the guidelines might lead to the adoption of more stringent regulation. They foresaw the conversion of the guideposts into clubs to beat the recalcitrant businessmen or union leaders into submission. Those who expressed this fear pointed out that, although the guidelines started out as simple educational devices designed to show business and labor the right path, they had sub-

sequently been used with varying degrees of forcefulness and effectiveness to keep the two parties on the charted path. The efforts by President Kennedy to put pressure on the steel industry to rescind a price boost and by President Johnson to employ government stockpiles to avert price increases in copper did little to quiet these fears.

Labor union leaders were particularly unhappy about the wage guidelines, viewing them as a betrayal of labor's cause by the Democratic party leaders. Union leaders argued that it was unfair to hamstring labor's efforts to raise the living standards of their members. They contended that if they followed the wage guidelines they would be, in effect, giving their blessing to the current distribution of income—a blessing they were far from willing to bestow. As a result, George Meany, president of the AFL-CIO, denounced the wage guidelines, announced labor's intention to disregard or violate them, and warned that candidates wearing the Democratic party label would no longer be assured of labor's support.

Despite this crescendo of criticism, the Johnson administration was reluctant to shelve the guidelines. (The formal guidelines were abandoned in January 1967.) Part of the appeal of wage guidelines lay in their flexibility and their informality. It was possible to apply them without resort to congressional debate or lengthy court litigation. Despite the outcries from business and labor, the guidelines were probably less risky politically than more drastic action might be. Furthermore, the guidelines were not a complete failure in helping to hold prices down, although their success was decidedly limited.[14] There is considerable room for the belief that businessmen (whether because of their fear that the government might take more severe measures or because of their growing sense of social conscience) came to accept the fact that the government was overseeing their price changes. Guidelines may have been particularly useful in checking anticipatory price increases, those made in the expectation of a new round of inflation.

The guidelines applied to wages displayed the greatest weakness. Even here, however, the government's efforts, although partially frustrated, were not a complete failure. Furthermore, it might be possible for the responsible government officials to combine exhortation and persuasion with not too subtle threats. For example, officials might hint that tariffs would be relaxed or that legislation that labor had on its "musts" list might not be pushed too strenuously. The appeal to the building construction workers to reduce their demands in 1966 combined with a sharp tightening of credit that severely curtailed construction is a good illustration of this use of the iron fist in the velvet glove. It should be quickly added, however, that it is exactly this quiet combination of cajolery and threat that many critics believe is the most alarming feature of a system of guidelines.[15]

Experience Elsewhere

Inflation during the past quarter of a century has by no means been limited to the United States. In fact, because this country never suffered the ravages of a modern war fought on its own soil, the United States' experience with inflation has been relatively mild compared to that of other countries. Because much of the inflation in other countries has been of the traditional demand-pull variety, their labor unions have come under less serious attack as instigators of in-flation. The familiar set of tools has been used to combat inflation, but there have been some interesting twists, including in one case (Sweden) a sharp departure from anything tried in the United States.

Some interesting variations on cost-push theory have also been developed abroad, particularly in Great Britain and Sweden. In both of these countries, some economists have stressed the importance of wage differentials and the competitiveness between unions as a cause of cost-push inflation. H. A. Turner points out that in the early 1950s, despite low rates of profit and high levels of unemployment in the industry, the British textile union sought a sizable increase in wages in order to match gains won by other unions.[16]

F. W. Paish and Josselyn Kennedy, on the other hand, argue that cost push can keep an inflation rolling once it is under way but deny that cost push can be the instigating factor. They maintain that those who argue to the contrary are ignoring the costs to the employer involved if he makes concessions when the supply of money is not tight and demand high.[17] One could, of course, with equal logic, argue that Paish and Kennedy ignore the costs to the employer in the form of lost production and a possible loss of markets if he chooses to resist the unions' demands.

Great Britain

Both during World War II and in the postwar years, Britain has experienced a very sharp rise in both its wage and price levels; by 1950 both were nearly three times what they had been immediately before the war. This rise was partially the result of the extremely low rates of unemployment prevailing in Britain during recent years; for most of the postwar period the rate of unemployment has averaged 1.6 percent or less (about 2.5 to 3 percent as measured in the United States). The relationship between inflation and collective bargaining in Britain has differed from the United States in a number of other important respects.

Because of the tight employment situation, Britain has experienced, although to a lesser degree, the "wage drift" phenomenon that has been quite familiar on the continent. The term "wage drift" indicates the tendency of many employers to pay wages in excess of those negotiated by the unions. Unlike the United States, where it is at least debatable whether or not wages would have risen as much in the absence of union pressure for increases, in Europe there is ample evidence that unions have been demanding less than they are capable of getting from many companies. Such circumspection comes from the system of industrywide bargaining. Unions are reluctant to ask for too much because of fear of what the demand would do to the marginal firms. It has been estimated by one group of students of British wages that wage drift accounted for 21 percent of the rise in wages between 1948 and 1957 in Britain.[18]

Wage drift has been made easier by the larger proportion of British workers who are covered by piece rates—one third as compared to 27 percent in the United States. Piece rates can be more easily adjusted to give added take-home pay without the increase being too obvious. Continued bonuses and spurious overtime have also added to the upward drift of wages.

In Britain there has been an increase (the exact extent of which is unknown) in bargaining on the local level. Local-level bargaining permits wage adjustments locally in keeping with the productivity in different plants, and British unions have thus come to play a larger role in the issue of cost-push inflation than they have in many countries on the continent, but their role is still markedly less than in the United States.

The attitude of the British government toward the problem of wages in some respects closely resembles that of the United States and in other respects is markedly different. Britain has relied, for example, on the traditional tools of monetary and fiscal policy to help check inflation. The implementation of both policies has been handicapped, however, by the sensitivity of the British general public to any increase in the rate of unemployment. In addition, the British government has, in a series of official white papers, attempted to set up wage guidelines and exhort union leaders to a responsible wage policy. A tripartite National Economic Council has been responsible for the study and evaluation of wage and price increases. The intention of either business or labor to demand increases is relayed to the board through an "early warning" system. This warning system was not made compulsory, however, and has not been a notable success. Even when the Labour party has been in power, the union leaders have not been overly cooperative and the attempts to have the TUC (Trades Union Congress) screen the demands of individual unions have done little to restrain wage demands. As a partial concession to the unrest among workers, wage guidelines in Britain, unlike those in the United States, made allowances for differing gains in productivity in various plants.

Until very recently a striking difference between British and American wage policy had been the fact that the British had never attempted direct wage controls—even during World War II they relied upon a system of compulsory arbitration instead. Britain finally had to resort to direct controls in 1966.

A major difference that still prevails is that the British government employs about one-fifth of the labor force (about 5 million in nationalized industries, etc.) and thus has an opportunity to set an example in holding down wages for other sectors of the economy. Some attempts have been made in this direction, but they have all collapsed after a short period of brave resolve.

On the whole, British labor unions have been much less sympathetic to the issue of inflation than American unions, and some of them have refused to acknowledge that the problem is serious. Often their views resemble those of Sumner Slichter. British union leaders are prone to argue that excessive emphasis on the danger of inflation has been detrimental to Britain's economic growth. They contend that much of the sting could be taken out of inflation if those on fixed incomes were assured of appropriate adjustments in their incomes as prices rose.

Quite frequently too, British labor leaders have denied that they are able to control their members' push for higher wages. In effect, they have declared that any promises to restrain their members would inevitably be broken. Leaders suggest that workers will never accept curbs on wages unless they are convinced that profits will also be held in restraint.

In the view of some British economists, the net result of all this has been to put England in a precarious trade position, to endanger its world markets, and to expose it to continued inflationary pressure.

In the summer of 1966, the British Labour party faced a renewed economic crisis compounded by a sharply worsening balance of payments position and a new round of wage and price rises. The Labour government had permitted a maritime strike to tie up British shipping for several weeks in the hopes of averting an inflationary settlement. The eventual settlement proved to be inflationary anyway; meanwhile precious foreign credits had been lost while British ships were idle. For the first time in its history the British government instituted a general freeze on all wage and price increases in the hope of restoring England's position in the world's markets. In the fall of 1967, however, despite repeated assurances of intentions to the contrary, Prime Minister Harold Wilson was compelled to devalue the pound. Britain's trade position at the time of this writing (1970) is improved but still precarious.

France

France has not until very recently experienced much (if any) inflation induced by union demands. Although the de Gaulle regime experienced some minor strikes among the coal miners and other groups, French unions on the whole have been too weak and too divided to exercise much influence on wages. Most observers agree that the sharp postwar rise in earnings of French workers can be attributed almost completely to the wage drift phenomenon. France, in the immediate postwar years, went through a violent inflationary expansion prompted by the agonies of reconstruction from the war. Several times the country was compelled to devaluate its currency in order to rectify her trade position. After the election of de Gaulle, however, the French economy achieved a degree of stability, and the government's program of directed planning played a large role in increasing this stability. Even under de Gaulle, however, French unions were restless because they felt that too little of the gains from the nation's growth was going into the workers' pockets. In the spring and summer of 1968, stimulated by a strike of French university students, French unions went out on strike across the country. The result was a serious disruption of French economic stability, a slowing of the country's rate of growth, and a not yet determined inflationary stimulus.

West Germany

Germany as a defeated nation suffered heavily from the war and experienced a sharp postwar inflation as a result. Like Italy and the other continental countries, West Germany has also experienced wage drift, and the German unions have been assigned little blame for the continued problem of inflation. Many German economists and government officials, in fact, credit the German unions with a high sense of public responsibility in refraining from making excessive wage demands.

Whether or not the behavior of German unions in this respect is based on a strong sense of social responsibility alone, however, is open to serious question. Certainly there are strong reasons for doubting whether German unions could have successfully advanced more powerful demands, even had they chosen to do so.

Among the factors hampering a more aggressive attitude by the German unions has been their members' deep-rooted fear of the alternative evils of inflation and unemployment. There is also a tendency for German workers to be satisfied with the status quo and more interested in security than higher wages. As a result, strikes have been virtually unknown in postwar Germany; only the Metal Workers have been willing to push their demands at the risk of a strike. The status of unions in Germany has not been high. Because of the shortage of labor, workers have been able to win wage increases with little effort by their unions. A high level of demand, coupled with a strong system of administered prices that permits companies great leeway in their pricing, has also encouraged employers to anticipate union demands.

The government has employed a wide variety of weapons in its battle against inflation. Wage and price controls were abandoned shortly after the war, but Germany has followed a very strict monetary policy and the central bank consistently has placed the goals of price stability and balance of payment equilibrium ahead of full employment. The German tax system is generally regressive, and thus tends to depress consumption. Several other aspects of the government's attack on inflation warrant brief mention. One of these techniques involves importing workers from countries like Italy that have a labor surplus to help meet Germany's critical labor shortage. Nearly 750,000 foreign workers were imported in the 1960s, but their employment has only ameliorated, not eliminated, the problem of labor shortages. Such workers are likely to be unskilled and thus unable to supply labor in the areas where it is most critically needed. In addition, the improved economic conditions in other countries have reduced the supply of available workers, and increases in the pool of imported labor have come to a virtual halt.

Additional steps taken to check inflation have included curtailment of construction (shortage of labor was particularly critical in this field) and the government's attempt to set a good example by holding down the wages it paid its own employees. This latter step has been largely unsuccessful because low morale and high turnover among its employees forced the government to meet competition from the private sector and to pay comparable wages. Although the governments of other countries have also generally found this policy unworkable, public employees have in some instances suffered when the private sectors have failed to follow the public sectors' lead.

The West German government has also established a Council of Economic Experts and this group, along with other officials, has continued to beseech both labor and management to use discretion in their price systems. Most economists agree that these appeals have not been particularly effective.

Sweden

The last European country in our survey is the only one to have escaped the ravages of World War II. Nevertheless, Sweden has experienced considerable inflation and has taken some novel steps to help hold it in check. Sweden's unemployment rate has been somewhat above that of Great Britain during the postwar years but distinctly below that of the United States.

Like many of the European countries, Sweden has a system of collective bargaining on an industrywide and even nationwide basis, and both employers and workers are highly organized. The LO employs a council of economists to advise it on wage policy. Because of industrywide settlements and the acute shortages of labor in some areas of the labor market, there has been a considerable amount of wage drift in the years since World War II. As much as 50 percent of the wage increase has been attributed to this phenomenon.[19]

Because of certain steps taken by the government that were quite effec-tive in restraining wages, there have been occasions when unions and employer associations agreed to a wage freeze for substantial periods. In general, the national associations of employers were more effective in restraining employers than were their union counterparts in restraining local unions. An employer who exceeded the agreed limits could be fined and might face a boycott by fellow employers. If a local union exceeded the proper boundaries, on the other hand, it might face a lockout and fellow locals might be locked out as well. It was during the periods when wages were frozen that wage drift became most pronounced and created serious discrepancies in wage rates between different groups of workers. White-collar workers who were not on incentive programs were particularly hard hit by wage drift. These discrepancies and the dissatisfactions they caused led to periodic and substantial upward adjustments in the general level of wages.

Despite the fact that the party in power in Sweden throughout the postwar years has been the party most favorable to labor, the government has stood ready to take action whenever it felt wage increases were unduly inflationary. Sweden's government has never instituted an "income policy" similar to that in Great Britain. Instead when pressures for higher wages developed the government imposed an added sales tax that sopped up much or all of the added purchasing power won by the wage increases. Unions soon learned that any attempt to win disproportionate gains would be countered by this use of government fiscal policy. Since Sweden also has a strong central labor organization able to exercise great influence on the bargaining practices of individual unions, Swedish unions did not seek excessive wages. Until recently, the rise in wages and prices could be blamed on Swedish unions only very slightly if at all. Thus although Swedish unions deny that their country has an income policy, in fact only the form is different—the underlying idea is still the same.

By the late 1960s, however, the picture had changed considerably. After a bitter struggle between employer and union groups that came close to turning into a giant lock-out and the worst labor crisis since the general strike of 1909, unions negotiated a three-year contract that boosted wages 8.4 percent in 1966, 8.9 percent in 1967, and 7.6 percent in 1968. The result has been a sudden upward surge in Swedish prices and a serious deterioration in her balance of payments position. Between 1960 and 1967 Sweden's price index rose 33 points, compared to a 13 point rise in the United States. The government has been trying to check this by increasing the bank rate to 6 percent, the highest since 1932, and by a reduction in government expenditures. Sweden has also placed more emphasis on a retraining program for the unemployed and less on the maintenance of full employment as a goal. By 1970 unemployment had risen to 2.5 to 3 percent as compared to the earlier rate of 1 to 1.5 percent.

Israel

Israel's inflationary difficulties also began with World War II and early in the war she adopted a program of strict price controls. After the war, inflation persisted largely because wages were initially set by the Histadrut to match those of unskilled workers in Western Europe, and were thus considerably higher than those warranted by Israeli levels of produc-

tivity. From the beginning the level of fringe benefits was in excess of that won by American workers. In addition, throughout the late forties and early fifties, Israeli labor had a wage program that adjusted wages automatically to rises in the cost of living index. These escalator clauses received sharp criticism from a number of economists, and in recent years a policy of attempting to hold the line on wages until productivity increases have an opportunity to catch up to wages has been adopted. To expedite this "catching-up" process the Histadrut has been trying to encourage gains in productivity through joint productivity councils. In addition, Israel has had inflation to accompany her rapid pace of economic growth. From 1955 to 1965 her GNP on the average rose by 10 percent per year.

The attempt to hold wage increases in check has meant that the relatively small differential between skilled and professional and industrial workers has been perpetuated. As a result, there has been considerable unrest among skilled and professional workers, including some strikes and the threats of strikes. In order to relieve the tension, the government has been forced to make some concessions in the form of higher wages to the skilled and professional workers, despite its desire to hold the line in order to improve Israel's trade position. The Israeli government has also attempted to fight inflation by launching a sizeable housing program (housing has been a pressing problem because of the influx of immigrants) and by encouraging consumer cooperatives, these measures serving to hold down rent and food prices.

In the summer of 1966, Israel abandoned a program of voluntary savings designed to cut consumer demand. These savings were to take the form of voluntary pay cuts to be deposited to the credit of the individual at the Bank of Israel. On the basis of early enthusiasm over the scheme the premier had even foregone a request from the legislature for additional taxes. Four months after the plan had been in operation, however, only $1,600 had been deposited! In early 1970, in the aftermath of the Six-Day War in the Middle East, the Israeli government directed that part of wages be paid in bonds to avert further expansions in consumer demand.

India and Mexico

Although both India and Mexico have experienced a great deal of inflation in the postwar years, in neither country can the problem be attributed in any significant degree to unions and collective bargaining. In both countries unions have been too weak and small to have an important impact. A substantial amount of the inflation, particularly in Mexico, has come from deliberate government policy designed to stimulate a more rapid pace of economic growth. Perhaps more than any other country in the world, Mexico has been successful in fostering growth through inflation. More recently the Mexican government has been displaying a degree of caution. The 1967 GNP rose by 7 percent, but a sizable trade deficit plagued the economy. India's moves in this direction have been both less deliberate and less successful but equally subject to criticism by orthodox economists.

Japan

Japan's postwar boom, which began in the latter half of the forties, ebbed in the fifties, and carried on through the sixties, has been every bit as great as Italy's or West Germany's. Favorable terms of trade, a high rate of investment, and the boost of the Korean and Vietnam wars have all contributed to Japanese economic growth, which for some years has attained an annual rate of increase of nearly 17 percent. In 1946 Japan's GNP was only $1 billion. By 1957 it had climbed to $21 billion and today it is over $100 billion. Even more remarkable, this phenomenal pace has been attained with relatively little inflation.

This is not to say that Japan has been entirely free of inflation; she has not. But Japan has had less inflation than any of the other countries examined and Japanese inflation has occurred only sporadically. Most important for our purposes, virtually none of Japanese inflation can be attributed to wages and the demands of unions.

Until recently, wages in Japan during the postwar years lagged behind gains in productivity; between 1950 and 1960 productivity gains rose 9 percent annually while wage increases rose only 6 percent. This phenomenon is due to several factors, including: (1) Japan's relatively large labor force, which was expanded after the war by the return of emigrés from Japan's short-lived "empire"; (2) the abundant supply of skilled workers; and (3) the resulting low bargaining strength of Japanese unions.

Throughout the 1960s there have been increasing signs of growing shortages of labor in certain fields, some of which have an overall unemployment rate of less than 1 percent. Both this fact and the growing bargaining strength of Japanese unions suggest that the smooth sailing of earlier years may be brought to an end. Interestingly enough, however, the chief pressure on prices has come from the smaller plants, which recently have had sharp increases in wage levels without offsetting gains in productivity. As a result, these small plants have led in passing their higher costs on to the public.

Summary and Conclusions

In only four of the countries in our survey, the United States, Great Britain, Israel, and Sweden, can unions be characterized as playing a major role in contributing to inflation. Of these four countries the most consistent criticism (although there is no general agreement on the extent of union responsibility) seems to be lodged against the unions of the United States and possibly those of Great Britain. In all the other countries, labor organizations are either too weak (India and France) or industrywide bargaining produces a kind of wage drift (Germany) that pushes wages above the levels sought by the unions.

It is also quite evident from our discussion of the countries in our survey that attempting to maintain a stable price level in the face of full employment and rapid economic growth is an extremely difficult task, whether or not an elaborate system of collective bargaining is in existence. Attempts at controls have ranged from voluntary guidelines, to indicative planning (France), to bipartisan or tripartite boards (Great Britain), to a complete freeze (Great Britain). None of these has proven successful.

NOTES

1. Note that the wage-push hypothesis does not contain anything that is basically contradictory to the marginal productivity theory. However, the picture changes if one assumes, as most wage-push theorists do, that the government will act to assure the maintenance of full employment. By acting in this manner, the government in effect shifts the demand curve to the right—a shift marginal productivity assumed would not occur in the short run.

2. William Beveridge, *Full Employment in a Free Society* (New York: Norton, 1945). A United Nations study group defined full employment as "a situation in which employment cannot be increased by an increase in effective demand." John M. Clark, *et. al, National and International Measures for Full Employment* (New York: United Nations, 1949), p. 13.

3. Walter A. Morton, "Trade Unionism, Full Employment and Inflation," *American Economic Review* (March 1950), pp. 13–39.

4. *Ibid.,* p. 18.

5. Morton himself has acknowledged the existence of wage-push inflation for the more recent period. "I am inclined to believe that cost-push has been actively present since 1951 and that wage-push has been an important though not the only factor in this cost-push." Walter A. Morton, "Wage-Push Inflation," Industrial Relations Research Association, *Proceedings,* (1958), p. 186. In that article Morton continued to emphasize that demand-pull factors have been important as he reemphasizes the importance of monetary and fiscal policy designed to stiffen the resistance of employers to union demands.

6. Gottfried Haberler, "Wage Policy, Employment and Economic Stability," in David McCord Wright (ed.), *The Impact of the Union* (New York: Harcourt Brace Jovanovich, 1951), p. 47.

7. A. W. Phillips, "The Relation Between Unemployment and the Rate of Change of Money Wage Rates in the United Kingdom, 1861–1957," *Economica* (November 1958), pp. 283–299.

8. Paul A. Samuelson and Robert M. Solow, "Analytical Aspects of Anti-inflation Policy," *American Economic Review* (May 1960), pp. 177–194.

9. William G. Bowen, *Wage Behavior in the Postwar Period: An Empirical Analysis* (Princeton, N.J.: Princeton University, Industrial Relations Section, 1960).

10. George L. Parry, *Unemployment, Money Wage Rates and Inflation,* (Cambridge, Mass.: Harvard University Press, 1966).

11. Milton Friedman, "Some Comments on the Significance of Labor Unions for

Economic Policy," in David McCord Wright (ed.), *The Impact of the Union* (New York: Harcourt Brace Jovanovich, 1951), pp. 204–234. Actually the possibility that long-term contracts stimulate anticipatory demands should not be neglected.

12. Charles Schultze, "Recent Inflation in the United States," in Richard Perlman (ed.), *Inflation: Demand-Pull or Cost-Push?* (Boston: Heath, 1965), p. 37.

13. Sumner Slichter, "Economics and Collective Bargaining," in *Economics and the Policy Maker* (Washington: Brookings, 1959).

14. The wage guidelines might conceivably have been more successful if the Council of Economic Advisors had done a better selling job to both management and labor and to the general public. On this point see the comments of John Dunlop, "Guideposts, Wages and Collective Bargaining," in George P. Shultz and Robert Z. Aliber (eds.), *Guidelines: Informal Controls and the Market Place* (Chicago: University of Chicago Press, 1966), p. 85. The difficulty of selling workers on the idea that they should accept less than they can get is obviously great, however.

15. The most favorable case for the guidelines has been made by John Sheahan. See his *The Wage-Price Guideposts* (Washington: Brookings, 1967).

16. H. A. Turner, "Inflation and Wage Differentials in Great Britain," in John T. Dunlop (ed.), *The Theory of Wage Determination* (London: St. Martin's, 1957), pp. 123–135. See also Gosta Rehhn, "The Problem of Stability: An Analysis of Some Policy Proposals," in Ralph Turvey (ed.), *Wages Policy Under Full Employment* (London: W. Hodge, 1952).

17. F. W. Paish and Josselyn Kennedy, *Policy for Incomes?* Hobart Paper 29 (London: London Institute of Economic Affairs, 1966).

18. Murray Edelman and R. W. Fleming, *The Politics of Wage-Price Decisions* (Urbana: University of Illinois Press, 1966), p. 177.

19. Bertil Ohlin has suggested that in Sweden, during the years immediately following World War II at least, much of the wage drift occurred in small plants that were able to grant increases without individually attracting public attention. Bertil Ohlin, *The Problem of Employment Stabilization* (New York: Columbia University Press, 1949), p. 15.

17
The Future of Collective Bargaining

The task of making collective bargaining work embodies one of the great challenges to what we call "the democratic process."
—George Taylor

. . . the greatest danger to collective bargaining is that it may do more and more for less and less to its ultimate undoing.
—Leonard Woodcock

□ EVEN before collective bargaining had acquired its name, it was the target of numerous hostile critics who proclaimed that it would never work or that its working would spell the doom of capitalism and free enterprise. It is not surprising, therefore, that today, less than two generations after collective bargaining won widespread acceptance in the United States, its early demise is predicted with unfailing regularity. Many of the early foes of collective bargaining have continued to repeat their warnings about the dire consequences of permitting free collective bargaining to operate.

Perhaps more surprising and certainly more disturbing to unions and other supporters of collective bargaining is the recent flood of criticism from individuals formerly deeply involved in the labor movement.[1] Many of these critics contend that the labor movement is losing its earlier idealism and spark and is concentrating instead on routine activities disparaged by the critics as being nothing more than "business unionism." Union leaders are pictured as fat cats who settle for higher wages for their current memberships rather than fighting on the front lines where poverty, discrimination, and exploitation still exist. The message of unionism goes unheard by the workers, the critics say, not only because it is directed toward ears that no longer listen, but also because the message itself is uninspired. We have always felt that this criticism of American labor unions constituted a misreading of the historical character of those unions. Unions in this country never could be characterized as being interested in widespread social and economic reform, but have always been most interested in improving the economic position of their own memberships, even when those gains were won at the expense of those outside the ranks of organized labor. Although it is probably true that unions have played a smaller role in the battle against current social evils than they might have, many of the expectations of greater effort are based on the false premise that the 1930s represented the true picture of union character.[2] Some critics seem to suggest that most or all of the social and economic problems besetting our country could be eliminated tomorrow if only unions would take a greater interest or that unions could solve them single-handedly if they would only try. As we have noted in previous chapters, American unions have begun to look to the government for additional aid in helping to combat problems of automation and unemployment, problems that are too large to be solved by collective bargaining alone. The extent to which unions should exert political pressure for legislation dealing with social issues rather than attempting to solve problems through collective bargaining is at least debatable.

If the failure of unions to push into new areas in either collective bargaining or political action is debatable, there is little question that there are other current developments that pose serious threats to the future of collective bargaining.

Collective bargaining in the absence of labor unions is difficult to imagine. Even if unions are not as guilty of a loss of initiative and spirit as some critics have charged, there are substantial reasons for worrying about their current state of health. The statistics presented in Chapter 2 indicate that unions have failed to grow in size proportionately to increases in the labor force. They have even lost ground slightly in terms of absolute numbers.

There is substantial evidence that the Taft-Hartley and Landrum-Griffin acts accurately reflected the public sentiment that the pendulum of power had swung too far in the direction of labor and that a balance needed to be restored. A growing fear of inflation and an impatience with work stoppages that could at worst be considered public inconveniences have been symptomatic of a growing public suspicion of labor unions. The findings of the McClellan Committee and rumors of widespread malfeasance among union leaders have done little to reassure the general public as to the worth of labor unions.

Increasing public disenchantment has led to the growth of government interference with collective bargaining. The continuation of the Cold War and local involvements such as the Vietnam War have led the government to place great stress on the maintenance of production despite the fact that one or both parties are dissatisfied with existing contracts. In a number of fields like rocketry, collective bargaining has been subjected to continuous pressure by government officials. Since the unions are the ones most

likely to be dissatisfied with an existing contract, they have borne the brunt of disapproving public opinion and governmental pressure.

It is easy to slip into an attitude in which all major strikes become national "emergencies" calling for government seizure when other methods of settlement fail. Collective bargaining, however, has always rested on the assumption that workers were free to withhold their labor when the pay did not satisfy them just as the businessman has been free to refrain from selling his product unless he could obtain a satisfactory price for that product.

However, although the number of manhours lost by strikes has continued to remain less than three-tenths of one percent of total yearly work hours, public acceptance of those strikes that occur has been less and less easy to win. In part this is the result of the emphasis on national defense just cited, but three other considerations have also played an important role.

First of all, the public has a fear of inflation. We have seen that in some countries, notably in West Germany, such fears have played an important role in restraining union leaders from making excessive demands lest those demands find little support from the rank-and-file membership. Fear of inflation has had a far less restrictive impact on union demands in this country, but it undoubtedly has had some effect in that direction. Until the summer of 1966, union demands were usually in accord with the guidelines laid down by the President's Council of Economic Advisors, and unions that strayed outside those boundaries faced the danger of government retaliation. Even in those years, however, it was always clear that the government had at its disposal few weapons that it could (or was willing to) deploy against a union determined to break the imposed limits. Forebodings about the effectiveness of the guidelines were confirmed when the Machinists won their airline strike in the summer of 1966 and made a settlement considerably in excess of the President's guidelines. Similar wage settlements at levels above those matched by gains in productivity have increased the general public's concern over inflation even when the union's justification is that it was only "catching up" with previous price increases.

Second, the public's preoccupation with economic growth has also hampered union demands. Economists and politicians alike have extolled the virtues of economic growth so regularly that it is difficult for citizens to view with anything but suspicion any institution that appears to impede that growth. Such actions as featherbedding or slowdowns and work stoppages are likely to be targets for strong public disapproval when there is an emphasis on raising output.

The third public concern, which is less easily articulated by many citizens than the first two, although it is closely related to them, is an appreciation of the interdependence of the various sectors of our economy. Since this interdependence is greater today than it has been in the past, the public is more likely to question whether or not the economy as a whole can afford to let labor and management settle their disputes by themselves at the expense of public convenience and protection. More than ever, the public does have a stake both in getting any specific dispute resolved and in the nature of the settlement made.

If one's goals are to permit the expansion of union power and to allow completely free collective bargaining, one must deny that periodic disruptions in production are too great a price to pay for a free labor movement actively pursuing its own interests through collective bargaining. Furthermore, one must not admit that settlements made under collective bargaining that are satisfactory to both parties can ever be so unsatisfactory to the general public that the forbidding of such settlements or their mandatory overthrow will become necessary. (Inflationary wage settlements are one obvious example of a case in which this issue might arise.)

A number of economists and labor experts basically sympathetic to the cause of labor have been reluctant to take the second position. When Willard Wirtz was Secretary of Labor he was concerned about the frequency with which what he regarded as "good" settlements were rejected by the rank and file. He warned union members that their insistence on still higher settlements might lead to government intervention.[3] John Dunlop has been critical of the Landrum-Griffin Act for this reason and has suggested that the power of final settlement should rest in the hands of the president of the international union.[4]

Other changes in our economy may also spell trouble for unions and collective bargaining. The growing proportion of women in the labor force may make the problems of organization more difficult. However, the earlier difficulty experienced in organizing female workers was due partly to the unwillingness of many unions to make the effort and partly to the fact that at an earlier period many women were in the labor force for only short periods of time. The success of the ILGWU demonstrates that the organization of women was never as difficult as pictured. Furthermore, today many women plan to be in the labor force on at least a semipermanent basis and are, therefore, likely to be more receptive to union overtures.

We have seen that white-collar unions have had great success in countries like Japan, Israel, and Sweden but have been only selectively successful in this country. Fear of displacement by automated equipment, increasing routinization of the job, and the basic conflicts that exist between the employer and the employee are problems that affect the white-collar worker as much as the blue-collar worker. We would therefore expect the total number of white-collar union members to continue to increase both in absolute and percentage terms. In order for our forecast to be realized, the white-collar workers will have to see the benefits that unionizing offers them and be willing to be affiliated with other parts of the labor movement rather than holding themselves apart as something special. Experience in Sweden suggests that separate federations of white-collar unions can be successful. Manual workers in the United States, however, have been less sympathetic to wage equality than have their Swedish counterparts. Thus white-collar workers who tend to oppose the erasing of differentials may be more open to systematic drives by the AFL-CIO to enroll them in its ranks. Interest on the part of the AFL-CIO to do so may be stimulated by the declining importance of some of the traditional strongholds of unionism such as the coal mines and the railroads and by the fact that since 1956 white-collar has exceeded blue-collar employment.

Just as the white-collar worker is likely to play an ever more important role in the ranks of organized labor, so also will the public employee. Both state and local governments have been providing an expanding source of employment in recent years (currently around 6 million) and the problems and frustrations faced by the public employee are often similar to those of his counterpart in the private sector.

Bargaining in this new area is likely to be fraught with difficulties for some time to come, not only because both parties are unaccustomed to their positions at the bargaining table, but also because the public sector has long been hard pressed for funds, and the situation has worsened as added functions have been undertaken.

On the one hand there is a newly organized group anxious to display their new-found strength in securing substantial gains and on the other a group of financially sorely pressed local and state governments. Although virtually every governmental unit in this country outlaws strikes by public employees, there have been over 35 strikes per year by public employees since 1942. Beginning in 1966 the number of strikes each year by public employees jumped to over 150 and by 1968 was in excess of 250. Attempts by states to write laws effectively outlawing such strikes have thus far proved largely futile. The correct prescription for the right amount of penalties is still to be found.

Some observers even doubt the propriety of restricting the right of public employees to strike. Can real collective bargaining develop in the absence of the right to strike? Few countries except Sweden and Canada, however, have been willing to permit such strikes. Even in these two countries, whenever the public interest is threatened other means of resolving the dispute are applied. If we do bar strikes by public employees, how can we be certain their interests will be protected? What penalties for strikes can be imposed that will remain within the limits set by a democratic society and still be effective? As things now stand, it is the weak unions (social workers, etc.), whose members are most badly in need of protection, that have been most severely punished by the government, while the stronger unions (the Transport Workers in New York City, for example) have been able to strike without fear of reprisals. A strike by our teachers, our sanitation men, or our highway crews is bearable at least for a short time. Can the same be said about a strike of our policemen or firemen?

With the increase in both white-collar and public employee unionism, new issues and new problems hitherto left untouched by collective bargaining are likely to emerge. In some cases these issues may be entirely new; more frequently they will be a variant of familiar themes in industrial relations. For example, a local board of education member complained to the authors that a local teachers' union was seeking jurisdictions on decisions previously left entirely to the board and administration.

Far from complete has been the acceptance of the Negro into the ranks of organized labor. It is now a decade and a half since the AFL-CIO at the time of its merger adopted a plank assuring equal bargaining rights for Negro workers. Although progress has not been totally lacking, it has been painfully slow and the actions of both the federation and its constituent unions have fallen far short of the written pledge. In many major cities black workers continue to press for recognition and admission to the jobs organized by the unions. The battles are likely to continue for some time in the future as the black man seeks his constitutional right of equal access to jobs.

Even in those unions where Negroes are now admitted freely, their opportunities to rise to the top are hindered. Union leaders have generally turned a deaf ear to pleas that the Negroes should be given any preferential treatment to atone for earlier discrimination. The number of skilled Negro workers has increased but is still pitifully small: given the tight labor market of the late 1960s progress should have been much more rapid.

There has been another significant change in the economy during the past half century that may make the road for unions more difficult as they seek satisfactory contracts under collective bargaining. A substantial number of firms today are in a position where they may not be at all adverse to a work stoppage. Not only does management realize that the primary responsibility for such stoppages will be placed at the doorstep of the unions, but it is able to weather such stoppages better than its ancestors were for two reasons. First, the firm may be so large and have such a dominant position in the market that it is able to overproduce existing consumer demand. A disruption of production in the form of a strike may hamper the company's market position less than might at first be expected and may even serve to strengthen it. Second, modern technology may enable a plant to run for protracted periods in the face of a walkout by the company's union employees. Prime examples of this can be found in the cases of the telephone company, the oil refineries, and the national television networks. Even Mohawk Airlines in the fall of 1966 was able to keep operations at 70 percent of capacity in the face of a strike by the Machinists. Clearly unions encounter increasingly numerous instances in which they will have to rethink the strategy of the strike and its attractiveness.

The growth of big business in the form of conglomerate mergers holds still another implication for collective bargaining. Not only is the bargaining strength of the company enhanced because of its greater financial resources, but the giant company often crosses industry lines, making it difficult for even an industrial union organized along the traditional jurisdictional lines to represent all of the workers in the company adequately. In the future, unions may find it necessary to grow larger as companies continue to expand. Unions may also have to cross jurisdictional boundaries previously largely regarded as sacred in order to match the opposition or work out programs of coordinated bargaining as they have at General Electric.

Another frequently neglected but important hurdle to continued union growth and successful collective bargaining is the very success that unions have experienced with bargaining in the past. Many young workers, arriving long after the battles have been won, find that contract negotiations have become routine affairs and that management's personnel officers display a great interest in workers' welfare. These newcomers forget or are unaware of the vital role the union has played in the past in assuring the stable labor relations that now exist. Whether a possible future trend toward longer-term contracts and the tendency of many contracts today to tie wage increases to annual increases in the company's productivity will add to this feeling of security and to the downgrading of unions' importance in workers' minds is problematic. Both practices have come under heavy fire from some representatives of both unions and management.

Already many contracts are set for two- or three-year periods and some students of labor relations have projected a trend toward five- and even ten-year contracts in the years to come. Tying wages to gains in productivity, a practice that began with the 1948 contract between General Motors

and the UAW, has also grown increasingly popular with time. When wages are tied to gains in productivity, the worker is likely to identify increases in his take-home pay with improvements in the company's efficiency rather than with the efforts of the union on his behalf.

The apathy of union members toward their union has been further reinforced by the need of the union to adapt to the increasing size of the modern corporation by developing industrywide or pattern bargaining. Increasingly, major decisions are taken out of the hands of local union leaders. Members thus come to view bargaining as a process far removed from them. We have noted in previous chapters that this has been a source of concern to labor leaders in other countries and the resulting wage drift (which occurs regardless of workers' efforts or apathy) has been an important contributing factor in the declining union membership in some of those countries.

As this book is being written (1970), the rank and file in the United States appears to be in revolt, insisting that they have some voice in the terms of the contract. These workers have repeatedly held up the ratification of contracts negotiated by the national's officers until adjustments in local conditions have been made. Whether or not this unrest will overcome the forces tending toward greater centralization remains to be seen. Perhaps some compromise will be the result, a compromise in which some items are standardized and negotiated at the national level while others are left to local option.

Given the thousands of contracts negotiated in this country each year, it is not surprising that the traditional critics of collective bargaining have been able to find choice bits of evidence to wave as proof of the generally unhealthy state of the entire process. Instances of "sweetheart contracts," where undercover deals between the employer and the union leaders were made at the expense of the union's membership, or cases where union leaders have used their economic power to coerce an employer into accepting extremely undesirable contracts have not been too difficult to find. All too often both parties have taken a short-sighted view and made settlements that, although they were to their immediate advantage, made future negotiations still more complicated. Collective bargaining has sometimes proved to be a farce as both sides turned stubborn and refused to make reasonable settlements.

Clearly there are other criticisms of collective bargaining that have more merit. Unions, upon occasion, do force upon management wage adjustments that are inflationary in their impact. Nor can collective bargaining be properly viewed as a panacea that solves all the problems of industrial relations without difficulty. Certain issues do lie outside its purview or at least there are some issues that thus far have remained largely untouched.

But when all the criticisms are put together and put into proper perspective, we find that faults are present in a decided minority of the total bargaining situations and that the gains achieved from bargaining have been far greater than the accompanying losses. These conclusions hold true whether bargaining is viewed from the perspective of workers, management, or the entire economy. Let us look for a moment at the major advantages accruing to each.

A system of collective bargaining provides two major services to most employers and a third to some. The first chief advantage lies in the improved system of plant communica-

tions that a collective bargaining system provides. As we noted in our discussion of grievances, the grievance machinery has had particular importance as a means by which management could communicate its point of view to the workers. A second major advantage is that the existence of a labor union also provides management with a more predictable and more consistent pattern of wage increases and labor conditions. Through the years as it deals with the union's leaders across the bargaining table at contract time and in the daily settlement of grievances, management comes to know what to expect by way of new demands and is thus able to gauge its production plans accordingly. A distinct advantage to a lesser number of employers is union recruitment of trained workers—a service that is performed by a number of the craft unions.

Since much of this book has dwelt on the gains accruing to workers from collective bargaining in the form of higher wages, greater fringe benefits, and protection from arbitrary treatment, it is not necessary to elaborate again upon the virtues of collective bargaining from the workers' viewpoint. The very real importance for workers of having some voice in the decisions that vitally affect their economic future, however, cannot be emphasized often enough.

Some important gains accruing to the economy from collective bargaining have been less frequently perceived. Health and safety standards in many plants have undoubtedly been far higher than they would have been in the absence of union pressure for the passage and enforcement of relevant legislation. Unions have probably also been an important stimulant to the efficiency of management, thereby promoting the use of more advanced technology and other labor-saving devices. This in turn has played an important part in fostering a more rapid pace of economic growth.

While it would be too dogmatic to state categorically that no new arrangement will ever replace collective bargaining, this book has suggested that it has been a remarkably viable and flexible instrument, one that has been able to adjust repeatedly to changing institutions and economic and social environments. George Taylor and others have suggested that there is nothing instinctive or natural about collective bargaining and that it is a cultivated method of handling industrial disputes.[5] Nevertheless, it appears to be easily the best method thus far devised and likely to remain with us for some time to come.

In projecting the future of collective bargaining, therefore, we dismiss as premature those predictions that contend that collective bargaining will soon collapse under the weight of its own inadequacies. But if collective bargaining is to be with us for the foreseeable future, what changes in its form will take place? The answer to this last question is obviously a difficult one to provide, but we will attempt to answer it by noting some of the trends now taking place in the various countries we have studied.

In the near future, certain trends already discernible are likely to continue. To an indeterminate extent the path to labor settlements may be further smoothed in this country by the emergence of early (before contract expiration) negotiations and the utilization of continuous bargaining. James P. Mitchell, Secretary of Labor during the latter half of the Eisenhower administration, first suggested continuous bargaining. He based his case on its behalf on the premise that modern contracts had become too complex to permit resolution on the basis of deadline bargaining.

Whether continuous bargaining will herald a new era of cooperation in industrial relations remains to be seen. While it worked reasonably well in the steel industry when first adopted, rank-and-file dissatisfaction with its results contributed to the defeat of David McDonald as president of the Steelworkers. The practice has done little to resolve some of the more difficult issues separating unions and management in the railroad industry.

As management and labor come to settle more and more of their disputes on a peaceful basis, it is likely that unions will participate more and more in management's decisions, particularly where those decisions even remotely involve the interests of workers. Whether some form of union-management cooperation in the traditional meaning of the term will subsequently develop appears more doubtful, but there appears to be an increasing realization on both sides of the right of what E. Wight Bakke has called "mutual survival."[6] Certainly there is evidence that the old doctrinaire ideology of the unions (in which management was a mortal enemy to be treated with deep suspicion at all times) has faded considerably in a number of European countries like France.

The role of the government is likely to increase in some countries and diminish in others depending on the previous historical role of government in industrial relations within a particular country. Government is likely to retain an important role in industrial relations in all the countries of the world, however.

One of the most provocative themes about the future of collective bargaining around the world appears in *Industrialism and Industrial Man,* a book written by four of the nation's leading industrial relations experts.[7] These experts argue that industrial relations in different countries are becoming more alike with the passage of time. We have found confirming evidence of such a trend among the countries we have examined, including:

1. There is less diversity in the scope of the bargaining unit. With the possible exception of Japan, the dominance of local plant bargaining in countries where it was formerly important (such as the United States) has declined. It seems highly unlikely, however, that the United States would ever move toward widespread industrywide bargaining. Although plantwide bargaining still accounts for about two-thirds of the bargaining agreements in the United States, 40 percent of the workers are covered by multiplant contracts. Meanwhile, in countries like France, Great Britain, and West Germany, where multiemployer bargaining has been the rule, unions have been emphasizing the importance of local bargaining. Since local bargaining in Britain is still on an informal basis it is difficult to measure its extent, but most observers agree that it is growing. In West Germany, unions have been working hard for "close to the undertaking" arrangements for bargaining. In France, the unions' early ideological opposition to plant bargaining is dwindling and many companies have attained a size where individual plant bargaining is now more feasible.

2. Similarities have also increased with regard to the range of items included in the collective bargaining contract. Judged by United States standards, many foreign labor unions in the past have neglected the key parts of collective bargaining contracts. Absent in many cases were provisions for seniority and union security. Even more striking, many unions in other countries have had little impact on the *sine qua non* of United States collective bargaining, wage rates, because of the existence of wage drift. While differences still exist, there has been some reduction. France and West Germany in particular have had unions fighting for fringe benefits of one form or another. Wage drift has been a source of great concern to union leaders in all of the countries where it is found and they have tried to make the role of unions in determining wage rates more significant. Although seniority provisions are spelled out in far less detail in contracts abroad than they are in the United States, the principle is by no means neglected elsewhere and continues to receive the attention of unions. The concept of union security, on the other hand, is still far more fully developed in this country than elsewhere.

3. Differences in the role of government in the various countries are also declining. France has historically been known as the country where the law dominated the field of industrial relations. In Britain, on the other hand, both parties to collective bargaining were left remarkably free. Gradually countries like France have relaxed some of their intricate legal controls over their collective bargaining systems, while countries like the United States and Great Britain, where few regulations (save the courts) have controlled unions, are now limiting more and more the freedom of unions to act. In the latter countries, concern over inflation and economic growth and the disruptive effect of nationwide strikes have been major reasons for this trend.

At least four underlying forces that promote the gradual narrowing of the differences in the various bargaining systems can be identified, although they can not be clearly ranked in importance.

The first of these is the growing force of technology, which shapes the character of the plant's work force, the nature of the work to be performed, and the resulting differences that emerge between labor and management. Technology results in the same challenges, the same problems, and the same stresses and strains whether the plant is located in the United States, Europe, or the Far East. Machinery tends to make workers more mobile, thereby reducing management's paternalism. This phenomenon is beginning to be evident even in Japan where workers for years have had life-long tenure and felt bound to a particular company. Japanese workers are beginning to move into the labor market just as workers in other countries did years earlier.

The second force toward uniformity is the rising educational level of people in all nations and the gradual decline of illiteracy. With rising standards of education, there is less chance that collective bargaining demands will be based on false premises and ideological standards; thus unworkable and illogical claims are less frequently pressed. In India, for example, employers have often been afraid to enter collective bargaining because the demands of the workers were often far in excess of the worth of the business.

Similarly, the mere passage of time works to eradicate the more extreme positions that make collective bargaining unworkable. Time provides an opportunity for a nation to experiment with its programs of collective bargaining and to learn what works well and what does not. Today, more than ever, the labor unions of each country can learn from past experience in other countries and can pick those variations that seem to work best and adopt them. Foreign labor movements are becoming more like our own, and American unions have made adaptations as well. Whether American labor unions will ever become as much of a political force as their counterparts in

Europe still seems doubtful on the basis of results of recent elections. Few would deny, however, that American unions are more politically active than they were a century ago.

Fourthly, communications have improved. Not only are we now in a position to export our industrial relations model where that seems desirable but we are better able to import from others as well. The importance of such institutions as the International Labor Organization in furthering a better understanding of how problems in various countries are handled for unions and managements should not be overlooked.

In explaining the historical international differences in collective bargaining Arthur Ross noted that each country "has its own historical background, its own political institutions, its own cultural tradition, its own distinctive style."[8] With the passage of time, the significance of all of these is likely to decrease as collective bargaining in all of the democratic nations continues to play a healthy and constructive role throughout the world. We began this book by noting the great diversity that characterized collective bargaining. It is likely that some of that diversity will continue to exist, but the differences will probably become less pronounced.

NOTES

1. See, for example, Paul Jacobs, *Old Before Its Time: Collective Bargaining at 28* (Santa Barbara, Calif.: Fund for the Republic, 1963); Paul Sultan, *The Disenchanted Unionist* (New York: Harper & Row, 1963); Sydney Lens, *The Crisis of American Labor* (New York: Barnes, 1961).

2. Our chapter in labor history suggested that the extent to which unions were more socially conscious in the 1930s was a product of the times, a period when unemployment touched one out of four members of the labor force. If unions have lost some of

their militancy today, reduced hostility on the part of employers toward labor unions should also be recognized as an important factor. Furthermore, it is not at all clear that labor takes a less active interest in politics than it did in the 1930s; perhaps its interest has simply not moved in the direction critics wished.

3. *The New York Times,* January 3, 1967, 16:5.

4. A. H. Raskin, "Why Labor Doesn't Follow Its Leaders," *The New York Times,* January 8, 1967, p. 6E. Not all students of the subject agree with Dunlop. Clyde Summers, for example, suggests that the rank-and-file is rarely more *radical* than the union's leadership and usually rejects a recommended agreement because of poor communications in the union or because the agreement lacks a clause important to the membership. Summers agrees, however, that only those workers actually on strike should be permitted to vote and those working in other plants not involved in the dispute should be barred from voting. Clyde Summers, "Ratification of Agreements," in John T. Dunlop and Neil W. Chamberlain (eds.), *Frontiers of Collective Bargaining* (New York: Harper & Row, 1967), pp. 75–102.

5. George Taylor, *Government Regulation of Industrial Relations* (Englewood Cliffs, N.J.: Prentice-Hall, 1948), p. 369.

6. E. Wight Bakke, *Mutual Survival* (New Haven, Conn.: Yale Labor and Management Center, 1946).

7. Clark Kerr, John T. Dunlop, Frederick Harbison, and Charles A. Myers, *Industrialism and Industrial Man* (New York: Oxford University Press, 1964).

8. Arthur Ross, "Prosperity and Labor Relations in Europe: The Case of West Germany," *Quarterly Journal of Economics* (August, 1962), p. 336.

BIBLIOGRAPHY

1. The Many Faces of Collective Bargaining

Davey, Harold W., Howard S. Kaltenborn, and Stanley H. Ruttenberg (eds.). *New Dimensions in Collective Bargaining.* New York: Harper & Row, 1959. Treats many of the topics covered in this book with respect to the United States.

Dunlop, John T., and Neil W. Chamberlain (eds.). *Frontiers of Collective Bargaining.* New York: Harper & Row, 1967. Twelve papers that are the product of three years of research of the Labor-Management Institute of the American Arbitration Association.

Friedland, William H. *Unions and Industrial Relations in Under-Developed Countries.* Bulletin No. 47. Ithaca, N.Y.: New York State School of Industrial and Labor Relations, 1963.

Galenson, Walter (ed.). *Comparative Labor Movements.* Englewood Cliffs, N.J.: Prentice-Hall, 1952. Detailed accounts of collective bargaining in Great Britain, Scandinavia, Australia, Germany, France, Italy, and Russia.

————— (ed.). *Labor in Developing Economies.* Berkeley and Los Angeles: University of California Press, 1963. Chapter 5, "Israel," by Irvin Sobel, is the one most relevant to users of the present book.

Galvin, Miles E. *Unions in Latin America.* Bulletin No. 45. Ithaca, N.Y.: New York State School of Industrial and Labor Relations, 1962.

Kassalow, Everett M. *Trade Unions and Industrial Relations.* New York: Random House, 1969. Emphasizes comparative materials.

Lester, Richard A. "Reflections on Collective Bargaining in Britain and Sweden," *Industrial and Labor Relations Review,* Vol. 10 (April 1957).

Selekman, Benjamin M. "Varieties of Labor Relations," *Harvard Business Review,* Vol. 27 (March 1949). Gives eight types of union-management relations ranging from open warfare to cooperation.

Sturmthal, Adolf (ed.). *Contemporary Collective Bargaining in Seven Countries.* Ithaca, N.Y.: Institute of International Industrial and Labor Relations, 1957. A survey of labor relations in Great Britain, Italy, France, West Germany, and the United States (among others) by leading experts.

Twentieth Century Fund. *How Collective Bargaining Works.* New York: Twentieth Century Fund, 1942. Somewhat dated but still a rich source of material on bargaining in various industries in the United States.

2. The History of Collective Bargaining—Here and Elsewhere

There are a large number of fine labor histories in print plus a journal with the title *Labor History.* Following are some of the more recent and readable that are also among the best.

Bernstein, Irving. *The Lean Years.* Boston: Houghton Mifflin, 1960. An account of the 1920s and early 1930s, including the U.S. labor movement.

—————. *Turbulent Years: A History of the American Worker 1933–1941.* Boston: Houghton Mifflin, 1970. Sequel to his earlier work.

Chamberlain, Neil W., and James Kuhn. *Collective Bargaining,* 2nd ed. New York: McGraw-Hill, 1965. Chaps. 1, 2.

Derber, Milton, and Edwin Young (eds.). *Labor and the New Deal.* Madison: University of Wisconsin Press, 1957.

Galenson, Walter. *The CIO Challenge to the AFL.* Cambridge, Mass.: Harvard University Press, 1960.

Pelling, Henry. *American Labor.* Chicago: University of Chicago Press, 1960.

Taft, Philip. *Organized Labor in American History.* New York: Harper & Row, 1964. A sympathetic account of "business" unionism.

Rayback, Joseph G. *A History of American Labor.* New York: Free Press, 1966. An excellent overall summary—particularly good on the early years.

3. Collective Bargaining and Governmental Policies

Bradley, Philip (ed.). *The Public Stake in Union Power.* Charlottesville: University of Virginia Press, 1959.

Chamberlin, Edward H. *The Economic Analysis of Labor Union Power.* Washington: American Enterprise Institute, 1963. A highly critical evaluation of union power.

Evans, Robert, Jr. *Public Policy Toward Labor.* New York: Harper & Row, 1965.

Mason, Edward S. "Labor Monopoly and All That," Industrial Relations Research Association, *Proceedings of the 8th Meeting* (1955), pp. 188–208. An often-reprinted article.

Meltzer, Bernard. "Labor Unions, Collective Bargaining and the Anti-Trust Laws," *University of Chicago Law Review,* Vol. 32 (Summer 1965).

Millis, Harry A., and Emily C. Brown. *From the Wagner Act to Taft-Hartley.* Chicago: University of Chicago Press, 1950. A thorough study of the NLRB for the time period indicated.

Shister, Joseph, Benjamin Aaron, and Clyde Summers, eds. *Public Policy and Collective Bargaining.* New York: Harper & Row, 1962. A series of articles by leading authorities edited for the Industrial Relations Research Association.

Timbers, Edwin. "The Problem of Union Power and Antitrust Legislation," *Labor Law Journal,* Vol. 16 (September 1965). An evaluation of the sources of union power, its misuses, and possible remedies.

Wellington, Henry H. *Labor and the Legal Process.* (New Haven, Conn.: Yale University Press, 1968).

4. The Bargaining Unit

Brooks, George W., and Mark Thompson. "Multiplant Units: The NLRB's Withdrawal of Free Choice," *Industrial and Labor Relations Review,* Vol. 20 (April 1967).

Chamberlain, Neil W. "The Structure of Bargaining Units in the United States," *Industrial and Labor Relations Review.* Vol. 10 (October 1956).

Jones, Dallas L. "The NLRB and the Multi-employer Unit," *Labor Law Journal,* Vol. 5 (January 1954).

Kennedy, Van Dusen. "Association Bargaining," *Monthly Labor Review,* Vol. 82 (May 1959).

Kerr, Clark, and Lloyd H. Fisher. "Multi-Employer Bargaining: The San Francisco Experience." in Richard A. Lester and Joseph Shister (eds.), *Insights into Labor Issues.* New York: Macmillan, 1948.

Pierson, Frank C. "Multi-Employer Bargaining." Reprint 4. Los Angeles: University of California Institute of Industrial Relations, 1949.

Weber, Arnold R. (ed.). *The Structure of Collective Bargaining.* New York: Free Press, 1961.

5. The Strategies of Collective Bargaining

Hicks, John R. *The Theory of Wages.* New York: Peter Smith, 1948.

Lindblom, Charles. "Bargaining Power in Price and Wage Determination," *Quarterly Journal of Economics,* Vol. 42 (May 1948).

Lovell, Hughes. "The Pressure Lever in Mediation," *Industrial and Labor Relations Review,* Vol. 6 (October 1952). Parts of this article were the basis for the present chapter.

McConnell, Campbell (ed.). *Perspectives on Wage Determination.* New York: McGraw-Hill, 1970, pp. 127–184.

Nash, J. F. "The Bargaining Problem," *Econometrica,* Vol. 18 (April 1950).

———. "Two Person Cooperative Games," *Econometrica,* Vol. 21 (January 1953). Neither of these two works by Nash is for the mathematical novice.

Pen, J. "A General Theory of Bargaining," *American Economic Review,* Vol. 42 (March 1952).

Stevens, Carl M. *Strategy and Collective Bargaining Negotiation.* New York: McGraw-Hill, 1963. An obvious source of inspiration for much that is in this chapter.

Walton, Richard E. "Leadership Strategies for Achieving Membership Consensus," Industrial Relations Research Association, *Proceedings of the 18th Annual Meeting* (December 1965). Another important source of aid in writing this chapter.

Zeuthen, Frederik. *Problems of Monopoly and Economic Warfare.* London: Routledge, 1930.

6. Wage Theory and Collective Bargaining

Cartter, Allan M. *Theory of Wages and Employment.* Homewood, Ill.: Irwin, 1959. A good review and analysis of wage theory.

Chamberlain, Neil W., Frank C. Pierson, and Thomas Wolfson, eds. *A Decade of Industrial Relations.* New York: Harper & Row, 1958. A series of articles written for the Industrial Relations Research Association. See particularly the article by Melvin Reder.

Dunlop, John T. *Wage Determination Under Trade Unions.* New York: Macmillan, 1944. One of the great modern-day classics on the subject.

McConnell, Campbell (ed.). *Perspectives on Wage Determination.* New York: McGraw-Hill, 1970.

Pen, J. *The Wage Rate Under Collective Bargaining.* Cambridge, Mass.: Harvard University Press, 1959.

Perlman, Richard (ed.). *Wage Determination: Market or Power Forces.* Boston: Heath, 1964. A series of articles debating the issue implicit in the title.

————. *Wage Theory.* New York: Wiley, 1969. A selective analysis of some of the current theories.

Ross, Arthur M. *Trade Union Wage Policy.* Berkeley: University of California Press, 1948. Should be read in connection with Dunlop.

7. Wage Patterns and Collective Bargaining

Bachman, Jules. *Wage Determination: An Analysis of Wage Criteria.* Princeton, N.J.: Van Nostrand, 1959.

Bloch, Joseph W. "Regional Wage Differentials," *Monthly Labor Review,* Vol. 66 (April 1945).

Douty, Harry M. "Union Impact on Wage Structures," Industrial Relations Research Association, *Proceedings of the 6th Annual Meeting* (1953).

Kennedy, Thomas. *The Significance of Wage Uniformity.* Philadelphia: University of Pennsylvania Press, 1949.

Lester, Richard A. "A Range Theory of Wage Differentials," *Industrial and Labor Relations Review,* Vol. 5 (July 1952).

Lewis, H. Gregg. *Unionism and Relative Wages in the United States.* Chicago: University of Chicago Press, 1963. A difficult but well-written book that thoroughly covers the subject.

McConnell, Campbell (ed.). *Perspectives on Wage Determination.* New York: McGraw-Hill, 1970. Part V.

Reynolds, Lloyd G., and Cynthia Taft. *The Evolution of Wage Structure.* New Haven, Conn.: Yale University Press, 1956. A careful study leads the authors to conclude that the impact of unions on wage structure has been minimal. Some comparative material on other countries.

8. Hours of Work

Dankert, Clyde E. "Shorter Hours—In Theory and Practice," *Industrial and Labor Relations Review,* Vol. 15 (April 1962).

————, Floyd C. Mann, and Herbert R. Northrup, eds. *Hours of Work.* New York: Harper & Row, 1965. A collection of articles written for the Industrial Relations Research Association.

Fogel, Walter, and Archie Kleingartner, eds. *Contemporary Labor Issues.* Belmont, Calif.: Wadsworth, 1966. Articles by the NAM, AFL-CIO, and Sam Levitan.

Greenbaum, Marcia. *The Shorter Workweek.* Bulletin No. 50 (Ithaca, N.Y.: New York State School of Industrial and Labor Relations (June 1965).

Henle, Peter. "Leisure and the Long Weekend," *Monthly Labor Review,* Vol. 89 (July 1966).

Lens, Sydney. "A Shorter Work Week?" *Commonweal*, Vol. 72 (April 29, 1960).

9. Seniority

Belfer, Nathan. "Hidden Costs in the Labor Agreement," *Current Economic Comment*, Vol. 2 (February 1955).

Kahn, Mark L. "Seniority Problems in Business Mergers," *Industrial and Labor Relations Review*, Vol. 8 (April 1955).

Mater, Dan H., and Garth L. Mangum. "The Integration of Seniority Lists in Transportation Mergers," *Industrial and Labor Relations Review*, Vol. 16 (April 1963).

Meyers, Frederick. "The Analytic Meaning of Seniority," Industrial Relations Research Association, *Proceedings of the 18th Annual Meeting* (1965).

Sayles, Leonard R. "Seniority: An Internal Union Problem," *Harvard Business Review*, Vol. 30 (January–February 1952).

Speed, John. *Seniority in Non-Unionized Companies.* New York: National Industrial Conference Board, 1950.

10. Fringe Benefits

Garbarino, Joseph W. *Health Plans and Collective Bargaining.* Berkeley and Los Angeles: University of California Press, 1960.

Goldner, William. "Area Pension Plans Under Collective Bargaining," *Labor Law Journal*, Vol. 3 (December 1952).

————. "Trade Union Structure and Private Pensions," *Industrial and Labor Relations Review*, Vol. 5 (October 1951).

Harbrecht, Paul P. *Pension Funds and Economic Power.* New York: Twentieth Century Fund, 1959.

Rottenberg, Simon. "Property in Work," *Industrial and Labor Relations Review*, Vol. 15 (April 1962). Interesting argument against job property rights and severance pay.

Seidman, Joel. "The Union Agenda for Security," *Monthly Labor Review*, Vol. 86 (June 1963). A general discussion of the various protections sought by workers including fringes and seniority.

U.S. Department of Labor. *Labor Mobility and Private Pension Plans.* Washington, D.C.: U.S. Government Printing Office, 1964.

————. *Severance Pay and Layoff Benefit Plans.* Washington, D.C.: U.S. Government Printing Office, 1965.

11. The Problem of Union Security

Glasgow, John M. "That Right to Work Law Controversy Again?," *Labor Law Journal*, Vol. 18 (February 1967). Glasgow argues that if unions add to democracy, they need strength in both membership and finances and that both are hurt by right-to-work laws.

Kuhn, James W. "Right-to-Work Laws—Symbols of Substance," *Industrial and Labor Relations Review*, Vol. 14 (July 1961).

Moore, Mack A. "The Conflict Between Union Discipline and Union Security," *Labor Law Journal*, Vol. 18 (February 1967). Argues that the problem is not union shops but too few limits on union discipline.

Pulsipher, Allan G. "The Union Shop—A Legitimate Form of Coercion in a Free Market Economy," *Industrial and Labor Relations Review*, Vol. 19 (July 1966).

Warshal, Bruce S. "Right-to-Work: Pro and Con," *Labor Law Journal*, Vol. 17 (March 1966).

12. The Issue of Management Security

Beal, Edwin, "Origins of Co-Determination," *Industrial and Labor Relations Review*, Vol. 8 (July 1955). This together with William H. McPherson's "Co-Determination in Practice," *Industrial and Labor Relations Review*, Vol. 8 (July 1955), provides a good introduction to the issues.

Berg, Ivar, and James Kuhn. "The Assumptions of Featherbedding," *Labor Law Journal*, Vol. 13 (April 1962).

Blum, Albert A. "Paternalism and Collective Bargaining," *Personnel Administrator*, Vol. 26 (January–February 1963).

Brown, Leo G. "The Shifting Distribution

of the Right to Manage," Industrial Relations Research Association, *Proceedings of the 1st Annual Meeting* (1948).

Chamberlain, Neil W. *The Union Challenge to Management Control.* New York: Harper & Row, 1948. One of the classics on the subject.

————. "Organized Labor and Management Control," *Annals of the American Academy of Political and Social Science,* Vol. 276 (March 1951).

Ginzberg, Eli, Ivar Berg, John L. Herma, and James K. Anderson. *Democratic Values and the Rights of Management.* New York: Columbia University Press, 1963.

Strauss, George, and Eliezer Rosenstein. "Worker Participation: A Critical View," *Industrial Relations,* Vol. 9 (February 1970). One in a series of articles on this subject in this issue.

Weinstein, Paul (ed.). *Featherbedding and Technological Change.* Boston: Heath, 1965.

13. Grievance Procedure and Grievance Arbitration

Bernstein, Irving. "Arbitration." in Arthur Kornhauser, Robert Dubin, and Arthur Ross (eds.), *Industrial Conflict.* New York: McGraw-Hill, 1954. See also "Grievance Negotiations" by Van Dusen Kennedy in the same book.

Davey, Harold W. "Hazards in Labor Arbitration," *Industrial and Labor Relations Review,* Vol. 1 (April 1948).

————. "Labor Arbitration: A Current Appraisal," *Industrial and Labor Relations Review,* Vol. 9 (October 1955).

McKelvey, Jean T. (ed.). *Critical Issues in Labor Arbitration.* Washington, D.C.: Bureau of National Affairs, 1957.

Slichter, Sumner, James J. Healy, and E. Robert Livernash. *The Impact of Collective Bargaining on Management.* Washington, D.C.: Brookings, 1960. Chaps. 23–26.

Stone, Morris (ed.). *Labor Grievances and Decisions.* New York: Harper & Row, 1965.

Witte, Edwin F. *Historical Survey of Labor Arbitration.* Philadelphia: University of Pennsylvania Press, 1952.

14. The Strike—A Breakdown and Continuation of the Bargaining Process

Chamberlain, Neil W. "The Problem of Strikes," *Proceedings of the 13th Annual Conference on Labor at N.Y.U.* (1960), pp. 421–448.

Gouldner, Alvin W. *Wildcat Strike.* Yellow Springs, Ohio: Antioch Press, 1954.

Hutchinson, John G. *Management Under Strike Conditions.* New York: Holt, Rinehart & Winston, 1966. What management can do in the face of a strike.

Kornhauser, Arthur, Robert Dubin, and Arthur Ross. *Industrial Conflict.* New York: McGraw-Hill, 1954. An invaluable book covering a wide range of discussions on the forms and settlements of industrial disputes.

Marshall, Howard D., and Natalie J. Marshall. "The Nonstoppage Strike—A Critique," *Labor Law Journal,* Vol. 7 (May 1956).

Ross, Arthur M., and Paul T. Hartman. *Changing Patterns of Industrial Conflict.* New York: Wiley, 1960.

Stern, James L. "Declining Utility of the Strike," *Industrial and Labor Relations Review,* Vol. 18 (October 1964).

Uphoff, Walter H. *Kohler on Strike: Thirty Years of Conflict.* Boston: Beacon, 1967. A fascinating account of one of the seamier stories in U.S. collective bargaining history.

15. Automation and the Threat of Unemployment

Bowen, Howard R., and Garth L. Mangum (eds.). *Automation and Economic Progress.* Englewood Cliffs, N.J.: Prentice-Hall, 1966. A summary of findings of the National Commission on Technology, Automation and Economic Progress.

Dunlop, John T. (ed.). *Automation and Technological Change.* Englewood Cliffs, N.J.: Prentice-Hall, 1962. Edited for the American Assembly. See particularly Chapter 5 by George H. Taylor.

Lebergott, Stanley M. (ed.). *Men Without Work: The Economics of Unemployment.*

Englewood Cliffs, N.J.: Prentice-Hall, 1964.

Rezler, J. S. *Automation and Industrial Labor.* New York: Random House, 1969.

Selekman, Benjamin M. "Resistance to Shop Change," *Harvard Business Review,* Vol. 24 (Autumn 1945).

Somers, Gerald G., Edward L. Cushman, and Nat Greenberg (eds.). *Adjusting to Technological Change.* New York: Harper & Row, 1963. A series of articles edited for the Industrial Relations Research Association.

U.S. Department of Labor. *Seminar on Manpower Policy and Program.* Washington, D.C.: U.S. Government Printing Office, 1966. Interesting article by Robert L. Heilbroner with comments by Ben R. Seligman.

Wolfbein, Seymour. *Employment, Unemployment and Public Policy.* New York: Random House, 1965.

16. Inflation, Economic Growth, and Collective Bargaining

Edelman, Murray, and R. W. Fleming. *The Politics of Wage-Price Decisions.* Urbana: University of Illinois Press, 1966. A study of how wage inflation has been handled in four European countries.

Marshall, Howard D. "Checking Wage-Push Inflation," *Labor Law Journal,* Vol. 11 (January 1960). Explores the problems attached to the various methods proposed to check wage-push inflation.

Perlman, Richard (ed.). *Inflation: Demand-Pull or Cost-Push?* Boston: Heath, 1965.

Shultz, George P., and Robert Z. Aliber

(eds.). *Guidelines: Informal Controls and the Market Place.* Chicago: University of Chicago Press, 1966. Part II on wage guidelines is particularly appropriate for students of collective bargaining.

Thorp, Willard, and Richard E. Quandt. *The New Inflation.* New York: McGraw-Hill, 1959.

17. The Future of Collective Bargaining

Jacobs, Paul. *Old Before Its Time: Collective Bargaining at 28.* Santa Barbara, Calif.: Fund for the Republic, 1963.

Kelly, Matthew A. "Adaptations in the Structure of Bargaining," Industrial Relations Research Association, *Proceedings, of the 19th Meeting* (1966), pp. 290–302. Argues that future bargaining in the United States is likely to be more decentralized with some items like pensions remaining standardized.

Lester, Richard A. *As Unions Mature.* Princeton, N.J.: Princeton University Press, 1958. Provides case studies of individual unions and a peek at developments in Great Britain and Sweden.

Levine, Solomon B., and Bernard Karsh. "Industrial Relations in the Next Generation," *The Quarterly Review of Economics and Business,* Vol. 1, (February 1961).

Selekman, Benjamin M. "Trade Unions—Romance and Reality," *Harvard Business Review,* Vol. 36 (June 1958). Argues that in the past we have tended to overromanticize our union movement with the result that we are disillusioned today.

INDEX

Korean War, 192
Kumar, Pradeep, 280

Labor Bill of Grievances (1906), 53
Labor injunction, use of, 47–49
Labor-Management Relations Act, 15, 30, 31, 41, 57, 58, 333; arbitration decisions and, 257, 258; bargaining unit and, 77, 78, 80, 82, 90; government policies, 46, 56, 58–61, 62, 64; major provisions of, 70; seniority system and, 179, 184; state right-to-work laws and, 219; strategies of collective bargaining, 103; strikes and, 269, 270, 272, 282, 283, 284; terms of, 58–61; union security and, 207, 208, 209, 211–213, 218–219
Labor-Management Reporting and Disclosure Act, 30, 31, 46, 61, 64–65, 212, 258, 333, 334; major provisions of, 71; terms of, 61–62
Labor Party (Mexico), 42
Labor Relations Adjustment Act: Indian, 39; Japanese, 262
Labor Standards Law (Japan), 177
Labour Party (Great Britain), 65–66, 237, 278, 324, 325
Landrum-Griffin Act. See Labor-Management Reporting and Disclosure Act
Landorganisation (Sweden), 37
Leave of absence, 190–191
Lester, Richard, 3, 90–91, 106, 126, 163, 276
Levinson, Harold M., 86, 87, 91, 133–134, 135, 136, 164–165
Lewis, H. Gregg, 134
Lewis, John L., 6, 27, 31, 59, 85, 110, 111, 192
Lloyd-LaFollette Act, 63
Lock-outs, 265
Loewe v. Lawlor, 49, 50
Luddites (movement), 243

McClellan Committee, 61, 333
McCormick Company, 135
McDonald, David, 111, 339
Macdonald, Robert M., 86, 87
McKersie, Robert, 156
Machinists Union, 334
Machlup, Fritz, 126
Maher, John, 138
Maintenance of membership, 217; meaning of, 208
Malthus, Thomas Robert, 122

Malthusian law, 122–123
Management: attitudes of, 8–11; authority in earlier times, 224–227; bargaining associations, 81; loss of rights, 234–236; protection of rights, 237–239; seniority system views, 180–183
Management security, contract time and, 224–245; in other countries, 240–243; reasons for concern about, 227–230; union position on, 236–237; views of management about, 230–234
Mann, Floyd C., 171
Manpower Development and Training Act, 303
Manufacturers' Association (Israel), 94–95
Marceau, LeRoy, 285
Marginal productivity, theory of, 123–131; criticisms of, 125–131; empirical research and, 131–136; opposition to research findings, 136–138; reaction of union leaders to, 138–141; unions as political body in economy, 144–145; union's standards for wages, 141–144. *See also* Wage theory
Marshall, Alfred, 11–12, 131
Marshall, John, 225
Marx, Karl, 34, 297
Marxism, 5, 165
Mayo, Elton, 268
Means, Gardiner, 9
Meany, George, 31, 90, 171, 321
Metal Polishers' Union, 49
Metal Trades Union (West Germany), 36
Mexico: automation and unemployment, 305; bargaining unit, 95; earnings in manufacturing, 312; fringe benefits, 204–205; government policies, 68–69; grievance procedure, 262–263; hours of work, 177; inflation and economic growth, 329; issue of management security, 243; labor unions, 41–43; strike pattern, 282; strikes, 281–282; union security, 210, 222; wage differentials, 167
Mill, John Stuart, 123
Millis, Harry A., 122
Mitchell, James P., 339
Modern Corporation and Private Property, The (Berle and Means), 9
Modified union shop, 208, 217–218
Mohawk Airlines, 336
Molestation of Workers Act (Great Britain), 34
Monopsony, 128–130

Reuther, Walter, 31, 32, 90, 103, 105, 111, 228
Revere Copper and Brass Company, 90
Reynolds, Lloyd, 126, 145, 158–159, 161, 168
Ricardo, David, 122–123
Right-to-work laws, 213
Robertson, A. Willis, 52
Robie, Edward A., 90–91
Rochdale Plan, 14
Roosevelt, Franklin D., 55, 62
Roosevelt, Theodore, 63
Ross, Arthur M., 84, 98, 133, 136, 145, 161, 207, 241, 259, 269, 270, 277–278, 341

Samuelson, Paul, 315–316
Schultze, Charles, 317–318
Seasonal unemployment, 291
Seaton, Louis, 119
Segal, Martin, 135–136, 162–163
Selective Service Act of 1940, 186
Senior, Nassau, 224
Seniority system, contract time and, 179–188; management's views on, 180–183; in other countries, 186–187; union's views on, 183–184; workers' views on, 184–186
Severance pay, 200–201
Shaw, Chief Justice, 47
Sherman Antitrust Act of 1890, 49, 50, 51
Shift differentials, 191–192
Shister, Joseph, 4
Shock theory, wages and, 139
Shultz, George, 145, 267
Sick leaves, 190–191
Sit-down strikes, 267–268
Six-Day War (1967), 329
Skill differentials, 152–153
Slichter, Sumner, 136, 230, 293, 294, 299, 308, 319–320
Sloane, Arthur A., 88
Slowdown strike, 268
Smith, Adam, 158, 225
Social Security, 200, 319; in Latin America, 203
Socialist Workers Associations (Germany), 36
Solow, Robert, 315–316
Stephens, Uriah, 23
Strategy, collective bargaining, 98–121; at bargaining table, 107–119; choice of bargaining unit, 104; game theory, 101; indifference curve approach, 98, 99–101; multiemployer bargaining, 104–106; size of team, 104; timing importance, 102–104

Strikebreakers, 270
Strikes, 265–287, 335; alternatives to, 284–286; attempts at solution, 282–284; classification of, 267–270; effects of, 271–275; foreign patterns, 277–278; function of, 265–267; legality, 270–271; in 1945–1968, 276; in other countries, 278–282; trends in, 275–277; work stoppages and time lost (1966–1967), 282
Structural unemployment, 291–292
Summers, Clyde, 112
Sumner, William Graham, 267
Supplementary Unemployment Benefits (SUB), 198–200
Sweden: automation and unemployment, 303–305; bargaining unit, 93–94; compulsory arbitration, 285; earnings in manufacturing, 312; government policies, 67; grievance procedure, 261; hours of work, 177; inflation and economic growth, 327–328; strike pattern, 282; strikes, 279; union movement, 37; union security, 221; wage differentials, 166
Swedish Confederation of Professional Associations (SACO), 37
Swedish Employers Confederation (SAF), 37
Sweetheart contracts, 338
Sylvis, William, 14
Sympathetic strikes, 267

Taft, Cynthia, 161, 168
Taft, Philip, 14
Taft, William Howard, 63
Taft-Hartley Act. See Labor-Management Relations Act
Taylor, George, 332, 339
Taylor Law (New York), 64
Teamster (magazine), 88–89
Teamsters Union. See International Brotherhood of Teamsters, Chauffeurs, Warehousemen and Helpers of America
Technological unemployment, 292–299
Tennessee Valley Authority (TVA), 33
Terborgh, George, 297
Textile Workers Union, 113
Thirteenth Amendment, 270
Trade Disputes Act (Great Britain), 65, 221
Trade Union Unity League (TUUL), 20, 26–27
Trade Unions Act (Great Britain), 65
Trades Union Congress (Great Britain), 34, 92, 221, 242, 324

Transport Workers Union, 336
Truman, Harry, 102, 226
Turner, H. A., 323
Typographical Society of New York, 19
Typographical Union, 103

Unemployment: automation and, 291–307; cyclical, 292; in Europe, 303–305; frictional, 291; seasonal, 291; structural, 291–292; supplementary fringe benefits, 198–200; technological, 292–299
Union Challenge to Management Control, The (Chamberlain), 226
Union security: contract time and, 207–223; agency shop, 218; argument against union shop, 215–217; arguments for union shop, 213–215; the check-off, 218; closed shop, 211–213; compulsory unionism, 210–211; decertification, 218–219; maintenance of membership clause, 217; modified union shop, 217–218; in other countries, 220–222; raiding by rival unions, 219–220; state right-to-work laws, 219; Taft-Hartley Act, 219
Union shop, 116; arguments for, 213–215; case against, 215–217; meaning of, 207–208; modified, 217–218
Unionism and Relative Wages in the United States (Lewis), 134
United Auto Workers (UAW), 32, 84, 86, 87, 103, 105, 119, 153–154, 161, 184, 199, 234, 274, 301, 337
United Electrical, Radio and Machine Workers, 90
United Mine Workers of America (UMW), 84–85, 102, 110, 192
United Mine Workers of America v. Pennington, 52
United Rubber Workers (URW), 173
United States Chamber of Commerce, 202
United States Department of Labor, 22, 193, 202, 265
United States Employment Service (USES), 186
United States Steel Corporation, 28
United States Supreme Court, 8, 27, 91, 257; antitrust laws and, 49–55; management security and, 225–227, 235, 238
United States v. Hutcheson, 51
United Steelworkers of America, 161, 174, 200, 301, 339

United Steelworkers of America v. Warrior and Gulf Navigation Company, 226–227, 235
United Trade Union Congress (India), 39

Vall, Mark van de, 221
Vietnam War, 333
Virginia Electric Band Power Company case, 56
Voluntary retirement, 195–196

Wage differentials: abroad, 165–167; between plants, 158–159; effect of, 159–160; geographical location, 162–164; impact of, 156–158; incentive programs, 156; income distribution and union demands, 164–165; industrial, 160–162; internal differences, 151–152; intraplant, 155; role of unions and, 153–155; skill, 152–153; union attitudes, 155–156
Wage patterns, contract time and, 149–169; differentials, 151–168; rigidity, 149–154
Wage theory: empirical research, 131–136; institutional market, 145–146; Malthusian Law, 122–123; opposing views of, 136–138; reaction of union leaders, 138–141; unions as political body in economy, 144–145; union's standards for wages, 141–144. *See also* Marginal productivity, theory of
Wages fund doctrine, 123
Wagner, Senator Robert, 54, 55
Wagner Act. *See* National Labor Relations Act
Wallace, Henry, 309
War Labor Board (World War II), 158, 190, 192, 248
Washington, Booker T., 29
Waterous Company, 78
Webb, Beatrice, and Sydney, 15–16, 33, 46, 159
Weimar Republic, 36
West Coast Longshoremen's Union, 212, 239, 299–300
West Germany: automation and unemployment, 303–305; bargaining unit, 93–94; codetermination in, 240–241; earnings in manufacturing, 312; fringe benefits, 204; government policies, 66–67; grievance procedure, 261; hours of work,

176, 177; inflation and economic growth, 326–327; labor productivity, 311; management security, 240–241; seniority system, 186–187; strike pattern, 282; strikes, 278–279; union movement, 36–37; union security, 221; wage differentials, 166

Whig Party, 47

White-collar unionism, 32–33, 78, 355

Wildcat strikes, 268, 270

Wilson, Harold, 325

Wilson and Company, 90

Wirtz, Willard, 207, 272, 334

Wisconsin Grain and Warehouse Commission, 272

Wolman, Leo, 229

Women workers, 152, 159; in Great Britain, 166

Woodcock, Leonard, 332

Work stoppages, meaning of, 265

Workers' Regional Confederation (Mexico), 42–43

World War I, 36, 40, 137

World War II, 18, 37, 137, 151, 158, 190, 192, 248, 320

Wortman, Max, 81

Xerox Corporation, 239

Yellow dog contracts, 53, 208, 226; meaning of, 48

Yuai Kai (society), 40